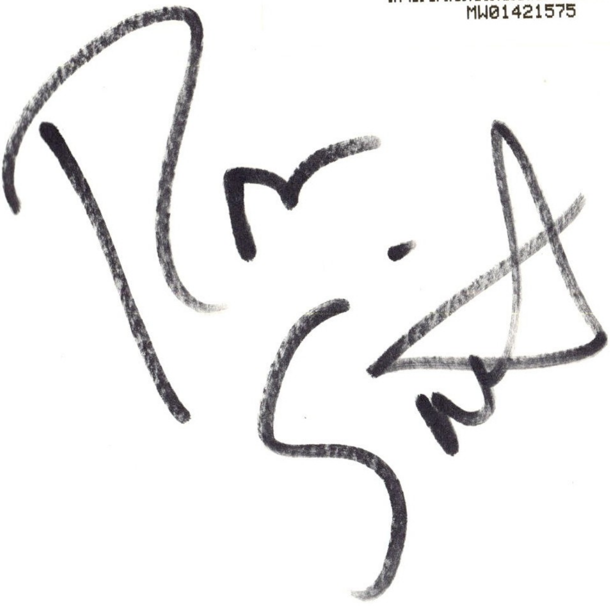

Minnesota Studies in the
PHILOSOPHY OF SCIENCE

HERBERT FEIGL, FOUNDING EDITOR

VOLUME XII

Rereading Russell: Essays in Bertrand Russell's Metaphysics and Epistemology

EDITED BY

C. WADE SAVAGE AND C. ANTHONY ANDERSON

UNIVERSITY OF MINNESOTA PRESS, MINNEAPOLIS

Copyright © 1989 by the Regents of the University of Minnesota

William Demopoulos and Michael Friedman, "The Concept of Structure in *The Analysis of Matter*," as reprinted from *Philosophy of Science* 52 (1985): 621–639. John Earman, "Concepts of Projectability and the Problems of Induction," reprinted by permission of the author and of the editor of *Noûs*, vol. XIX (1985): 521–535.

All rights reserved. No part of this publication may be reproduced, stored in a retrieval system, or transmitted, in any form or by any means, electronic, mechanical, photocopying, recording, or otherwise, without the prior written permission of the publisher.

Published by the University of Minnesota Press
2037 University Avenue Southeast, Minneapolis MN 55414.
Published simultaneously in Canada
by Fitzhenry & Whiteside Limited, Markham.
Printed in the United States of America.

Library of Congress Cataloging-in-Publication Data

Rereading Russell: essays in Bertrand Russell's metaphysics and epistemology / edited by C. Wade Savage and C. Anthony Anderson.
p. cm. – (Minnesota studies in the philosophy of science ;
v. 12)
Includes index.
ISBN 0-8166-1649-3
1. Russell, Bertrand, 1872-1970. I. Savage, C. Wade.
II. Anderson, C. Anthony. III. Series.
Q175.M64 vol. 12
[B1649.R94]
501 s--dc19
[192]   88-27841
CIP

The University of Minnesota is
an equal-opportunity educator and employer.

Contents

Note on References	vii
List of Abbreviations	ix
Preface	xi
Introduction	3
Russell's Reasons for Ramification *Warren Goldfarb*	24
Russell's Theory of Logical Types and the Atomistic Hierarchy of Sentences *Nino B. Cocchiarella*	41
Russell's Paradox, Russellian Relations, and the Problems of Predication and Impredicativity *Herbert Hochberg*	63
The Significance of "On Denoting" *Peter Hylton*	88
Russelling Causal Theories of Reference *Richard Fumerton*	108
Russell on Indexicals and Scientific Knowledge *Janet Farrell Smith*	119
Sense-Data in Russell's Theories of Knowledge *C. Wade Savage*	138

Russell's 1913 *Theory of Knowledge* Manuscript *David Pears*	169
The Concept of Structure in *The Analysis of Matter* *William Demopoulos and Michael Friedman*	183
On Induction and Russell's Postulates *R. M. Sainsbury*	200
Concepts of Projectability and the Problems of Induction *John Earman*	220
Giving up Judgment Empiricism: The Bayesian Epistemology of Bertrand Russell and Grover Maxwell *James Hawthorne*	234
Russell on Order in Time *C. Anthony Anderson*	249
Cause in the Later Russell *Elizabeth R. Eames*	264
Portrait of a Philosopher of Science *Kenneth Blackwell*	281
References	297
Notes on Contributors	305
Author Index	311
Subject Index	313

Note on References

Various methods of citing references are employed in the book. Some papers provide full references in the endnotes; others list the references separately. References are located at the end of the paper in some cases, at the end of the book in others. Some papers cite the Russell entries by employing the abbreviations on pp. ix-x; most do not.

List of Abbreviations

ABR	*The Autobiography of Bertrand Russell*, 3 volumes
AMa	*The Analysis of Matter*
AMi	*The Analysis of Mind*
Essays	*Essays in Analysis*
FG	*An Essay on the Foundations of Geometry*
HK	*Human Knowledge: Its Scope and Limits*
IMP	*Introduction to Mathematical Philosophy*
IMT	*An Inquiry into Meaning and Truth*
KEW	*Our Knowledge of the External World*
LA	"Logical Atomism"
LK	*Logic and Knowledge*
MMD	"My Mental Development"
MPD	*My Philosophical Development*
ML	*Mysticism and Logic*
MLT	"Mathematical Logic as Based on the Theory of Types"
NSD	"The Nature of Sense-Data – A Reply to Dr. Dawes Hicks"
NTF	"On the Nature of Truth and Falsehood"
OD	"On Denoting"
OP	"On Propositions: What They Are and How They Mean"
OT	"On Order in Time"
PFM	*Portraits from Memory*
PL	*A Critical Exposition of the Philosophy of Leibniz*
PLA	"The Philosophy of Logical Atomism"

PM	*Principia Mathematica*, 3 volumes
POM	*The Principles of Mathematics*
PP	*The Problems of Philosophy*
RUP	"On the Relations of Universals and Particulars"
RSDP	"The Relation of Sense-Data to Physics"
TK	*Theory of Knowledge*
UCM	"The Ultimate Constituents of Matter"

Preface

This volume evolved over several years from a conference at the Minnesota Center for Philosophy of Science on Bertrand Russell's later epistemology, ontology, and philosophy of science – the philosophy of *The Analysis of Matter* (1927), *An Inquiry into Meaning and Truth* (1940), *Human Knowledge: Its Scope and Limits* (1948), and *My Philosophical Development* (1959). The evolution has been significant, in both the contents and the conception of the volume. Some of the essays were presented at the conference; some were written by conferees afterward; and some were written by additional invitation. All were originally prepared for the volume, although two have since appeared elsewhere. Some of the essays deal with Russell's later period; some deal with earlier periods; and some deal with all periods. The volume thus covers the entire body of Russell's metaphysics, epistemology, and philosophy of science; and it reveals continuities running through the often noted differences among various phases of his philosophy. To mention a few of the more striking continuities, the outline for much of the later Russell can be found in *The Problems of Philosophy* (1912); the methodology of *The Analysis of Matter* (1910–13) is explicitly modeled on that of *Principia Mathematica* (1910); and his later event ontology resembles the ontology of sensed and unsensed sensibilia developed in *Our Knowledge of the External World* (1914).

Russell was one of the founders of twentieth-century analytic philosophy of science, along with Ernst Mach, Moritz Schlick, and others. In addition to his technical contributions in logic and mathematics, he devised an empiricist ontology to accommodate the Einsteinian theory of relativity and also quantum mechanics, one in which space, time, force, and matter are analyzed in terms of a causal framework of perceptual and nonperceptual events. And he developed an empiricist theory of knowledge to accompany his scientific ontology, one in which the principles of nondemonstrative inference are generalizations from scientific practice. The technical contributions have been widely studied and employed. But their relation to the philosophical contributions needs more examination. We hope the present volume will help to stimulate work of this sort.

Russell saw, perhaps more clearly than anyone (except possibly Einstein), both the value and the danger of science to the contemporary world. At times he despaired of the cruelty and stupidity of his fellow humans, as evidenced by their suicidal pursuit of ever more destructive weapons of war, but his faith that scientific enlightenment is the only solution did not waver. He articulated the scientific ideal with courage, wisdom, and humanity. He is one of the noblest philosophers in history and an incomparable model for philosophers of science.

We in the Minnesota Center are conscious of a special debt to Russell. Our founder, Herbert Feigl, regarded Russell as one of his mentors. Our director from 1971–81, Grover Maxwell, considered himself a disciple of Russell. He suggested the conference that led to this volume, and we greatly regret that he did not live to see the project accomplished.

We are indebted to David Maytum for assistance in preparing the manuscript, and to Ruth Wood for the index.

REREADING RUSSELL

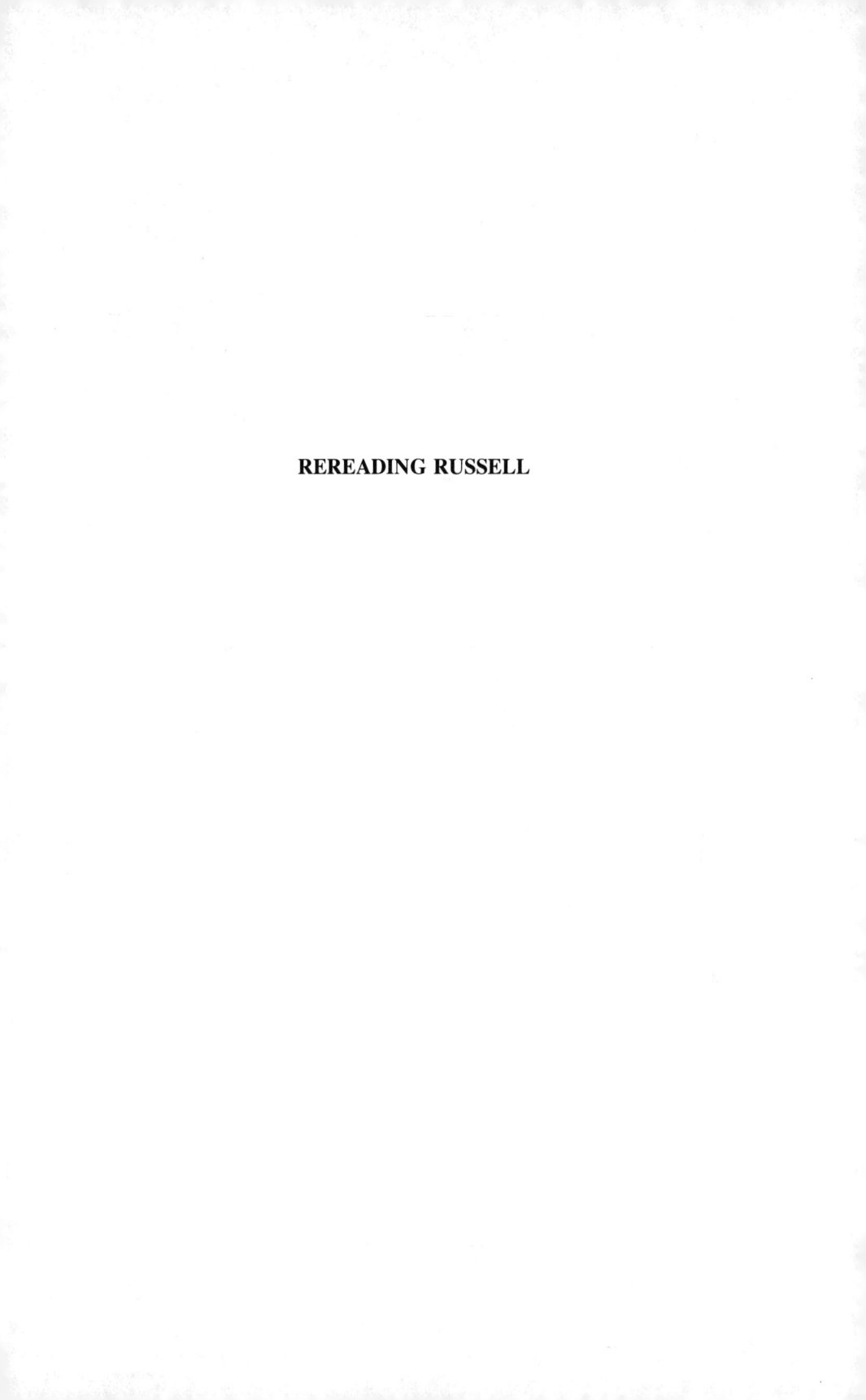

C. Wade Savage and C. Anthony Anderson

Introduction

Bertrand Russell is generally acknowledged to be one of the most important philosophers of the twentieth century, and many regard him as the most important. He is the chief architect of *Principia Mathematica* (1910-13), the three-volume masterpiece that established symbolic, or mathematical, logic; and he is one of the founders—if not the principal founder—of analytic philosophy, which applies the methods of logical analysis to philosophical projects and problems. And yet a large part of his metaphysics and epistemology, especially what we here call the "later philosophy," has been neglected and undervalued.

One aim of this volume is to direct attention to Russell's later metaphysics and epistemology, by which we mean the logic, ontology, theory of knowledge, and philosophy of science of his later writing. However, the later work cannot be properly understood except as a development of the earlier, and so we have prepared a volume that deals with Russell's metaphysics and epistemology in all its phases, early and late, with the exception of the preanalytic work.

The general aim of the volume is to emphasize the unity (if not the continuity) and integrity of Russell's metaphysical and epistemological writings. In a well-known barb, C. D. Broad said: "Mr. Bertrand Russell produces a new system of philosophy each year or so, and Mr. G. E. Moore none at all" (Broad, p. 79). Wittgenstein implied that the trouble with Russell's work after *PM* was that he had run out of problems to solve (Wittgenstein, 1967, p. 82). Both remarks are, at best, extreme exaggerations, and are seen to be so when the entire body of Russell's writing is examined and its development is studied. We accept Russell's own mature characterization in *My Philosophical Development* (1959, p. 11):

> There is one major division in my philosophical work: in the years 1899-1900 I adopted the philosophy of logical atomism and the technique of Peano in mathematical logic. This was so great a revolution as to make my previous work, except such as was purely mathematical, irrelevant to everything that I did later. The change in these years was a revolution; subsequent changes have been of the nature of an evolution.

It is true that his views evolved, for example, from phenomenalism to neutral monism to structural realism. But the development is orderly and well motivated. The changes of mind, contrary to Broad's suggestion, are neither capricious nor frivolous. It is probably true that—as with most philosophers—Russell's later philosophy was less creative than the earlier. But the reason was not that he ran out of problems or solutions, and merely recycled earlier solutions to the same problems, as Wittgenstein's remark implies. Problems set and not solved during the early period were addressed and sometimes solved during later periods. For example, changes in his early views regarding sensation (acquaintance) and sense-data required a new account of the way in which knowledge is based on experience, and such an account is offered in *An Inquiry into Meaning and Truth* (1940). Perhaps the most notable example is the problem of induction, which was first addressed in *The Problems of Philosophy* (1912), but not solved to Russell's satisfaction until the last two parts of *Human Knowledge: Its Scope and Limits* (1948) were completed.

We will provide an outline of Russell's most important work in metaphysics and epistemology, and then briefly speculate on the reasons for failure to appreciate its unity and for neglect of the later phase. It is convenient for our purposes to divide this work into five historical periods.

I. The preanalytic period (1893–99), during which Russell was under the sway of Kantian and German idealist philosophy, as interpreted by various of his teachers and former teachers at Cambridge University. The most important works during this period were *A Critical Exposition of the Philosophy of Leibniz* (1900), which examines Leibniz's logic and the hidden ontology built on it, and *An Essay on the Foundations of Geometry* (1897), an expanded version of his fellowship dissertation, which justifies a class of Euclidean and non Euclidean geometries (those with constant curvature) by Kantian arguments. In *My Philosophical Development* (1959b), his comprehensive intellectual autobiography, Russell says that "Einstein's revolution swept away" this early geometrical work, and he disowns nearly all his philosophical work during the period (pp. 40ff.). In 1899 Russell and G. E. Moore led a celebrated rebellion against idealism. Although realism is the philosophy of both Russell's early and late analytic periods, English idealism (Berkeley, Hume, and Mill) in the form of phenomenalism and neutral monism dominated his middle analytic period.

II. The logical period (1900–10), during which he conceived the idea of deriving mathematics from logic, and developed a symbolic logic for the purpose. The conception was born when he met the Italian mathematician, Guiseppe Peano, at a conference in Paris and was immediately led to a study of the latter's work and method of symbolism. The conception was sketched in *The Principles of Mathematics* (1903b), and in "Mathematical Logic as Based on the Theory of Types" (1908) and other papers (see the collections edited by Marsh [1956a] and by Lackey [1973a]). Russell's most widely read philosophical work, "On Denoting" (1905a), is among these papers. The conception was finally developed in full technical detail in the three volumes of *Principia Mathematica*, written over a ten-year interval in collaboration with A. N. Whitehead and published in 1910, 1912, and 1913. PM is, without doubt, Russell's most important contribution to philosophy, and quite possibly the most important philosophical work of the twentieth century so far. Although the focus was on technical logic during this period, Russell's early analytic philosophy was developing at the same time; consequently, there is some artificiality in distinguishing this period from the first of the three subsequent philosophical periods.

III. The early analytic period (1911-18), during which Russell extracted his method of logical analysis and synthesis from the logical work of the previous period, and used it to develop his metaphysics and epistemology. *The Problems of Philosophy* (1912) is a sketch of his early metaphysics and epistemology. It holds that we have "acquaintance" with sense-data and abstract universals, and that other existing things are known only by "description." *Theory of Knowledge* (1984) is a development of the doctrines of acquaintance, judgment, certainty, and truth sketched in PP. It was written in 1913, suppressed because of Wittgenstein's criticism of its doctrines, and published posthumously by the Russell Archives in 1984. *Our Knowledge of the External World* (1914b) is the development of a phenomenalist epistemology and associated philosophy of physics, and together with "The Relation of Sense-data to Physics" (1914c) constitutes Russell's phenomenalist phase. "The Philosophy of Logical Atomism" (1918b) is Russell's classical presentation of analytic philosophy, the method of analyzing entities and sentences into their logical atoms. *An Introduction to Mathematical Philosophy* (1919), written while Russell was serving a six-month prison sentence for allegedly seditious opposition to Britain's involvement in World War I, is a nonspecialist overview of PM and an introduction to its underlying philosophy.

IV. The middle analytic period (1919-27), during which Russell perfected the application of his analysis to physics and extended its application to psychology, thus achieving an empiricist philosophy he hoped would be acceptable in itself and compatible with contemporary physics and psychology. The first work of the period is *The Analysis of Mind* (1921), which extends the phenomenalist analysis of matter in KEW and RSDP to mental entities, analyzing both minds and bodies into collections of sensations, in the manner of Hume and William James. Two semipopular expositions of science were published next: *The ABC of Atoms* (1923), and *The ABC of Relativity* (1925). These were followed by a popular exposition of his philosophy, *An Outline of Philosophy* (1927a). The last work of the period is *The Analysis of Matter* (1927b), which analyzes the central concepts of physics—force, matter, space, and time—into *events*. Events are held to include sensed and unsensed sensibilia, and midway during the book it is suggested that some events may not be perceivable even in principle. With the admission of unperceivable events, the basic ontology becomes unambiguously unambiguously realist.

V. The late analytic period (1928–59), during which the realist shift at the end of the previous period is consolidated, and major deferred problems are addressed. The stated purpose of *An Inquiry into Meaning and Truth* (1940) is to discover the relation between our empirical knowledge and the experience on which it is based; and it develops an extensional hierarchy of statements built up from basic propositions (sense-datum statements, in an earlier incarnation) to describe the relation. In *The Philosophy of Bertrand Russell* (1944), a volume in the Library of Living Philosophers, there is an informative memoir by Russell, entitled "My Mental Development," and a useful "Reply" to the articles of criticism and commentary contained in the volume. In *Human Knowledge* (1948), Russell's philosophy achieves its final form. The epistemology is Humean empiricist. In the last two parts he treats the long-deferred problem of induction, and concludes that inductive inference cannot be justified by probability theory or in any other manner, although its principles can be described. The metaphysics is a return to the briefly sketched structural realism of PP (though cleansed of most subsistent, abstract entities), which holds that whatever the perception-independent world may consist in, only the logical structures that it shares with our sensations can be known. *My Philosophical Development* (1959b) is Russell's final summation and commentary on his metaphysics and epistemology. Its summaries and explanations are of great importance in interpreting his work, and occasionally it provides a final development to the doctrine being summarized.

By Russell's later philosophy, we mean the philosophy of the late analytic period together with AMa, which is a transitional work. There are several possible reasons for the neglect of this later work and for failure to appreciate the unity and integrity of Russell's philosophy. *First*, PM and the associated books and articles on logic comprise work so focused, subtle, and creative that Russell's later philosophical efforts can seem pale by comparison. *Second*, after PM a large part of Russell's writing was devoted to science, religion, education, history, biography, political science, world affairs, education, and other nonphilosophical topics. As a consequence, his philosophical writing has an appearance of discontinuity: it is spread out over a period of some fifty years, making it difficult to trace and appreciate its patterns and continuities. The difficulty is increased by his unhelpful habit of not mentioning previous developments in each new book. *Third*, most of Russell's philosophical work is found in books prepared for an audience not limited to professional philosophers. The first such book was PP, the so-called shilling shocker (that is, a popular book sold for a shilling), which Wittgenstein hated. Russell tells us that after completing PM he wished to descend from the cold beauty of mathematics to the human level, and to communicate with the world at large. His termination from Cambridge after being convicted of sedition, and his harsh financial circumstances (most of his fortune had been given to charity), undoubtedly contributed to his decision to write for a general audience. One unfortunate effect was that much of his philosophical work is composed in too casual and unself-critical a manner to avoid the usual professional criticisms of such efforts—some deserved, some not.

Finally, just after World War II, Russell's philosophy came under attack by a new generation, who, under the influence of the later Wittgenstein, developed British linguistic philosophy. Russell called this school "the new philosophy" and declared that he had no sympathy with it. In 1956 he wrote a review (reprinted in MPD, pp. 215–30) of J. O. Urmson's book of the same year, *Philosophical Analysis: Its Development between the Two World Wars*, a book that attempts to present the objections of the later Wittgensteinian school both to logical positivism and to Russell's analytic philosophy. Russell says of the school (MPD, p. 216): "Its positive doctrines seem to me trivial and its negative doctrines unfounded. I have not found in Wittgenstein's *Philosophical Investigations* anything that seemed to me interesting and I do not understand why a whole school finds important wisdom in its pages." He concludes with these words (MPD, p. 230):

> Philosophers from Thales onwards have tried to understand the world. Most of them have been unduly optimistic as regards their own successes. But even when they have failed, they have supplied material to their successors and an incentive to new effort. I cannot feel that the new philosophy is carrying on this tradition. It seems to concern itself, not with the world and our relation to it, but only with the different ways in which silly people can say silly things. If this is all that philosophy has to offer, I cannot think that it is a worthy subject of study. The only reason that I can imagine for the restriction of philosophy to such triviality is the desire to separate it sharply from empirical science. I do not think such a separation can be usefully made. A philosophy which is to have any value should be built upon a wide and firm foundation of knowledge that is not specifically philosophical. Such knowledge is the soil from which the tree of philosophy derives its vigour. Philosophy which does not draw nourishment from this soil will soon wither and cease to grow, and this, I think, will be the fate of the philosophy that Mr. Urmson champions with an ability worthy of a better cause.

Such pronouncements strengthened the conviction of the new generation of philosophers that Russell was out of touch and out of fashion. In later years some were uncharitable enough to speculate that he had become senile. The speculation reached its peak in 1967 when Russell organized an international tribunal to try the United States for war crimes in Vietnam, and published a biting little book of essays entitled *War Crimes in Vietnam*. Commenting on this episode, A. J. Ayer says in his biography, *Russell* (1972): "The proceedings of this tribunal were ill-received at the time but the evidence which has since come to light has largely vindicated them" (p. 34). And, "I last saw him [Russell] on his ninety-fifth birthday and found him physically active and intelligently alert. The rumour which was put about by his political adversaries that he became senile is quite without foundation" (p. 32).

By inference from the history of ideas, one may reasonably hope that future developments will correct both Russell's assessment of the new philosophy and its assessment of his philosophy, and will incorporate the most attractive features of both in some new synthesis. It would be gratifying if this volume contributed to such a development.

The essays presented here are divided into five topic groups.

The *first group* (Goldfarb, Cocchiarella, and Hochberg) deals with Russell's philosophy of mathematics and ontology: the project of PM to derive mathematics from logic (logicism), the theory of types that Russell devised to eliminate the paradoxes that threatened the project, and the varieties of logical atomism that grew out of the project.

The *second group* (Hylton, Fumerton, and Smith) treats Russell's philosophy of language: his theory of descriptions from POM to OD and its uses, his related theory of proper names, and his theory of indexicals in IMT.

The *third group* (Savage, Pears, and Demopoulos and Friedman) is concerned with Russell's epistemology, and to some degree his metaphysics: his theory of sensational and perceptual data both early and late, his early theory of judgment and Wittgenstein's criticism of it, and his structural realism as articulated in AMa.

The *fourth group* (Sainsbury, Earman, and Hawthorne) treats Russell's theory of nondemonstrative inference in HK: the status of his postulates of inductive inference, his rejection of induction as a postulate of inference, and his apparent adoption of a Bayesian theory of confirmation in which the postulates are used to assign prior probabilities.

The *fifth group* (Anderson, Eames, and Blackwell) addresses Russell's philosophy of science and metaphysics: his analysis of instants in terms of events, his treatment of the fundamental concept of causality both early and late, and his quasi-religious lifelong devotion to science and to its philosophy.

The following summaries of these essays are designed not merely to indicate the contents but also to assist readers who are not specialists in the topic areas. They are, of course, no substitute for the essays themselves.

Philosophy of Mathematics and Ontology

Warren Goldfarb: Russell's Reasons for Ramification

Goldfarb is concerned to show that Russell had good reasons for adopting a *ramified theory of types*, rather than the less complicated *simple theory of types* that Ramsey and other logicians recommended in criticizing his logic. Gödel and Quine are also among the critics. They insist that sets are real, i.e., language- and mind-independent entities; and they hypothesize that Russell adopted the ramified theory because he subscribed to an antirealist, constructivist interpretation of sets, an interpretation on which sets come to exist only as they are constructed (defined) by set theoreticians. Their evidence that Russell is a constructivist is his use of the vicious-circle principle in his theory of types. This principle is most precisely stated for propositional functions, which take propositions as values and individuals (or propositions) as arguments. For example, the propositional function, *Red(x)*, takes as value the proposition that the fire hydrant is red where the fire hydrant is its argument. The vicious-circle principle holds that the definition of a propositional function—and hence of the set of arguments to that function— cannot require the function to be an argument of itself, since the function does not exist until it is constructed (defined).

Goldfarb argues, against the Gödel-Quine interpretations, that Russell regarded propositional functions and the classes defined by them as independent, real entities, and was not a constructivist. His reason for ramification therefore cannot have been the one suggested by Gödel and Quine. Rather, it is the reason he explicitly offers: without the ramified theory certain paradoxes arise. Ramsey classified these as *semantic* paradoxes, because he believed they arise from the particular language being used, and he dismissed them as of no importance to logic. He contrasted them with the *logical* and mathematical paradoxes, such as Russell's famous paradox of the class of classes that are not members of themselves, which can be avoided by means of a simple, nonramified theory of types. But Goldfarb argues that the so-called semantic paradoxes arise from the misuse of propositional functions, which are abstract entities and therefore logical objects like propositions and classes. Consequently, the semantic paradoxes are as important to logicians as those that arise from the misuse of classes. As Ramsey himself concedes, the Grelling paradox and the other semantic paradoxes require ramification for their solution. Hence Russell's reason for ramification was correct: it is to avoid paradoxes that logicians and mathematicians need to avoid.

Goldfarb believes, however, that Russell cannot be rescued from the well-known difficulty of the ramified theory. As Russell knew and Ramsey confirmed, mathematics cannot be derived from a ramified logic without adding to it the axiom of reducibility. Ramsey argued persuasively that the axiom of reducibility is not a logical axiom, and that in consequence the logicist project of deriving mathematics from logical axioms cannot be accomplished in the ramified theory of types.

Nino B. Cocchiarella: Russell's Theory of Logical Types and the Atomistic Hierarchy of Sentences

Russell's ontology becomes increasingly anti-Platonist, or nominalist, as his thought matures. Cocchiarella's thesis is that this process ultimately leads Russell to deny the real existence of propositional functions, and thus deprives him of the machinery required to define numbers in such a way that the theory of numbers is derivable from logic. The required definition treats numbers as classes of classes, or as propositional functions of propositional functions, if we use Russell's definition of a class as the extension of a propositional function. Cocchiarella traces the process of nominalization from POM to IMT. In POM and other early works propositions and propositional functions were held to be real, i.e. to be logical subjects. But in PM propositions were declared to be logical fictions, incomplete symbols, and therefore not logical subjects. In PLA, written under the influence of Wittgenstein, facts suffered a similar fate (though they would later be resurrected as events in IMT). And in IMT so did propositional functions.

Cocchiarella notes that the atomism of IMT is very severe: its simples are limited to particulars (including concrete facts, or events) and n-adic relations (including properties, which are 1-adic, or monadic, relations). A linguistic hierarchy is built on these simples consisting of atomic sentences, truth-functional combinations of atomic sentences, and generalizations on the subjects and predicates of such sentences. The only doctrine of types required is a fragment of the simple theory: it stipulates only that n-adic predicates have n terms. The usual paradoxes cannot arise in this hierarchy because propositional functions are not real, that is, are not logical subjects, and therefore cannot be arguments of propositional functions. (Or as in Ramsey's proposal, and Russell's in the second edition of PM, a propositional function can appear in a proposition only through its values.)

Cocchiarella claims that the resulting logic is merely a fragment of second-order logic and that arithmetic cannot be derived from it in the manner of PM. For the derivation requires propositional functions to be logical subjects, that is, entities capable of being subjects of propositions and arguments of propositional functions. For example, the number 2 is the class of all pairs, or the property possessed by all properties whose extensions are pairs, or the propositional function that takes as arguments all propositional functions whose arguments are pairs. But the number 2 cannot be so defined in the logic of IMT, since propositional functions cannot be arguments of propositional functions. Thus, Russell's later nominalism destroys his earlier logicism.

Herbert Hochberg: Russell's Paradox, Russellian Relations, and the Problems of Predication and Impredicativity

Russell employed what is now known as the simple theory of types to resolve the paradox arising from the set of all sets not members of themselves, and also the companion paradox arising from the property of not being a property of itself, the property of *impredicability*, I. Impredicability is defined as follows: f is an impredicable property $= df f$ is not f, or, in symbols, $I(f) = df \neg f(f)$. For example, redness is impredicable since redness is not red (or any other color). Russell contended that it is illegitimate to substitute I for the variable f, in the definition of impredicability, because it violates the rule that the instance of a property must be of lower type than the property, or, in other terms, the rule that the argument of a propositional function must be of lower type than the function. Hochberg proposes to resolve the paradox without employing any theory of types. (He rejects the attempt to resolve it by employing a definite description to define I, on the ground that this requires the identity of extensionally equivalent functions.) He argues that impredicability is not a property but a relation: the relation of non-self-exemplification, $\neg \phi(\phi)$, the relation a property ϕ has to itself when it does not exemplify itself. On this suggestion, $\neg \phi(\phi)$ is like the relation, $\neg Lxx$, the relation of a thing not being to the left of itself. He claims that the paradox arises from erroneously supposing that $\neg \phi(\phi)$ is a property and can be substituted for property variables such as f in the definition of impredicability. Blocking the paradox thus requires only the familiar distinction between properties and relations.

In the course of his argument, Hochberg examines Russell's attempt in TK to account for the sense of relational propositions (a topic also discussed in the papers by PEARS and SAVAGE), and proposes an interpretation designed to meet Wittgenstein's objections. Russell's doctrine is that relational order is to be defined on the pattern of the following example: $Lab = df(a\ L_1\ [Lxy, a, b])$ & $(b\ L_2\ [Lxy, a, b])$; that is, a is to the left of b if and only if a has first place in the relational fact which has form Lxy and contains particulars a and b, and b has second place. Hochberg argues that relational terms such as L_1 and L_2 cannot be avoided in such analyses, either by the Wiener-Kuratowski definition of ordered pairs and other n-tuples, or by any other means.

The notion of logical form is used by Hochberg to resolve Bradley's "paradox." Bradley argued that if the exemplification of a property by an object is a (two-term) relation, then that relation must be exemplified by the property and object, which requires a further (three-term) relation of exemplification, and so on ad infinitum. Hochberg avoids the difficulty by treating exemplification as a logical form that "shows itself" (cf. Wittgenstein, 1961) in the fact, instead of a relational constituent of the fact.

Hochberg concludes with a discussion of the ramified theory of types. He maintains (in agreement with GOLDFARB) that the theory is necessary to block certain paradoxes that should be regarded as logical, and that the Ramsey-Wittgenstein interpretation of quantifiers as infinite conjunctions or disjunctions will not do the job. But then to derive arithmetic from the theory requires the axiom of reducibility, and it is not a logical axiom.

Philosophy of Language

Peter Hylton: The Significance of "On Denoting"

According to the theory of denoting in OD, "The present king of France is bald" is analyzed as meaning, $(\exists x)(Rxf\ \&\ (y)(Rxf \supset y = x)\ \&\ Bx)$, read as "There is an x such that x is a male ruler of France, and only one such, and x is bald." On the standard account, this theory of descriptions was adopted to explain the meaningfulness of such expressions as "the present king of France" without requiring that they denote existing, or even subsisting, entities. Hylton brings objections against this account, and offers a better one. The main objection is that the earlier theory of POM—according to which "all men," "some men," "a man," and "the man" express *denoting concepts* and not objects—avoids subsistent entities as effectively as does the theory of OD. Consequently, there must be motivation and significance for the theory of OD that the standard account has missed.

The main significance of OD, according to Hylton, lies in its doctrine that the grammatical (surface) form of a sentence need not correspond to its logical form (the form of the underlying proposition), and that analysis is required to discover the logical form. The analysis of the sentence in our example shows in the underlying proposition that there is no constituent corresponding to the present king of France, for the constituents are the relation of being male ruler, the property of baldness, France, and (or one interpretation) the variable, x. The status of the quantifiers and connectives is unclear. Furthermore, France will not be a constituent in the completely analyzed proposition, since proper names are held to be disguised descriptions. (For proper names see FUMERTON.) The distinction between grammatical and logical form forced Russell and other analytic philosophers to pay explicit attention to expressions of propositions, to *language*. Words and sentences could no longer be regarded as transparent, but had to be regarded as potentially misleading and capable of producing metaphysical error.

According to Hylton, it is important to distinguish two kinds of analysis: eliminative and noneliminative, and to realize that the theory of descriptions can be employed in either kind. The analysis of our sentence whose subject is the present king of France is of the second kind, since it does not eliminate the thing that exists when such sentences are true. Similarly, Russell's use of the theory of descriptions prior to 1913 to analyze sentences about physical objects does not eliminate the thing that is the bearer of the sense-data. But his analysis of physical-object sentences after 1913 (in KEW and elsewhere) does eliminate the subject of the sentence, leaving only sense-data and relations between them.

Richard Fumerton: Russelling Causal Theories of Reference

The theory of denoting in OD is applied by Russell, not only to definite descriptions such as "the present king of France," but also to ordinary proper names, such as "Aristotle" and "Mont Blanc." On this application, ordinary proper names are held to be disguised descriptions. For example, the name "Dedefre" might be defined as follows:

(*) Dedefre = *df* the Egyptian ruler who built the second pyramid.

Fumerton defends this theory of names from several objections, the strongest of which is associated with the causal theory of proper names. He then shows how to enlist the causal theory to defend Russell's theory, a maneuver described by the paper's title.

Several objections to (*) are considered: (1) "Dedefre" is a rigid designator, but the descriptive phrase is not; (2) (*) is not logically necessary, or at least not analytic, and definitions should be; (3) different speakers associate different descriptive phrases with the name, so none can provide the definition. Fumerton shows how each of these objections can be met. The most serious objection is one usually brought by the causal theorist: (4) (*) may be false (e.g., Dedefre may have built the *third* pyramid) even when "Dedefre" is meaningfully and referentially used to say something true, for example, that Dedefre is an Egyptian. From such cases the causal theorist concludes that Russell's theory cannot be correct, and that the reference of names is fixed, not by descriptions, but by a causal chain beginning with the referent of the name and ending with its utterance on the occasion in question.

Fumerton replies that the description of the causal chain posited by the causal theorist can be used to improve Russell's definition of the proper name, as follows:

(**) Dedefre = *df* the person whose being called by some name resulted (by a long and complicated causal chain) in the present utterance of the name "Dedefre."

This definition employs a description that satisfies the requirements of Russell's theory as well as the causal theory of reference.

The most serious objection to his suggestion is that the defining phrase in (**) cannot be substituted for "Dedefre" in all contexts. Substituting the definiens in the sentence, "Dedefre is an Egyptian," we obtain, "The person whose being called by some name resulted (by a long and complicated causal chain) in the present utterance of the name 'Dedefre' is an Egyptian." In the new sentence the name "Dedefre" is mentioned but not used (not uttered); consequently, the new sentence removes the referent for "the present utterance of the name 'Dedefre,' " which then becomes meaningless. Fumerton's reply, in brief, is that the defining description need not be substitutable for the name. It is sufficient that the description express an intended content that we associate with the name on occasions of its use, that is, on occasions when there is a referent for "the present utterance."

Janet Farrell Smith: Russell on Indexicals and Scientific Knowledge

Indexicals are *strict (logically proper) names* whose denotation generally varies from use to use. The most important examples are "I," "this," "now," and "here." In her paper Smith contends that Russell was right to hold in IMT and HK that strict names are indispensable, but that he was wrong to hold that indexicals are completely interdefinable. She considers objections to both doctrines by Bar-Hillel in reaching her conclusions.

Carnap held in *The Logical Structure of the World* that every name can be replaced by a description: for example, names of entities in space and time can be replaced by a description mentioning the spatiotemporal coordinates (locations) of the entity. Russell objected that unless the chain of definitions terminates in names, it must become either an infinite regress or a circle. The origin of any spatiotemporal coordinate system must be named by "(0, 0, 0, 0)" (three spatial coordinates and one temporal), and any description that replaces this name must refer to the same coordinate system (circular) or to another coordinate system (regressive). Consequently, according to Russell, names are indispensable.

Bar-Hillel objects that Russell's thesis that names are indispensable in a scientific language has been incorrectly inferred from their indispensability in *learning* the language. Smith defends Russell from the objection. She concedes that indexicals are not necessary to designate simple particulars, since there are no particulars in the ontology of HK; and that names are not necessary to accomplish unique reference, since definite descriptions can do that. But she insists that names are epistemologically necessary to express one's awareness of one's own sensory experience, on which all empirical knowledge is based.

Russell maintains in IMT that "I" can be defined as "the person experiencing this." Bar-Hillel objects that "I" is not ambiguous, whereas "the person experiencing this" is ambiguous. The latter phrase may refer to something experienced by the speaker, or by the speaker and someone else. After examining several attempts to escape it, Smith accepts this objection. She concludes by connecting the basis of the objection to Russell's doctrine that indexicals have a twofold meaning, public and private, that enables the speaker to relate public knowledge to its private basis in experience.

Epistemology and Metaphysics

C. Wade Savage: Sense-Data in Russell's Theories of Knowledge

Sense-Data in Russell's early theory of knowledge are the completely certain, immediate, precise data of experience on which all our empirical knowledge is allegedly based. They are immediately sensed by what Russell calls *acquaintance*, and they provide the ground and test for the basic perceptual knowledge (judgments of perception) from which all other empirical knowledge is obtained by deductive or inductive inference. Russell maintains that he "abandoned" sense-data in 1921, but it is clear that he continued to employ sensory or perceptual data of some sort in his later theory of knowledge. Savage attempts to discover precisely what the "abandonment" consists in, and how the later notion of perceptual data differs from the earlier. Some commentators have claimed that Russell abandoned little more than the term "sense-data," others that he abandoned sense-data in favor of fallible percepts. Savage attempts to show that the correct interpretation lies between these two extremes.

Through an examination of preabandonment texts, especially PP and TK, Savage builds a case that even during this early period Russell did not hold—in spite of contrary appearances—that sense-datum judgments are absolutely certain or infallible. For in the completely developed view of TK, the process of analyzing the sense-data on which sense-datum judgments are based is not infallible and therefore cannot produce indubitable judgments. Accordingly, the preabandonment doctrine is consistent with Russell's postabandonment insistence that nothing is absolutely certain.

Nonetheless, the notion of absolutely certain data is retained in the postabandonment view, on Savage's interpretation, as a ideal toward which we should strive. In Russell's later theory of knowledge, sense-data become the sensory core of perceptual experiences, the part of the experience that is causally most dependent on the stimulus, and a part that can only in theory be completely separated from the conscious and unconscious inferences that inevitably surround it. The more of these inferences one strips away, the purer the datum; and the purer the datum, the more reliable the scientific inferences based on it. The process of purifying data is extremely difficult, and at some points Russell suggests that it requires the aid of a psychological theory. This suggestion, though of great interest, is shown to lead to difficulty.

Savage suggests that the Russellian view of data may be precisely the view required to reconcile the traditionally opposed correspondence and coherence theories of empirical knowledge.

David Pears: Russell's 1913 *Theory of Knowledge* Manuscript

Pears examines that part of TK that Russell suppressed, apparently because of Wittgenstein's severe criticism, for the light that it throws on the development of logical atomism. In this part of the manuscript Russell tried to explain a subject's ability to understand contingent propositions (judgments) such as "a is to the right of b" (abbreviated "aRb") merely by means of S's acquaintance with the constituents, a, R, and b, of the proposition. But he encounters two problems: (1) acquaintance with the constituents does not explain why S groups them together in a meaningful combination rather than some meaningless one, and (2) it does not explain how S knows that the combination selected is a meaningful one. Reliance on what Pears calls *extensional* acquaintance (roughly, acquaintance not involving any knowledge) prevents Russell from bringing S's intention or knowledge of types of objects into the explanation. And so he is led to hypothesize that S has acquaintance with the form of the fact, xFy, a sort of schema into which S fits the constituents. According to Russell, what it means to say that S is acquainted with the form is that S knows the general logical fact,

($\exists x$)($\exists y$)($\exists F$)(xFy), read as "There is an individual x, and an individual y, and a relation, F, such that x has the relation F to y."

Pears considers three alternative construals of these general logical facts: that they are contingent, that they are necessary, and that they are self-evident. He finds that there are insuperable problems on each construal, and offers evidence that some of these problems were urged against Russell by Wittgenstein in his *Notebooks 1914–1916*.

The most important problem, according to Pears, is that even if we grant that S has acquaintance with a, R, b, and xFy, this still fails to explain how S knows that the combination aRb makes sense. Pears suggests that it is precisely this problem that Wittgenstein had in mind in his celebrated objection to Russell's theory of judgment in a letter written in June 1913, while Russell was at work on the sections of TK that would later be suppressed.

Pears argues that Wittgenstein's rejection of Russell's theory of judgment was an important step in the development of his picture theory of meaning in the *Tractatus*, with its doctrine that to know an object is to know the combinations into which it can enter. If S knows the objects, or constituents of facts, in this sense, then knowledge of the postulated form of the fact is unnecessary.

William Demopoulos and Michael Friedman:
The Concept of Structure in *The Analysis of Matter*

The metaphysical theory of AMa—its theory of theories—is usually called *structural realism*. It holds that the objective, scientific properties (and relations) of the world are the *structural* properties, which are known indirectly, by description; and that the subjective, ordinary properties are the *intrinsic* properties, which are known directly, in sensation. Structural properties are second-order properties, properties of properties. For example, the transitivity of the relation of being to the left of something is a structural property. The left-of relation is first-order, and also intrinsic (at least if taken to be a relation of the observer's visual field).

The authors take the central feature of structural realism to be its claim that the reference of theoretical predicates of a scientific theory can be explained non-reductively in terms of the reference of the perceptual or observable predicates of the theory. Structural realism therefore has important similarities to Ramsey's view that theoretical terms are not constants but rather existentially quantified variables, and consequently do not refer to particular entities. It is also similar to Carnap's view that a scientific theory is a partially interpreted formal system, a system in which only the observation terms are given interpretations. The authors examine M. H. A. Newman's little-known objection to Russell's structural realist view, and then identify counterpart objections to views similar to Russell's.

Newman's objection is presented as follows. Any set of empirical objects of sufficient cardinality can be used to construct any structure, since a structure is simply a set of sets of objects. On the structuralist view scientific theories are about the existence of structures, which are properties and relations of at least second-order, or in set-theoretical terms, sets of sets of sets of...objects. But since the existence of such structures is constrained only by considerations of cardinality, scientific theories on this philosophical view are not empirical, or at least not empirical in various important respects. If we could distinguish "empirically important" from empirically unimportant structures, then we could require that scientific theories postulate only the existence of the former. But the distinction cannot be drawn within a purely structuralist framework.

Newman's objection is compared to Putnam's recent objection to the Carnapian view of scientific theories as partially interpreted formal systems, which can be summarized as follows. Any model (true interpretation) of the observational part of a theory can be used to define a model of the theoretical part, if the cardinality of its domain is sufficiently great; so the truth of the theoretical part is guaranteed for some interpretation. Since it does not matter which interpretation is chosen for the theoretical part on a Carnapian view, the truth of that part is automatically guaranteed, and the theory is therefore trivial.

The general suggestion is that all structuralist theories of scientific theories succumb to the same difficulty: they carry the unwanted and unacceptable implication that scientific theories are not empirical, or at least not as empirical as they should be.

Nondemonstrative Inference

R. M. Sainsbury: On Induction and Russell's Postulates

In HK Russell claimed that we need a priori knowledge of contingent propositions — what he called the postulates of scientific inference — in order to know anything other than our own data. A second, connected claim was that these postulates would also serve to characterize the kinds of nondeductive reasoning we in fact take to be valid.

Sainsbury's paper aims to clarify the first of these claims and to assess its truth. He supports Russell's view that principles of evidence — i.e., generalizations setting out the characteristics propositions must have for one set of them to confer rational credibility on another — cannot all be established by the data without circularity. But he does so for reasons different from Russell's. Russell seems to think that principles of evidence must be known if ordinary nondeductive reasoning is to be correct, and in this he was mistaken. On the other hand, Russell was right in thinking that there is a genuine philosophical question about whether the principles can be known, and if so, how.

Sainsbury suggests that this philosophical question is simply a reformulation of the problem of skepticism about induction. Since Russell's attempt to show that all principles of evidence are contingent fails, it would seem natural to try to meet skepticism about induction by proposing that some principles of evidence are necessary and knowable a priori. But this gambit is unsuccessful, Sainsbury argues, for skepticism reemerges on the view that the principles of evidence are necessary. Where principles of evidence are held to be contingent, the skeptical doubt is simply whether the principles are true. Where the principles are held to be necessary, the skeptical doubt is whether merely *credible* beliefs (data) can lead by the use of the principles to *true* beliefs. Consequently, there is no epistemological issue of substance that rests on the question of whether the principles of evidence are contingent or necessary.

John Earman: Concepts of Projectability and the Problems of Induction

Earman attempts to state the conditions under which, according to probability theory, inductions from and projections of observed patterns are correct. The most familiar sort of induction infers a general hypothesis from its instances and, appropriately, is called *general* induction. An example is the inference that all swans are white from observations of some number of white swans and no observations of nonwhite ones. Inferring from the same evidence that the next swan encountered will be white is called *instance* induction. Earman formulates the conditions under which, assuming Bayes's theorem of probability theory, the (posterior) probability of a hypothesis, or of its next instance, goes to 1 (i.e. to certainty), given infinitely accumulating evidence.

Instance induction is treated first. Earman distinguishes between *future-moving* induction, which is based on evidence obtained in the future, and *past-reaching* induction, which is based on evidence already obtained in the past. He also distinguishes between *strong* induction, in which the probability of the inferred instances goes to 1, and *weak* induction, in which the probability of the inferred instances merely increases continually. He cites proofs that a nonzero prior probability for a hypothesis is a sufficient condition for strong future-moving induction to one of its instances, and a necessary condition for weak future-moving instance induction. He shows that a nonzero prior is not sufficient for past-reaching induction, unless one assumes that differently ordered sequences of evidence are exchangeable; and he suggests that exchangeability is a version of the principle of uniformity of nature, whose truth probability theory cannot decide. He concludes that Humean skepticism regarding instance induction is either defeated, or at least not supported, by these results.

Earman goes on to show that general induction to a hypothesis, H, is not strongly projectable if H has rival hypotheses that are assigned high nonzero prior probabilities; but that if H is assigned a nonzero prior, then it is weakly projectable. Consequently, strong induction, which of course is the most desirable, requires that competing hypotheses be given low prior probabilities; and it will be difficult to justify these assignments by any rational means. (HAWTHORNE examines ways of justifying them.)

Earman examines the treatment of induction by Russell, Reichenbach, Goodman, and others in the light of the foregoing results. He finds Russell's treatment in HK disappointing. For Russell failed to distinguish future-moving and past-reaching induction, and although he discovered the objection to induction based on Goodmanian (nonprojectable) predicates, he failed to see that the objection does not apply to future-moving induction, and that this sort of induction is acceptable. Also, Russell failed to realize that competing hypotheses prevent projection of all except observable hypotheses, whether these contain Goodmanian predicates or not. Earman concludes with a pessimistic prognosis for anything but a minimalist theory of objective projectability, i.e., something like the theory offered in the first half of his paper. And he criticizes the attempts of Jaynes, Keynes, Russell, and Reichenbach to obtain a more ambitious theory. Subjectivist probability is not criticized but is deemed the province of cognitive psychology.

James Hawthorne: Giving Up Judgment Empiricism:
The Bayesian Epistemology of Bertrand Russell and Grover Maxwell

Hawthorne's paper compares the views of Russell and Grover Maxwell on induction. He notes that Maxwell agreed with Russell on nearly all points, including the point that judgment empiricism is false. (Judgment empiricism is the thesis that all synthetic statements are a posteriori [non-a priori], i.e., confirmable by the data of experience.) Only on one point was there disagreement: Russell proposed five postulates, or principles, governing nondemonstrative inference; and Maxwell found these inadequate. Hawthorne suggests that this disagreement flows from a general failure to appreciate Russell's Bayesian framework, and the role of the postulates in that framework. Hawthorne's theme is that Russell was really a Bayesian, and employed both the special and the general forms of Bayes's theorem as forms of nondemonstrative (inductive) inference.

The most familiar version of Bayes's theorem is

$Pr(H/E) = Pr(H)Pr(E/H) \div Pr(E)$,

where $Pr(H/E)$ abbreviates "the probability of hypothesis H given evidence E," and E is a finite conjunction of any number of evidential statements. Where H is a general hypothesis, such as "All swans are white," and the evidential statements are instances, "Swan #1 is white," "Swan #2 is white," etc., H entails E, and $Pr(E/H) = 1$. The version of Bayes's theorem used by Russell is stated as follows:

(*) The probability of a general hypothesis (or of the next instance of the hypothesis) goes to 1 as the number of instances of positive evidence goes to infinity.

Keynes's results are used to show that (*) is true if the following two conditions are satisfied: (1) the prior probability of the hypothesis is nonzero (or finite, as Russell says), and (2) the probability of any piece of evidence given the falsity of H falls below some value, q, less than 1. Apparently Russell believed that (2) is true for all empirical hypotheses. And Hawthorne suggests that the purpose of the postulates of nondemonstrative inference was to assign nonzero prior probabilities so as to satisfy (1).

The generalized version of Bayes's theorem shows how the probability of a hypothesis is affected by rival hypotheses. Both Russell and Maxwell held that every hypothesis has an infinite number of rivals (though most of these will seem artificial), and they realized that the number of such rivals must be reduced to a finite, small number if Bayes's theorem is to confirm a hypothesis for a practically obtainable amount of evidence. The reduction is obtained by assigning a finite, small number of hypotheses nonzero probabilities. Accumulating evidence can then eliminate all but one of these. The assignment of prior probability is made with the assistance of the five postulates of nondemonstrative inference. Hawthorne finds this use of the postulates implicit in, or at least consistent with, Russell's treatment.

Hawthorne believes that even if Maxwell had interpreted Russell in the manner just described, he would have found the postulates inadequate because too narrow in scope. According to Maxwell, there is only one postulate for assigning prior probabilities, and it is the following rule: order and weight the probabilities of rival hypotheses intuitively. His basis for this rule is that humans have evolved in such a way that they now possess the innate ability to select hypotheses close enough to the truth that evidence will favor one of them. Hawthorne points out that an idea very like this can be found in HK.

Philosophy of Science and Metaphysics

C. Anthony Anderson: Russell on Order in Time

Russell's program of replacing inferred entities by logical constructions was applied to instants of time in KEW and generalized in AMa to accommodate the theory of relativity. Still later, in a little-studied paper, "On Order in Time" (OT, 1936), Russell brings the full logical machinery of PM to bear on the question of the possibility of usefully defining instants as certain classes of events. Here his conclusion is negative: "...the existence of instants [constructed out of events] requires hypotheses which there is no reason to suppose true" (OT, p. 216).

Anderson argues that Russell underestimated what he had accomplished in OT. Adopt as a primitive the relation that holds between events x and y if and only if x wholly precedes y. Define "x overlaps y" as "x does not wholly precede y and y does not wholly precede x." Finally, define "x ends before y ends" as

"Some event is wholly preceded by x and overlaps y." Using these definitions (which are Russell's) Anderson proposes as the best axioms for Russell's project: (1) no event wholly precedes itself, and (2) if x ends before y ends and y wholly precedes z, then x wholly precedes z. Russell's definition of an instant of time is as a class consisting of exactly those events that overlap every event in that class. It appears that many of the important properties of instants of time follow from axioms (1) and (2).

One thing that does not follow is that any instants *exist*. Earlier, in AMa, Russell had used the axiom of choice (actually an equivalent well-ordering principle) to prove the existence of instants, but he came to have doubts. Anderson explains the proof and urges that from an extensional point of view (which Russell would reject) the postulate is correct and the argument is convincing.

Anderson shows, however, that some further assumptions about events are necessary. Instants of time should form a *compact* series — there should be an instant between any two. Russell claimed to prove that certain simple conditions suffice to guarantee compactness. Anderson shows, by counterexample, that the conditions are not sufficient. It appears that Russell must simply assume as an additional axiom that there is an event between any two nonoverlapping events. Further axioms may be necessary to guarantee the continuity of the series of instants.

Anderson argues that these results — in some ways less and in some ways more than Russell thought he had established — are not defeated by objections that Russell presented earlier, or by objections arising from the theory of relativity. And he tries to defend constructionalism here against a general refutation based on Benacerraf's objection to defining numbers in terms of sets. Basically the defense is that equally good alternative definitions of points have not been shown to exist, and that even if alternatives exist, any one of the definitions may still be better than none. He concludes that epistemological (and even aesthetic) considerations support the adoption of a Russellian construction.

Elizabeth R. Eames: Cause in the Later Russell

Eames argues that Russell's later analysis of causation was unlike his early analysis. In his early realist period (that of PP), Russell held that inferences from sensations (percepts) to the physical objects that cause them are uncertain, since the cause can never be observed. In RSDP and KEW, physical objects are analyzed as structures of sensed and unsensed (but sensible) sensibilia. This analysis is accompanied by an analysis of cause of the empiricist, Hume-Mill variety: cause is defined in terms of observable regularities, and metaphysical ingredients are excluded from the definition. In his final, realist phase in AMa and HK, Russell constructs physical objects out of structures of observable *as well as unobservable* events defined in causal terms. Since the causes may not be observable, an empiricist analysis can no longer be employed, and Russell is forced to formulate postulates that govern inferences from observable effects to unobservable causes. These postulates are undesirable from an empiricist point of view for two reasons. First, they contain metaphysical notions, such as *production* and *power*. Second, they cannot be empirically confirmed.

There is a further difficulty. In AMa and HK Russell holds that if inferences from the data of perception are to be reliable, then perceptual experience must be analyzed and purified, to separate it from the encrustations of habit, memory, and expectation that may well not be veridical. His idea is that the purer the sensory datum the greater its causal dependence on the physical stimulus to perception. Thus to identify the relatively pure datum requires making causal judgments. However, causal judgments are based on data, and the more reliable the judgment the purer the data. Causal judgment requires the purification of data, and the purification of data requires causal judgment; thus, the process of obtaining data is circular.

In summary, the necessity of metaphysical causal postulates, as well as circularity in the basis of causal concepts, are difficulties for Russell's later philosophy of science, and for any view, like Maxwell's, based on it.

Kenneth Blackwell: Portrait of a Philosopher of Science

It is widely known that as an undergraduate at Cambridge Russell concentrated on mathematics, and that his early research was in the foundations of geometry. Blackwell corrects and expands this picture with information from Russell's early writings and from documents in the Russell Archives. Annotated books from Russell's library show that he was reading widely in physics during his twenties and thirties, and published and unpublished memoirs show that during this period he was trying to fit current physics into the Kantian-Hegelian framework obtained from various of his mentors at Cambridge. Although Russell rejected Kant and Hegel, from these efforts emerged the project of PM, the project of deriving arithmetic from logic.

Blackwell suggests that Russell's devotion to science was quasi-religious, arising from his deep need for certainty, and was possibly a substitute for his lost adolescent religiosity. He supports this interpretation by references to Russell's early writing on religion and science, and his later writings on science. In one of the latter we find (*The Scientific Outlook*, 1931, p. 102):

> [Science] belongs with religion and art and love, with the pursuit of the beatific vision, with the Promethean madness that leads the greatest men to strive to become gods. Perhaps the only ultimate value of human life is to be found in this Promethean madness. But it is a value that is religious, not political, or even moral.

In another passage Russell says that the mystic, the lover, the poet, and the scientist are all seekers after knowledge, and that they desire to know the object of their pursuit, not for power or any other manipulative end, but because in the "mystic union" that such knowledge brings "the object in and for itself sheds happiness upon the lover."

Blackwell notes that these remarks by Russell are continuous with others made near the end of his life in "The Expanding Mental Universe" (1959, p. 397). There Russell claims that seers, poets, and scientists all undergo an "expansion of the ego," in which they come to "embrace... distant portions of space and time" and steadily approach a God-like view of the universe "as one vast whole, without any here-now, without that partiality of sense and feeling to which we are, in a greater or lesser degree condemned." The suggestion is that Russell's preoccupation with science and its philosophy is metaphysically, even religiously grounded. For he views the aim of scientific knowledge as a mystical union of the ego with the whole universe.

Warren Goldfarb

Russell's Reasons for Ramification

I

Russell introduced a form of ramification in his 1906 paper "On 'Insolubilia' and Their Solution by Symbolic Logic."[1] There it is applied to propositions. Extended and somewhat modified, ramification is the central component of the theory of types as it is presented in "Mathematical Logic as Based on the Theory of Types" in 1908 and in *Principia Mathematica*.[2] That is, Russell did not separate the theory of orders, which embodies the ramification of propositional functions, from the theory of types. A disentanglement of these two notions was first urged by Ramsey in 1925, when he formulated a simple theory of types.[3] Ramification could then, and only then, be seen as a superposition of a theory of orders on a basic type-theoretic structure.

For over sixty years now, ramification has elicited an intriguing bipolar reaction. Those who have most shared Russell's motivations in the philosophy of mathematics have thought it confused or misguided (thus Ramsey, and also Carnap, Gödel, and Quine).[4] Yet many whose basic outlook is rather more distant from Russell's have found the notion alluring, have continued to study its nature and consequences (although often in settings removed from the theory of types), and have argued for its importance in foundational studies.[5]

Ramification of a domain of abstract entities is the result of requiring that legitimate specifications of such entities be predicative. Briefly put, a specification is predicative if it contains no quantifier that ranges over a universe to which the entity specified belongs.[6] (Obviously, we speak of specifications in an interpreted language.) The predicativity requirement allows a specification to license an existence claim only if the entity whose existence is inferred lies outside the universes of the quantifications in the specification. Thus, the requirement will yield a hierarchy of entities: those at any given level of the hierarchy are just those that are specifiable using quantifiers that range only over lower levels of the hierarchy. Ramification is just this division of entities into levels.

There is a particular philosophical cast that, it seems, has to be put on the nature of the entities under discussion in order for the predicativity requirement, and hence for ramification, to be justified. This philosophical cast, roughly put, is nonrealist and in a sense constructivist: these entities do not subsist independently of us, but are created or legitimized by our being able to specify them. (I have said "in a sense constructivist" because the specifications need not be constructive in the ordinary sense. There is no constraint of effectiveness, and no prohibition of quantifiers with infinite ranges.) It is, to be sure, not an easy matter to spell out such a constructivist view, particularly if the legitimacy of classical (truth-functional) logic is also to be supported. Yet it does seem clear that some such view will entail the predicativity requirement. Since it is first the specification that legitimizes the entity specified, that specification can in no way depend on the existence of the entity. Therefore, the ranges of the quantifiers in the specification cannot include the entity.[7]

My interest, however, is in the converse claim, namely, that ramification is justified *only* on such a constructivist view (and hence that, implicitly at least, Russell held such a view). This claim was forwarded by Gödel in "Russell's Mathematical Logic":

> If, however, it is a question of objects that exist independently of our constructions, there is nothing in the least absurd in the existence of totalities containing members which can be . . . uniquely characterized only by reference to this totality. (p. 136)

The point is echoed by Quine in *Set Theory and Logic*, speaking of classes as the entities in question:

> For we are not to view classes literally as created through being specified. . . . The doctrine of classes is rather that they are there from the start. This being so, there is no evident fallacy in impredicative specification. It is reasonable to single out a desired class by citing any trait of it, even though we chance thereby to quantify over it along with everything else in the universe. (p. 243)

Given this analysis, by now enshrined as the common wisdom, the bipolar attitude toward ramification that I have mentioned becomes most understandable. The sort of constructivism that Gödel and Quine impute to Russell is, it seems, simply out of place in a logicist. For constructivism bespeaks a shift in the very conception of existence, a shift away from realism; whereas one point of logicism, and other classical theories of mathematics—including that which Gödel espoused—is to vindicate, in one way or another, our full-bloodedly realistic talk about mathematical entities. What work and attention ramification has received over the past sixty years has issued from authors with markedly proof-theoretic leanings.

Now the claim that a constructivist view must underlie ramification is not implausible, and it is even possible to read some of Russell's remarks as pointing to such a view. Yet constructivism does seem inconsonant with Russell's usual overarching manner of talking about existence.[8] In the period of the *Principles of Mathematics*, Russell espoused a strong variety of realism.[9] Subsequently, he became ontologically more and more parsimonious. This parsimony is achieved by elimination and reduction, using the devices of incomplete expressions and logical constructions. That is, statements apparently about certain entities are systematically paraphrased, so that they can be held true without any commitment to those entities. Thus Russell is able to shrink the class of things whose existence must be assumed. But, throughout, his conception of what it is to be an entity does not change. There is no notion of a sort of existence, different from the full-blooded kind in being reliant on our specifications.

Thus, it seems to me that the imputation of constructivism to Russell stands in need of refinement. Gödel and Quine make Russell out to have a general vision of what the existence of abstract entities comes to, and thus to be adopting constructivism as a fundamental stance toward ontology. That does not seem accurate to Russell. Rather, the justification for ramification rests on the particular sorts of entities to which it is applied, namely, propositions and propositional functions. To understand this, we must see more clearly why these entities are central to Russell's logical enterprise and what special features of their structure Russell exploits. The results might have the appearance of constructivism, but Russell's most basic reasons for ramification are not the outgrowth of such a general position; rather, they are far more particular to the nature of the entities he treats.

Attention to the importance of propositions in Russell's conception of logic will also clarify the other widely recognized root of the predicativity requirement. Russell's logical theorizing always proceeds in response to the paradoxes, both set-theoretic and semantic. Now, Ramsey pointed out that the former are blocked by simple type theory alone. The others are not, but they involve notions like truth, expression, and definability (indeed, that is why we call them "semantic"). Therefore, Ramsey argued (as had Peano before him), their solution need not come from the logical theory itself. Thus, it appears, it was a misguided desire on Russell's part that the logical system do more than is appropriate that led to ramification. However, it seems to me that Russell's treating the two sorts of paradoxes as one is not a gratuitous blunder: his view of the aims of logic precludes any sharp separation of them.

In what follows, I shall examine Russell's conception of logic and the theories of propositions that it spawns. The general themes of this conception, canvassed in section II, explain the centrality of propositions and propositional functions to logic and support Russell's view that logical structures must preclude the possibility of semantic paradox. In section III, I examine those features of propositions and propositional functions—features that arise from their intensionality—that undercut any immediate link between ramification and constructivism. Russell's particular theories of propositions, sketched in section IV, exhibit the mechanisms through which ramification is generated, and cast some light on various oddities in *Principia Mathematica*.

Russell's reasons for ramification rest on a wealth of rather intricate views; they cannot be accurately summarized by a label or a quick diagnosis. I hope here to be making a first step towards the fuller treatment that they demand.

II

Russell took logic to be completely universal. It embodies all-encompassing principles of correct reasoning. Logic is constituted by the most general laws about the logical furniture of the universe: laws to which all reasoning is subject. The logical system provides a universal language; it is the framework inside of which all rational discourse proceeds.

For Russell, then, there is no stance outside of logic: anything that can be communicated must lie within it. Thus there is no room for what we would call metatheoretic considerations about logic. Logic is not a system of signs that can be disinterpreted and for which alternative interpretations may be investigated: such talk of interpretations would presuppose just the sort of exterior stance that Russell's conception precludes. In particular, the range of the quantified variables in the laws of logic is not subject to change or restriction. These ranges must be fixed, once for all, and fixed as the most general ranges possible.

The conception of the universality of logic that I have just outlined is intrinsic to Russell's logicism.[10] Although prior to his coming under the influence of Wittgenstein Russell did not have much to say about the status of the laws of logic, he did draw strong philosophical consequences from the reduction of mathematics to logic. These consequences rest on the complete generality that Russell took logic to have. For logic, on his conception, is not a special science. It invokes no concepts or principles peculiar to one or another particular area of knowledge. Rather, it rests only on assumptions that are involved in any thinking or reasoning at all. In this way, Russell could take the logicist reduction to show that no special faculties (such as Kantian intuition) need be postulated in order to account for mathematics.

This conception points also to what has to figure among the "logical furniture of the universe" whose laws are at issue. Logic is the universal framework of rational discourse; this suggests that its primary objects of study will be the vehicles of judgment, that is, the entities to which a person who judges is primitively related. For Russell (in his earlier period), the vehicles of judgment are propositions.[11] Logic will provide laws that govern all propositions, and will thus exhibit the bounds of discourse: the bounds, so to speak, of sense. Now, that there are general laws of propositions depends essentially on the fact that propositions are complex. Hence part of the task of logic is to display what this complexity consists in. The branch of logic that Russell sometimes calls "philosophical logic" provides the general framework for the analysis of propositions: the categories of building blocks from which propositions are made, and the ways in which they are fitted together. In this way propositional functions—functions whose values are propositions—also come to figure centrally among the entities that logic treats.

The centrality of propositions underlies Russell's view that the logical system must treat the semantic paradoxes. Now Russell did recognize a distinction between these and the set-theoretic paradoxes. In "On 'Insolubilia,' " he presents a "simple substitutional theory" that eliminates classes, relations, and propositional functions. He goes on to say:

> The above doctrine solves, as far as I can discover, all paradoxes concerning classes and relations; but in order to solve the *Epimenides* we seem to need a similar doctrine as regards propositions. (p. 204)

(This "similar doctrine" is his earliest form of ramification, discussed in section IV.) The distinction, then, is simply a distinction of subject matter. Just as the set-theoretic paradoxes are about classes and relations, and to solve them logic must inquire into the nature of these entities, the Epimenides paradox and its ilk are about propositions and propositional functions, and logic must inquire here too. Indeed, given Russell's conception of logic, the semantic paradoxes are more important to it. Since the structure of propositions is the very center of logic's attention, the semantic paradoxes pose a greater threat.

Although Ramsey shared Russell's view of the centrality of propositions to logic, he denied that logic bears the responsibility for solving the semantic paradoxes. In "The Foundations of Mathematics," Ramsey gives an account of propositions, using infinitary truth-functions, that supports the simple—rather than ramified—theory of types. He claims that this system need not concern itself with the semantic paradoxes, insofar as

> [they] are not purely logical, and cannot be stated in logical terms alone; for they all contain some reference to thought, language, or symbolism, which are not formal but empirical terms. So they may be due not to faulty logic or mathematics, but to faulty ideas concerning thought and language. (p. 21)[12]

Thus the semantic paradoxes are to be blocked not by laws about the structure of propositions but rather by special features of the notions like truth and definability that are invoked in them.

A brief look at Ramsey's solution of the Grelling paradox (that of the adjective "heterological") will show why his position would be unacceptable to Russell. Ramsey notes that the paradox depends upon a relation of expression between a word (an adjective) and a propositional function. He then urges that "expression" is ambiguous, and that there is a hierarchy of expression relations. Once this is taken into account, the definition of "heterological" leads to no contradiction.

Now Russell, I think, would ask why there is no relation that sums up (is the union of) the different expression relations that Ramsey postulates. (Such a union would reintroduce the paradox.) Since in the absence of ramification the propositional functions expressed are all of the same type, nothing in the nature of the relata of these relations would preclude such a union. Particularly given his acceptance of arbitrary infinitary truth-functions, Ramsey must take the impossibility of summing the relations to be merely factual, perhaps of a natural or empirical sort. Given his notion of proposition, this position is of doubtful coherence – particularly in view of the a priori reasoning that engenders it.

In fact, the ramified theory of types, even with the axiom of reducibility, does prevent precisely this summation. As Church has rigorously substantiated, ramification – in particular, the differing orders of the propositional functions involved – precludes the existence of a single expression relation that could generate Grelling's paradox.[13] The impossibility here flows from the nature of the entities at issue, not from any ad hoc restriction. Thus the hierarchical structure of semantic relations arises from purely logical considerations; it is not a fact of a special science. No conclusion of a special science could block a union of levels of a hierarchy; only a logical impossibility could do so.

There is another criticism that Russell could make of Ramsey's diagnosis of the semantic paradoxes, one specific to the Epimenides. In this paradox, Ramsey would presumably take the notion of truth to be the culprit, and claim that special features of that notion – perhaps some ambiguity in the phrase "is true" – forestall the reflexivity that yields contradiction. (This would be similar to a Tarskian approach.) However, Russell's view of propositions enables one to dispense with all explicit mention of truth in logic. The proposition, e.g., that no proposition having property φ is true can be expressed as

(1) $(p)(\varphi p \supset \neg p)$.

Hence this proposition does not contain the notion of truth. Now, the acceptability of this manner of expression rests on the construal of truth as a property of propositions (rather than of sentences, as in Tarski), and, to some extent, on Russell's view that propositions are both nameable and assertible by sentences; i.e., propositions both are complex entities on all fours with other objects and are the objects of judgment. As a result of these views, the notion of truth simply disappears, through formulations like (1). Moreover, Ramsey agrees with Russell, at least to the extent of accepting formulations like (1); this forms the basis of his redundancy theory of truth.[14]

The Epimenides paradox can then be generated with no use of semantic notions. All that is required is a value for the propositional function φ in (1) that is uniquely satisfied by the proposition expressed by (1). Such a propositional function, it seems, would not be hard to imagine. Thus, it appears, a Ramseyan solution to the paradox is simply not available. The weakness of the extralogical assumptions needed for the paradox makes it clearer why for Russell the nature of propositions themselves must figure in any solution. (In fact, ramification blocks the paradox by precluding the proposition expressed by (1) from being a member of the range of the quantified variable in (1).)[15]

I have been talking of the central role of propositions in Russell's logic, and have so far ignored the other principal sort of entity Russell considers, namely, classes. Now the system of *Principia* makes no class-existence assumptions; rather, Russell eliminates classes in favor of propositional functions. He sees this "no-class theory" as the solution to the problems that had vexed him for many years. For mathematics, it seems, requires classes; yet the paradoxes had raised pervasive questions about their existence. Such questions could not be solved merely by devising a consistent theory of classes and leaving it at that. For this would make the theory a special science, whereas Russell sought to justify classes as *logical* objects: as objects guaranteed by principles implicit in all reasoning. Only thus could the reduction of mathematics to class theory be a logicist reduction, and bear more weight than a mere interpretation of one branch of mathematics in another.[16]

For this reason Russell worries not just about which classes exist but about the very nature of a class. In the *Principles of Mathematics* a central issue is that of how a class is a unity: what logical operation binds the members together into a single object, so that the class can serve as a logical subject. In the *Principles* theory there is a general feature of discourse that is of help here, namely, the quantifier-words. For at that time, Russell took *all* φ's to be a denoting concept that denotes the class of φ's. Since "all" is a logical word if anything is, the logical nature of classes is thereby vindicated. However, this route is not open to Russell after the demise of the *Principles* theory of denoting concepts in 1905 (for more on this theory, see Hylton's contribution to this volume).

Given all this, the attractions of the no-class theory for Russell are obvious. The paradoxes show that the straightforward naive views fail for both propositional functions and classes. But whereas Russell's fundamental conception of logic demands an account of propositions and propositional functions, classes are additional, and pose further questions. The no-class theory enables Russell to be agnostic about the existence of classes and to say nothing about their nature.

III

Important consequences about the nature of ramification follow from the fact that Russell's logic treats propositions and propositional functions rather than classes. Indeed, Russell never envisaged a ramification of classes. When in "Mathematical Logic as Based on the Theory of Types" or in *Principia* he speculates about the existence of classes, he treats them as all of the same order, and he asserts that the existence of classes would imply the axiom of reducibility. Now the claim that ramification necessarily bespeaks constructivism is, it seems to me, most plausible if ramification of classes is at issue. If all the members of two classes are of like logical category, then the intrinsic nature of these classes can provide no ground for a difference in *their* logical category. To support any such distinction, some feature extrinsic to the identity of the classes would have to be brought in. To support ramification in particular, this extrinsic feature would have to reflect something about how the classes are characterized. But to justify in turn the role that a feature extrinsic to the identity of the class is now taken to play, it would have to be maintained that the feature is essential to the existence of the class. The constructivism implicit in such a view is clear.[17]

Thus it appears that the close connection between ramification with respect to classes and constructivism depends on the fact that we have a conception of the nature of the class that works "from below." The identity of a class is determined by its membership; yet ramification would demand that categorical distinctions be made among classes on grounds over and above membership.

Matters are different, however, with propositions and propositional functions. For these are intensional entities. The identity of a propositional function is not determined by the objects of which it is true, nor is the identity of a proposition determined by its truth-value. This opens the possibility that intrinsic features of propositions and propositional functions could support the categorical distinctions that ramification demands. If so, the immediate link between ramification and constructivism that exists for classes would be severed.

Our conception of the nature of a proposition or propositional function comes not "from below" but rather by way of the manner in which the proposition or propositional function is expressed. This points to a distinction in the notion of specification when applied to propositions and propositional functions, as opposed to classes. To specify a class is to give a propositional function that is true of all and only the members of that class. The specification can be understood on its own; given such an understanding, it is a further question whether or not a given class is the one specified. That is, the specification by itself does not tell us which entity *is* the one specified. This space between the specification and the entity specified does not exist in the case of propositions and propositional functions. Here, to understand the specification is to understand the proposition or propositional function specified. That is, the specification immediately tells us which entity is the one meant.

For Russell, understanding is – like judging – a relation to the propositions and propositional functions expressed by our words. To understand a sentence is to grasp the proposition expressed by the sentence.[18] Thus, for propositions and propositional functions, it makes no sense to speak of first understanding a specification and then going on to investigate which entity is specified; for that entity is given in the understanding of the specification. With classes, clearly, matters are different: a specification can be understood, that is, a propositional function can be grasped, yet there can still be a question as to which class is specified.

Indeed, for this reason I find the terminology of "specification" completely misleading in the realm of propositions and propositional functions. The closest analogue to class specifications here would be descriptions like "the last proposition conjectured by Fermat," descriptions the understanding of which is independent of the particular propositions specified. Such "indirect" specifications do not figure in Russell's logical system. Rather, the comprehension axioms for propositions and propositional functions that are implicit in the system involve not so much the specification of these entities as the presentation of them. One is not characterizing a proposition or propositional function: one is giving it. I shall therefore use "presentation" rather than "specification" in this connection.

This helps explain, I think, why no comprehension axioms are explicit in *Principia*. When Russell talks about the existence of classes, he clearly recognizes that the issue concerns which principles of the form

$$(\exists \alpha)(x)(x \epsilon \alpha \equiv Fx)$$

are to be accepted.[19] From a modern perspective, a theory of propositions and propositional functions would have to answer the analogous questions: for which formulas F and Gx (and for what orders of the variables p and φ) are

$$(\exists p)(p = F)$$

and

$$(\exists \varphi)(\varphi \hat{x} = G\hat{x})$$

to be accepted?[20] But Russell never comes close to formulating this or to having axioms of this form. The mathematical power of such axioms is obtained by means of generalization and instantiation, as in

$$\frac{H(G\hat{x})}{(\exists \varphi)H(\varphi \hat{x})} \quad \text{and} \quad \frac{(\varphi)H(\varphi \hat{x})}{H(G\hat{x})}.$$

The absence of such axioms springs from the idea that, once the presentation $G\hat{x}$ is given, one needs no special principle to yield the existence of the propositional function. Rather, in using the formula $G\hat{x}$ in our sentences at all, we are using that propositional function in our propositions. Thus, inferences like the preceding appear to be purely logical, and not the result of special existence assumptions.

The role of presentations of propositions and propositional functions also lies behind Russell's not distinguishing among the various formulations of the vicious-circle principle. One formulation is "no totality may contain members that are definable only in terms of that totality"; the others use "presuppose" and "involve" instead of "are definable only in terms of." Gödel points out that, prima facie, these are three distinct principles, and he claims that only the first yields ramification, whereas only the second and third are plausible without recourse to constructivism ("Russell's Mathematical Logic," p. 135). But if definitions are not external to the entities under consideration, as they are to classes but are not — if they are presentations in my sense — to propositions and propositional functions, then the distinction among these formulations seems to collapse. For, in that case, to say that a totality is necessarily involved in any presentation of a proposition is to say that the totality is involved in the proposition.

In pointing to what I have called the lack of space between the intrinsic nature of a proposition or propositional function and the manner in which it is presented, I do not mean to be suggesting that the existence of such an entity is dependent on its having been presented. That would lead to an extreme constructivism involving a notion of temporality, of the sort to which Quine alludes (*Set Theory and Its Logic*, p. 243). It may appear, however, that every such entity must be in some sense presentable. Indeed, Ramsey and Gödel speak of Russell's system as treating only "nameable" entities. Yet the terms "presentable" and "nameable" must be approached with caution; they cannot be used here in any ordinary sense. Certainly, presentability construed as nameability in the language of *Principia* is not at issue. Indeed, Russell never tells us — nor does he think he needs to tell us, in the logical writings — what the basic building blocks of presentations are. The logical vocabulary of *Principia* is a mere skeleton: any notions the special sciences (or epistemology) might arrive at are to be added to its vocabulary. Logic does not set any limits on which predicates and relations (i.e., elementary propositional functions) exist. Even to speak of propositions as "in principle presentable" is somewhat misleading. This is shown by a claim Russell makes concerning a consequence of the hypothesis that classes exist: he says that if α is a class, then $\hat{x} \in \alpha$ is an elementary propositional function (*Principia*, p. 166). Now, if classes exist, there are too many of them to be even potentially nameable; thus these elementary propositions also fail to be nameable. In short, the notion of "presentability" that is at issue does not involve even the notion of a possible language. It is, so to speak, an ontological rather than a linguistic notion. Thus it provides no ground for the sort of criticisms that Ramsey and Gödel make.

Since logic sets no limits to the elementary functions, it may appear that it can provide no information at all about presentations of propositions. This appearance is deceptive. Consider, for example, the Epimenides paradox. Here we present (or so it seems) a proposition like:

Every proposition hereby asserted is false.

Now our understanding of this proposition is *as* a universal one, with a quantifier over propositions. That is, the complexity represented by the quantifier is built into the proposition. Since logic does tell us what sorts of complexity can figure in the structure of propositions, this proposition and ones like it can be treated by logic, even in ignorance of what the basic building blocks of propositions generally—that is, what the elementary propositions and propositional functions—are.

I have been arguing that the intensional nature of propositions and propositional functions makes it in principle possible to justify ramification without reliance on a constructivist view of these entities. This does not yet provide any justification. The substantive constraints on the complex structures of propositions and propositional functions that comprise ramification rely on the details of the theory of these entities that Russell adopts. To those details I now turn.

IV

Unfortunately, in *Principia* and the writings leading up to it, Russell never lays out any comprehensive theory of propositions. (This is in marked contrast to the *Principles*, in which the nature of propositions is investigated at length.) One clear reason for this absence is that, during this period, Russell's views frequently shift. Often, several different theories seem to be espoused simultaneously. Hence I shall here be engaging in somewhat speculative reconstruction.

One rather startling view that Russell expresses in *Principia* is that propositions simply do not exist. On page 44 he writes,

> What we call a "proposition"... is not a single entity at all. That is to say, the phrase which expresses a proposition is what we call an "incomplete" symbol; it does not have meaning in itself, but requires some supplementation... when I judge "Socrates is human" the meaning is completed by the act of judging.

This view is of a piece with Russell's "multiple-relation" theory of judgment, about which Russell subsequently writes at length. It does not appear that this view is consistent with the logic of *Principia* (see Church, "Comparison," p. 748). Luckily, the view seems to play no real role in Russell's explanations of his logical system. In what follows, I shall take the charitable course of ignoring it.

As background, let me recall Russell's early view of propositions. A proposition is a complex of entities; ordinarily, it is that complex which, if true, is identical with the fact that makes it true. Thus the constituents of a proposition are, ordinarily, the entities that the proposition is about; for example, the proposition that Mont Blanc is higher than the Zugspitze literally contains two mountains, as well as the relation *higher than*. I have said "ordinarily" since, in the *Principles of Mathematics*, there are exceptions that arise in connection with denoting concepts. As a result of "On Denoting," the exceptions disappear.[21]

The theory of descriptions of "On Denoting," and, indeed, the general notion of incomplete expression there introduced, puts into prominence the role of quantified variables. In line with the early view of propositions, Russell takes variables to be actual constituents of propositions, that is, to be entities underlying the use of a letter like "x" or "φ" in the same way that an object underlies the use of its name. To the obvious question of what these entities are, Russell has no answer, but does not seem overly perturbed by this. In "On Denoting" he says, "I take the notion of the *variable* as fundamental," and explains no further (p. 104). Note that Russell speaks of "the variable" as though there were only one. In this period Russell took variables to be completely unrestricted: all variables range over everything. Since every variable confers the same generality, the particular identity of a variable is needed only for its role in cross-referencing. Thus, in a sense, there is only *the* variable—that is, the notion of unrestricted variation—to explain.

Indeed, during this period Russell stresses the complete generality of variables. He takes the lack of restrictions on range to arise from the universality of logic, especially from the idea that anything expressible at all can be expressed inside its framework. (See, e.g., "On 'Insolubilia,' " p. 206. Such reasons also seem to underlie his dissatisfaction with the primitive theory of types discussed in Appendix B of the *Principles of Mathematics*.) The retention of unrestricted generality is a great advantage he sees in the "substitutional theory" he develops in 1906. In that theory, classes and propositional functions are eliminated in favor of propositions and a primitive notion of substitution of one entity for another in propositions.[22] The set-theoretic paradoxes are avoided, even though the basic language contains no type restrictions, because of the form of the contextual definitions through which class variables can be introduced. Were the basic language to be extended by means of these definitions, the class variables so introduced *would* have to be restricted as to type. In other words, any putative formula in the extended language that violates type restrictions could not be reduced by means of the contextual definitions to a formula of the basic language.

However, Russell recognizes in the third section of "On 'Insolubilia' " that the theory as he had so far laid it out does not block the semantic paradoxes. Hence he takes it a step further and denies that any but elementary propositions exist: that is, he suggests, there are no propositions that contain bound variables. Thus paradox-engendering forms like $(p)(\varphi p \supset \neg p)$ do not express propositions; a fortiori, there is nothing they express that can instantiate the universal variable, and paradox is blocked. Of course, Russell then has to show how to make sense of quantified statements at all. He does this by talking of ambiguous statements:

> "For all values of x, $x = x$" I take to be an ambiguous statement of any one of the various propositions of the form "$x = x$." There is thus not a new proposition, but merely an unlimited undetermined choice among a number of propositions. (p. 207)

It is hard to extract a coherent theory from Russell's sketchy remarks here, but I take it that what he has in mind is, roughly, that judgment, assertion, truth, and so on relate only to elementary propositions. The force of applying such notions to quantified statements is captured by more complex ways in which the notions can be related to elementary propositions. Thus, he says:

If we want to say what is equivalent to "I am making a false statement containing n apparent variables," we must say something like: "There is a propositional function $\varphi(x_1, x_2, \ldots, x_n)$ such that I assert that $\varphi(x_1, x_2, \ldots, x_n)$ is true for any values of $x_1, x_2, \ldots, x_n$ and this is in fact false." (p. 208)

Statements are logical fictions, and "there is no way of speaking of statements *in general*: we can speak of statements of propositions, or statements containing one, two, three,... apparent variables, but not of statements in general." (p. 207)

Russell does not give the contextual definitions needed here (and there may well be serious problems in this, particularly with regard to alternating quantifiers and nonprenex statements). But it seems clear that what he envisages still preserves the virtues of the substitutional theory. In the basic language, all variables range over the whole universe; now, though, the universe contains none but elementary propositions. If the contextual definitions are used to extend the language by introducing variables for quantified propositions, the form of those definitions would require a hierarchy of such variables. Indeed, his remarks suggest that to quantify over n-quantifier statements is really to use $n + 1$ quantifiers in the basic language; thus, one cannot quantify over all statements, and, more particularly, one cannot in an n-quantifier statement quantify over n-quantifier statements. A ramified structure is thereby induced by the contextual definitions, although none exists in the basic language.[23]

The sort of ramification that results, however, is more finely grained than that which would arise from a constraint of predicativity. *Any* additional quantifier affects the order of a statement; that is, order is determined by the number of quantifiers, not by their range. To be sure, the constraint of predicativity is obeyed, but as a special case. No statement can contain a quantifier that ranges over a domain of which that statement is a member, since that would require a statement to contain simultaneously n and $n + 1$ quantifiers.

Russell seems to jettison this theory: there is no hint of it in "Mathematical Logic as Based on the Theory of Types," and no subsequent assertion that elementary propositions are real while others are logical fictions. (This may be due to difficulties in giving the appropriate contextual definitions or in finding a satisfactory account of judgment and other propositional attitudes; more likely, Russell may feel that his later official view that *no* propositions exist supersedes it.) Nonetheless, as we shall see, remnants of the 1906 view persist in *Principia*.

In "Mathematical Logic," Russell's view is quite different from that exhibited in the substitutional theory. Propositional functions are now taken as legitimate entities; with their reappearance, the realistic view of propositions as complexes also returns. Moreover, variables no longer have unlimited generality; rather, a variable ranges only over the entities of one order. These two points are closely related. Once propositional functions are allowed, with the concomitant idea that every well-formed open formula of the language expresses one, paradoxes like the Russell paradox will immediately arise unless some restrictions are put on the variables. Fortunately, the admission of propositional functions allows Russell to think that restrictions in the ranges of variables are consonant with the universality of logic. For, he argues, those restrictions come from the ranges of significance of the propositional functions. That is, inherent in a propositional function is a range of arguments to which the propositional function can be applied with sense. In this way, the restrictions on variables are intrinsic rather than stipulated ad hoc; they do display the bounds of sense.

I shall not examine Russell's tenuous arguments for the coincidence of ranges of significance and orders. I wish only to point to a consequence of having variables that lack complete generality. Once such variables are used, the question of the nature of the variable (as an entity) becomes far more urgent. Different variables can have different ranges; it then appears that our understanding of a proposition or a propositional function that contains quantified variables will depend quite heavily on an understanding of what those ranges are. The variable must carry with it some definite information; it must in some way represent its range of variation. Therefore, I would speculate, Russell takes a variable to presuppose the full extent of its range. Now, since the identity of a proposition or propositional function depends on the identity of the variables it contains, and the variables presuppose their range of variation, even the weakest form of the vicious-circle principle suffices to yield ramification. Indeed, Russell may perhaps even think of the variable as *containing* all the entities over which it ranges; in that case, the only principle needed is that a complex entity cannot contain itself as a proper part. In any case, the ramification engendered is just the sort required by the constraint of predicativity. In short, in this theory ramification springs from the strongly realistic picture Russell has of propositions and propositional functions, and in particular of the nature of variables.

In *Principia Mathematica* it is by and large this theory of 1908 that is put to work. However, in both the philosophical discussions and the technical work there are remnants of the 1906 view. For example, in the Introduction, chapter II, part III, Russell distinguishes between first truth, which elementary propositions can have, and second truth, the truth of propositions that contain one quantified variable. He takes second truth to be parasitic on first truth. This leads him to a distinction of orders of propositions on the basis of the number of quantifiers they contain, a clear shadow of the 1906 view. Yet in part IV of the same chapter, he distinguishes orders of propositions on the basis of the sorts of variables they contain, in the standard ramified manner. Both views are reflected in subsequent technical work. The more finely grained ramification that stems from 1906 motivates his grounding quantificational logic in *9 by *defining* the truth-functions of quantified propositions in terms of quantifications of truth-functions of elementary ones. This is unnecessary on the 1908 view; and in *10, he starts quantificational logic over again, giving what he calls an "alternative method." This method is a more standard axiomatic approach, consonant with the fully realistic view of quantified propositions of 1908. There are other curiosities in the text that exhibit the presence of two distinct theories.[24] Thus, it seems to me that the murky beginning sections of *Principia* will be illuminated if the influence of these competing theories is traced through.

Conclusion

I have been emphasizing how the issues surrounding ramification look when we bear in mind the conception of logic that focuses on propositions and propositional functions. Russell's logicism comes down to the idea of trying to obtain mathematics from the laws of these intensional entities; in this way, his basic conception of logic is less mathematical than Frege's. Russell's logicist enterprise fails, as is shown by the need for the axiom of reducibility (which cannot be justified on any grounds but expediency); this failure may indeed show, as Gödel says, that there is irreducibly mathematical content in mathematics.

Many features of the project give rise to ramification. Russell is no constructivist, although a semblance of constructivism can arise from the tight connection between how these intensional entities are presented and what they are. In fact, Russell tends toward realism, but a realism modified by his concern to investigate how intelligible claims on reality could function. Criticisms of ramification from a "Platonist" point of view simply ignore this concern. However muddled Russell sometimes gets, he seems to have grasped the extremely subtle points that such a concern can unearth.[25]

Notes

1. B. Russell, "On 'Insolubilia' and Their Solution by Symbolic Logic," in Russell, *Essays in Analysis*, ed. D. Lackey (New York: Braziller, 1973), pp. 190–214.

2. B. Russell, "Mathematical Logic as Based on the Theory of Types," (1908), in J. van Heijenoort (ed.), *From Frege to Gödel: A Sourcebook in Mathematical Logic* (Cambridge, MA: Harvard University Press, 1967), pp. 150–82. A. N. Whitehead and B. Russell, *Principia Mathematica*, vol. 1 (Cambridge: Cambridge University Press, 1910).

3. F. P. Ramsey, "The Foundations of Mathematics" (1925), in F. P. Ramsey, *The Foundations of Mathematics and Other Logical Essays* (London: Routledge & Kegan Paul, 1931), pp. 1–61.

4. R. Carnap, "On the Logicist Foundations of Mathematics" (1931), in P. Benacerraf and H. Putnam (eds.), *Philosophy of Mathematics: Selected Readings* (Cambridge: Cambridge University Press, 1983), pp. 41–52. K. Gödel, "Russell's Mathematical Logic," in P. A. Schilpp (ed.), *The Philosophy of Bertrand Russell* (LaSalle, IL: Open Court, 1944), pp. 125–53. W. V. Quine, *Set Theory and Its Logic* (Cambridge, MA: Harvard University Press, 1969).

5. See, e.g., H. Weyl, *Das Kontinuum* (Leipzig: Veit, 1918), S. Feferman, "Systems of Predicative Analysis," *Journal of Symbolic Logic*, 29 (1964), pp. 1–30, and I. Hacking, "What Is Logic?" *Journal of Philosophy*, 76 (1979), pp. 285–319.

6. In the Russellian setting, the notion of predicativity has to be amplified to preclude quantifiers that range over universes containing anything that "presupposes" the entity specified. For the amusing history of the word "predicativity," see Quine, *Set Theory and Its Logic*, p. 242.

7. Clearly, this argument relies upon a premise to the effect that the sense of a specification depends in some way on the ranges of the quantifiers it contains. Interestingly enough, it is this

premise—rather than the thesis that certain entities are first legitimized by their specifications—that Carnap denies in "Logicist Foundations."

8. I do not use Russell's ontological terminology. For him, existence means existence in space and time. Abstract entities thus do not exist; they have Being (they *are*). Since I prefer to avoid the grammatical awkwardness, and am not concerned with any contrast between concreta and abstracta, I use "existence" for Russell's "Being."

9. B. Russell, *The Principles of Mathematics* (London: Allen & Unwin, 1903).

10. Fuller accounts of this conception can be found in J. van Heijenoort, "Logic as Calculus and Logic as Language," *Synthèse*, 32 (1967), pp. 324–30; W. Goldfarb, "Logic in the Twenties: The Nature of the Quantifier," *Journal of Symbolic Logic*, 44 (1979), pp. 351–68; and P. Hylton, "Russell's Substitutional Theory," *Synthèse*, 45 (1980), pp. 1–31. Hylton also discusses in more detail the relation between this conception and the philosophical upshot Russell took logicism to have.

11. This move, although natural, is not inevitable. Although Frege had a similar conception of logic, he distinguished between the vehicles of judgment (thoughts) and the entities that logical laws are about (objects, including the truth-values, and functions). Russell, of course, rejected the basic points on which Frege's distinction rests: the theory of sense and reference and the notion that sentences refer to truth-values.

12. Ramsey continues, "If so, they would not be relevant to...logic, if by 'logic' we mean a symbolic system, though of course they would be relevant to logic in the sense of the analysis of thought"; and, in a footnote: "These two meanings of 'logic' are frequently confused." This rather glib distinction suggests that Ramsey is not, in the end, in agreement with key features of Russell's conception of logic. Perhaps it explains how Ramsey could introduce infinitary truth-functions so cavalierly, a step justly criticized by Gödel as undercutting the whole point of a logicist reduction ("Russell's Mathematical Logic," p. 142).

13. A. Church, "Comparison of Russell's Resolution of the Semantical Antinomies with That of Tarski," *Journal of Symbolic Logic*, 41 (1976), pp. 747–60.

14. See F. P. Ramsey, "Facts and Propositions" (1927), in *Foundations of Mathematics and Other Logic Essays*, p.143.

15. Cf. *The Principles of Mathematics*, p. 527, where Russell considers a paradox that, as far as I know, does not reappear in his writings. This paradox would be classified as semantic, from our point of view; but it is engendered by means that, for Russell, involve no nonlogical notions. (I am grateful to Leonard Linsky and to C. Anthony Anderson for calling my attention to this passage.)

16. An interest in showing classes to be logical objects also lies behind Frege's criticizing Cantor at the same time as adopting the notion of extension (and, later, course-of-values) of a concept in order to obtain classes. Of course, Frege and Russell have different conceptions of what it is to be a logical entity.

17. Even the simple theory of types looks unnatural if taken directly as a theory of classes. While there might be arguments from our conception of classes to the need for a cumulative hierarchy, I see none for a noncumulative hierarchy of classes, one that precludes all mixed-level classes.

18. Sentences and, in general, words and symbols play no role in Russell's characterizations of understanding, judgment, assertion, and inference. That is why such use-mention errors as exist in his writings rarely turn out to have vicious effect.

19. See B. Russell, "On Some Difficulties in the Theory of Transfinite Numbers and Order Types" (1906), in *Essays in Analysis*, pp. 135–64, especially section II.

20. Russell uses the circumflex as an abstraction operator: if Fx is an open sentence, then $F\hat{x}$ expresses the propositional function that, for each argument a, yields as value the proposition expressed by Fa. He discusses this operator in the Introduction to *Principia*, p. 15; but in the body of that work it is introduced almost on the sly, in *9.131. Cf. Hylton, "Russell's Substitutional Theory," p. 27.

21. B. Russell, "On Denoting" (1905), in *Essays in Analysis*, pp. 103–19.

22. Details of this theory are given in Hylton, "Russell's Substitutional Theory." Note that it is entities that are substituted one for another, not words or names. Hence this theory is quite distinct from what is currently called "the substitutional theory of quantification."

23. Here I disagree sharply with Hylton's reading of this section of "On 'Insolubilia' " ("Russell's Substitutional Theory," pp. 22–26).

24. A more minor example is his definition of predicative function. In the Introduction (p. 51),

Russell identifies the predicative functions with the first-order ones. Thus a predicative function of individuals is one whose quantifiers, if any, range only over individuals. This is in keeping with standard ramification. But in *12 he calls a propositional function predicative only if it is elementary, a definition that the more finely grained ramification of 1906 would support.

25. I am greatly indebted to Peter Hylton for many illuminating conversations and much useful advice. I would also like to thank Burton Dreben, Leonard Linsky, and Thomas Ricketts for helpful discussions.

Nino B. Cocchiarella

Russell's Theory of Logical Types and the Atomistic Hierarchy of Sentences

Russell's philosophical views underwent a number of changes throughout his life, and it is not always well appreciated that views he held at one time came later to be rejected; nor, similarly, that views he rejected at one time came later to be accepted. It is not well known, for example, that the theory of logical types Russell described in his later or post-PM philosophy is not the same as the theory originally described in PM in 1910–13; nor that some of the more important applications that Russell made of the theory at the earlier time cannot be validated or even significantly made in the framework of his later theory. What is somewhat surprising, however, is that Russell himself seems not to have realized that he was describing a new theory of logical types in his later philosophy, and that as a result of the change some of his earlier logical constructions, including especially his construction of the different kinds of numbers, were no longer available to him.

In the original framework, for example, propositional functions are independently real properties and relations that can themselves have properties and relations of a higher order/type, and all talk of classes, and thereby ultimately of numbers, can be reduced to extensional talk of properties and relations as "single entities," or what Russell in POM had called "logical subjects." The Platonic reality of classes and numbers was replaced in this way by a more fundamental Platonic reality of propositional functions as properties and relations. In Russell's later philosophy, however, "a propositional function is nothing but an expression. It does not, by itself, represent anything. But it can form part of a sentence which does say something, true or false" ([MPD], p. 69). Surprisingly, Russell even insists that this was what he meant by a propositional function in PM. "Whitehead and I thought of a propositional function as an expression containing an undetermined variable and becoming an ordinary sentence as soon as a value is assigned to the variable: 'x is human,' for example, becomes an ordinary sentence as soon as we substitute a proper name for 'x.' In this view...the propositional function is a method of making a bundle of such sentences" ([MPD], p. 124). Russell does realize that some sort of change has come about, however, for he admits that

"I no longer think that the laws of logic are laws of things; on the contrary, I now regard them as purely linguistic" (ibid., p. 102).

How an uncountable reality of classes and numbers can be reduced to a countable reality of "linguistic conveniences," Russell never explained; but it is clear that he thought that such a reduction was already accomplished in PM, i.e., that PM could sustain a nominalistic construal of propositional functions. Now whether or not PM can sustain such an interpretation is not our concern here (though, given the axioms of reducibility and infinity, we think it cannot); for what Russell failed to see was that the theory of types he described and was committed to in his later philosophy was but a fragment of the theory described in PM, and that in fact the analysis of classes and numbers given in PM cannot be given in this fragment. This new theory of types was dictated by what Russell later called "the technical form of the principle of atomicity," namely, the thesis that "all propositions are either atomic, or molecular, or generalizations of molecular propositions; or at least, that a language of which this is true, and into which any statement is translatable, can be constructed" (IMT, pp. 250f.). The "logical language" in question here is what Russell called "the atomistic hierarchy of sentences" (ibid., p. 187), and it amounts, as we shall see, to but a fragment of second-order predicate logic. Russell does also allow for a hierarchy of "languages" constructed on the basis of the atomistic hierarchy, but this additional hierarchy, as we shall also see, turns out to be essentially a nominalistic construal of ramified second-order logic. That is, ramified second-order logic is all that is left in Russell's later philosophy of his original theory of types. This system is not only much weaker than Russell's original logic, but, even worse, on grammatical grounds alone it cannot sustain Russell's analysis of classes and numbers. For, despite Russell's misleading notation otherwise (in his 1925 introduction to PM), propositional functions (construed as expressions) cannot occur as (higher-order) abstract singular terms in ramified second-order logic, and yet it is precisely their occurrence as such that is essential to Russell's analysis of classes and numbers.

Now it is not whether PM can sustain a nominalistic interpretation that is our concern in this essay, as we have said, but rather how it is that Russell came to be committed in his later philosophy to the atomistic hierarchy and the nominalistic interpretation of propositional functions as expressions generated in a ramified second-order hierarchy of languages based on the atomistic hierarchy. We shall pursue this question by beginning with a discussion of the difference between Russell's 1908 theory of types and that presented in PM in 1910. This will be followed by a brief summary of the ontology that Russell took to be implicit in PM, and that he described in various publications between 1910 and 1913. The central notion in this initial discussion is what Russell in his early philosophy called the notion of a logical subject, or equivalently that of a "term" or "single entity." (In PM, this notion was redescribed as the systematically ambiguous notion of an "object.") As explained in Cocchiarella (1980), this notion provides the key to the various problems that led Russell in his early philosophy to the development of his different theories of types, including that presented in PM. This remains true, moreover, even when we turn to Russell's later philosophy, i.e., to his post-PM views, except that then it is described as the notion of what can and cannot be named in a logically perfect language. The ontology of these later views is what Russell called logical atomism, and it is this ontology that determines what Russell described as the atomistic hierarchy of sentences. In other words, it is the notion of what can and cannot be named in the atomistic hierarchy that explains how Russell, however unwittingly, came to replace his earlier theory of logical types by the theory underlying the atomistic hierarchy of sentences as the basis of a logically perfect language.

1. The 1910 versus the 1908 Theory of Logical Types

An important fact that is commonly overlooked in most of the literature on the theory of logical types is that the theory Russell described in PM in 1910 is not the same as the theory he described in "Mathematical Logic as Based on the Theory of Types" (1908)—unless, that is, one assumes that both propositions (as objective truths and falsehoods) and propositional functions are for Russell "single entities" in both theories. Russell did not assume this, however, and in fact while propositions are single entities in "Mathematical Logic," propositional functions, or so Russell then thought, were nonentities. Two years later, in PM, propositional functions are reckoned as single (nonlinguistic) entities, and propositions are reconstrued by Russell as not being single entities after all. The difference, apparently, was the result of Russell's shifting from a propositional theory of belief or judgment to his famous multiple-relations theory (which he later rejected in 1913 as a result of criticisms by Wittgenstein). Thus, according to Russell in PM, "what we call 'a proposition' (in the sense in which this is distinguished from the phrase expressing it) is not a single entity at all," and in fact "the phrase which expresses a proposition is what we call an 'incomplete' symbol" (p. 44). We should note, incidentally, that being a single entity is what Russell also means by being capable of being a logical subject.

To see what this difference between the two theories comes to, let us turn to Alonzo Church's formal characterization of Russell's ramified types, hereafter called r-types, and orders.[1]

(1) There is an r-type i to which all and only individuals belong, and whose order is stipulated to be 0.

(2) If $m \in \omega$, $n \in \omega - \{0\}$, and $\beta_1, \ldots, \beta_m$ are given r-types, then there is an r-type $(\beta_1, \ldots, \beta_m)/n$ to which belong all and only m-ary propositional functions of level n and with arguments of r-types $\beta_1, \ldots, \beta_m$, respec-

tively; and the order of such a function is $N + n$, where N is the greatest of the orders corresponding to the types $\beta_1, \ldots, \beta_m$ (and $N = 0$ if $m = 0$).

The notion of the *level* of a propositional function ϕ of r-type $(\beta_1, \ldots \beta_m)/n$ is needed here, it should be noted, as a counterpart to Russell's nonsyntactical use (in 1910) of the notion of an apparent (or "bound") variable. Thus if N is the greatest of the orders corresponding to $\beta_1, \ldots, \beta_m$, and k is the greatest of the orders of the apparent variables occurring in ϕ (in Russell's nonsyntactical sense), then $n = 1$ if $k \leq N$, and $n = k + 1$ if $N < k$. Since ϕ is said to be *predicative*, according to Russell, when "it is of the lowest order compatible with its having the arguments it has" (PM, p. 53), then in terms of the notion of level, it follows that ϕ is *predicative* if, and only if, $n = 1$.[2]

Now the preceding definition recognizes both propositions and propositional functions as single entities. Propositions of order n, for example, are represented here as 0-ary propositional functions of level n, i.e., as propositional functions of r-type ( )/n, where "( )" represents the null sequence. This of course is merely a convenience of terminology, since propositions are really not propositional functions in the intended sense. That both propositions and propositional functions are "single entities" is acknowledged here in the fact that both can occur as arguments of propositional functions, or as "logical subjects" of the resulting propositions. For example, an individual can stand to a propositional function of r-type $(\beta_1, \ldots, \beta_m)/n$ in a predicative relation of r-type $(i, (\beta_1, \ldots, \beta_m)/n)/1$; and where belief is a predicative relation between an individual and a proposition of order n, belief will be a propositional function of r-type $(i, (\ )/n)/1$.

Church is not unaware that Russell rejected propositions as single entities in 1910, and that he did so on the basis of his multiple-relations theory of belief. Church claims, however, that the "fragmenting of propositions" that is involved in the multiple-relations theory also requires the "fragmenting of propositional functions" (1976, p. 748), and therefore if propositional phrases are to be analyzed as incomplete symbols then phrases for propositional functions must also be so analyzable. The result would mean that the only category or type that was really fundamental with respect to quantification was that of the individuals, since only individuals would then remain as real single entities. The result, in other words, would mean that the theory of logical types was reducible to first-order logic. Such a reduction was certainly not intended by Russell, and in any case, or so Church argues, "it is probable that the contextual definitions [i.e., analyses of phrases for propositions and propositional functions as incomplete symbols] would not stand scrutiny" (ibid.).

Actually, Church is not correct in thinking that the fragmenting of propositional functions that is involved in Russell's multiple-relations theory means that propositional functions are ultimately to be eliminated as single entities. For although the propositional functions that occur in a belief or judgment on this theory are indeed "fragmented" in the sense of analysis, nevertheless each propositional function, as well as the "fragments" of that function that result upon analysis, retains its status as a single entity in the belief or judgment complex. Consider, for example, the judgment that all men are mortal as made by some person A. The truth of this judgment, according to Russell, is a "second-order truth" (PM, p. 45), and that this is so can be seen in the following analysis:

$Judges(A, (x)[\hat{\phi}!x \supset \hat{\psi}!x], \hat{x}$ is a man, $\hat{x}$ is mortal).

We assume in this analysis that $\hat{x}$ is a man and $\hat{x}$ is mortal are predicative propositional functions of r-type $(i)/1$ and that $(x)[\hat{\phi}!x \supset \hat{\psi}!x]$ is a propositional function of r-type $((i)/1, (i)/1)/1$, and therefore of order 2. The judgment is said to have second-order truth because 2 is the maximum of the orders of the propositional functions occurring in its analysis. Note that the propositional phrase "all men are mortal" does not occur in this analysis as a singular term even though it may appear to so occur (when appended to "that") in the English sentence, "A judges that all men are mortal." This is what Russell meant by saying that propositions are no longer to be reckoned as single entities. The phrases for the propositional functions that result from the analysis of "A judges that all men are mortal," on the other hand, all occur as singular terms in the final analysis, and it is for this reason that the propositional functions they represent must be reckoned as single entities. Indeed, without including propositional functions among the single entities combined in a judgment or belief complex, there would simply be no multiple-relations theory of belief at all.

This is not to say that the multiple-relations theory of belief is a viable theory after all (or at least not without serious reconstruction). Our point rather is that as far as Russell was concerned in 1910–13, propositional functions are single entities (of different r-types and orders) and can be quantified over as such, but that the same cannot be said of propositions. That is, propositions (in the sense of objective truths and falsehoods) are not single entities according to the Russell of 1910, and therefore they cannot be quantified over as such. This means modifying Church's characterization of r-types by excluding all r-types of the form $(\ )/n$, where $n \in \omega - \{0\}$; or, in other words, by requiring in clause (2) of the definition of r-type that $m \in \omega - \{0\}$ as well.

Note that rejecting propositions while retaining propositional functions in no way affects Russell's logical reconstruction of mathematics. For it is propositional functions, and not propositions, that are essential to that reconstruction. This is so because a statement about a class, i.e., a statement in which an expression for a class occurs as a singular term, is to be analyzed, according to Russell, as a statement about the extension of a propositional function; and the latter, assuming that propositional functions can be single logical subjects, is in turn to be analyzed as a statement about some (or preferably *any*) propositional function materially equivalent to the propositional function in question. Thus, reading "$\hat{z}(\psi z)$" as "the class defined by ψ," Russell gives the following contextual analysis for statements in which a class appears as a single logical subject (PM, p. 188):

$$f\{\hat{z}(\psi z)\} =_{df} (\exists\phi)((x)[\phi!x \equiv \psi x] \,\&\, f\{\phi!\hat{z}\}).$$

In this analysis, needless to say, it is essential that a propositional function can occur as a single logical subject of the analysans. In Russell's 1908 theory, on the other hand, it is propositions and not propositional functions that are reckoned as single entities; and in that regard Russell's logical reconstruction of mathematics is very much in question, since it is not r-types of the form ( )/n that are then to be excluded but rather all r-types for propositional functions that are not of this form.

Russell's pre-1910 rejection of propositional functions as single entities goes back as far as 1903, incidentally, when, as a result of his paradox, Russell was led to claim that "the ϕ in ϕx is not a separate and distinguishable entity: it lives in the propositions of the form ϕx and cannot survive analysis" (POM, p. 88). Thus, since being a separable entity is the same for Russell as having the capacity of being a logical subject, there can be no propositions of the form $\psi(\phi)$, and therefore none of the form $\phi(\phi)$ or $\sim\phi(\phi)$ as well, on this earlier view of Russell's. In other words, it was by "the recognition that the functional part of a propositional function is not an independent entity" (ibid.) that Russell sought to avoid the contradiction that would otherwise result when his paradox was applied to propositional functions as single entities. (See Cocchiarella [1980], section 4, for a fuller discussion of this point.)

Despite his rejection in POM of propositional functions as single entities, Russell still found it "impossible to exclude variable propositional functions altogether" (POM, p. 104); that is, he still admitted quantification with respect to such variables. This was because on Russell's view "wherever a variable class or variable relation [in extension] occurs, we have admitted a variable propositional function which is thus essential to assertions about every class or about every relation" (ibid.). This view was later developed by Russell into his famous "no classes" theory, first in the form of the substitutional theory of 1906, then in the form of the 1908 theory of types, and finally in PM. (See Cocchiarella [1980], sections 6-8 for a fuller discussion of this development.) It was only in the 1910 theory of logical types, however, that Russell was finally able to give a coherent account of his "no classes" theory, for it is only in the 1910 theory that quantification over propositional functions as independently real entities is finally recognized.

2. Propositional Functions as Properties and Relations in Russell's 1910–1913 PM-Ontology

"Pure mathematics," Russell wrote in 1911, "is the sum of everything that we can know, whether directly or by demonstration, about certain universals"

([1911], p. 293). The certain universals in question here are the independently real propositional functions that occur as "single entities" in the analyses Russell gave in PM of our talk of classes and numbers. "Logic and mathematics force us, then," according to this Russell of 1911, "to admit a kind of realism in the scholastic sense, that is to say, to admit that there is a world of universals and of truths which do not bear directly on such and such a particular existence. This world of universals must *subsist*, although it cannot *exist* in the same sense as that in which particular data exist" (ibid.).

Propositional functions, accordingly, are universals for Russell in his 1910–13 PM ontology, and as such they may also be called properties and relations (in intension). This was already suggested by Russell in "The Regressive Method of Discovering the Premises of Mathematics" (1907; reprinted in 1973a, p. 281), where two of his "principles" for mathematical logic are as follows:

> Any propositional function of x is equivalent to one assigning a property to x.
>
> Any propositional function of x and y is equivalent to one asserting a relation between x and y.

But these two "principles" were said by Russell in "The Regressive Method" to be "less evident" than the others he listed there for mathematical logic; and, as already indicated, Russell attempted to do without them completely in "Mathematical Logic" (1908). Nevertheless, regardless of his earlier hesitancy, and sometimes outright rejection, it is clear that Russell did assume these "principles" in his 1910–13 PM ontology.

Another assumption that Russell also made in his 1910–13 ontology, albeit only implicitly, was that some properties and relations are simple while others are complex. This assumption goes back as far as POM where it is described as the distinction between properties and relations that are or are not logically analyzable in terms of other properties and relations. That is, if properties and relations "have been analyzed as far as possible, they must be simple terms, incapable of expressing anything except themselves" (POM, p. 446); and if they are otherwise analyzable, then they must be complex. Of course, for Russell, throughout the period in which he was a logical realist, logical analysis is the same as ontological analysis; i.e., "where the mind can distinguish elements [in a logical analysis], there must *be* different elements to distinguish" (ibid.).

This assumption is not itself a consequence of the comprehension principle for properties and relations, incidentally; for despite the validity of the latter in PM, where propositional functions are properties and relations, nothing follows about properties and relations being themselves complex if they are specified in an instance of that principle by a complex expression for a propositional function. In other words, the complex/simple distinction is not essential to the validation of the comprehension principle (as is all too frequently assumed in the literature).

Nevertheless, it is a sufficient condition if we also assume that the language of PM is "a logically perfect language" in the sense that complex expressions for propositional functions represent (onto)logical analyses of those propositional functions as independently real universals. This in fact was what Russell assumed in 1910–13, at least implicitly, and, as we shall see, it is not unrelated to the nominalistic validation of the comprehension principle in his later philosophy where the complexity of a propositional function is none other than its syntactical complexity as an expression. Of course properties and relations will then be distinguished from propositional functions, and in fact Russell will then in general speak of them only as simple.

The comprehension principle, incidentally, really has two forms that are valid in PM, but only one that is valid in the theory of logical types of Russell's later philosophy. These are

$$(\exists f)(x_1)\ldots(x_m)[f(x_1,\ldots,x_m) \equiv \phi],$$

and

$$(\exists f)\, f = \phi(\hat{x}_1,\ldots,\hat{x}_1),$$

where f is a variable of r-type $(\beta_1,\ldots,\beta_m)/n$ that does not occur free in ϕ, $x_1,\ldots,x_m$ are variables of r-types $\beta_1,\ldots,\beta_m$, respectively, and the bound variables in ϕ are all of an order less than the order of f. Here the second form implies the first, but not conversely. The second form, given Russell's analysis of identity, is an abbreviation of

$$(\exists f)(\psi)[\psi!\{f\} \equiv \psi!\{\phi(\hat{x}_1,\ldots,\hat{x}_m)\}],$$

which requires that propositional functions be "single logical subjects"; and this form is not even meaningful in ramified second-order logic where all propositional functions are of r-types of the form $(i,\ldots,i)/n$, for arbitrary "level" n; i.e., where propositional functions (of arbitrary "level") have only individuals as arguments. In other words, strictly speaking, only the first form remains "significant" in Russell's later philosophy.

Nothing comparable can be said of Russell's analysis of classes, on the other hand. That is, there is no form of that analysis that remains significant in Russell's later philosophy. This is because expressions for classes are to occur as singular terms, and Russell's analysis, as described in section 1, requires that expressions for propositional functions must then also occur as singular terms; and yet it is precisely that type of occurrence that is not "significant" in ramified second-order logic.

3. Russell's 1910–1913 Commitment to Abstract Facts

In 1910–11, Russell described his ontology as consisting simply of "an ultimate dualism" of universals and particulars. That is, "the disjunction, 'universal-particular' includes all objects. We might also call it the disjunction 'abstract-concrete' " (1910–11, p. 214). The particulars of this dualism are "particular existents" or "entities which can only be subjects or terms of relations, and cannot be predicates or relations" (1911–12, p. 109). (A "predicate" for Russell at this time was always a property or quality, or what he also called a concept.) A universal, on the other hand, is "anything that is a predicate or a relation" (ibid.), but which may also be a "subject" or "term" of a relation.

Particulars, incidentally, are the individuals of PM; i.e., they are the objects of r-type i. This terminology differs from that Russell used earlier in POM where the word "individual" was taken as synonymous with "term" and "entity," or having the capacity of being a logical subject (cf. POM, p. 43). This means that universals were also construed as individuals in POM, since as logical subjects they were also "terms." In PM, on the other hand, particulars and only particulars are individuals, i.e., are of r-type i, which is not to say that universals have lost their individuality or capacity to occur as "terms" of other universals. The matter is really terminological, in other words, for the word used in PM to cover the individuality of both particulars and universals is "object." That is, both particulars and universals are "objects" in PM, though of course they are objects of "essentially different types" (PM, p. 24). As propositional functions, moreover, universals are also of different types among themselves, since some may be arguments or "terms" of others. "The division of objects into types," according to Russell, "is necessitated by the vicious circle fallacies which otherwise arise" (ibid., p. 161).

Among particulars Russell included not just "existents" but "all complexes of which one or more constituents are existents, such as this-before-that, this-above-that, the-yellowness-of-this," etc. ([1910–11], p. 213). In 1912, Russell sometimes called these complex particulars events, and other times facts. For example, my seeing the sun and my desiring food are "events" that happen in my mind (PP, p. 49); and when "I am acquainted with my acquaintance with the sense-datum representing the sun,...the whole *fact* with which I am acquainted is, 'Self-acquainted-with-sense-datum' " (ibid., pp. 50–51). Note that one of the ways that we can have knowledge of such a complex particular is "by means of *acquaintance* with the complex fact itself, which may (in a large sense) be called perception, though it is by no means confined to objects of the senses" (ibid., p. 136).

The importance of events or facts as complex particulars in Russell's 1910–13 ontology is that they provide the basis of his new theory of truth; that is, the theory in which truth and falsehood are no longer properties of propositions as independently real single entities, but are rather "properties of beliefs and statements" (PP, p. 121). (Note that a *statement* for Russell is always the overt expression of a judgment or belief.) For example, in the case of a simple statement, such as that a has the relation R to b, "we may define *truth*...as consisting in the fact that there is a complex *corresponding* to the discursive thought which is the judgment.

That is, when we judge '*a* has the relation *R* to *b*,' our judgment is said to be *true* when there is a complex '*a*-in-the-relation-*R*-to-*b*,' and is said to be *false* when this is not the case" (PM, p. 43).

We should note that truth and falsehood are no more univocal in Russell's new theory than they were in his earlier 1908 theory when they were properties of propositions of different orders. In particular, although beliefs or statements are themselves particular complex occurrences (and therefore are particulars), the kind of truth or falsehood each will have will depend on the highest order of the propositional functions occurring as "terms" in the belief or statement complex. For example, a statement of "this is red" is said to have *elementary truth or falsehood*, while a statement of "all men are mortal," as already explained in section 1, will have *second-order truth*. Similarly, a statement of "Napoleon had all the (predicative) properties of a great general" will have *third-order truth or falsehood* (cf. Cocchiarella [1980], p. 104); and of course, there can be statements or beliefs with *fourth-order truth or falsehood*, and so on. Instead of a hierarchy of propositions as abstract entities that may be true or false, in other words, Russell's 1910-13 framework has only a hierarchy of truth and falsehood as properties of particular occurrences of beliefs and statements.

The hierarchy of truth and falsehood as properties of beliefs and statements as complex particulars fits in well with Russell's 1910-11 "ultimate dualism" of universals and particulars; i.e., with his claim that "*the disjunction 'universal-particular' includes all objects*" (1910-11, p. 214, emphasis added). By 1912, however, Russell came to realize that not all of the facts he needed in his "realism in the scholastic sense" could be construed as events or complex particulars. That is, with respect to Russell's "abstract-particular" disjunction, which he had originally identified in 1910 with the "universal-particular" disjunction, there are *abstract facts* as well as concrete facts (events). These are "facts about universals," and, according to Russell, "they may be known by acquaintance to many different people" (PP, p. 137). For example, "the statement, 'two and two are four' deals exclusively with universals" (ibid., p. 105), and therefore the complex that makes it true is not an event or complex particular but an abstract fact. The statement itself, to be sure, as a statement made by someone at some particular time, is an event or complex particular, and as a statement about classes of classes of individuals (or rather about predicative propositional functions of predicative propositional functions of individuals) the truth it has is a property of third-order (the order of the identity relation in this case). But still, since the fact that makes this statement true "deals exclusively with universals," i.e., with objects that "*subsist* or *have being*, where 'being' is opposed to 'existence' as being timeless" (ibid., p. 100), then the fact itself must subsist and belong to "the world of being" (ibid.).

Russell's commitment to abstract facts, it should be emphasized, cannot be brushed aside here as something that can be avoided, as though his original "ultimate dualism" of universals and particulars might suffice after all. Consider, for example, comparing Russell's ontology of universals and particulars, and now abstract facts as well, with an event ontology that is combined with the ontological commitments of one or another set theory. In the latter, there are no facts other than events (if the identification of concrete facts with events is to be retained at all), and, in particular, there are no set-theoretical facts regarding pure sets (i.e., sets whose transitive closure contains no elements other than the empty set). Nor are any set-theoretical facts really needed, moreover, to account for the truth of statements of membership in a set. For a set, at least on the iterative concept, has its being in its members, and in that regard a set's existence (or "being," as Russell would say) is all that is needed to account for the truth or falsehood of statements ascribing membership in that set. That is, the being of a set consists in its having just the members that it has, and therefore no fact over and above the being of the set itself is needed to account for membership in the set. A property or relation (in intension), on the other hand, does not have its being in its instances, and for that reason its being cannot alone account for the truth of statements ascribing that property or relation to its instances. The usual gambit logical realists make here to account for such truth is to posit propositions as objective truths and falsehoods in themselves, i.e., as independently real single entities. Russell, however, had deliberately removed that option, and in consequence, he was forced to fall back on abstract facts as an additional category of his ontology beyond the events or concrete facts that make up the world of existence. In his later philosophy, when "all the propositions of mathematics and logic are assertions as to the correct use of a certain small number of words" ("Is Mathematics Purely Linguistic?" in *Essays*, p. 306), these abstract facts are replaced by truths that are "purely linguistic." What Russell failed to see, however, was that such a replacement did not result in an equipollent system of logic.

4. Logical Atomism and the Doctrine of Logical Types

The status of facts as "objects" or complex single entities that can be named was important to Russell in the 1910-13 framework, and in general he went out of his way to use only perfect nominalizations of sentences (where the verb has been completely deactivated) to refer to such facts. That is why he used examples like "my seeing the sun," "my desire for food," "a in the relation R to b," and "a having the quality q," as opposed to the imperfect nominalizations "that I see the sun," "that I desire food," etc. Indeed, he sometimes even used hyphens to emphasize the perfect nominalization in question, such as in "this-before-that," "this-above-that," and "the-yellowness-of-this." Such nominalizations were necessary, according to Russell, insofar as we can be directly acquainted with the facts in question. For acquaintance is a binary relation and is to be represented by a two-place predicate expression taking only singular terms as argument expressions.

A problem does arise here regarding the logical status of facts, however. For example, insofar as the concrete fact denoted by "this-before-that" is a particular, it must be of the *r*-type *i* of individuals. But as a complex, a fact has a logical structure, and according to Russell the complexity of that structure must somehow be represented in its logical type, which for us is its *r*-type. That is, as a complex a fact must have an *r*-type other than *i*; and therefore, assuming that no object is of more than one *r*-type, facts really cannot be particulars after all. This argument, or at least one with the same conclusion, was apparently forced on Russell sometime in 1913 by Ludwig Wittgenstein. Whatever his initial reluctance, and it must have been great since it meant giving up completing the manuscript of his 1913 *Theory of Knowledge*, Russell came to accept the conclusion by the end of 1913.

Now it is significant that in accepting this conclusion Russell went on to claim that "only particulars can be named" (PLA, p. 267) and therefore that facts cannot be named at all. For example, in January 1914, Russell wrote that although "an observed fact...does not differ greatly from a simple sense-datum as regards its function in giving knowledge," nevertheless "its *logical* structure is very different...from that of sense: *sense* gives acquaintance with particulars, and is thus a two-term relation in which the object can be *named* but not asserted,...whereas the observation of a complex fact, which may be suitably called perception, is not a two-termed relation, but involves the propositional form on the object-side, and gives knowledge of a truth, not mere acquaintance with a particular" ([1914c], p. 147). In other words, it was no longer even meaningful, no less true, for Russell that "the complex '*a*-in-the-relation-*R*-to-*b*' may be capable of being perceived...as one object" (PM, p. 43). That is, this perception was no longer "a relation of two terms, namely, '*a*-in-the-relation-*R*-to-*b*,' and the percipient" (ibid.). And the reason, Russell claims, is that the *logical structure* of a fact precludes its being the sort of entity that can be named, i.e., the sort of entity that can stand as a "term" in a relation. "You cannot name a fact.... You can never put the sort of thing that makes a proposition to be true or false in the position of a logical subject" (PLA, p. 188).

Before taking up this rather extraordinary claim, let us note that as so far defined no *r*-type is the *r*-type of a fact, and therefore in a trivial sense no fact can be a "logical subject" according to the theory of *r*-types. The reason why this is so is that every *r*-type other than *i* is the *r*-type of a propositional function, and facts are not propositional functions. Resurrecting propositional *r*-types of the form ( )/*n* for facts will not do, moreover, since these fail to indicate both the number and the *r*-types of the constituents of a fact.

We can rectify this situation, however, if we assume along with the Russell of the 1910–13 ontology that every fact consists of some one relation actually relating the remaining constituents of that fact. (This assumption of Russell's goes as far back as the *Principles*; cf. POM, p. 52.) For example, the relation that Russell calls "formal implication" (and represented by $(x)[\hat{\phi}!x \supset \hat{\psi}!x]$ in section 1) is the relating relation of a general fact (cf. PM, p. 138), and "the asymmetrical relation of predication" is the relating relation of a fact corresponding to a true subject-predicate sentence (cf. 1911–12). Following Russell's later usage (adopted from Wittgenstein's *Tractatus*), we shall call the relating relation of a fact the *component* relation of that fact, whereas the "terms" or "logical subjects" of that relation will be called simply the *constituents* of the fact. We can now revise the definition of *r*-type given in section 1 by supplementing that definition with the following clause:

(3) If $m, n \in m - \{0\}$, $m \geq 2$, and $\beta_1, \ldots, \beta_m$ are given *r*-types, then there is an *r*-type $[(\beta_1, \ldots, \beta_m)/n]$ to which belong all and only facts whose component relation is of *r*-type $(\beta_1, \ldots, \beta_m)/n$ and whose constituents are of *r*-type $\beta_1, \ldots, \beta_m$ respectively; and the order of such a fact is the order of its component relation.

Of course it now follows that no concrete fact is a particular, since particulars are all of *r*-type *i* and no fact is of *r*-type *i*. But that—as far as the theory of logical types as the theory of *r*-types is concerned—has nothing to do with Russell's new or post-PM claim that you cannot name a fact, or that a fact cannot be a logical subject.

There is no reason, for example, at least as far as the theory of *r*-types is concerned, why there cannot be different types of relations of acquaintance, just as there are on Russell's multiple-relations theory different types of relations of belief. Only one of these acquaintance relations will in fact be a relation between individuals; others will be relations between individuals and facts (of a given *r*-type) or between individuals and universals (of a given *r*-type). (Russell also called acquaintance with universals *conceiving*; cf. 1910–11, p. 212.) Also, as far as the theory of r-types is concerned, there is no reason why all and only individuals should be particulars, i.e., why particulars should constitute a distinct logical category. After all, if concrete facts can be logical subjects, then why shouldn't they be called complex particulars, just as Russell in fact did so call them in his 1910–13 ontology?

It is not just facts that Russell now says cannot be named, it should be noted, but anything that suggests "the form of a proposition" (PLA, p. 205). A property or quality, for example, cannot be named by a nominalized predicate, since "a predicate," according to Russell's new or post-PM view, "can never occur except as a predicate. When it seems to occur as a subject [i.e., as a nominalized predicate], the phrase wants amplifying and explaining, unless, of course, you are talking about the word itself" (ibid.). Similarly, "a relation can never occur except as a relation, never as a subject" (ibid., p. 206). "All propositions in which an attribute or a relation *seems* to be the subject," in other words, "are only significant if they can be brought into a form in which the attribute is attributed or relation relates. If this were not the case, there would be significant propositions in which an attribute or a relation would occupy a position appropriate to a substance, which would be contrary to the doctrine of types, and would produce contradictions" (LA, pp. 337–38).

Note that here we have another extraordinary claim: *facts and universals cannot be logical subjects, and therefore cannot be named, because that would be contrary to the doctrine of types and would produce contradictions*. What is so extraordinary about this is that facts and universals are logical subjects in the theory of r-types, and as a theoretical account of the doctrine of logical types, the theory of r-types was designed explicitly so as not to produce contradictions. Apparently, Russell has somehow replaced his earlier version of the doctrine of logical types with a new or much restricted version, and it is not at all clear how well aware he was of the consequences of this move.

Note also that on this new version of the doctrine of types, Russell must reject his multiple-relations theory of belief, as well of course as the view that we can be acquainted with facts and universals. Thus, besides "the impossibility of treating the proposition believed as an independent entity, entering as a unit into the occurrence of the belief" (PLA, p. 226), there is now also "the impossibility of putting the subordinate verb on a level with its terms as an object term in the belief" (ibid.). "That is a point," Russell observed, "in which I think that the theory of judgment which I set forth once in print some years ago was a little unduly simple, because I did then treat the object verb as if one could put it as just an object like the terms, as if one could put, 'loves' on a level with Desdemona and Cassio as a term for the relation 'believe' " (ibid.) in the case of Othello believing that Desdemona loves Cassio. (Note that Russell uses "verb" to stand for both the word and the attribute or relation the word stands for; cf. PLA, p. 217.)

It is clear, as these observations indicate, that Russell has changed or seriously modified his 1910–13 ontology, and that somehow the change involves a new version of the doctrine of types. Thus, in 1924 Russell writes that "the doctrine of types leads to... a more complete and radical atomism than any that I conceived to be possible twenty years ago" (LA, p. 333), which in this case includes the 1910–13 ontology. This complete and radical atomism is of course Russell's form of logical atomism, the justification of which he claims is none other than "the justification of analysis" (PLA, p. 270). On this view, "you can get down in theory, if not in practice, to ultimate simples, out of which the world is built, and...those simples have a kind of reality not belonging to anything else" (ibid.); i.e., each simple has a kind of reality or mode of being that is unique to the entities of that kind (and which is the same as its logical type). "Simples...are of an infinite number of sorts. There are particulars and qualities and relations of various orders, a whole hierarchy of different sorts of simples" (ibid.). Aside from simples, "the only other sort of object you come across in the world" is facts (ibid.). That is, in the ontology of logical atomism, there are only simples and facts. Everything else is what Russell called a "logical fiction" (cf. PLA, pp. 253f).

The hierarchy of different sorts of simples that is in question here, it should be noted, is not the hierarchy of r-types (where properties and relations can be logical subjects). For by the "order" of a relation Russell means in this context only the degree or adicity of that relation (cf. PLA, pp. 206f). That is, he does not mean "order" in the sense defined in section 1. In that regard, the r-types of the hierarchy of simples, i.e., of particulars, qualities, and relations of various "orders" now intended by Russell, can be indicated as follows, namely: i, $(i)/1$, $(i, i)/1$, $(i, i, i)/1$, and so on ad infinitum. (Note that as simples, no quality or relation has a "level" higher than 1; i.e., each is "predicative" in the sense of section 1). It is only first-order properties and relations, in other words, and even then only *simple* first-order properties and relations, that are involved in the ontology of logical atomism. Of course, quantifiers that "refer" to these simple properties and relations are no less significant than quantifiers that refer to particulars as individuals, which means that some restricted form of second-order logic is needed for the representation of this ontology. Indeed, the sentences of this restricted form of second-order logic are precisely what Russell later called the *atomistic hierarchy of sentences*; i.e., the hierarchy of sentences obtained from atomic sentences by the three operations of *substitution*, *combination*, and *generalization* (cf. IMT, p. 187).

Note that by the operation or principle of *substitution* Russell only means that an atomic sentence $R_n(a_1, \ldots, a_n)$ "remains significant if any or all of the names are replaced by any other names, and R_n is replaced by any other n-adic relation" (ibid., p. 185). Truth-functional or molecular compounds of atomic sentences are then obtained by iterated application of the stroke-operation of combination (having the truth-table of "either not...or not..."). Finally, "given any sentence containing either a name 'a' or a word 'R' denoting a relation or predicate, we can construct a new sentence in two ways" (ibid.), according to Russell, by the operation of *generalization*; i.e., quantification is significant with respect to both the subject and relation or predicate positions of atomic sentences. The resulting "hierarchy" of sentences, needless to say, consists only of second-order sentences; that is, it consists of sentences that are significant in second-order logic where there are no higher-order universals of an r-type $(\beta_1, \ldots, \beta_m)/n$, where β_i, for some i, is the r-type of a property or relation. This means that expressions for the higher-order universals that Russell took numbers to be in his 1910–13 ontology are no longer significant in his new theory of types. And yet, according to Russell's version of the principle of atomicity, "Everything we wish to say can be said in sentences belonging to the 'atomistic hierarchy' " (IMT, p. 160).

5. Propositional Functions as Linguistic Conveniences

In considering whether the atomistic hierarchy of sentences "can constitute an 'adequate' language, i.e., one into which any statement in any language can be translated" (IMT, p. 187), Russell asks if we can "be content with names, predicates, dyadic relations, etc., as our only variables, or do we need variables of other kinds?" (ibid.). This question, we are told, "is concerned with generalization and is relevant in solving the paradoxes" (ibid.). The other kinds of variables Russell has in mind here are propositional variables and propositional function variables (or what Russell also called variable propositions and variable functions).

By a proposition in his post-PM view Russell means not an objective truth or falsehood but "a sentence in the indicative" (PLA, p. 185), i.e., "a sentence asserting something" (ibid.). In other words, "a proposition is just a symbol," and in particular "it is a complex symbol in the sense that it has parts which are also symbols" (ibid.). (Russell sometimes also means by a proposition an image-proposition [cf. "On Propositions" (1919) and AMi]; but we shall ignore image-propositions here since they correspond only to atomic sentences and do not contain propositional functions.) A propositional function, similarly, "is simply *any expression containing an undetermined constituent, or several undetermined constituents, and becoming a proposition as soon as the undetermined constituents are determined*" (ibid., p. 230). Of course, as an expression that can be mentioned and talked about as such, a propositional function is a "single entity." But being mentioned is not the same as being used, and as for its use in logical syntax "the only thing really that you can do with a propositional function is to assert either that it is always true, or that it is sometimes true, or that it is never true" (ibid.); that is, otherwise than being referred to as an expression, "a propositional function is nothing" (ibid.). This means that as an expression that is being used rather than mentioned, a propositional function cannot occur as the grammatical subject of a proposition. This is why Russell in his 1925 introduction to the second edition of PM claims that "there is no logical matrix of the form $f!(\phi!\hat{z})$. The only matrices in which $\phi!\hat{z}$ is the only argument are those containing $\phi!a, \phi!b, \phi!c, \ldots$, where $a, b, c, \ldots$, are constants" (p. xxxi), and of course these are matrices in which $\phi!\hat{z}$ does not occur as a singular term or logico-grammatical subject. Indeed, this is precisely what Russell means by his new fundamental assumption that "*a function can only appear in a matrix through its values*" (p. xxix).

Note that by a matrix Russell means in this context any propositional function (expression) that "has elementary propositions as its values" (p. xxii), where an elementary proposition is either an atomic proposition or a truth-functional compound of atomic propositions (p. xvii). Note also that an n-adic relation symbol R_n "cannot occur in a atomic proposition $R_m(x_1, \ldots, x_m)$ unless $n = m$, and then can only occur as R_m occurs, not as $x_1, x_2, \ldots, x_m$ occur" (ibid.); i.e., relation symbols are not allowed to occur as singular terms (the way they were allowed to occur, e.g., in Russell's 1910–13 multiple-relations theory of belief or in what he then called *higher-order matrices*). Finally, note that what "$\phi!a$" stands for, according to Russell, is any elementary proposition that contains an atomic sentence of the form $R_n(a, b_1, \ldots, b_{n-1})$. That is, $\phi!a$ is an elementary proposition in which, strictly speaking, $\phi!\hat{z}$ does not occur as an "argument" at all once we are given the predicate and relation symbols upon which any application of Russell's logical syntax is to be based. This is why Russell says in his 1925 introduction to PM that the "peculiarity of functions of second and higher-order is arbitrary" (p. xxxii), and that in fact by adopting predicate and relation variables (i.e., predicate variables of different adicities) we can avoid the notation for propositional functions altogether (ibid.). In other words, no new variables are really needed, according to Russell, beyond those already occurring in the atomistic hierarchy of sentences.

Because "the logic of propositions, and still more of general propositions concerning a given argument, would be intolerably complicated if we abstained from the use of variable functions" (ibid.), Russell does go on to include propositional variables and function variables in his new logical syntax. But, despite appearances to the contrary, these new variables all belong to ramified second-order logic; i.e., they are not allowed to occur as singular terms or logico-grammatical subjects of the new sentences formed by their addition to the atomistic hierarchy. Russell's notation can be deceptive in this regard, however, for even though "there is no logical matrix of the form $f!(\phi!\hat{z})$" (p. xxxi), i.e., a matrix where f is a second-order variable of r-type $(i/1)/1$, nevertheless, according to Russell, there are logical matrices of the form $f!(\phi!\hat{z}, x_1, x_2, \ldots, x_n)$, where "we call f a 'second-order function' because it takes functions among its arguments" (ibid.). A matrix of this form, however, "is always derived from a stroke-function

$$F(p_1, p_2, p_3, \ldots, p_n)$$

by substituting $\phi!x_1, \phi!x_2, \ldots, \phi!x_n$ for $p_1, p_2, \ldots, p_n$. *This is the sole method for constructing such matrices*" (ibid., emphasis added). Note that the propositional variables $p_1, \ldots, p_n$ do not occur in a stroke-function as singular terms, but as "arguments" of a sentential connective (viz., the stroke connective having the truth-table of "either not...or not..."). This means that the substitution of $\phi!x_1, \phi!x_2, \ldots, \phi!x_n$ for $p_1, p_2, \ldots, p_n$ in a stroke-function does not result in a proposition in which $\phi!\hat{z}$ occurs as a singular term, despite appearances to the contrary in Russell's way of representing this substitution as $f!(\phi!\hat{z}, x_1, x_2, \ldots, x_n)$. In other words, despite appearances, f is not occurring in this matrix as an $(n + 1)$-ary second-order variable of r-type $((i)/1, i, \ldots, i)/1$, but as an n-ary second-order variable of r-type $(i, \ldots, i)/2$. This is why Russell says that "*since ϕ can only appear through its values it must appear in a logical matrix with one or more variable arguments*" (ibid., emphasis added).[3]

Now in regard to generalization and the ramification of propositional functions, note that according to Russell "when we have a general proposition $(\phi).F\{\phi!\hat{z}, x, y, \ldots\}$, the only values ϕ can take are matrices, so that functions containing apparent variables are not included" (ibid., p. xxxiii). However, "we can, if we like, introduce a new variable to denote not only functions such as $\phi!\hat{x}$, but also such as

$(y).\phi!(\hat{x}, y), (y, z).\phi!(\hat{x}, y, z), \ldots, (\exists y).\phi!(\hat{x}, y), \ldots;$

in a word, all such functions of one variable as can be derived by generalization from matrices containing only individual variables" (ibid.). For this purpose, Russell introduces the variables ϕ_1, ψ_1, χ_1, etc.; i.e., "the suffix 1 is intended to indicate that the values of the functions may be first-order propositions, resulting from generalization in respect of individuals" (ibid.). "Theoretically," according to Russell, "it is unnecessary to introduce such variables as ϕ_1, because they can be replaced by an infinite conjunction or disjunction" (ibid.).

Of course, "when the apparent variable is of higher-order than the argument, a new situation arises. The simplest cases are

$(\phi).f!(\phi!\hat{z}, x), (\exists \phi).f!(\phi!\hat{z}, x).$

These are functions of x [where f is of r-type $(i)/2$, and not of r-type $((i)/1, i)/1$ as might appear from Russell's notation], but are obviously not included among the values for $\phi!x$ (where ϕ is the argument)" (ibid., p. xxxiv). Russell's original reason for this restriction of the values of $\phi!x$ was that paradoxes would otherwise ensue, including in particular his own paradox of predication. But that reason assumes that f is of r-type $((i)/1, i)/1$ in the preceding examples, and not of r-type $(i)/2$, as is required in Russell's new "atomistic" theory. That is, given Russell's fundamental new assumption that "a function can only appear in a matrix through its values," his own paradox is not even formulable, since it depends on propositional functions being expressions that can occur as singular terms of second-order matrices (or, as in Frege's *Grundgesetze*, on propositional functions having certain abstracts as their singular term counterparts). In other words, no paradox would be forthcoming in Russell's new or restricted logical syntax even if we were to allow the "values" of $\phi!x$ to include propositional functions in which ϕ occurs as a bound variable. (This of course is just the situation that obtains in standard impredicative second-order logic.)

There is a reason, nevertheless, why the "values" of $\phi!x$ should not include propositional functions in which ϕ or another function variable has a bound occurrence, and that is Russell's new or post-PM nominalistic construal of propositional functions. For "in the language of the second-order, variables denote symbols, not what is symbolized" (IMT, p. 192), and in that regard, of course, they cannot themselves be among the symbols they "denote." That is, bound propositional function variables are to be given a substitutional and not an "objectual" interpretation (as they were in Russell's original 1910-13 theory). On this interpretation, to attempt to make the "values" of $\phi!x$ include propositional functions that contain bound occurrences of ϕ "is like attempting to catch one's own shadow. It is impossible to obtain one variable which embraces among its values all possible functions of individuals" ([1925b], p. xxxiv).

Of course, "we can adopt a new variable ϕ_2 which is to include functions in which $\phi!\hat{z}$ can be an apparent variable" (ibid.), but then "we shall obtain new functions" (ibid.), and in this way go on to adopt new variables ϕ_3, ϕ_4, etc. Each of the new variables will belong to a language one order higher than the language whose propositional functions are the substituends or "values" of those variables, and therefore of course none of the substituends or "values" of these new variables can contain bound occurrences of those variables themselves. But all of these variables, it should be emphasized, will be variables of ramified second-order logic; i.e., they will have as substituends only propositional functions of individuals, albeit functions of higher and higher "levels," and in that sense of higher and higher "orders" as well. For, as defined in section 1, the order of an m-ary propositional function of r-type $(i, \ldots, i)/n$ will be the same as its level, and of course that is why the languages generated by the addition of the new variables will be one order higher than the language whose propositional functions are the substituends or "values" of those variables. This means that the higher-order languages of Russell's later philosophy are not the higher-order languages of the simple theory of types, and indeed this is why according to Russell, "my hierarchy of languages is not identical with Carnap's or Tarski's" (IMT, p. 60). For on Russell's "atomistic" view, "what is necessary for significance is that every complete asserted proposition should be derived from a matrix by generalization, and that, in the matrix, the substitution of constant values for the variables should always result, ultimately, in a stroke-function of atomic propositions. We say 'ultimately,' because, when such variables as $\phi_2\hat{z}$ are admitted, the substitution of a value for ϕ_2 may yield a proposition still containing apparent variables, and in this proposition the apparent variables must be replaced by constants before we arrive at a stroke-function of atomic propositions. *We may introduce variables requiring several such stages, but the end must always be the same: a stroke-function of atomic propositions*" (ibid., p. xxxv, emphasis added). In other words, ultimately, according to Russell, "there is...no reason to admit as fundamental any variables except name-variables and relation-variables (in intension)" (IMT, p. 192), where the latter cannot themselves occur as singular terms. That is, in the end, according to Russell, a proposition is significant only if it can be translated into the atomistic hierarchy of sentences.

It is in this sense, accordingly, that propositional functions are merely linguistic conveniences in Russell's later philosophy. And, indeed, as a claim about the reducibility of the truth-conditions of ramified second-order logic to the truth-conditions of the atomistic hierarchy of sentences, such a view is completely unproblematic. Where Russell errs in his later philosophy is in thinking that everything that could be said in his original theory of types can also be said in the atomistic hierarchy, or what comes to the same thing, that his earlier theory of types is equipollent to ramified second-order logic. In particular, Russell's own analysis of classes in terms of propositional functions is no longer available to him in his later philosophy; and apparently the reason he failed to see this was his new way of representing a logical matrix. Russell's claim, accordingly, that "truth in pure mathematics is syntactical" ([MPD], p. 220) and that "numbers are classes of classes, and classes [as propositional functions] are symbolic conveniences" (ibid., p. 102), cannot be justified, since in order to talk of numbers as classes of classes, we must first be able to use expressions for classes as singular terms, which in Russell's framework ultimately means that we must be able to use propositional functions as abstract singular terms, and not merely as expressions that can be asserted as being always true, or sometimes true, or never true.

6. Russell's Weakened Form of the Principle of Atomicity

As originally formulated by Wittgenstein, the principle of atomicity is the thesis that "every statement about complexes can be analyzed into a statement about their constituent parts, and into those propositions which completely describe the complex" (*Tractatus*, 2.0201). For Russell, the technical form of this principle became, as we have said, the thesis that every significant sentence can be translated into the atomistic hierarchy of the sentences of an ideal or logically perfect language (whose logical syntax turns out to be that of ramified second-order logic). But since, according to Russell, all complexes are facts and facts cannot be named, it follows that the names of such a language can only denote simple particulars.

This makes the practical application of such a language very difficult, if not impossible, it should be noted, since Russell himself always maintained that what we take to be a simple particular may in the end really be complex and susceptible to further analysis. Indeed, by 1940, Russell came to the conclusion that "everything that there is in the world I call a 'fact.' The sun is a fact; Caesar's crossing the Rubicon was a fact; if I have a toothache, my toothache is a fact" (HK, p. 43). Facts in this sense, it should be noted, "are to be conceived as occurrences" (IMT, p. 268), i.e., as events.

Events, from 1914 to 1940, were the original simple particulars of Russell's atomist ontology, with ordinary physical objects being somehow analyzed as complexes consisting of a "compresence" of events (cf. LA, p. 341). That analysis is very much in doubt, however, insofar as complexes cannot be named and ascribed properties and relations in Russell's atomistic hierarchy. That is, just as Russell's earlier analysis of classes and numbers is no longer significant in his new logical syntax, so too his analysis of physical objects as a series of events is at least problematic, if not also nonsignificant in its allowing such complexes to have properties and stand in various relationships to one another. In addition, most, if not all, events will have an internal complexity of their own, and so they will not really be the simple particulars of an atomist ontology after all.

Russell never doubted the adequacy (or availability within the atomistic hierarchy) of his analysis of physical objects as complexes of events, it must be said; but he did agree, at least from 1940 on, that most events, notwithstanding their status as particulars, were themselves complexes. Their constituents, it turned out, or at least so Russell proposed, were simple qualities. Thus, from 1940 on, events were no longer the simple particulars of Russell's atomist ontology, but were reconstrued as complexes of simple qualities. For Russell, this meant that words for qualities, such as "red," "blue," "hard," "soft," etc., are "names in the syntactical sense" (IMT, p. 89) of his ideal language. For example, according to Russell, "wherever there is, for common sense, a 'thing' having the quality C, we should say, instead, that C itself exists in that place, and that the 'thing' is to be replaced by the collection of qualities existing in the place in question. Thus 'C' becomes a name, not a predicate" (ibid., p. 93). This does not mean that properties and relations in general can now be named; for Russell continued to insist right until the end that "relation-words ought only to be employed as actually relating and that sentences in which such words appear as subjects are only significant when they can be translated into sentences in which the relation-words perform their proper function of denoting a relation between terms. Or as it may be put in other words: verbs are necessary, but verbal nouns are not" ([MPD], p. 173).

What is important about this modification in Russell's ontology is that simple qualities are not the only particulars there are. That is, in Russell's ideal language of the atomistic hierarchy, at least from 1940 on, names may denote not only simple qualities but complexes of such as well (cf. HK, p. 84). This in fact is what Russell means by the weakened form of the principle of atomicity; that is, the form in which the principle "is not to be applied to everything that is in fact complex, but only to things named by complex names" (IMT, p. 251). "A name N may be in fact the name of a complex, but may not itself have any logical complexity, i.e. any parts that are symbols. This is the case with all names that actually occur. Caesar was complex, but 'Caesar' is logically simple, i.e., none of its parts are symbols" (ibid.). On the other hand, "though 'Caesar' is simple, 'the death of Caesar' is complex" (ibid.), and according to the principle of atomicity, it is to be analyzed into a statement about its constituent parts. In other words, although facts in the sense of events can be named in Russell's later philosophy after all, complex names of facts must still be analyzed and are not allowed to occur as names in the logical language based on the atomistic hierarchy of sentences (cf. IMT, p. 309).

This weakening of the principle of atomicity does allow Russell to translate sentences about physical objects into the logical language of his atomistic hierarchy, even though physical objects are ultimately themselves complexes of events, which in turn are complexes of compresent simple qualities. The translation, however, must never be such as to syntactically represent physical objects both as particulars and as complexes, since statements about complexes as single entities or "logical subjects" will have no counterparts in the atomistic hierarchy. How satisfactory a resolution of the problem of the practical application of Russell's ideal language this comes to in the end, we shall not attempt to assess here. For it still remains true in any case that Russell's original analysis of classes and numbers in terms of propositional functions as single entities will have no counterpart in his atomistic hierarchy of sentences.

Notes

1. Cf. Church, "Comparison of Russell's Resolution of the Semantical Antinomies with that of Torski," *Journal of Symbolic Logic*, 41 (1976), pp. 747–60. We take ω to be the set of natural numbers; thus, "$m \in \omega$" is read "m is a natural number," and "$n \in \omega - \{0\}$" is read "n is a natural number other than 0." We assume, incidentally, that the definition applies to expressions as well as to what the expressions stand for.

2. This notion of "level" should not be confused with Frege's. It corresponds, though not exactly, to Russell's notion of "order" in PM. We have retained Church's terminology here, since we are after all using his characterization of the r-types. We should note, however, that we use the phrase "ramified second-order logic" with its now standard meaning (as described, e.g., in Church [1956], section 58), i.e., as referring to the system of all the propositional functions that have r-types of the form $(i, \ldots, i)/n$, for arbitrary "level" n. These functions have only individuals as arguments, and therefore, as defined earlier their "order" is the same as their "level." This means that functions of every "order" are among the functions of ramified *second-order* logic, even though they always have only individuals as their arguments. I believe, incidentally, that a confusion of the different notions of order and level in part explains why Russell failed to see that the theory of types in his later philosophy was not the same as the theory he described in PM.

3. We should note, incidentally, that the use of the exclamation mark following the variable f no longer means that f is "predicative" in the sense defined in section 1. Rather, in Russell's 1925 introduction to PM, it simply means that the function has elementary propositions as its values (see p. xxviii).

Herbert Hochberg

Russell's Paradox, Russellian Relations, and the Problems of Predication and Impredicativity

Russell's paradox and the resultant distinction of logical types have been central topics of philosophical discussion for almost a century. In this essay I claim that a more fundamental distinction, that which distinguishes properties and relations as monadic, dyadic, etc., provides a basis for blocking Russell's paradox as applied to properties, not sets, without distinctions of type (or equivalent distinctions). The distinction also points to fundamental features of predication that bear on the nature of relations, the extension of relations, the problem of the analysis of relational order, and questions about symmetrical relations (identity) and purported monadic relational properties (self-identity). In particular, an early unpublished analysis of relational order that Russell proposed is examined in detail and contrasted with the standard set-theoretical analysis of Wiener and Kuratowski. I argue that the analysis of Kuratowski presupposes a basic ordering relation, and hence does not provide an analysis of order, whereas a modification of Russell's analysis provides a viable alternative analysis. The discussion of Russell's paradox and relational predication brings out a connection with Bradley's lesser-known paradox of predication, which, like the Russell paradox, is found to stem from a mistaken conception of the exemplification relation.

Though I argue that a *Principia*-style schema without type distinctions avoids the familiar paradox involving self-predication, I defend Russell's rejection of impredicative properties, and his use of a ramified theory of orders, from Ramsey's arguments attacking Russell's claim that a "vicious circle" is involved in the use of impredicative predicates. This discussion involves a consideration of Ramsey's view of quantification, which he derived from Wittgenstein. As both the ramified theory, involving Russell's axiom of reducibility, and the acceptance of impredicative predicates are found to be problematic, I conclude that complex predicate abstracts involving predicate quantifiers should not be taken to represent properties.

I. Self-predication and Paradox

Russell and others have held that the Russell paradox arises for both properties and classes, given an unrestricted comprehension rule. The paradox is sometimes mistakenly said to arise from the introduction of a certain expression into a schema. Thus, if one introduces a predicate "I" defined by:

(1) $I(f) = df \neg f(f)$

so that we have:

(2) $(f)[I(f) \equiv \neg f(f)]$,

which we instantiate to:

(3) $I(I) \equiv \neg I(I)$,

we have a contradiction. Quine has stressed the point that this is mistaken since the paradox results only when one holds that the property (or class) I exists.[1] The paradox does not arise from the mere introduction of "I" into the schema by (1). Thus, the additional assumption of "$(\exists f)(f = I)$" or "$(\exists f)(g)[f(g) \equiv \neg g(g)]$" is needed to generate (3). This, for Quine, is implicit in the instantiation from (2) to (3), since, as Quine sees it, one is committed to the existence of something if one instantiates to a sign "for it" or existentially generalizes from such a sign. The instantiation from (2) to (3) also involves letting "I" occupy subject place, even though we define the sign, in (1), only as it occurs in predicate place. This, too, fits with Quine's notions of "ontological commitment," since, for Quine, we arrive at the paradox of (3) only by means of an instantiation of (2), or an equivalent rule for substitution covering the free variable in (1), which presupposes the appropriate existential claim. Thus, Quine and others avoid the paradox by adopting a comprehension axiom warranting existential statements like "$(\exists f)(g)[f(g) \equiv \ldots g \ldots]$" if restrictions on the context "$\ldots$" are satisfied. The restrictions limit instantiations to "non-problematic" predicates. Russell's theory of types amounts to such a restrictive comprehension axiom, since it excludes contexts like "$\neg f(f)$" as ill formed, hence blocking existential statements like "$(\exists f)\neg f(f)$."

The use of a definition like (1) is problematic in that while "I" is a defined predicate, it cannot be replaced in (3). This is not only due to the use of "I" in both subject and predicate place in (3), while it occurs only in predicate place in the definiendum of (1). What is also peculiar is the use of the free variable "f" in both subject and predicate place in the definiens. These peculiarities suggest that the definition in (1) is not really a definition. But we can define "I" by the use of an abstract in the form of a definite description:

(4) $I = df\ (f)(g)[f(g) \equiv \neg g(g)]$.

One can now attempt to generate the Russell paradox, along lines Russell sometimes used in the exposition of it, by use of the law of excluded middle.[2] Thus,

(5) $I(I) \vee \neg I(I)$

is taken as an instance of "$p \vee \neg p$," and the paradox supposedly results since each disjunct in (5) entails its negation. But the matter is not so simple. Replacing "I" by its definition, given in (4), in "$I(I)$," we get

(6) $(\iota f)(g)[f(g) \equiv \neg g(g)]\{(\iota f)(g)[f(g) \equiv \neg g(g)]\}$,

with the use of braces in (6) to set off the occurrence of the description in subject place. If we retain standard features of Russell's theory of descriptions in our "type-free" notation, (6) is readily seen to entail (in fact it is equivalent to):

(7) $E!(\iota f)(g)[f(g) \equiv \neg g(g)]$,

which is the existential condition Quine takes to be necessary to generate the paradox. (6) and (7) are easily seen to be contradictions upon expansion of the descriptions. Replacing "I" by its definition in "$I(I)$" we get:

(8) $\neg (\iota f)(g)[f(g) \equiv \neg g(g)]\{(\iota f)(g)[f(g) \equiv \neg g(g)]\}$.

By Russell's theory of descriptions we now face the familiar ambiguity of scope. If we take the scope to be secondary, then (8) may be read as the denial that there is a unique Russell property that applies to itself. Upon expansion of the description in (8), (8) is clearly not a contradiction. If we take the scope (or α scope) as primary, (8) is contradictory. But, to treat the scope as primary is not to take (8) as an instance of "$p \vee \neg p$." Thus, a well known feature of the theory of descriptions blocks the attempt to derive a paradox by the use of "$p \vee \neg p$." One may then allow the predicate "$(\iota f)(g)[f(g) \equiv \neg g(g)]$" into a type-free schema without paradox, just as one may allow "$(\iota f)(f \neq f)$" as a predicate. One can no more claim that "$E!(\iota f)(g)[f(g \equiv \neg g(g)]$" holds than one can adopt "$E!(\iota f)(f \neq f)$." However, there is a problem involved in treating "I" as an abbreviation of a definite description or lambda abstraction in a calculus where predicates are taken to represent properties, rather than classes.

The problem is easily seen in a simpler context. Let "R" and "S" be two predicates that we take to stand for properties, say being red and being square. If we limit ourselves to lower functional logic we may define a predicate "RS" by

(D_1) $RS(x) =_{df} R(x) \& S(x)$

or use an abstract

$R(\hat{x}) \& S(\hat{x})$

so understood that

(D_2) $[R(\hat{x}) \& S(\hat{x})](y) =_{df} R(y) \& S(y)$

is assumed. But, if we consider "RS" or "$R(\hat{x}) \& S(\hat{x})$" in a higher functional calculus, (D_1) and (D_2) do not suffice. They do not provide for the elimination of the defined signs in all contexts where such signs occur as subject signs, as in

"$(\exists f)(f = RS\,)$" and "$(\exists\phi)\phi(RS\,)$" or in "$(\exists f)(f = [R(\hat{x})\ \&\ S(\hat{x})])$" and "$(\exists\phi)\phi[R(\hat{x})\ \&\ S(\hat{x})]$." Hence, we may use definite descriptions (or lambda abstracts) so that "RS" and "$R(\hat{x})\ \&\ S(\hat{x})$" are construed in terms of "$(\iota f)(x)[f(x) \equiv (R(x)\ \&\ S(x))]$." But, doing this presupposes that we hold that only one property has the extension had by RS, namely, RS itself. This is precisely what we should not assume if we take predicates to stand for properties, rather than classes.[3] Making such an assumption amounts to the introduction of an extensionality axiom. Even if one holds that necessary or logical equivalence guarantees identity, as Carnap once suggested, one presupposes a variant of an extensionality axiom. Aside from the familiar problems associated with such a claim, it simply amounts to a stipulation regarding "identity conditions" for complex properties. Moreover, it would not only force one to hold that there is only one tautologous and one contradictory property, but it also goes against the obvious point that complex properties with different constituents are different—$R\hat{x}\ \&\ \neg R\hat{x}$ and $G\hat{x}\ \&\ \neg G\hat{x}$, for example. To avoid making an unwarranted assumption about equivalence as a condition of identity, we should not use such definite descriptions (or lambda abstracts where such abstracts are construed "extensionally") to define expressions like "RS" or "$R(\hat{x})\ \&\ S(\hat{x})$," where the latter are taken to stand for a property: the property we would normally take as being red and square. We can then take the juxtaposition of "R" and "S" in "RS" or the use of "&" in "$R(\hat{x})\ \&\ S(\hat{x})$" to be devices for forming compound predicates, from other predicates, that represent "complex" properties. The explicit use of "&" in "$R(\hat{x})\ \&\ S(\hat{x})$," and its implicit use in "RS," is not as a truth-functional connective. Rather, "&" operates as a primitive sign that is used to form predicates from predicates. The predicates formed by its use are, then, undefined complex predicates. Hence, we require

(9) $(y)([R(\hat{x})\ \&\ S(\hat{x})](y) \equiv [R(y)\ \&\ S(y)])$

as an instance of an axiom schema governing the use of "&" *in* predicate expressions. Not having (D_1) or (D_2), (9) is not a consequence of any definitional pattern.

The same situation arises in a type-free schema in the case of contexts like

(10) $R(R)$

and

(11) $\neg R(R)$.

We can form the predicates

(12) $\hat{\phi}(\hat{\phi})$
(13) $\neg\hat{\phi}(\hat{\phi})$

by abstraction. But, there is a problem about how to treat such predicate abstracts in sentential contexts. So long as we have taken predicates to stand for properties, we cannot treat such abstracts as abbreviations of definite descriptions, such as "$(\iota f)(g)[f(g) \equiv \neg g(g)]$." Just as we may not use "$(\iota f)(x)[f(x) \equiv (R(x) \& S(x))]$" in a calculus where the predicates are taken to stand for properties, so we may not use "$(\iota f)(g)[f(g) \equiv \neg g(g)]$," and, hence, we may use neither "I," defined as in (4), nor (13), construed as an abbreviation for "$(\iota f)(g)[f(g) \equiv \neg g(g)]$."

(13) must then be construed as a primitive complex predicate that is not eliminable by definition. Hence, as in the case of "$R(\hat{x}) \& S(\hat{x})$," a question arises about the treatment of such abstracts in sentential contexts. Again, let us consider a simpler case. From the contexts "$(\exists x)R(x)$" and "$(\exists f)f(a)$," where "a" is a proper name, we may construct the abstracts "$(\exists x)\hat{f}(x)$" and "$(\exists f)f(\hat{x})$" and read them, respectively, as "applying to something" and "having some property." If we then consider the appropriate sentences used to attribute such properties to R and a, respectively, to be

$$[(\exists x)\hat{f}(x)](R)$$

and

$$[(\exists f)f(\hat{x})](a)$$

we must assume, as instances of axiom schemata for such abstracts,

$$[(\exists x)\hat{f}(x)](R) \equiv (\exists x)R(x)$$

and

$$[(\exists f)f(\hat{x})](a) \equiv (\exists f)f(a),$$

in order to have the predicate abstracts carry the "sense" intended. Therefore, it is simpler, following Russell and Whitehead in PM, to express the attribution of $(\exists x)\hat{f}(x)$ to R by replacing the occurrence of "f" by "R" to yield "$(\exists x)R(x)$," and employ a similar pattern in the case of "a" and "$(\exists f)f(\hat{x})$." This way of construing such predicate abstracts can be taken to be a reason for denying that such abstracts stand for properties if their use is limited to predicate place. Where such abstracts function as subject terms, as in "$\phi[(\exists)\hat{f}(x)]$," no such replacement is possible, just as in the earlier case of "RS" and "$R(\hat{x}) \& S(\hat{x})$." In the present cases we do not construct the predicate abstract by combining predicate signs, as in the case of "$R(\hat{x}) \& S(\hat{x})$," but by "abstracting from" a constant predicate (or "open sentence" if one prefers). Interestingly enough, just as one may deny that such abstracts stand for properties, if they are confined to use in predicate place, since, for example, "$[\exists(x)\hat{f}(x)](R)$" is merely an alternative rendition of "$(\exists x)R(x)$," one may also object to taking such abstracts to stand for properties if they are not so confined. For, in the latter circumstances, such abstracts must be construed as undefined but complex predicates, since they are not eliminable, as subject terms, by axiom schemata or rules of replacement. Ruling out such properties on such grounds would, of course, rule out the Russell property.[4] But ruling out the Russell property by denying that complex, yet undefined, predicates stand for properties is not a resolution I wish to pursue here. Rather, there is a more fundamental point about the abstract "$\neg \hat{\phi}(\hat{\phi})$" and the "Russell property" that will block the paradox.

Given the abstract "$\neg \hat{\phi}(\hat{\phi})$" as a sign for the "Russell property," one may then, purportedly, form

(14) $\neg \hat{\phi}(\hat{\phi})[\neg \hat{\phi}(\hat{\phi})]$,

as the relevant self-predication.[5] By our understood replacement rule we would take the subject abstract to replace each token of "$\hat{\phi}$" in the predicate term and obtain

(15) $\neg [\neg \hat{\phi}(\hat{\phi})[\neg \hat{\phi}(\hat{\phi})]]$,

which contradicts (14). One might object to the legitimacy of "$\hat{\phi}(\hat{\phi})$" and "$\neg \hat{\phi}(\hat{\phi})$" as predicate expressions, since their use as predicates leads to an unending application of the replacement rule. Thus, by that rule, (15) will generate another statement, equivalent to (14), that will generate yet another statement, and so on. One will never arrive at a statement where the abstract in predicate place is removed by application of the replacement rule. This is reminiscent of the peculiarity of "I," defined as in (1), as it occurs in (3) and, hence, points to another way of dismissing the Russell paradox. But there is still a more fundamental point to be made about $\neg \hat{\phi}(\hat{\phi})$. This we can see by considering the argument purportedly establishing the paradox. Supposedly, given the derivation of (15) from (14), one concludes that (14) is contradictory and hence that $\neg \hat{\phi}(\hat{\phi})$ cannot apply to itself. And, if we assume that it does not, i.e., assume (15), then by the replacement rule we obtain

(16) $\neg [\neg [\neg \hat{\phi}(\hat{\phi})[\neg \hat{\phi}(\hat{\phi})]]]$,

which is the other strand of the familiar paradox. Thus, assuming our replacement rule and that either (14) or (15) holds, we seem to arrive at the familiar contradiction.

The appearance is deceiving and illustrates a crucial point about the "Russell property." Neither (15) nor (16) is obtained by a legitimate application of the replacement rule. The purported Russell property $\neg \hat{\phi}(\hat{\phi})$ is really a two-term relation, and the abstract "$\neg \hat{\phi}(\hat{\phi})$" a two-term relational predicate. Yet to arrive at (15) and (16) we replaced a monadic predicate variable abstract "$\hat{\phi}$" by a two-term relational predicate. Once again, the point is easily seen in a simpler case.

Consider the sentence "Ra." We form an abstract by abstraction on the sign "a" and obtain "$R\hat{x}$," which we may take to be another sign for the property *being an R*, i.e., R itself. If we abstract from the predicate sign and obtain "$\hat{\phi}a$," we get a sign for *being a property of a*. Suppose we abstract from both signs and obtain "$\hat{\phi}\hat{x}$." What do we have a sign for? One obvious answer is *the relation* exemplification that obtains between properties and objects. Thus, we can take

(17) $\hat{\phi}\hat{x}(R, a)$

to be a way of stating that a has R and, by appropriate use of the replacement rule, take (17) to yield "Ra." The crucial point is that "$\hat{\phi}\hat{x}$" is a relation sign and that we must apply the replacement rule to two sign tokens to obtain "Ra" from (17). Notice also that one replaces the token of "$\hat{\phi}$" in (17) by a monadic predicate, "R." The same situation is present in the case of "$\hat{\phi}(\hat{\phi})$" and "$\neg \hat{\phi}(\hat{\phi})$." They are relation signs, just as "$\hat{\phi}\hat{x}$" is. The Russell property is really a relation, not a monadic property. $\hat{\phi}(\hat{\phi})$ may be taken as the relation of self-exemplification for monadic properties and $\neg \hat{\phi}(\hat{\phi})$, the Russell "property," as the relation of non-self-exemplification for monadic properties. Thus, (14) is not well formed, irrespective of a theory of types, since "$\neg \hat{\phi}(\hat{\phi})$" is a relational predicate that is used as a monadic predicate in (14). In place of (14) we should seek to use

(18) $\neg \hat{\phi}(\hat{\phi})[\neg \hat{\phi}(\hat{\phi}), \neg \hat{\phi}(\hat{\phi})]$

to state that the Russell relation applies to itself, i.e., that it stands in the relation to itself. One would then seek to derive the contradiction by replacing "$\neg \hat{\phi}(\hat{\phi})$" for each occurrence of "$\hat{\phi}$" in the predicate expression "$\neg \hat{\phi}(\hat{\phi})$" in (18). But, whereas "$\neg \hat{\phi}(\hat{\phi})$" is a two-term relation sign, "$\hat{\phi}$" is a monadic predicate abstract and must be replaced by a monadic predicate sign. Recall (17) and the replacement of "$\hat{\phi}$" by "R." Thus, such a replacement in (18) is illegitimate.[6] The derivation of the paradox is also blocked if we seek to use

(19) $(g)[\neg \hat{\phi}(\hat{\phi})g \equiv \neg g(g)]$

in place of the replacement rule, for (19) must be modified to

(20) $(g)[\neg \hat{\phi}(\hat{\phi})(g, g) \equiv \neg g(g)]$

to be well formed, given that "$\neg \hat{\phi}(\hat{\phi})$" is a relational predicate. But, then, we can, *at best*, only instantiate to

(21) $\neg \hat{\phi}(\hat{\phi})[\neg \hat{\phi}(\hat{\phi}), \neg \hat{\phi}(\hat{\phi})] \equiv \neg [\neg \hat{\phi}(\hat{\phi})[\neg \hat{\phi}(\hat{\phi})]]$

and not to

(22) $\neg \hat{\phi}(\hat{\phi})[\neg \hat{\phi}(\hat{\phi})] \equiv \neg [\neg \hat{\phi}(\hat{\phi})[\neg \hat{\phi}(\hat{\phi})]]$.

But, even (21) is illegitimate, since we instantiate a relation sign for a monadic predicate variable, "g," to obtain the right-hand side of the biconditional. Thus, (21) is not only not contradictory, it is not even well formed.

Taking the Russell property as a relation, as we should, the Russell paradox does not arise for properties and relations in a type-free schema that distinguishes between monadic and relational properties and predicates in the familiar way. The paradox does arise for classes, without the familiar restrictions, and for a schema that would permit definite descriptions of properties, based on extensional conditions, as in (4), and where (7) is assumed. But the use of such descriptions for properties is problematic in its own right. Thus, for properties and relations, one may recognize self-predication and the Russell relation without paradox, if one employs a viable schema for the representation of properties. Such a schema need not employ either a version of type theory or a corresponding restricted comprehension rule. The distinction between monadic and relational properties suffices as a restriction that prohibits the paradox. Thus, we may conclude that a fundamental feature of exemplification or predication suffices to block the paradox. It is worth recalling that Russell once took the "fact" that particulars were of one kind while attributes were of logically different kinds, monadic, dyadic, etc., to be the ultimate distinguishing feature between particulars and attributes (properties).

II. Properties, Relations, and Identity

Besides the difference between classes and properties that prevents the use of a sign like "$(\iota f)(g)(f(g) \equiv \neg g(g))$" for a property, another reason the paradox arises for classes, but not for properties, is that there is no distinction for classes like that between monadic, dyadic, etc., attributes. Taken "in extension," as one says, a dyadic relation is a class, though a class of ordered pairs or, following the Wiener-Kuratowski procedure, a class of two-membered classes (whose members, in turn, are classes). Thus, one can speak of the class of classes that are not members of themselves. In the case of attributes one must speak of the dyadic relation of non-self-exemplification that monadic attributes stand in (or do not) to themselves. It is clear that a monadic Russell property does not exist since "$(\exists f)(g)(f(g) \equiv \neg g(g))$" is paradoxical. Moreover, if one claims that there is a monadic property had by all properties that stand in the Russell relation to themselves,

(23) $(\exists f)(g)(f(g) \equiv \neg \hat{\phi}\hat{\phi}(g, g))$,

a paradox results as well, since, by the replacement rule, we arrive at "$(\exists f)(g)(f(g) \equiv \neg g(g))$" from (23). This means that the abstract "$(g)(\hat{\phi}(g) \equiv \neg g(g))$," taken as an abstract standing for a monadic property that applies to any monadic property that is a Russell property, stands for an empty property. The class of monadic Russell properties is empty. No paradox results, however, from recognizing $(g)((\hat{\phi})(g) \equiv \neg g(g))$ as an attribute (see note 5), just as no paradox results from recognizing $\neg \hat{\phi}\hat{\phi}$ as a dyadic relation.[7] Moreover, as no paradox results from "$(\exists R_2)(R_2 = \neg \hat{\phi}\hat{\phi})$" or "$(\exists R_2)(g)(R_2(g, g) \equiv \neg \hat{\phi}\hat{\phi}(g, g))$" or "$(\exists R_2)(g)(R_2(g, g) \equiv \neg g(g))$," it is clear that there are several ways in which one can say that the Russell relation exists without paradoxical consequences.

The relation $\hat{\phi}(\hat{\phi})$ poses a problem ignored in the preceding discussion. Suppose one considers "$\hat{\phi}(\hat{\Psi})$" to represent monadic exemplification for properties. Thus

(24) $\hat{\phi}(\hat{\Psi})(G, G)$

would express the self-exemplification of G, and (24) would be equivalent to "$G(G)$."

To say that G exemplifies G is to say that G stands in *the relation of exemplification* to G (itself). But if one also recognizes $\hat{\phi}(\hat{\phi})$ we have a second situation obtaining: that G stands in the relation of self-exemplification to G. The situations would be different since one involves $\hat{\phi}(\hat{\Psi})$ while the other involves $\hat{\phi}(\hat{\phi})$. Yet, both "$\hat{\phi}(\hat{\Psi})(G, G)$" and "$\hat{\phi}(\hat{\phi})(G, G)$" are equivalent to "$G(G)$," by the understood replacement rule. This points to the peculiarity of recognizing a relation of self-exemplification, as well as a relation of exemplification. It is problematic to take "$\hat{\phi}(\hat{\phi})$" to stand for a relation, since what we have when we use "$\hat{\phi}(\hat{\phi})$" in "$\hat{\phi}(\hat{\phi})(G, G)$" is simply a case of the use of "$\hat{\phi}(\hat{\Psi})$." There is no more a relation of self-exemplification in addition to that of exemplification than there is a relation of self-identity in addition to the identity relation. What can lead one to recognize such an additional relation is the confusion whereby one takes such a relation to be a monadic property, which is easily done. Thus, one may think of *self-identity* as a monadic property that an entity exemplifies, and not as a reflexive relation. Being a monadic property, it is then different from a reflexive relation. But this is mistaken. If we take "$\hat{x} = \hat{y}$" as a predicate for the identity relation, then "$\hat{x} = \hat{x}$" only appears to be a monadic predicate, since it involves two tokens of the same type. Consider "$L\hat{x}\hat{y}$" to represent the relation of being to the left of. It is clearly absurd to take "$L\hat{x}\hat{x}$" to represent the further relation, or property, of *being to the left of itself*. There are really two questions involved. First, is there an additional relation or monadic property in the case of *self-identity* and *being to the left of itself*? Second, if there is, is it a monadic property or a relation? It is clear that we do not have a monadic property. For when one asserts that an object a is not to the left of itself and is to the left of an object b, it must be that one denies that the object a stands to itself as it stands to the object b. That is, what is denied is that *the pair* (a, a) stands in the very same relation that obtains of *the pair* (a, b). But, even if it is taken to be a relation, $L\hat{x}\hat{x}$ would have to be taken to hold of the pair (a, a) only when the relation $L\hat{x}\hat{y}$ holds of the pair. To recognize $L\hat{x}\hat{x}$ in addition to $L\hat{x}\hat{y}$ is not only pointless by Occam's razor, but introduces the difficulty of forcing one to recognize the distinct situations involving the different relations, while having both "$L\hat{x}\hat{y}(a, a)$" and "$L\hat{x}\hat{x}(a, a)$" being elliptical for "Laa." But, then, we no more have "$L\hat{x}\hat{x}$" standing for a relation than for a monadic property. What goes for $L\hat{x}\hat{x}$ goes for self-identity and $\hat{\phi}(\hat{\phi})$. Thus, neither "$\hat{\phi}(\hat{\phi})$" nor "$\neg \hat{\phi}(\hat{\phi})$" stands for a relation. The purported Russell relation $\neg \hat{\phi}(\hat{\phi})$ may thus be avoided, and with it the purported paradox disappears in yet another way.

III. Relations and Order

Not acknowledging $L\hat{x}\hat{x}$, $\hat{x} = \hat{x}$, and $\hat{\phi}(\hat{\phi})$ as relations, for the preceding reasons, shows something further about relational predication. It has been common to construe properties in extension as classes. Relations, then, are taken as classes of ordered pairs or, following the Wiener-Kuratowski procedure for the construal of such pairs, as classes of classes. This means that in taking relations as classes, one either recognizes a further kind of entity—an ordered pair—or treats relations like $L\hat{x}\hat{y}$, which obtain among particulars, as higher-order classes of classes of classes, as opposed to monadic properties of objects, which become first-order classes of particulars. By so treating relations one obliterates a logical distinction between monadic and relational properties by, in effect, treating relations as monadic properties of ordered pairs. Yet, by so doing one appeals to a different logical distinction: that between the objects, particulars as opposed to pairs, or that between the order of classes relative to the particulars, since relations like $L\hat{x}\hat{y}$ become classes of classes of classes of particulars.

In the case of the use of the Wiener-Kuratowski procedure there is an interesting consequence. The pair (a, a) becomes the class $\{\{a\}\}$, a one-membered class of a unit class of a particular. This, in a way, correlates with the notion that signs like "$\hat{x} = \hat{x}$," "$L\hat{x}\hat{x}$," and "$\hat{\phi}(\hat{\phi})$" are signs for monadic properties. Yet, there is also an obvious correlate of the point that "$\hat{x} = \hat{x}$," etc., are not signs for monadic properties, for the appropriate class for a monadic property of objects a, b, etc., would be $\{a, b, \ldots, \}$, whereas the appropriate class correlated to the relational predicate "$\hat{x} = \hat{x}$" would contain $\{\{a\}\}$, $\{\{b\}\}$, etc. The difference between a and $\{\{a\}\}$ as members of the extension of predicates reflects the difference between a monadic property and a reflexive relation. Of course, if one thinks of "open sentences" being satisfied, one can speak of "$x = x$" and "Gx" both being satisfied by, say, a, and hence of classes of objects of the same kind as the extensions of both "predicates." But this already overlooks the relational form of "$x = x$" by treating it along the lines of "Gx & Hx." In both cases there are two tokens of an individual variable, but no relational predicate occurs in "Gx & Hx."

Russell was long preoccupied by the problems posed by the analysis of relational facts. One problem he was concerned with was that of the logical form of propositions. That problem would be resolved by recognizing different exemplification relations for monadic, dyadic, etc., facts. Thus, one difference between the facts expressed by "Ga" and "Lab" would be that the former involved the two-term exemplification connection expressed by "$\hat{\phi}\hat{x}$," while the latter would involve a three-term connection expressed by "$\hat{R}\hat{x}\hat{y}$." The exemplification connection would be the form of the fact. But such a form would not suffice to distinguish the facts expressed by "Lab" and "Lba." Russell's most detailed attempt to deal with the problems of relational predication occurs in the recently published *Theory of Knowledge*.[8] It has been suggested that his solution of the difficulty was similar to the Wiener-Kuratowski procedure in that he appeals to higher-order relations.[9] But this is not accurate. What Russell did was to suggest coordinating a relation, say $L\hat{x}\hat{y}$, to two relations, say L_1 and L_2, which were relations that obtained between objects, like a, and "complexes," as nonlinguistic entities. Thus, the fact or proposition[10] that-Lab was the fact or proposition to which a stood in the relation L_1 and to which b stood in the relation L_2. The complex that-Lab was thus denoted by a definite description:

(R$_1$) $(\iota p)[(aL_1p) \& (bL_2p)]$.

Such an analysis is problematic, since it distinguishes aLb from bLa by holding that the first stands in one relation to a, while the second stands in another relation to a. This means that one assumes that one may distinguish two entities by means of relational properties. Ironically, Russell had, following Moore, earlier argued that one could not do this.

This problem is avoided by modifying Russell's analysis and doing the following. Let us take "$(L\hat{x}\hat{y}, a, b)$" to indicate a "complex" that obtains when one of the two particulars is to the left of the other, without specifying any "order." Let L_1 and L_2 be relations between a particular and the complex indicated by "$(L\hat{x}\hat{y}, a, b)$." Then

(R$_2$) $[aL_1(L\hat{x}\hat{y}, a, b)] \& [bL_2(L\hat{x}\hat{y}, a, b)]$

can be taken to state that a is the first element, and b the second, of an instance of $L\hat{x}\hat{y}$. Hence, "Lab" and (R$_2$) express the same proposition or situation. But (R$_2$), unlike "Lab," makes no use of order in several senses. First, conjunction is commutative.[11] Second, the sign "$(L\hat{x}\hat{y}, a, b)$," like a set sign, makes no use of the order of the terms. Thus, $(L\hat{x}\hat{y}, a, b) = (L\hat{x}\hat{y}, b, a) = (a, b, L\hat{x}\hat{y}) = $ etc. Third, given the difference in the kinds of terms of L_1 and L_2—individuals and situations or propositions—one can take "$aL_1(L\hat{x}\hat{y}, a, b)$" and "$(L\hat{x}\hat{y}, a, b)L_1a$" to state the same thing: that the particular a is the first term of an instance of a left-of relation (with b).

Russell's use of a description rather than a sign like "$(L\hat{x}\hat{y}, a, b)$" avoids the redundancy of one of the conjuncts of (R$_2$). (Actually, given the redundancy in (R$_2$) one may take "Lab" to be analyzed in terms of one conjunct.) But his description is peculiar. For Russell replaces a *sentence*, such as "Lab," by a *description*, since we understand that the sentence "Lab" stands for a complex that the description picks out. We, at best, have "Lab" as an abbreviation for the description, but it is not an abbreviation for a sentence, unless

(R$_3$) E!$(\iota p)[(aL_1p) \& (bL_2p)]$

is the appropriate sentence, a sentence Russell uses to assert that the complex exists. Russell's use of a description instead of an unordered complex sign like "$(L\hat{x}\hat{y}, a, b)$," may be partly motivated by an apparent circularity in the use of such a complex. He takes the relation $L\hat{x}\hat{y}$ to be determined by L_1 and L_2. And, if we think of specifying what "*Lab*" asserts in terms of (R_1) or (R_3), as opposed to (R_2), we see an apparent problem with (R_2) that is not present in (R_3) or (R_1).[12] The problem is only apparent. For "L_1" and "L_2" are used in different ways in (R_2), on the one hand, and (R_1) and (R_3) on the other. Russell's L_1 and L_2 determine $L\hat{x}\hat{y}$ as well as the order of the terms a and b in the expressed proposition or situation. By using (R_2), one takes L_1 and L_2 simply to supply the order. Thus, whereas Russell would require two completely different relations, playing the roles analogous to L_1 and L_2, in the case of another two-term relation, say *below*, "L_1" and "L_2" may be used for such a relation, as those terms are used in (R_2). As referred to in (R_2), the relations L_1 and L_2 simply determine the order of terms, and not the relation involved. Thus, there is no circularity in the use of "L_1" and "L_2" in (R_2). Rather the pattern recognizing ($L\hat{x}\hat{y}$, a, b) separates the two features involved: the content supplied by one relation rather than another *and* the ordering of the terms standing in the relation. On the pattern, L_1 and L_2 are the basis for the analysis of order in propositions (or situations or facts). Moreover, one does not appeal to Russell's vague talk of L_1 and L_2 "determining" $L\hat{x}\hat{y}$. For what this amounts to is simply the running together of the two quite different aspects of a relational fact: the content supplied by the relation and the order of the terms.

The Wiener-Kuratowski procedure appears to offer an alternative analysis of order without appealing to ordering relations like L_1 and L_2. But this is misleading. If one were to employ such a procedure in the analysis of facts or propositions, one would have to introduce higher-order classes or some correlate of such classes as constituents of facts or propositions. Either alternative is problematic. For not only are additional entities introduced, but the ordering relations are not avoided. It is easy to see why they are not. Suppose one takes $L\hat{x}\hat{y}$ to be a property of the class { {a}, {a, b} }, and thus takes the fact that $-Lab$ to be the exemplification of $L\hat{x}\hat{y}$ by that class. It is clear that two relations, say *is a member of a unit class in* and *is not a member of a unit class in*, are implicitly employed in the analysis of relational facts by the use of classes like { {a}, {a, b} }. The former relation replaces L_1 as an ordering relation, since we understand that a is the first element, as in the standard definition

$\langle a, b \rangle$ = df { {a}, {a, b} }.

The appeal to order is not eliminated by the use of the Wiener-Kuratowski procedure. Rather, one uses a property (really a relation) like *being a member of a unit set* as an ordering property instead of something like *being the first member of a pair*. In short, what the procedure shows is that a property like *being a member of a unit set* can be used to order a pair of elements. When we have an ordered pair, $\langle a, b \rangle$, we have two elements, and one is the first of the pair and the other is the second. We express that by the linear ordering of the signs in "$\langle a, b \rangle$." With

"{{a}, {a, b}}" we take *is the member of the unit set* to perform the role of *is the first*.[13]

We may conclude that Russell has proposed a way of analyzing relational facts that appeals to ordering relations that are not really avoided by procedures of the Wiener-Kuratowski type. On the pattern suggested here, derived from Russell's, one need not introduce classes as constituents of facts nor appeal to ordered pairs as basic entities. However, on such a pattern, the analysis of a fact or situation, such as that — Lab, involves the particulars, a and b; the relation $L\hat{x}\hat{y}$;[14] the ordering relations L_1 and L_2; the unordered compound ($L\hat{x}\hat{y}, a, b$); and compounds like $aL_1(L\hat{x}\hat{y}, a, b)$.[15]

IV. Bradley's Paradox, Russell's Paradox, and Exemplification

While Russell's paradox has preoccupied philosophers and logicians since the turn of the century, Bradley's paradox of predication has received relatively little attention. Yet it is far more threatening, since it involves the claim that predication is incoherent. There are many ways of construing the problem posed by Bradley. One way that is germane to the preceding discussion of Russell's paradox and to Russell's concern with relational predication is the following. We take an atomic sentence "Ga" to state that a particular has or exemplifies a property. The existence of the indicated fact — the particular exemplifying the property — is the truth condition for the sentence. The fact is taken to consist of the particular, a, and the property, G, in the exemplification relation, $\hat{\phi}\hat{x}$. But, supposedly, it cannot be so taken. For there must be a further constituent: a three-term exemplification connection that obtains of G, a, and $\hat{\phi}\hat{x}$. Thus, the fact must be construed to consist of a, G, and $\hat{\phi}\hat{x}$ in the three-term exemplification relation. But, then, there must be a further constituent connecting these four constituents, and so on. The supposed problem can be taken to be that to acknowledge $\hat{\phi}\hat{x}$ as a constituent of the fact that a is G is to prohibit allowing one to specify the factual truth condition for the sentence "Ga," since it is not the fact consisting of a and G in the relation $\hat{\phi}\hat{x}$. For that purported fact turns out to be a fact containing the three-term connection that, in turn, must be construed as a fact containing a four-term relation and so on. Frege, it should be noted, took Bradley's problem to be a serious problem prior to Bradley's statement of it. He suggested one type of response to it, a response that Russell adopts at some places. This response holds that properties (or at least relations) do not require connecting relations to combine with particulars. This is a, if not *the*, fundamental difference between particulars and properties. It is a logical feature of a property or relation that it provides the connecting link in a fact (or proposition). In this vein one may say that the various logical kinds of properties — monadic, dyadic relations, etc. — provide the logical form of the facts in which they attributively enter. There has been a second type of response to Bradley's problem. This is to hold that there is an exemplification connection (or many such) but that such connections need not, in turn, be related to what they connect. This singular feature of an exemplification relation is marked by classifying it as a *tie*, a *nexus*, or a *logical* relation.

The Fregean response suffers from giving each property a further, yet common, role in a fact or proposition. The alternative response faces the charge of stipulating that exemplification relations are unique in order to avoid Bradley's problem. It is thus an ad hoc solution. What I wish to argue is that the construal of exemplification as a logical form provides us with a solution that is not ad hoc.

Consider a list of primitive monadic, dyadic, etc., predicates representing properties and relations. Exemplification could not be represented by one of the basic dyadic predicates. For we must have

(E_1) $Ex(G, a) \equiv Ga$

and, in general,

(E_2) $(f)(x)[Ex(f, x) \equiv fx]$

as logical truths, with "Ex" representing exemplification. But there is no justification for (E_1) and (E_2) being such truths if "Ex" is a primitive predicate. Moreover, it is clear that one appeals to such a relation, exemplification, by the use of sentential patterns like "fx" and "Ga." In effect, sentence structure is taken to represent such a relation. Yet, there is a trap one must avoid in making such a claim. The sentence "Ga" represents the purported fact that a is G. How, then, does the structure of the sentence represent exemplification? The point of the question is that as "a" represents an object and "G" a property, the sentence pattern represents the fact that a is G, and not the structure of the fact. The abstraction device provides a way of representing the structure, with "$\hat{\phi}\hat{x}$" as a sign for the exemplification relation and "$\hat{\phi}\hat{x}(G, a)$" as an alternative rendition of "Ga." In a way, "$\hat{\phi}\hat{x}$" is not a constituent sign of "Ga" as "G" and "a" are, but in that we form "$\hat{\phi}\hat{x}$" by abstraction and in that "$\hat{\phi}\hat{x}(G, a)$" is an alternative rendition of "Ga," one can see what is meant by the claim that the sentence structure of "Ga" represents the exemplification relation. For it is clear that a sign like "$\hat{\phi}\hat{x}$" presupposes sentential patterns, since without such patterns one could not form "$\hat{\phi}\hat{x}$" by abstraction. Hence, without such patterns one could not have "$\hat{\phi}\hat{x}$" on a list of signs standing for relations. Thus, we already recognize and represent exemplification by the use of "Ga." Removing the content terms "G" and "a" from "Ga" we are left, by abstraction, with "$\hat{\phi}\hat{x}$," which represents the form of monadic exemplification between a particular and a property. The exemplification relation $\hat{\phi}\hat{x}$ may then justifiably be called the form of monadic atomic facts containing particulars and properties.

Bradley's paradox may then be taken to amount to the claim that to recognize the form of a fact, as a constituent of a fact, requires acknowledging that there is a further form with respect to which the first form is a constituent among constituents. Or, to put it another way, the claim is that one cannot specify the form of a fact, since whatever one takes to be the form will merely be a constituent requiring a further form. But, in view of the contrast between the form $\hat{\phi}\hat{x}$, and the content constituents, G and a, of the fact that—Ga, Bradley's problem loses its force. For clearly, there is nothing ad hoc about the difference between a form and the things, particulars and properties, that are "in" it. It is worth recalling that monadic exemplification can be represented by a sign like "$\hat{\phi}\hat{x}$" only if we already represent it by the sentential juxtaposition of the subject and predicate signs. And, if we introduce "$\hat{\phi}\hat{x}$" and, subsequently, from

$\hat{\phi}\hat{x}(G, a)$

form something like

$\hat{R}(\hat{\phi}, \hat{x})$

and subsequent abstracts, then the members of the series of sentences

$\hat{\phi}\hat{x}(G, a)$
$\hat{R}(\hat{\phi}, \hat{x})[\hat{\phi}\hat{x}, G, a]$
....

all "reduce" to "Ga," by the understood replacement rule. Ironically, Bradley's purported paradox would be bothersome only if such a reductive chain were not present. One way of avoiding such a reductive chain would be to introduce "Ex" as a primitive predicate representing exemplification; but then we do not get (E_1) and (E_2) as formal truths.

There is a further irony. Even if one holds that the fact that-Ga is to be analyzed as the fact that—$\hat{\phi}\hat{x}(G, a)$, and so on, one cannot conclude that we have not specified the form of the fact that—Ga unless one also holds that we can only specify the form of a fact that is not further analyzable. Such a position involves a kind of assumption characteristic of the atomism of Russell and Wittgenstein. And it is only on such an assumption that we could make our version of the Bradley problem a paradox.

We can see another point. On the Fregean-style resolution of Bradley's problem, a property (concept) supplies the form to a proposition. This is revealed by the use of the sign "$G\hat{x}$". What then happens when a property exemplifies another? It would appear that both properties "carry" conflicting forms into the proposition or fact. Thus one can be led to deny that properties can be subjects in prepositions or facts—as Frege and Russell, at times, were led to do in their respective ways and as Wittgenstein may also have done in the *Tractatus*. Separating the form from the property or concept, as Russell did at other places, avoids this pointless problem, for the property $G\hat{x}$ can enter into the form $\hat{\phi}\hat{x}$ or the form $\hat{\Psi}(\hat{\phi})$. Or, if we have a general form for monadic predication without regard to types, say $\hat{\phi}\hat{\alpha}$, where α can be either a property or a particular, then $G\hat{x}$ can combine in such a form as either attribute or term. All the "$\hat{x}$" in "$G\hat{x}$" reveals is that the attribute referred to is a monadic attribute of particulars and not that it must be "predicated" in a fact or proposition.

Bradley's purported paradox can be seen to be a reflection of the fact that, given a procedure for producing abstracts, we can carry on the series of abstracts

$\hat{\phi}\hat{x}$
$\hat{R}(\hat{\phi}, \hat{x})$
$\hat{R}_3(\hat{R}, \hat{\phi}, \hat{x})$
. . . .

and the series of sentences

$\hat{\phi}\hat{x}(G, a)$
$\hat{R}(\hat{\phi}, \hat{x})[\hat{\phi}\hat{x}, G, a]$
$\hat{R}_3(\hat{R}, \hat{\phi}, \hat{x})[\hat{R}(\hat{\phi}, \hat{x}), \hat{\phi}\hat{x}, G, a]$
. . . .

indefinitely. But this is not paradoxical, unless one stipulates that the successive members of the series reveal the correct logical form of the previous members. What is then paradoxical is that one can never state or show the form of a fact correlated to an atomic sentence. Without such a stipulation, the series of sentences is no more paradoxical than the fact that we can generate, with an appropriate *truth* predicate, the series

Ga
$T'Ga'$
$T'T'Ga''$
. . . .

What one may conclude is that it is pointless to introduce "$\hat{\phi}\hat{x}$," by abstraction, as a predicate expression. For, as we noted earlier, doing so presupposes the recognition of exemplification by the very use of sentential structure. Thus, the "paradoxes" of Russell and Bradley stem from a common implicit and, in a way, unrecognized assumption: that exemplification is, logically, a relation and, hence, representable by a predicate. This overlooks the fundamental difference between what is a logical form and the "objects" that may *stand in* a form. This, in turn, invites one to hold that the objects and the form stand in a form and so on. Recognizing the difference, one avoids both paradoxes while acknowledging the form $\hat{\phi}\hat{x}$. But this involves rejecting $\hat{\phi}\hat{x}$ as a relation among relations. Thus, Russell's paradox and Bradley's paradox disappear, with respect to the attribution of properties, without appealing to types or to a special relation that does not require to be related in turn.

Wittgenstein rejected Russell's paradox in the *Tractatus* by an appeal to logical form in a Fregean manner.[16] Taking the appropriate predicate form for a monadic predicate to be "ϕx" he rejected the pattern "$\phi(\phi)$," since "ϕx" could only be a subject term for a predicate whose form was "$\Psi(fx)$." Hence, as its form is "ϕx" and not "$\Psi(fx)$," no predicate of the first form can be its own argument. But Wittgenstein's claim either over-relies on the use of "ϕx" in place of "ϕ" or builds the type distinction into the predicate form. His solution either repeats Russell's in different words or simply and arbitrarily forbids the substitution of "ϕx" for "x" in "ϕx." Wittgenstein's appeal to logical form to reject Russell's paradox is thus quite different from the use of logical form in this essay. Yet, the rejection of Bradley's paradox I have advocated is in keeping with Wittgenstein's insistence that form be shown, not represented.

V. Wittgenstein, Ramsey, and the Ramified Theory of Types

So far, the discussion of Russell's paradox has focused on the role of the exemplification relation and the consequent connections of the paradox with Bradley's attack on the exemplification relation and with issues raised by a consideration of relations. By so doing, I have avoided a problem concerning versions of Russell's paradox that arise in complex contexts, and which involves further issues raised by so-called impredicative properties. Thus, consider

(25) $I(f) = df\,(\exists g)[(g = f)\ \&\ \neg f(g)]$.

To claim that "I," or the abstract "$(\exists g)[g = \hat{f})\ \&\ \neg \hat{f}(g)]$" that it abbreviates, is a relational abstract, as "$\neg \hat{\phi}\hat{\phi}$" is, poses a number of problems, though I believe one can block the ensuing paradox along such lines. Aside from that, (25) involves a context that is *impredicative* in the sense that a quantifier is used to form a sign for a property and that property is in the range of the quantifier. Thus, we are concerned with impredicative contexts relevant to Russell's ramified theory of types. I will argue (1) that Russell was correct, as opposed to Ramsey and Carnap, to rule out such impredicative properties; (2) that the ramified theory of types is problematic; and hence, (3) that contexts like "$(f)fa$" do not yield abstracts, "$(f)f\hat{x}$," which represent properties whether or not one takes the quantifier to be general or restricted by considerations of ramification. The argument for (1) will rule out contexts like (25).

Russell's ramified theory of types was intended to avoid functions like $(f)f\hat{x}$ and $(\exists f)f\hat{x}$ as well as $\neg\hat{\phi}(\hat{\phi})$ and an unrestricted truth property. Ramsey argued that the ramified theory was an unnecessary complication.[17] His argument was twofold. First, he argued that Russell's claim that a "vicious circle" was involved in the recognition of impredicative functions was unfounded. Russell had held that impredicative functions "presupposed" a totality, the functions comprising the domain of the quantifier, and hence could not belong to such a totality. Thus, they could not be elements of the domain of the quantifier. Ramsey argued that impredicative functions only apparently posed a problem due to our inability to itemize an infinite list of functions. He might have meant that it would be mistaken to think we could not determine whether a function, $(f)fx̂$, applied to it. For it is obvious that we do not determine such matters by going through an infinite list. We know that $(f)fx̂$ does not apply to anything, since it is a contradictory function, just as we know that $(\exists f)fx̂$ applies to everything, since it is an analytic function. Ramsey clearly argued that there was nothing wrong with including an item in a totality it "presupposed." Thus, for example, in the case of the conjunction "p & q" we have an item that is logically equivalent to a "totality"

(26) p & q & (p & q),

of which it is an "element." Thinking of the quantifiers in Wittgenstein's fashion, Ramsey took "$(f)fx̂$" and "$(\exists f)fx̂$" to represent an infinite conjunctive and disjunctive function, respectively. And, as in the case of (26) and "p & q," he saw nothing wrong with one argument of such functions being the function itself. Second, Ramsey noted no contradiction was forthcoming from permitting *impredicative* functions, as opposed to *self-predicative* functions like $\neg\hat{\phi}(\hat{\phi})$, which violated a simple type restriction.[18] Ramsey's rejection of ramified type theory has prevailed, and there has been little interest in the ramified theory of types. But, even aside from its dependence on Wittgenstein's problematic view of quantification, Ramsey's argument is not cogent. Russell's worry about a "vicious circle" is well founded.

Russell's worry is that the quantifier has to be specified as governing a domain of "objects." The issue is, then, whether impredicative functions "involving" a quantifier may belong to the domain. It is as if Russell thinks of "introducing" the quantifier with respect to a domain. Hence, nothing in that domain can be specified by use of the quantifier. To speak of "involving" and "introducing" a quantifier is vague, and unfortunately it must be. For it is not clear just what quantifiers are construed to be, as nonlinguistic items, if they are construed to be *anything* at all, and how, as nonlinguistic items, they are construed to be related to impredicative properties (as the correlates of impredicative predicates). Linguistically, the matter is clearer. A quantifier (sign) and its bound variable are constituents of the sign for the impredicative property. But leaving aside problems about the nature of quantification, we can see the force of Russell's worry in another way. Whatever we take the quantifiers to be, the quantification signs are understood in terms of their connection with the rules of universal instantiation and existential generalization. These rules are the correlates of truth tables for the connectives, for the rules codify the use and, in that sense, the "meaning" of the quantifiers (signs). Suppose we take "$(f)fx̂$" and "$(\exists f)fx̂$" to stand for properties—the property of having every property and the property of having a property. Then,

(27) $(\exists f)fx̂(a)$

states that *a* has the property of having some property. The existential quantification from (27), over the predicate, would be

(28) (∃g)g(a).

But (28) is not a generalization of (27): it *is* (27), by the understood replacement rule. Thus, there is no sense to the notion of an existential generalization from "(∃f)fx̂" in (27). (A related point can be made about the purported universal instantiation involving "(f)fx̂" and "(g)g(a).") This points up Russell's worry. His concern can be taken to be that for (28) to be true *a* must have some property. Yet, if we allow "(∃f)fx̂" to stand for a property, satisfying that property could not be the instance that warrants the existential generalization, since to say that *a* has (∃f)fx̂ is to state the existential generalization. But, then, we do not use the quantifier in an appropriate way in going from (27) to (28). This puts quite specifically the point that functions that *presuppose* the use of a quantifier to specify them may not belong to the domain of quantification. Ramsey's argument overlooks a fundamental asymmetry between the case of the quantifiers and the case of conjunction. Moreover, if, as Ramsey suggests, "(∃f)fx̂" represents an infinite disjunctive function, one constituent of which is the infinite disjunctive function itself, then, like the familiar case of the label on the bottle, which contains a picture of a bottle with the label, we have an embedded infinite regress with respect to specifying the function.

There are three issues involved. First, there is a question about whether we can specify the meaning and use of the quantifier "(∃f)" if we include (∃f)fx̂ in the domain of properties over which the quantifier ranges. I have argued that we cannot. Second, there is a question as to whether including (∃f)fx̂ in that domain is like the case of "*p* & *q*" and "*p* & *q* & (*p* & *q*)," where we have a constituent included in a totality to which it is equivalent. The cases are not the same for the simple reason that the specification of the meaning and use of "&" is provided by the truth table for that sign and not, as in the case of the quantifier, by an inference rule connecting the sign to a specified domain of "entities." Third, there is a question as to whether construing the quantifiers in terms of infinite disjunctive and conjunctive functions enables one to avoid the problem raised by the first question and to hold that such infinite functions can unproblematically be specified, while containing "themselves" as "*p* & *q* & (*p* & *q*)" unproblematically contains "*p* & *q*." This third question is complex. For it involves, as a first step, the construal of the quantifiers in Wittgensteinian fashion in terms of the connectives. This is, at least, problematic. It also involves the additional issue regarding the claim that there is no problem in specifying the infinite disjunctive (and conjunctive) function even if we construe the quantifiers in terms of the connectives. My concern here is with this second step and not with the general problem raised by the Wittgensteinian interpretation of quantification. The problem is not about the specification of the meaning and use of the quantifiers, since that is supposedly resolved by the Wittgensteinian move. Rather, the problem is about the specification of the infinite functions, given that such functions are elements of themselves.

In a sense Ramsey has a point. Given an infinite domain of functions or properties $F_1, F_2, \ldots, F_n, \ldots$ and an infinite conjunctive function, ϕ_1, compounded from them, we may assume that we have an infinite conjunctive function, ϕ_2, compounded from the original F_i and ϕ_1. ϕ_2 is logically equivalent (hence identical) to ϕ_1. Ramsey makes use of this point, but he does so in an illegitimate way. For he includes ϕ_1, identified with ϕ_2, among the original F_i. One can see how he may be thinking. Since "p & q" is the logical product of "p," "q," and "p & q" and hence *is* "p & q (p & q)," a conjunction can contain itself. So, if "$(f)fa$" is a conjunction it can contain itself. Moreover, when we consider conjunction in terms of a truth table for "p & q," it is understood that "p" and "q" may be replaced by any propositional signs, including conjunctions like "p & q" and "p & q & (p & q)." Hence, in a way, we have a domain of propositions over which "&" ranges, and that domain includes conjunctive compounds. One may then think of specifying conjunction in terms of applying to a domain that includes conjunctions, and hence applying to a totality that includes itself. But there is a significant difference in the case of Ramsey's infinite functions. *Given* an infinite conjunction C, which contains a conjunct K, we may identify C with C & K. The problem is with the specification of C if we take it to include itself as a conjunct. Ramsey cannot specify such a function in general. For he is faced with an infinite embedded and self-referential series. By contrast, we can specify both the truth functional connective expressed by "&," by the truth table, as well as the field of propositions to which it applies. Identifying "p & q" with "p & q & (p & q)" does not preclude specifying *the* conjunction. Allowing a function to be one of the original F_i over which "(f)" ranges and the logical product of functions compounded from the F_i does preclude specifying the function in some cases.

If one allows for functions like $(f)f\hat{x}$ and $(\exists f)f\hat{x}$, one should resort to something like ramification to avoid impredicative properties and preserve the asymmetry of the instantiation and generalization rules. But the ramified theory has an insoluble problem. Russell and Whitehead introduced the axiom of reducibility to overcome problems connected with their definition of identity as

$$x = y. =: (\phi) :\phi!x . \supset .\phi!y \; Df^{19}$$

and with the need in mathematics for statements "which will usually be equivalent to what we have in mind when we (inaccurately) speak of 'all properties of x.' "[20] They were concerned with the status of the axiom as a truth of logic and with whether or not it could be deduced from other logical truths.[21] But there is a more basic problem that Wittgenstein noted in a letter to Russell:

Your axiom of reducibility is

:$(\exists f):\phi x \equiv {}_x f!x;$

now is this not all nonsense as this proposition has only then a meaning if we can turn the ϕ into an *apparent* variable.... The axiom as you have put it is only a schema and the real Pp ought to be

:$(\phi):(\exists f):\phi(x) \equiv {}_x f!x,$

and where would be the use of that?[22]

Wittgenstein's point is that the axiom cannot be stated without an unrestricted quantifier that violates the restrictions of the ramified theory of types. What one can state are indefinitely many axioms (or meta-axioms or statements in a background language) for various orders of functions. It is as if one were to state in a metalanguage or background schema that there is an axiom for every order or function of the system. But this background statement involves a quantified expression not governed by "the axiom" itself. Any statement of the axiom violates the point of the ramified theory of types. Yet, without such an axiom, or something equivalent to it, the problems Russell and Whitehead noted about the ramified theory of types remain.[23]

Wittgenstein's criticism overlooks a distinction that lies behind Russell's way of stating the axiom. The distinction was based on the supposed difference between "all" and "any." As Russell put it in 1908:

> If ϕx is a propositional function, we will denote by "$(x).\phi x$" the proposition "ϕx is always true.".... Then the distinction between the assertion of all values and the assertion of any is the distinction between (1) asserting $(x).\phi x$ and (2) asserting ϕx where x is undetermined. The latter differs from the former in that it cannot be treated as one determinate proposition.... In the case of such variables as propositions or properties, "any value" is legitimate, though "all values" is not. Thus we may say: "p is true or false, where p is any proposition," though we can not say "all propositions are true or false." The reason is that, in the former, we merely affirm an undetermined one of the propositions of the former "p is true or false," whereas in the latter we affirm (if anything) a new proposition, different from all the proposition of the form "p is true or false." Thus we may admit "any value" of a variable in cases where "all values" would lead to reflexive fallacies.[24]

and, specifically about the axiom of reducibility, as formulated by Wittgenstein above, Russell writes:

This is the axiom of reducibility. It states that, given any function ϕx, there is a predicative function f!x such that f!x is always equivalent to ϕx. Note that, since a proposition beginning with "($\exists$f)" is, by definition, the negation of one beginning with "(f)," the above axiom involves the possibility of considering "all predicative functions of x." If ϕx is *any* function of x, we can not make propositions beginning with "(ϕ)" or "($\exists \phi$)," since we can not consider "all functions," but only "any function."[25]

The real problem, however, is whether Russell's distinction between "all" and "any" (and its connection with his notions of "undetermined value," "ambiguous denotation," "ambiguous statement" and "statement about an ambiguity") makes his statement of the axiom viable. What is of course specious about Russell's claim, aside from questions about his account of "denotation," is, first, the claim that we can assert an indeterminate proposition by the use of a free (real) variable, and second, the use of a free variable with the "power" of a universally quantified (apparent) variable while holding that no determinate proposition is asserted. His overlooking of Russell's discussion of "any" and "all" notwithstanding, Wittgenstein's point is well taken. Moreover, even on his own terms, Russell's view is in trouble. First, he must admit that some primitive proposition of *Principia* cannot be symbolized but must be expressed in words. And he goes on to suggest the introduction of a new symbolic device to carry the sense of the words. Thus the symbol "[ϕy]" is introduced in the primitive proposition

$$:[\phi y] . \supset .(x).\phi x$$

to symbolize "ϕy is true however y may be chosen."[26] Second, Russell's discussion of the use of a free variable in the axiom of reducibility is inconsistent with the primitive proposition of *Principia* amounting to the rule of universal generalization.

*9.13 In any assertion containing a real variable, this real variable may be turned into an apparent variable of which all possible values are asserted to satisfy the function in question.[27]

Of course one can point out that it does not apply in such a case because the resulting universal generalization is an "illegitimate" statement. But that merely points up the specious use of a free variable to state the axiom of reducibility. Given the cogency of Wittgenstein's criticism, one may conclude that with or without ramification, abstracts like "$(f)f\hat{x}$" and "$(\exists f)f\hat{x}$," involving quantifiers, should not be taken to stand for properties. Hence, we may conclude that there are no "complex properties" represented by such quantified abstracts.

We may consider paradoxes of the Russell type to be of two kinds. One kind, the "pure" paradoxes of predication, involves only negated elementary subject-predicate contexts, such as "$\neg \phi(\phi)$," for monadic properties, "$\neg R(R,R)$" for dyadic relations, and so on. These are all blocked by the same considerations leading to the construal of "$\neg \hat{\phi}(\hat{\phi})$" as, at best, a relational abstract and by the basic distinction between monadic, dyadic, etc., predicates. In this vein "$\neg \hat{R}(\hat{R},\hat{R})$" will be a three-term relational abstract, and so on. The other kind of paradox, making use of complex quantified contexts, like "$(\exists g)((g = f)$ & $\neg f(g))$," involves the use not only of a term in an "unstratified" context but also of a quantifier ranging over such a term. Thus, even if one could not block such versions of the paradox by construing abstracts like "$(\exists g)((g = \hat{f})$ & $\neg \hat{f}(g))$" as relational abstracts (and I believe that one can block them in this way), they can be blocked by not acknowledging "impredicative" properties. Hence, assuming that one allows ramified predicate abstracts to stand for properties, which I have argued we should not do, the paradoxes arising from quantified contexts can be blocked by a variant of Russell's ramified theory of "orders," which does not make use of a type distinction as that is normally construed. Consider a familiar way of presenting the distinction between simple and ramified type theory – a way of presentation that is, though familiar, *not* an accurate account of the theory of Russell and Whitehead. One distinguishes *types* of predicates and properties – properties of 0-level objects, properties of properties of 0-level objects, and so on. These are properties of the first type, the second type, and so on. Within each type of property one then distinguishes orders of properties.[28] In type 1, for example, the properties of the first order are taken to be, say $f_1^{1,1}$, $f_2^{1,1}$, $f_3^{1,1}$,...which constitute the domain for a first type, first-order quantifier "$(f_1^{1,1})$." Then, an abstract like "$(f_1^{1,1})f_1^{1,1}(\hat{x})$" would be a predicate of order 2, type 1. Such an abstract does not represent a property in the domain of properties over which "$(f_1^{1,1})$" ranges. Modify the familiar presentation so that we do not distinguish types, but simply consider a domain of properties G^1_1, G^1_2, G^1_3, of order 1, but where we allow contexts like "$G^1_1(G^1_1)$." Yet, the quantifier "(f^1_1)," ranging over the properties (predicates) of order 1, will be taken to form an abstract "$(f^1_1)f^1_1(\hat{x})$" of order 2, and hence that abstract (predicate) will not represent a property in the domain of "(f^1_1)." Such a ramified theory of orders does not make the type distinction, but the separation of properties into orders will block the paradoxes making use of quantified contexts, as in "$(\exists g)((g = f)$ & $\neg f(g))$." However, such a theory, by recognizing complex properties represented by ramified abstracts, faces the problems that led to (and are involved in) the axiom of reducibility. But, whatever one might come to hold about the representation of properties by abstracts containing predicate quantifiers, the main concern of my discussion has been with what I have called the "pure" paradoxes of predication. These, I have argued, should be looked at and resolved in terms of the distinction that Russell took to be the essential demarcation between properties and particulars – the division of properties into monadic, dyadic, etc. – and the early insights Russell had regarding the need to acknowledge logical forms.[29]

Notes

1. W. V. O. Quine, *Set Theory and Its Logic* (Cambridge, MA: Harvard University Press, 1963), p. 39.

2. B. A. W. Russell, *Introduction to Mathematical Philosophy* (London, Allen & Unwin, 1953), p. 136.

3. For a detailed consideration of this point see H. Hochberg, "Properties, Abstracts, and the Axiom of Infinity," *Journal of Philosophical Logic*, 6 (1977), pp. 193–207. Russell often speaks of "propositional functions" in connection with predicate abstracts. He uses such a notion in many ways. Here I will take predicates and predicate abstracts to represent properties or attributes. In short, "propositional functions" will be construed as attributes, which fits with one of Russell's uses of "propositional function."

4. For other recent attempts to rule out the Russell paradox without recourse to type theory or the standard restrictions on a comprehension axiom see H. Castaneda, "Ontology and Grammar," *Theoria*, 42 (1976), pp. 44–93; N. Cochiarella, "Whither Russell's Paradox of Predication," in *Logic and Ontology*, ed. M. Munitz (New York: New York University Press, 1973), pp. 133–58; R. Grossmann, "Complex Properties," *Nous*, 6 (1972), pp. 153–64.

5. The abstract "$(g)(\hat{\phi}(g) \equiv \neg g(g))$" would be an abstract for a property that applied to *any* Russell property; i.e., it would apply to any property that applied to all monadic properties that did not exemplify themselves. Interestingly, the self-predication involving such an abstract leads to contradiction with the replacement rule, but the denial of such a predication does not (as in the case of (8) with secondary scope).

6. Hence, (18) is not really well formed. One cannot, then, say that the Russell relation does not (or does) apply to itself. As on the theory of types, the crucial statements are ill formed.

7. One must keep in mind that when an abstract like "$(g)(\hat{\phi}(g) \equiv \neg g(g))$" occurs in predicate place, as in "$[(g)(\hat{\phi}(g) \equiv \neg g(g))](R)$" one obtains "$(g)(R(g) \equiv \neg g(g))$" by replacing the occurrence of "$\hat{\phi}$" by "R," but when such an abstract occurs in subject place, no replacement of "$\hat{\phi}$" is permitted.

8. B. A. W. Russell, *Theory of Knowledge*, vol. 7 of *The Collected Papers of Bertrand Russell*, ed. E. Eames et al. (London: Blackwell, 1984).

9. D. Lackey, "Russell's 1913 Map of the Mind," in *The Foundations of Analytic Philosophy*, ed. P. French, et al. (Minneapolis: University of Minnesota Press, 1981), pp. 125–42.

10. Russell speaks of a "complex." What he has in mind is a fact, the existence of which provides a ground of truth for a sentence or proposition. Since the problem of order arises in the case of propositions (as nonlinguistic entities), facts, and "possibilities" or "situations," I will speak indiscriminately, in this discussion, of facts, complexes, propositions, and situations.

11. It would be foolish to object that the conjunction (R_2) makes use of order, since we cannot interchange "*a*" and "*b*" in the different conjuncts. For it is clearly not order that is made use of, as the conjuncts can be commuted (recall, also, that only one is needed). Rather, what differentiates them is the occurrence of "*a*" in one and "*b*" in the other as in "*Fa & Gb*" and "*Fb & Ga*" These latter conjunctions do not differ in the order of the terms "*a*" and "*b*." They differ in that "*a*" goes with "*F*" in one and with "*G*" in the other, and similarly for "*b*." This is not a question of the order of the terms "*a*" and "*b*" in "*Fa & Gb*" and "*Fb & Ga*."

12. Another reason for the use of a description would be an attempt to deal with the problems posed by the nonexistence of the complex in the case of a false sentence. Thus, Russell attempts to avoid the problems connected with "possible" and "negative" facts by the use of descriptions, just as he avoids a corresponding problem about nonexistent objects.

13. It is as if both the set sign "$\{\{a\}, \{a, b\}\}$" and the sign "$\langle a, b \rangle$" are used to implicitly express the fact that there is a pair of elements *and* that *a* is the first element of the pair.

14. The rejection of unordered complexes or ordering relations forces one, I believe, to hold that relational order is not analyzable and, hence, that facts like *Lab* and *Lba* cannot be distinguished by means of differing constituent entities. The difference between those facts cannot then be accounted for. (For an argument that relational facts are unanalyzable and that introducing basic ordered pairs amounts to accepting different *unanalyzed ordered complexes*, see my "Logical Form, Existence and Relational Properties," in *The Foundations of Analytic Philosophy*, pp. 215–37.) But I see no objections to acknowledging L_1, L_2, and ($L\hat{x}\hat{y}$, *a*, *b*) other than tedious, vague, and oversimplified declarations about what is or is not given in experience. Russell, by the way, took himself to be *acquainted*

with ordering relations and logical forms. Gustav Bergmann has recently proposed an analysis of relational order based on the Wiener-Kuratowski procedure. In effect, Bergmann introduces unordered pairs, say (a, b), as complex entities, and then forms further unordered pairs, say $(a, (a, b))$, etc. While there are several problems with Bergmann's analysis (see his "Notes on Ontology" and my "Intentionality, Structure, and Bergmann's Ontology," both in *Nous*, 15 [1981], pp. 131-54 and 155-64, respectively) the fundamental defect relevant to the present discussion is his attempt to do without ordering relations, like L_1 and L_2. His analysis fails for the same reasons that the Wiener-Kuratowski procedure does not give us an analysis of order in facts, propositions, or other ordered complexes. If Bergmann were to acknowledge ordering relations, then a modification of his analysis would be similar to the modification of Russell's pattern. In place of $(L\hat{x}\hat{y}, a, b)$ we would have the unordered complex (a, b) with $aL_1(a, b)$ replacing $aL_1(L\hat{x}\hat{y}, a, b)$. Thus, the fact that-*Lab* could be analyzed in terms of $aL_1(a, b)$ & $bL_2(a, b)$ & L (a, b); (a, b) being *the term* of the predicate "*L*." This involves accepting two kinds of complexes: those like (a, b) which do not contain properties, and those like $L(a, b)$, which do.

15. Relational order is analyzed, on the modification of Russell's view, in that facts like that-Lab and that-Lba are not taken to consist of the same constituents in a "different arrangement." They contain different constituents. Relational order may be taken to be unanalyzed in that (1) basic ordering relations, L_1 and L_2, are acknowledged, (2) complexes like $(L\hat{x}\hat{y}, a, b)$ are acknowledged, and (3) the difference in kind between particulars, like a, and complexes, like $(L\hat{x}\hat{y}, a, b)$, as terms of the ordering relations L_1 and L_2, is crucial to the analysis. (As William Demopoulos put it, a kind of "type" distinction is employed.) The situation is similar to the case of predication. In one sense, a philosopher like Russell offers an analysis of predication by recognizing a fundamental relation, or tie, or logical form of exemplification as involved in a fact. In another sense, as the ontological ground of predication is taken to be a basic relation or form, it is unanalyzed.

16. See 3.333 in L. Wittgenstein, *Tractatus Logico-Philosophicus*, trans. D. F. Pears and B. F. McGuiness (London: Routledge & Kegan Paul, 1961), p. 31.

17. F. P. Ramsey, "The Foundations of Mathematics" and "Mathematical Logic" in *The Foundations of Mathematics*, ed. R. B. Braithwaite (London: Routledge, 1931), pp. 1-61 and 138-55, esp. 38-54, 77-79.

18. Ramsey, "Foundations of Mathematics," p. 41.

19. A. N. Whitehead and B. A. W. Russell, *Principia Mathematica*, 2nd ed. (Cambridge: Cambridge University Press, 1950), vol. 1, p. 57.

20. Ibid., p. 166.

21. In the second edition Whitehead and Russell suggested that the axiom of reducibility was equivalent to the assumption that "any combination or disjunction of predicates is equivalent to a single predicate" (pp. 58-59). But they noted that the "combination or disjunction is supposed to be given intentionally" (p. 59). Thus, while they were thinking somewhat in the vein of Ramsey and Wittgenstein, about the quantifiers, they were concerned about the specification of Ramsey's infinite functions.

22. Printed in L. Wittgenstein, *Notebooks, 1914-1916*, trans. G. E. M. Anscombe (New York: Harper & Row, 1969), p. 122.

23. There is an additional problem concerning whether or not the axiom of reducibility is really a metalinguistic statement about *predicates*, not functions, that specify classes. This complication I ignore.

24. B. A. W. Russell, "Mathematical Logic as Based on the Theory of Types," reprinted in *Logic and Knowledge*, ed. R. C. Marsh (New York: Macmillan, 1956), pp. 66-67. For a link with Russell's earlier account of denoting see B. A. W. Russell, *The Principles of Mathematics* (London: Allen & Unwin, 1956), p. 94.

25. "Mathematical Logic as Based on the Theory of Types," p. 87.

26. Whitehead and Russell, *Principia Mathematica*, p. 132.

27. *Ibid.*

28. For presentations along such lines see I. M. Copi, *Symbolic Logic*, 4th ed. (New York: Macmillan, 1973), p. 302; R. Carnap, *Logical Syntax of Language* (London: Routledge & Kegan Paul, 1959), p. 86; W. and M. Kneale, *The Development of Logic* (Oxford: Oxford University Press, 1962), p. 659.

29. *Principia Mathematica*, p. xix.

Peter Hylton

The Significance of "On Denoting"

No one doubts that "On Denoting" marks a significant change in Russell's philosophical views.[1] My main aim in this essay is to see exactly what the significance of the article is in the development of Russell's philosophy, and thus of twentieth-century analytic philosophy more generally. My interest is thus in the consequences of the view set forth in OD, not in Russell's reasons for coming to hold that view. The two issues, however, cannot be completely separated, partly because the general issue of the significance of OD is confused by some of Russell's statements of his reasons for adopting the views of that article. One such statement is as follows:

> [Meinong] argued, if you say that the golden mountain does not exist, it is obvious that there is something that you are saying does not exist—namely the golden mountain; therefore the golden mountain must subsist in some shadowy Platonic world of being, for otherwise your statement that the golden mountain does not exist would have no meaning. I confess that, until I hit upon the theory of descriptions, this argument seemed to me convincing.[2]

This sort of statement suggests the following account of Russell's reasons for adopting the view of OD. According to Russell's views before OD, the meaningfulness of a sentence such as "The golden mountain does not exist" or "The present king of France is bald" demanded that there be a golden mountain or a present king of France. Russell's theory of meaning thus committed him to accepting the being (or the subsistence, as it is sometimes put) of nonexistent golden mountains, kings of France, and even worse ontological excesses involving round squares, even primes other than 2, and what not. The significance of OD, according to this account, is that it reformed Russell's theory of meaning in such a way that he could accept the meaningfulness of the sentence "The king of France is bald" without having to accept that there is, in any sense, a king of France; similarly, the existence of meaningful sentences that purport to be about golden mountains, round squares and so on is shown not to imply that these expressions correspond to objects that have being.

This account is misleading both in its implications about Russell's views before OD and, consequently, in its claim about Russell's reasons for abandoning those views in favor of the OD view. An understanding of exactly how the account is misleading will put us in a better position to assess the significance of OD. I shall, therefore, adopt the following strategy. In section I, I shall set out the relevant views of Russell from the period before OD. In section II I shall draw upon these views to argue that the preceding account of Russell's reasons for adopting the OD view is incorrect. This section will be largely negative in its immediate aim. I shall not attempt to give Russell's actual reasons for adopting the OD view, though I shall indicate the direction in which I think those reasons lie. In section III, finally, I shall discuss the significance of OD for Russell's philosophy. I shall argue, in particular, that a number of fundamental ideas of twentieth-century analytic philosophy, ideas that we take for granted, can be seen as coming into Russell's philosophy through that article. My claim will be that it is hard for us fully to assess the significance of that article precisely because we do take those ideas for granted.

I

Two general doctrines of Russell's from the period before OD are directly relevant. The first, to which I shall return in the last section, is that Russell's concern in this period is never with words and sentences, but with propositions and their constituents.[3] On one of the rare occasions when he talks explicitly about words he says:

> *Words* all have meaning, in the simple sense that they are symbols which stand for something other than themselves. But a proposition, unless it happens to be linguistic, does not itself contain words: it contains the entities indicated by words. Thus *meaning in the sense in which words have meaning is irrelevant to logic*.[4]

By a proposition's being "linguistic" Russell here means that it is *about* words, in which case it would (as we shall see in a moment) *contain* words. But in general a proposition is not made up of words, or of ideas; propositions are objective nonmental entities that are, as Russell puts it, "independen[t] of any knowing mind" (*Principles*, p. xvii). Although Russell does talk about meaning in the sense in which word have meaning, he does so only to dismiss this sense as philosophically irrelevant: he is certainly not concerned to advance any theory of meaning in this sense. Thus his statement that words are all "symbols which stand for something other than themselves" is not to be taken as a philosophical theory of meaning,[5] and when Russell speaks of "the entities indicated by words" he is not using "indicate" as a technical term.

The second general doctrine that will be relevant is one that we have already anticipated. This is that a proposition, in the standard case, *contains* the entities that it is about (and thus the entities indicated by the words that express it). Thus the proposition expressed by the sentence "Socrates is mortal" contains Socrates, or Socrates is a *constituent* of the proposition (as is mortality and, it seems, a relation between them—though this last point is problematic.) It may seem obscure and paradoxical to claim that anything so concrete as a human being could be a constituent of anything so abstract as a proposition, but this is Russell's claim.[6] Some of the air of paradox may be dispelled by remarking that the distinction between abstract objects and concrete objects is not a fundamental one for Russell. Human beings and propositions, numbers and mountains, all *are*, or have being, in exactly the same sense. Human beings happen to have the additional property of *existing* at some moments of time and points of space (and not at others), but it is being, not existence, that is Russell's fundamental (and in a sense his only) ontological category. Thus for Russell human beings and propositions are not so heterogeneous as to make it absurd that a proposition should contain a human being. It is Russell's view, then, that the constituents of a proposition in general include the things which that proposition is about. This doctrine is clearly stated in his correspondence with Frege. Taking as an example perhaps the most concrete object that he could think of, Frege had said "Mont Blanc with its snowfields is not itself a component part of the thought that Mont Blanc is more than 4,000 meters high" (letter of November 13, 1904). Russell's reply, in a letter dated the December 12, 1904, is as follows:

> I believe that in spite of all its snowfields Mont Blanc itself is a component part of what is actually asserted in the *Satz* "Mont Blanc is more than 4,000 meters high." We do not assert the thought, for this is a private, psychological matter: we assert the object of the thought, and this is, to my mind, a certain complex (an *objectiver Satz*, one might say) in which Mont Blanc is itself a component part.[7]

(I leave the German *Satz* untranslated here. In its first use one might substitute "sentence" or "statement." In the second use, Russell seems to use *objectiver Satz* as German for "proposition." His claim is that the object of thought is objective, neither psychological nor made up of words, and can have things as concrete as mountains among its components.)

I turn now to *denoting*, understood as a technical term of Russell's view in *Principles*.[8] The Russellian doctrine that the things that are the subject matter of the proposition are also, in the ordinary case, constituents of the proposition is crucial to an understanding of denoting. That notion is to be understood as a mechanism for bringing about exceptions to this general rule. The proposition expressed by "Socrates is mortal" *contains* Socrates and is *about* Socrates. The proposition expressed by "The teacher of Plato is mortal," however, contains the denoting concept *The teacher of Plato*, but it is not *about* that denoting concept—it is about Socrates. Denoting is Russell's explanation of—or at least his label for—this kind of (supposed) phenomenon. Thus he says:

> A concept *denotes* when, if it occurs in a proposition, the proposition is not *about* the concept, but about a term connected in a peculiar way with the concept. (*Principles*, 56)

"Term" here is used simply to mean "thing" or "object," in the widest possible sense—everything, Russell says, is a term (see, e.g., *Principles*, 47). "Denoting" is Russell's name for the "peculiar way" in which a concept may be connected with a term or combination of terms; in the technical sense it is not a relation between words and things but a relation between things of a particular kind (denoting concepts) and things in general. It is in virtue of this relation that a proposition may be *about* things which it does not contain: if a proposition contains a denoting concept it is about the things which that concept denotes, and not about the denoting concept itself. Denoting is a relation between a denoting concept and the object (or objects) it denotes. It is in no sense a psychological or linguistic relation, as Russell makes quite clear:

> The notion of denoting, like most of the notions of logic, has been obscured hitherto by an undue admixture of psychology. There is a sense in which *we* denote, when we point to or describe, or employ words as symbols for concepts; this, however, is not the sense that I wish to discuss. But the fact that description is possible... is due to a logical relation between some concepts and some terms, in virtue of which such concepts inherently and logically *denote* such terms. It is this sense of denoting which is here in question. (*Principles*, 56)

The presence of a denoting concept in a proposition is indicated by the fact that a denoting phrase occurs in sentences expressing the proposition. Denoting phrases are, typically, phrases formed with "a," "any," "all," "every," "some," or "the." (I shall call phrases formed with "the" definite descriptions, and phrases formed with one of the other words indefinite descriptions.) As an example of the use of the theory of denoting concepts, consider the proposition expressed by the sentence "I met a man." What constituent of this proposition corresponds to the words "a man"? One might be tempted to say that, if Jones is the man I met, then Jones is the corresponding constituent of the proposition. A moment's thought, however, shows that this sort of answer will not do. To begin with, it seems to have the consequence that the two sentences, "I met a man" and "I met Jones," express the same proposition in the case where it is in fact Jones whom I met. This is most implausible. Worse, the suggested answer seems to leave us with no account at all of the proposition expressed by "I met a man" if this sentence occurs in a hypothetical context or is negated or is simply false. If, in fact, I met no one then I can still *say* "I met a man" and express a proposition thereby, and this proposition is presumably the same one I would have expressed by the same words if I had in fact met Jones. It is, after all, the same proposition that would be false in the one case and true in the other. Russell's answer to this sort of difficulty is to say that the proposition in question contains the denoting concept, *a man*. Similarly, we have also the denoting concepts *some man*, *every man*, *any man*, and *all men*. Each of these denoting concepts, Russell says, denotes a different combination of men. Thus he says that *all men* denotes all men taken together, whereas *every man* denotes all men taken severally rather than collectively; *a man* denotes the constant disjunction of men; and so on (see *Principles*, 59–61). Russell devotes considerable subtlety to discussing the exact nature of each of these combinations of objects.

It is important to realize that Russell's reasons for developing the theory of denoting concepts go right to the heart of his philosophy at this period. He does not hold the theory because it enables him to solve some puzzles that he just happens to come across. On the contrary, the theory of denoting is directly connected with the attempt to reduce mathematics to logic that is the overarching aim of *Principles*. The most important link here is the variable. The propositions of logic and mathematics, according to Russell, are wholly general in nature. They contain no constants except logical constants; all their other constituents are variable (*Principles*, 8). The variable, according to Russell, is "*the* characteristic notion of Mathematics" (*Principles*, 87), and an understanding of the nature of the variable, he says, is "absolutely essential to any theory of Mathematics" (ibid.). It is in terms of denoting that Russell attempts to give an explanation of the variable, and thus of generality. The denoting concept *any term* is closely connected with the variable; the variable is explained by means of this denoting concept, and thus also by means of the theory of denoting. Thus it is that Russell can say that "*any* is presupposed in mathematical formalism" (89). Because the theory of denoting concepts explains the nature of generality, it also explains how we can talk about the infinite:

> With regard to infinite classes, say the class of numbers, it is to be observed that the concept *all numbers*, though not itself infinitely complex, yet denotes an infinitely complex object. *This is the inmost secret of our power to deal with infinity*. An infinitely complex concept, though there may be such, certainly cannot be manipulated by the human intelligence; but infinite collections, owing to the notion of denoting, can be manipulated without introducing any concepts of infinite complexity. (*Principles*, 72; emphasis added)

Further indication of the importance to Russell of the problems that he attempted to solve by the theory of denoting comes in a passage of the preface of *Principles*. Russell is writing of the development of his intellectual concerns that led him to write the book: "I was led to a re-examination of the principles of Geometry, thence to the philosophy of continuity and infinity, and thence, with a view to discovering the meaning of *any*, to Symbolic Logic" (p. xvii). Russell introduces the theory of denoting primarily in the hope of explaining the variable, and thus the nature of generality, which he holds to be essential to logic and mathematics.

The reasons that we have so far discussed for the introduction of denoting apply to indefinite descriptions; rather different considerations apply to definite descriptions. Such phrases, according to Russell, indicate denoting concepts that in turn denote the individual uniquely described by the definite description (if such there be). Here again there is a connection with the reduction of mathematics to logic. The application of denoting to definite descriptions is crucial to Russell's account of the role of definition in mathematics: to define an object (or a class), we find a class or a class of classes) of which it is the sole member; we can then define it as *the* member of that class (cf. *Principles*, 31, 63). More generally, denoting explains how a statement of identity can ever be informative. If a proposition corresponding to such a statement simply contained the same object twice over, then it is hard to see how it could be other than trivial. But on Russell's account an ordinary statement of identity (i.e., one that is *not* trivial) corresponds to a proposition that contains on the one hand an individual and, on the other hand, a denoting concept that, it is claimed, uniquely denotes the given individual; or it contains two distinct denoting concepts that it is claimed, uniquely denote the same individual. I shall quote Russell at some length on this point:

> But the question arises: Why is it ever worthwhile to affirm identity? This question is answered by the theory of denoting. If we say "Edward VII is the King," we assert an identity; the reason why this assertion is worth making is that, in the one case the actual term occurs, while in the other a denoting concept takes its place.... Often two denoting concepts occur, and the term itself is not mentioned, as in the proposition "the present Pope is the last survivor of his generation." When a term is given, the assertion of its identity with itself, though true, is perfectly futile, and is never made outside the logic-books; but where denoting concepts are introduced, identity is at once seen to be significant. (*Principles*, 64)

II

The theory of denoting concepts is rejected in OD—later uses of the word "denotes" by Russell are not in the technical sense but as synonyms for "indicates" or "refers." We have now seen enough of the theory to discuss what changes in Russell's philosophical views are effected by this rejection. I shall, to begin with, argue that the theory of OD—the theory of nondenoting, if you like—is not required to free Russell from a commitment to the being of the present king of France and his like. This is not to say that Russell in *Principles* does not accept the being of entities that seem to be no more respectable than the king of France. In a notorious passage he admits chimeras and Homeric gods as among the things that *are* (427). What I do wish to claim is that the theory of denoting concepts gives Russell a way of avoiding such ontological commitments, so that it cannot be held that such avoidance is possible only after OD. The supposed ontological commitment arises from the old problem: unless something *is*, in some sense, how can we say anything about it? How can we even deny that it is? The influence of this problem on Russell is clear. The passage about Homeric gods continues: "...if they were not entities of a kind, we could make no propositions about them" (*Principles*, 427). This argument is straightforward only so long as you hold it to be true, without exception, that the entities which a proposition is about—or purports to be about—must occur in the proposition. For then an entity must indeed be, in some sense, if there is to be a proposition that purports to be about it. But the theory of denoting concepts is, as I emphasized, a means of allowing exceptions to the general rule that the things a proposition is about must occur in the proposition. According to the theory of denoting concepts, the proposition expressed by the sentence "The present king of France is bald" does not contain the present king of France; it contains a denoting concept, *the present king of France*, and this is not an actual or possible human being of any kind, bald or not; it is a denoting concept. But then, given the theory of denoting concepts, it is far from obvious that the possibility of propositions that purport to be about the present king of France is enough to show that there *is* a present king of France. The question turns on whether there can be denoting concepts that do not denote anything. Russell's view, even in *Principles*, is that there can be such denotationless denoting concepts. He says this explicitly in section 73: "It is necessary to realize, in the first place, that a concept may denote although it does not denote anything." This admission raises certain problems for Russell, some of which have to do with the null-class, which he changed his mind about in the course of writing *Principles*. But in spite of these problems his view is clear: there can be denoting concepts that do not in fact denote anything.

Russell in *Principles* thus has resources at his disposal that would enable him to deny being to the present king of France. He can do this while still accepting that the sentence "The present king of France is bald" expresses a proposition. According to the theory of denoting concepts, this proposition does not contain the present king of France (as the corresponding proposition about Socrates would contain Socrates); it contains instead the denoting concept *the present king of France*. Given that a denoting concept may lack a denotation, nothing in Russell's account of the proposition demands that there be a present king of France, in any sense of "be." If Russell did not explicitly draw this conclusion in *Principles* it is perhaps because at that stage he saw no reason to deny being to the present king of France, but also because the sort of puzzles that are associated with the alleged king were simply not on his mind when he wrote the book. It was, I think, Russell's renewed study of Meinong beteween 1903 and 1905 that led him to consider these issues seriously.[9] When he does consider them seriously, he uses the theory of denoting in just the way that I suggested to deny being to the present king of France. He also treats at least some proper names in the same way that he treats definite descriptions. I quote from "The Existential Import of Propositions," written before OD:[10]

> "The present king of England" is a denoting concept denoting an individual; "The present king of France" is a similar complex concept denoting nothing. The phrase intends to point out an individual, but fails to do so: it does not point out an unreal individual, but no individual at all. The same explanation applies to mythical personages, Apollo, Priam, etc. These words have a meaning, which can be found by looking them up in a classical dictionary; but they have not a *denotation*; there is no individual, real or imaginary, which they point out. (Lackey, p. 100; *Mind*, 1905, p. 399)

The theory of denoting concepts—the theory that is rejected in OD—thus allows Russell to claim that there need be no object corresponding to a definite description or a proper name, even though that description or that name has a use in sentences that express propositions. Before he wrote OD Russell had come to recognize this and to exploit the theory of denoting concepts to show that there need be no king of France, even though we can meaningfully say "The king of France is bald." Getting rid of the present king of France and his like cannot, therefore, have been the reason for rejecting the theory he held before OD.

Russell's later statements about OD, as we have seen, stress the ontological economy which that article effected. One might therefore think that reasons for rejecting the pre-OD theory had to do with a desire to avoid the need for denoting concepts. The relevant ontological economy, on this view, would have to do not with the king of France but with the denoting concept *the king of France*. This view is perhaps encouraged by Russell's own insistence on the need for a "robust sense of reality" in logic.[11] Denoting concepts, mysterious and unexplained entities, might seem to offend a robust sense of reality just as much as nonexistent kings of France; and for Russell to talk about the latter when he means the former is perhaps an understandable piece of carelessness. There thus seems to be some reason to think that Russell adopted the OD theory for the sake of the ontological economy that it effected by eliminating the need for denoting concepts. In fact, however, this view is also seriously misleading. The issues here are extremely complex, and I shall not discuss them in any detail. I shall instead simply make two rather dogmatic remarks. First, there is no sign that Russell in 1905 was much concerned with ontological economy for its own sake. The rejection of the theory of denoting concepts was based not on a desire to eliminate entities but on difficulties that arise within that theory when it is thought through. Some of these difficulties come to the surface in the notorious "Gray's *Elegy*" passage of OD (pp. 111–113); other difficulties are discussed by Russell in works that are still unpublished.[12] Second, OD did have crucial ontological consequences for

Russell's philosophy, but these consequences are quite different in kind from the elimination of denoting concepts (see pp. 100–101, below). One can thus explain the connection that Russell makes between OD and ontological economy without supposing that this economy consisted in the elimination either of the king of France or of the corresponding denoting concept.

III

I turn now to the issue of the general significance of OD for Russell's philosophy. Besides the ontological consequences of the article, this significance consists chiefly in the effects it has on Russell's view of the nature of propositions, of their relation to sentences, of philosophical analysis, and thus of the aim and nature of philosophy itself. These changes contribute to the development of a conception of logical form, and to the idea that words and sentences might themselves be of philosophical interest. In *Principles*, as we have seen, Russell's view is that propositions and their constituents are what is philosophically important, and that words and sentences are more or less irrelevant. Russell continues, after OD, to hold that words are not philosophically important for their own sake, but he is subject to pressures that force him to make them the subject of explicit attention.

Let us now turn to the details of OD to see why it should have the consequences I have attributed to it. "The principle" of the new theory of OD, Russell says, is "that denoting phrases never have any meaning in themselves, but that every proposition in whose verbal expression they occur has a meaning" (OD, Lackey, p. 105). I shall explain this. Consider the sentence "All numbers are prime." This is a meaningful sentence; for Russell it is thus the verbal expression of a proposition. The *Principles* theory of denoting took it for granted that this proposition would contain a constituent corresponding to the words "all numbers"; since this phrase is a denoting phrase, that constituent is not all the numbers but rather the denoting concept *all numbers*. Whether there actually is anything that this denoting concept denotes is, as we have seen, a further question. The words "all numbers," according to the *Principles* view, thus indicate or stand for a constituent of the proposition that is expressed by the sentence in which those words occur. In the sense of "meaning" in which it is words that have meaning, those words have a meaning; their meaning is the denoting concept for which they stand. The new theory advanced in OD also has to account for the fact that a sentence such as "All numbers are prime" expresses a proposition. The new theory, however, does not presuppose that this proposition contains a constituent corresponding to or indicated by the words "all numbers." In fact, the theory claims that there is no such constituent: this is what Russell means in OD and later by saying that denoting phrases are "incomplete symbols" or have "no meaning in themselves" or "no meaning in isolation." The theory then goes on to explain how sentences containing denoting phrases can express propositions, even though denoting phrases have no meaning in themselves.

I shall put the point of the previous paragraph in a slightly different way. Meinong, according to Russell's account, seems to have been willing to argue as follows:

1. "The king of France is bald" expresses a proposition.

hence: 2. "The king of France" is a meaningful expression, which therefore corresponds to a constituent of the proposition.

hence: 3. the king of France is, in some sense.

The *Principles* theory of denoting concepts enables one to block this argument by denying the step from (2) to (3). "The king of France" corresponds to a constituent of the proposition, but this constituent is a denoting concept, not an actual or possible king.[13] The OD theory, by contrast, blocks the argument by denying the step from (1) to (2). The phrase "The king of France," according to that theory, corresponds to no constituent of the proposition that is expressed by a sentence containing those words; we are misled into thinking that there is such a constituent because we take the form of the sentence closely to resemble the form of the proposition that it expresses. The theory is then left with the task of explaining the true form of the propositions expressed by "The king of France is bald" or "All numbers are prime" in such a way as to make it clear that the propositions contain no constituents corresponding to the denoting phrases "the king of France" and "all numbers." The details of the way in which the theory accomplishes this task are familiar enough to require only a very brief explanation. Russell takes as fundamental and indefinable the variable and the notion of a proposition containing a variable and the notion of a proposition containing a variable being "always true," or true for all values of the variable, as we might put it (OD, Lackey, p. 104). The proposition corresponding to "All numbers are prime" is then said to contain, beside these notions, the properties or propositional functions... *is a number* and... *is prime*. Spelled out, the proposition has this form:

"If x is a number, then x is prime" is always true.

Or, in quantificational notation:

$(x) (Nx \supset Px)$.

If this is the true form of the proposition, then it is clear that the proposition contains no constituent corresponding to "all numbers." "$(x) (Nx)$" is patent nonsense, while "$(x) (Nx)$" is a sentence saying that all objects are numbers, and this is certainly not what "all numbers" stands for. Definite descriptions are treated in a way that is slightly more complicated, but with the same results. Denoting concepts disappear in favor of the variable, the notion of a proposition containing a variable being "always true," and propositional functions; with the denoting concept eliminated there is no constitutent of the proposition that could be held to correspond to, or to be indicated by, the definite description.

A general consequence of the new theory put forward in OD is that the grammatical arrangement of words in a sentence will in most cases be a poor guide to the logical arrangement of constituents in the proposition that the sentence expresses. Grammatically, the sentence "The king of France is bald" is a subject-predicate sentence, as is "Socrates is bald." We have seen that the theory of denoting concepts gives a complex account of the corresponding proposition, but this account preserves the segmentation of the sentence. According to the theory of denoting concepts, the proposition contains one constituent corresponding to the subject-phrase ("the king of France") and one constituent corresponding to the predicate-phrase ("is bald"). That the constituent corresponding to the subject-phrase is a denoting concept does not alter the fact that the proposition is segmented into subject-constituent and predicate-constituent. For all its complexity, the theory of denoting concepts does not call this segmentation into question. The form of the proposition, and the way in which it divides into logical units, is taken to be identical with the superficial form of the sentence and the way in which it divides into grammatical units. (Similar remarks apply to sentences that contain indefinite descriptions, provided that one holds that such sentences also have a subject-predicate form—and it is the most superficial form that is in question here.) Now Russell in *Principles* had assumed that the superficial grammatical form of a sentence is in general a good guide to the form of the proposition it expresses:

> Although a grammatical distinction cannot be uncritically assumed to correspond to a genuine philosophical difference, yet the one is prima facie evidence of the other, and may often be most usefully employed as a source of discovery. Moreover, it must be admitted, I think, that every word occurring in a sentence must have *some* meaning; a perfectly meaningless sound could not be employed in the more or less fixed way in which language employs words. The correctness of our philosophical analysis of a proposition may therefore be usefully checked by the exercise of assigning the meaning of each word in the sentence expressing the proposition. (*Principles*, 46)

OD does away with the idea of a congruence between sentences and propositions. There comes to be a sharp break between the grammatical form of the sentence and the form of the proposition it expresses—logical form, to anticipate a later terminology. This is perhaps clearest in the case of definite descriptions. The proposition expressed by "The king of France is bald" has a structure that is most accurately reflected by the sentence:

$$(\exists x)(Fx \ \& \ Gx \ \& \ (y)(Fy \supset y = x))$$

or, in prose (following Russell's example in OD):

> It is not always false of x that x is the king of France and that x is bald and that "if y is the king of France then y is identical with x" is always true of y.

There is a fundamental difference between the structure of the subject-predicate sentence that would normally be used to express the proposition and the sentence (whether in symbols or in prose) that is said to express the proposition in a way that accurately reflects its structure. There is no similarity of form between them. The gap here is so marked that the form of the sentence cannot be taken as even an approximate guide to the form of the proposition it expresses.

This contrast between grammatical form and logical form has crucial consequences for Russell's view of philosophical analysis and of philosophy itself.[14] According to *Principles*, the process of philosophical analysis does not affect the way a proposition divides into units. This segmentation was assumed to be the same as that of the sentence; the form or structure of a proposition was not a primary concern in analysis. Philosophical analysis was chiefly concerned with the entities making up the proposition, not with the form of the proposition. We have already seen that Russell's account, in *Principles*, of the proposition expressed by "All numbers are prime" would take it for granted that this proposition contained one constituent corresponding to "all numbers" and another corresponding to "is prime." The philosophical work, on this account, is to analyze these constituents (or, in the case of simple constituents, to perceive them clearly). This is, in fact, what most of the philosophical analysis in *Principles* does. It analyzes particular concepts, such as *is prime*, or *is a number*. This sort of philosophical analysis takes the form of a proposition and its segmentation into units for granted, and is primarily concerned to analyze those units.

The conception of philosophical analysis that comes to dominate Russell's work after OD is crucially different. Here the main work of analysis concerns the form of propositions, or logical forms; the chief problem is to find the logical form that is masked by the grammatical form of a given sentence or kind of sentence. The analysis of a particular expression comes to be, generally, a matter of analyzing the sentences in which the expression occurs to find the logical form of the propositions that such sentences express. Alongside these specific results about particular concepts there are also general results about all propositions of a given form, or about what logical forms a proposition can have. Russell comes to see philosophy as consisting largely, at least, of discovering, investigating, and cataloguing logical forms. The study of logical forms is, Russell claims, a part of logic, and it is this part of logic that he has in mind when he speaks of logic as the essence of philosophy[15] or when he says that "philosophy...becomes indistinguishable from logic."[16] Contrasting philosophy with the synthetic method of the special sciences, Russell says:

> ...in philosophy we follow the inverse direction: from the complex and relatively concrete we proceed towards the simple and abstract by means of analysis, seeking in the process, to eliminate the particularity of the original subject-

matter, and to confine our attention entirely to the logical *form* of the facts concerned. (KEW, pp. 189-90; emphasis in the original)

I turn now to what I take to be the ontological significance of the conception of philosophical analysis that is introduced in OD. This significance is that sentences that appear to be about entities of one kind are shown by the analysis to be really about entities of a different kind. As an example, consider the definition that forms the basis of Russell's mature theory of types. Russell assumes that there are propositional functions, i.e., intensional entities that yield propositions when applied to objects. I shall follow Russell in using expressions of the form "$\psi\hat{z}$" or "$\phi!\hat{z}$" to refer to these entities. Where f is any property of propositional functions, we can introduce symbols of the form "$f\{\hat{z}(\psi z)\}$" by means of the following definition:[17]

$$f\{\hat{z}(\psi z)\} =_{df} (\exists\phi)[(x)(\phi!x \equiv \psi x) \& f(\phi!\hat{z})].$$

In virtue of this definition, the truth-value of "$f\{\hat{z}(\psi z)\}$" depends only upon the extension of the propositional function $\psi\hat{z}$. The symbol "$\hat{z}(\psi z)$" thus operates (in the context "$f\{\hat{z}(\psi z)\}$") as if it stood for an extensional entity – the class of objects of which the propositional function $\psi\hat{z}$ is true. But in fact the symbol "$\hat{z}(\psi z)$" does not stand for any kind of entity: it is an incomplete symbol. The definition gives a sense to expressions of the form "$f\{\hat{z}(\psi z)\}$," and shows that some such expressions can be true, without implying that there is an entity for which "$\hat{z}(\psi z)$" stands. Sentences that appear to be about classes are shown to be in fact about propositional functions, so that the truth of such sentences is shown not to imply the existence of classes. Analyzing sentences (which appear to be) about classes shows that the truth of these sentences does not require that there be classes. In such a case analysis is elimination.

It is important to realize that the use made of the notion of an incomplete symbol in the theory of descriptions does not have the sort of ontological consequences I emphasized in the previous paragraph. What is crucial to those consequences is the idea that we can have a body of *true* sentences (which purport to be) about classes without supposing that there are classes. The analogue of this does not hold for definite descriptions. There is no body of truths (which purport to be) about the present king of France, and there could be no body of truths about the present queen of England if there were no such woman.[18] The theory of descriptions claims that propositions expressed by sentences that contain definite descriptions do not themselves contain entities for which the definite descriptions stand. But if such sentences are true then there must be such entities, even though they are not in the corresponding propositions. If it is true to say "The F is G," then there must be a unique entity that is F. When we are dealing with a body of true sentences (of the ordinary kind), e.g., when we are analyzing a theory we hold to be true, the significance of the theory of definite descriptions is not ontological but, in the broad sense, epistemological. The theory changes the account of the entities that must be in the propositions corresponding to the sentences (and thus of the entities with which we must be acquainted in order to understand the sentences), but it does not change the account of the entities that there must be in the world in order for the sentences to be true.

The notion of an incomplete symbol thus has an ontological significance that is not exploited in the theory of descriptions. This sort of ontological significance, unlike the elimination of the king of France, is something that could not readily be duplicated by the theory of denoting concepts. The idea that analysis is elimination is not explicitly contained in OD, but it is a natural consequence of the conception of analysis that this article introduces. For Russell the paradigm of eliminative analysis was the definition I gave earlier as an example, i.e., the definition of statements that purport to be about classes in terms of propositional functions. In spite of its simplicity, this definition was of crucial importance to Russell. By showing that there need be no classes, the analysis seemed to enable him to find an escape from the class paradox.[19] This is why he frequently links the theory of descriptions with the paradox, although the connection is by no means obvious on the face of it. He says, for example:

> When the *Principles of Mathematics* was finished, I settled down to a resolute attempt to find a solution to the paradoxes.... Throughout 1903 and 1904, my work was almost wholly devoted to this matter, but without a vestige of success. My first success was the theory of descriptions.... This was, apparently, not connected with the contradictions, but in time an unsuspected connection emerged. (MPD, p. 79)

Strictly speaking, the connection here is not directly with the theory of descriptions but rather with the notion of an incomplete symbol. But Russell introduced the notion of an incomplete symbol in the context of the theory of descriptions, and once introduced the notion rather obviously lends itself to the sort of ontological use that makes the elimination of classes possible.

Although the analysis of sentences containing class expressions was, for Russell, the paradigm of eliminative analysis, the idea of analysis as elimination came to be central to other parts of his philosophy. This can be clearly seen in two areas that were among his major concerns in the period (roughly) 1905–18. The first is his theory of judgment. The basis of this theory is that judgment is not a two-place relation, between a person and a proposition, but a many-place relation between a person and the various entities that (according to the old view) are constituents of the proposition. (This theory is usually known as the "multiple-relation theory," for this reason.) A corollary of this is that there are no propositions. Phrases that appear to refer to or express propositions are said to be incomplete symbols;[20] such phrases can occur meaningfully in various contexts even though there are no propositions.

The second major concern of Russell's is his epistemology. This is both more complicated and more interesting from the present point of view, for it shows the contrast between the two uses of incomplete symbols that I have distinguished. Before 1913 or 1914 Russell only employs the nonontological use of incomplete symbols in his discussion of sentences that appear to refer to physical objects. He thus holds that if our ordinary and scientific beliefs are correct then there really are physical objects quite independent of sense-data. We cannot grasp propositions containing physical objects, but our real interest is in the truth or falsity of these propositions. There is thus a problem about what principles of inference it is legitimate to use in deriving these propositions from propositions about sense-data. There is also a more subtle issue about how we understand such propositions at all. Russell's answer is that in a sense we do not. The propositions that we are really interested in are *described* by propositions that we *do* grasp (see "Knowledge by Acquaintance and Knowledge by Description," *Mysticism and Logic*, p. 158).

This curious position results from the fact that Russell uses the theory of descriptions to eliminate physical objects from the propositions expressed by certain sentences that might appear to be about physical objects, without taking the further step of eliminating physical objects from the world. So while physical objects do not occur in any proposition that we can directly grasp, still there must be physical objects if those propositions are to be true. In 1913 or 1914 he takes the further step and analyzes sentences that appear to be about physical objects in such a way that the existence of physical objects is not required for the truth of those sentences. Such sentences now appear to express propositions that neither contain nor describe physical objects; the sentences are true provided that sense-data occur in the right patterns. This is the view that physical objects are "logical constructions" or "logical fictions." With this view there are no longer ungraspable propositions that are merely described by the propositions we do grasp. The problem of inference to the unknown disappears and is replaced by the problem of showing that it is possible to analyze or translate sentences about physical objects into sentences about sense-data. Russell was sufficiently impressed by this new technique to say, "The supreme maxim in scientific philosophizing" is "Wherever possible, logical constructions are to be substituted for inferred entities" ("The Relation of Sense-Data to Physics," *Mysticism and Logic*, p. 115).[21]

A further important feature of the new conception of analysis is that nothing in the process of analysis itself enables us to tell when analysis is complete.[22] Analysis is complete when the true form of the proposition has been attained, but Russell has no clear criterion for when this has happened. When we have substituted a definite or indefinite description for each denoting phrase, we may well find that our descriptions contain proper names that may in turn need to be analyzed as definite descriptions. Russell's examples, "The king of France" and "The author of *Waverley*" make this clear, since both "France" and "*Waverley*" are themselves names. It is also true that we cannot think of successive stages in the analysis as closer and closer approximations to the true form of the proposition. The reason for this is that carrying the analysis a stage further, analyzing something previously left unanalyzed, may yield a sentence of completely different form. There is no reason to think that every stage of analysis yields a form that is closer to the true form of the proposition than are all previous stages, so the picture of closer and closer approximations to the real form of the proposition cannot be applied. What this suggests is that there is a need for external constraints on the process of analysis that are not intrinsic to the process but are imposed upon it. There is no explicit sign that Russell is aware of this need, but it may have affected him nevertheless. In particular, one of the reasons for the importance of the notion of acquaintance may be that it provides an external constraint on the process of analysis. The notion of acquaintance is present in Russell's philosophy from *Principles* onward, but its role becomes much more important in OD and after. One reason for this may be that the notion of acquaintance tells you what the ultimate entities of analysis are: they are the entities with which you are acquainted. The process of analysis is complete — and the true form of the proposition discovered — when all entities with which you are not acquainted have been eliminated. The new conception of analysis thus demands that the notion of acquaintance should bear much more weight than it had done before OD. On the other hand, it is also true that this conception of analysis makes possible a more realistic notion of acquaintance, i.e., one more closely tied to actual sensory experience.[23] Because analysis is indefinitely extendable, any putative object with which it is implausible to say that we are acquainted can be thought of as analyzable, and thus as not being an object of acquaintance. (Strictly one should say: expressions that might appear to refer to objects with which we are not acquainted can be thought of as analyzable.)

The contrast between grammatical form and logical form, together with the conception of analysis that accompanies it, forces Russell to pay explicit attention to words and sentences. Language begins to become a subject of philosophical interest in its own right. In part this is something of which Russell is aware and explicitly accepts; in part it is a matter of pressures that force him in a direction his explicit doctrines do not acknowledge. The change in Russell's overt view is to be understood in terms of the break between grammatical form and logical form. The assumption of congruence between sentences and propositions had served, before OD, to make it easy for Russell to ignore words (see, for example, *Principles* 46, quoted earlier, p. 98). That assumption makes words and sentences a transparent medium through which propositions and their constituents may be grasped. The medium may be essential, but just because of its transparency nothing more need be said about it. Words themselves need never be the subject of explicit attention. This sort of attitude is in sharp contrast with Russell's later emphasis on the dangers of being misled by grammar. His later attitude is that the grammatical form of the sentence will usually be quite different from the logical form of the proposition, and that many philosophical mistakes arise precisely from the neglect of this distinction. Thus in Lecture One of "The Philosophy of Logical Atomism" he says:

> Some of the notions that have been thought absolutely fundamental in philosophy have arisen, I think, entirely through mistakes as to symbolism.[24]

Because Russell comes to believe that symbols are fundamentally misleading, he also comes to think that symbolism is of great philosophical importance—not because it is really the thing we mean to talk about in philosophy but because it will mislead us if we do not pay attention to it. This is quite explicit in a well-known passage, also from Lecture One of "The Philosophy of Logical Atomism":

> There is a good deal of importance to philosophy in the theory of symbolism a good deal more than at one time I thought. I think the importance is almost entirely negative, i.e. the importance lies in the fact that unless you are fairly self-conscious about symbols, unless you're fairly aware of the relation of the symbol to what it symbolizes, you will find yourself attributing to the thing properties which only belong to the symbol. That, of course, is especially likely in very abstract subjects such as philosophical logic, because the subject-matter that you are supposed to be thinking about is so exceedingly difficult and elusive that...you do not think about it except perhaps once in six months for half a minute. (p. 185)

Perhaps more important than this somewhat grudging overt admission of the importance of language is the pressure that Russell is under, contrary to his explicit doctrines, to take language as the real subject with which he is dealing. One way in which this arises is from the fact, which we have already examined, that the new conception of analysis makes it hard to tell when an analysis is complete. The proposition itself, whose form is given by the final stage of analysis, becomes inaccessible, and our attention is focused on stages of analysis that may be short of the final stage. But all that we have at these stages are *sentences*. A single proposition, after all, is expressed equally by the unanalyzed sentence and by the fully analyzed sentence and by all the sentences that constitute the various stages of analysis between the two. So philosophical progress may consist in the transition from one sentence to another. Russell may say that this is progress only because the second sentence more nearly reflects the form of the proposition, but nothing in the process of analysis itself gives these words any force. Once the relation between sentences and the propositions that they express becomes problematic, the idea that one sentence can "reflect" the form of a proposition more accurately than another has to carry more weight than it can bear. As Russell becomes more conscious of symbols—of words and sentences—it becomes clear that analysis essentially concerns sentences; the references to propositions become *pro forma*.

I have argued that the significance of OD is *not* that it shows that there can be names or definite descriptions that occur in meaningful sentences without referring to anything. The significance of the article has to do rather, I have claimed, with the idea of analysis as elimination, and with the development of certain conceptions of logical form and of philosophical analysis. Perhaps most important, the article is a crucial step on the way to the idea that language is a primary philosophical concern. These ideas are so fundamental to analytic philosophy as it has developed since 1905 that it is hard to put them in a historical perspective. Those who are, even in a remote sense, the heirs of Russell, tend to take absolutely for granted the notion of logical form, the corresponding view of philosophical analysis, and the idea of elimination by analysis. I do not mean that we all accept the philosophical views embodied in these ideas. I mean, rather, that we all take it for granted that there are such ideas, that the philosophical views that they embody are available options—even if we think that these views need to be revised in some way. Such an attitude makes it difficult to appreciate an article whose significance lies largely in its contribution to the development of these ideas. For this requires that we see those ideas as the product of a historical process, that we realize that they were not always philosophical commonplaces but came to be so over a particular period of time and for traceable reasons. In short, we have to cease taking those ideas for granted. This is even more clearly true of the view that language is an important subject of philosophical study. It is hard to detach oneself enough from this idea to ask where it came from, and why it came to have such a hold over so many philosophers. Yet if one takes this idea for granted, it is hard fully to appreciate not only the significance but also the substance of OD. That article was written against the background of a view according to which the question, what are the constituents of the proposition expressed by a given sentence, is a real question with a right answer that is independent of how we choose to analyze the sentence—a fact of the matter that is independent of us. This assumption, I claimed, is one that OD itself helped to undermine, but OD cannot be fully understood unless one realizes that this was Russell's assumption.[25]

Notes

1. B. Russell, "On Denoting," first published in *Mind* (1905); reprinted in Russell, *Essays in Analysis*, ed. D. Lackey (New York: Braziller, 1973) and cited by page number in Lackey. I shall abbreviate the title of this article as OD, and cite it by page number in Lackey.

2. *My Philosophical Development* (London: Allen & Unwin, 1959), p. 84. See also P. Schilpp, ed., *The Philosophy of Bertrand Russell*. The Library of Living Philosophers (Evanston, IL: Open Court, 1946), pp. 13–14.

3. G. E. Moore, who was closely associated with Russell in this period, manifests a similar lack of interest in words. He makes, for example the following remark about what he means by a "definition of good": "A definition does indeed often mean the expressing of one word's meaning in other

words. But this is not the sort of definition I am asking for. Such a definition can never be of ultimate importance in any study except lexicography.... My business is solely with that object or idea, which I hold, rightly or wrongly, that word is generally used to stand for. What I want to discuss is the nature of that object or idea"; *Principia Ethica* (Cambridge: Cambridge University Press, 1903), p. 6.

4. *Principles of Mathematics* (London: Allen & Unwin, 1903; 2nd ed. 1937), section 51, second emphasis mine. I shall quote from the second edition of this book, which is identical with the first except for a new introduction and the consequent renumbering of the pages of the preface. Except for citations from the preface, I cite by section number, not page number. I shall abbreviate this work as *Principles*.

5. Contrast Sainsbury, *Russell*, (London: Routledge & Kegan Paul, 1979), p. 16.

6. Compare Moore, "The Nature of Judgment" (*Mind*, 1899). Moore argues that propositions are made up of what he calls "concepts," which are objective, nonmental entities. He then claims that these concepts also make up the world: "It seems necessary, then, to regard the world as formed of concepts" (p. 182).

7. G. Frege, *Wissenschaftlicher Briefwechsel* (Hamburg: Felix Meiner Verlag, 1976), pp. 250–51. I have followed the translation of Hans Kaal in *Philosophical and Mathematical Correspondence* (Chicago: University of Chicago Press, 1980), p. 169.

8. It is important to note that "denoting" and its cognates are technical terms in Russell's early philosophy. But even in that period he sometimes uses these words in a looser sense, and this becomes more common in OD and after, when there is no longer a use for "denoting" in the technical sense. I shall always use these words with their technical sense. The only serious ambiguity that arises is that Russell constantly speaks of the "theory of denoting" in OD and afterward, meaning the later theory, whereas this name would more naturally be used for the earlier theory. I shall call the earlier view "the theory of denoting concepts" to avoid this ambiguity.

9. See "Meinong's Theory of Complexes and Assumptions" published in *Mind* (1904); and Russell's review of *Untersuchungen zur Gegenstandstheorie und Psychologie*, published in *Mind* (1905). Both of these works are reprinted in Lackey (ed.), *Essays in Analysis*.

10. First published in *Mind* of July 1905; reprinted in Lackey.

11. *Introduction to Mathematical Philosophy* (London: Allen & Unwin, 1919), p. 170. Compare *Logic and Knowledge*, ed. R. C. Marsh (London: Allen & Unwin, 1956), p. 223.

12. See especially "Points About Denoting," "On the Meaning and Denotation of Phrases," "On Meaning and Denotation," and "On Fundamentals," all in the Russell Archives at McMaster University. I am grateful to the Archives for allowing me access to these and other unpublished works of Russell.

13. If one equates a Fregean thought (*Gedanke*) with a Russellian proposition—as Russell is inclined to do—then Frege's view here is analogous to the *Principles* view. The sense (*Sinn*) of "the king of France" is a constituent of the thought expressed by a sentence containing those words, but the king of France himself is not a constituent of that thought. The thought thus contains an entity (a Fregean sense) corresponding to the definite description. The two views are different in ways I shall not attempt to discuss, but the analogy that I have given explains why Russell speaks of his view as "very nearly the same as Frege's." (OD, p. 104; see also *Principles*, 476.)

14. Compare Wittgenstein: "It was Russell who performed the service of showing that the apparent logical form of a proposition need not be its real one." *Tractatus Logico-Philosophicus*, trans. D. F. Pears and B. F. McGuiness (London: Routledge & Kegan Paul, 1961), 4:0031. For the view that the crucial point of OD has to do with the notion of logical form, see also David Kaplan, "What is Russell's Theory of Descriptions?" Reprinted in *Bertrand Russell, A Collection of Critical Essays*, ed. David Pears (New York: Anchor Books, 1972).

15. *Our Knowledge of the External World* (London: Allen & Unwin, 1926; 1st ed. 1914), chapter 2, esp. p. 67.

16. "Scientific Method in Philosophy" (1918, reprinted in *Mysticism and Logic* [London: Allen & Unwin, 1963]), p. 84.

17. See "Mathematical Logic as Based on the Theory of Types," in *Logic and Knowledge*, p. 89; and also *Principia Mathematica*, proposition *20.01, vol. I, p. 190.

18. Taken literally, this claim is false. According to the theory of descriptions there is a body of truths (purportedly about the present king of France [or at least containing the words "the present the

king of France" in subject position]), e.g., "The present king of France does not exist," "It is not the case that: the present king of France is bald," "Either grass is green or the present king of France is bald," and so on. But there can be no true sentences that purport to ascribe an intuitively simple property to the present king of France, i.e., no true atomic sentences containing "the present king of France" in subject position. When I wish to make this qualification I shall speak of true sentences *of the ordinary kind* that purport to be about something.

19. Russell always speaks as if the elimination of classes by defining them in terms of propositional functions were crucial for the solution of the paradox. Unfortunately, it is unclear why he should hold this, for one can state a direct analogue of the class paradox for propositional functions, provided one makes sufficiently strong assumptions about propositional functions. I suspect that Russell's view is that the restrictions that enable one to avoid the paradox are completely arbitrary and untenable if stated as restrictions on classes, but are somehow natural as restrictions on propositional functions. See Warren Goldfarb, "Russell's Reasons for Ramification," this volume.

20. This is importantly distinct from the idea that propositions are themselves symbols, but the distinction is easy to blur. Russell often says that classes (for example) are incomplete symbols, meaning that symbols that appear to refer to classes are incomplete symbols, and that in fact there are no classes (or no classes are being assumed in the theory). This is simply shorthand and does not indicate any confusion on Russell's part. The same shorthand used about propositions, however, is less innocent. Russell does come to hold that propositions are just symbols, and the shorthand both eases and disguises the transition.

21. Russell attributes the use of this technique in physics to Whitehead (see *Mysticism and Logic*, pp. 88, 116). These applications demand considerable logical and mathematical sophistication, but the fundamental technique is the one that Russell had already used in the philosophy of mathematics.

22. I owe this insight to Warren Goldfarb.

23. One cannot, of course, both have a realistic (in this sense) notion of acquaintance and hold that we are acquainted with abstract objects. Russell continues to hold this belief in an unequivocal form until at least 1912 – see *Problems of Philosophy*, chapter 5.

24. *Logic and Knowledge*, pp. 185–86.

25. I thank Burton Dreben and Warren D. Goldfarb for their helpful conversations about the subject of this essay, and for their criticisms of an earlier draft. Comments by Thomas G. Ricketts and Catherine Elgin, and a question from Wade Savage, also resulted in changes I am glad to have made.

Note added in proof:

This essay left my hands almost exactly six years ago. There is much in it that I would now put quite differently; to attempt to do so would, however, be to write a wholly new piece. There is, however, one implication that now seems to me definitely wrong. I strongly suggest that Russell's elimination of classes was made possible only by the theory of incomplete symbols introduced in OD, i.e., that no analogue of the definition of (symbols for) classes in terms of propositional functions is possible in the theory of denoting concepts. This now seems wrong; given sufficient ingenuity in manipulating the theory of denoting concepts, I think it can be made to serve this purpose. I think it remains true, however, that Russell thought that the theory of incomplete symbols was required for the elimination of classes.

Peter Hylton, August 1988

Richard Fumerton

Russelling Causal Theories of Reference

Russell's theory of definite descriptions[1] has long been viewed as a classic example of how careful philosophical analysis can dissolve puzzles within a relatively clean ontology. Despite many attacks and the development of alternative views, Russell's analysis of definite descriptions has survived as the accepted theory because it provides the most straightforward philosophical account of the following data: (1) that meaningful assertions can be made using definite descriptions that fail to denote; (2) that there is something I believe when I believe that the F is G even when there is no F; (3) that certain intensional and modal statements using definite descriptions are referentially opaque.[2] Other philosophical accounts of definite descriptions attempt to handle these same phenomena, of course, but what strikes so many of us is the simplicity with which Russell handles the problems. The uncontroversial facts about the behavior of definite descriptions are handled without such ontological nightmares as nonexistent entities, with machinery no more complex than the quantifiers of predicate logic.

Given the nature of the problems Russell's theory of definite descriptions was designed to solve, it is no wonder that he and others tried to extend the analysis to ordinary proper names.[3] It certainly appears that there can be meaningful false statements expressed using proper names that fail to denote, that there can be belief in such statements, and that there is failure of substitutivity of co-referential names in belief contexts and (more controversially) modal contexts. What could be more natural for a Russellian than to construe ordinary proper names as disguised definite descriptions? The analysis of definite descriptions could resolve not one but two sets of puzzles.

As anyone who follows the literature knows, Russell's attempt to apply his analysis of definite descriptions to ordinary proper names has not fared as well as the theory of definite descriptions itself. It is now in danger of being displaced as the received view by the so-called causal theory. The causal theorists succeeded in putting Russellians on the defensive with a number of persuasive arguments. You can't keep a good Russellian down, however, and attempts were made to recover from these objections. One such attempt involves an effort to "steal" whatever is plausible in a causal theorist's account of how names refer and simply incorporate the relevant aspect of the causal theory in the very definite descriptions that Russellians offers as capturing the sense of ordinary names. Needless to say, some causal theorists have cried foul, and it is the legitimacy of the Russellians' attempt to borrow from the causal theory that I wish to explore in the remainder of this paper. Let us begin, however, by providing at least a brief sketch of the causal theorists' attack on the Russellian theory of names and the alternative they provide.

Objections to Russell's Analysis of Names

I shall focus on just two sorts of criticisms directed by causal theorists at Russellian analyses of ordinary names. The first involves modal considerations and the charge that there are simply too many definite descriptions associated with many names to allow anything but an ad hoc selection of one as *the* meaning of the name. The second argument is that for some ordinary names that we successfully use in making assertions, we find ourselves unable to associate with those names any *definite* description at all. Let us examine each of these in turn.

The modal arguments against Russellian analyses of ordinary names gained prominence in Kripke's now classic "Naming and Necessity."[4] Unfortunately, a great deal of needless confusion was generated by somewhat careless presentations of these arguments, presentations that often seemed insensitive to critical distinctions between *de re* and *de dicto* modality. Thus Kripke sometimes seemed to argue that one could not identify the meaning of "Aristotle" with some definite description, the F, for it is obvious that Aristotle did not have to be F. As stated, the argument seems to involve a non sequitur, however, for the most natural reading of the modal operator in this context is *de re*. It is true that Aristotle did not have to be F, but then the F did not have to be F either, and so this *de re* modal claim cannot constitute an argument against viewing "Aristotle" and "the F" as synonymous. Kripke is perfectly aware of the relevance of making this distinction between *de re* and *de dicto* modality (which he seems to view as analyzable in terms of scope distinctions),[5] but I fear his original arguments still gain too much initial credibility by capitalizing on the equivocation.

Having made the distinction between *de re* and *de dicto* interpretations of modal claims, Kripke and his followers still seem to think that one can distinguish names from definite descriptions by pointing out that the former are rigid while the latter are nonrigid designators. A rigid designator is an expression that names the same thing in all possible worlds. But once the metaphor of possible worlds is dropped, a rigid designator is only an expression with which we can talk about the individual designated in all counterfactual situations, and it is obvious that definite descriptions *can* be used as rigid designators. We can talk about what would have happened to the F if it had not been F. If one wants to accommodate Kripkean intuitions about the rigid reference of names, one can do so by construing them as equivalent to definite descriptions but with the added convention that modal statements involving names should always be given *de re* interpretations.

Although the causal theorist may not agree, it seems to me that if one wants to use modal considerations to attack Russellian analyses of ordinary names in terms of definite descriptions, the clearest, and still very effective, way is to focus on analyticity. To claim that "Aristotle" has the same meaning as some definite description, or conjunction of definite descriptions, or disjunction of conjunctions of definite descriptions is, trivially, to claim that certain statements using the term "Aristotle" are analytic. If "Aristotle" means "the F," then the statements "If Aristotle existed he was F" and "If one and only one thing was F that thing was Aristotle" are analytic. And causal theorists are certainly right in suggesting that it is extremely difficult for most of us to come up with some definite description "the F," such that we can confidently claim the analyticity, and the a priori knowledge, of the statement that if Aristotle existed he was F and if something was the only F that thing was Aristotle. This problem seems particularly difficult when there are a great many definite descriptions we associate with a name and it seems so very arbitrary to select some one or a few as more central than the rest.[6] To be sure, one can make some sophisticated moves to counter the problem of having to make ad hoc choices. The so-called cluster theory attempts to reconcile our intuition that there is no one definite description the satisfaction of which is necessary for the name "Aristotle" to denote, with the idea that it *must* be by associating "Aristotle" with descriptions that its having a denotation is possible. Thus one might hold that "most" of the definite descriptions we associate with a name must denote if that name is to successfully refer. More formally one can view the name as equivalent in meaning to a disjunction of conjunctions, with the number of conjuncts in each conjunction a matter too vague to admit of any precise specification. In rejecting this suggestion causal theorists might well turn to their second objection based on the observation that we use names with which we associate few or in some cases *no* definite descriptions.

It seems relatively uncontroversial, causal theorists argue, that I can successfully refer using a name with which I associate only one or two definite descriptions or even using a name when I cannot think of a single *definite* description denoting the individual about whom I am speaking. In the latter case the Russellians obviously have their problems, but even in the former we seem often unwilling to allow that successful reference using the name is parasitic upon the successful denotation of the definite descriptions. I vaguely recall that Dedefre was the Egyptian leader who built the second pyramid at Giza. That definite description and definite descriptions derived from it (e.g., the Egyptian leader who either had or did not have brown hair and who built the second pyramid at Giza) are about the only definite descriptions I can come up with that *might* denote Dedefre. On the other hand if I assert that Dedefre was an Egyptian (say, in answering the

$64,000 question) I will not view my statement as false just because it so happens that he built the *third* pyramid at Giza.

But surely this just shows that there must be some other definite description I associate with the name "Dedefre." In the "Meaning of 'Meaning' " Putnam argues that language is so complex a tool that we will naturally need specialists to whom we defer concerning the reference of many terms.[7] Perhaps Russellians can borrow this idea and argue that for most of us the definite descriptions we associate with "Dedefre" are parasitic for their denotation upon the successful reference of others. Perhaps, I mean by "Dedefre" the man who is called "Dedefre" by the experts in Egyptian history. But who are "the experts"? At best this must be viewed as an elliptical description. Suppose the experts on Egyptian history are split down the middle as to whether Dedefre built the second or the third pyramid and that the matter is so central to their concept of Dedefre that they define (for themselves) the name "Dedefre" in correspondingly different ways. Does this mean that *I* will fail to refer when I stand by my claim that, whatever else he was, Dedefre was an Egyptian?

Russelling a Causal Analysis

Causal theorists have a solution to all these problems, of course. Unless I am the first user of a name, the referent of my use of a name is parasitic upon the use of the person from whom I (causally) acquired the name. And unless that person initiated the use of the name, the referent of his use of the name is parasitic upon the use of the person from whom he acquired the name, and so on back to the original "baptism."[8] The referent of a name on a given occasion of its use is a function of its causal origin. The causal "theory" has justifiably been criticized as far too vague in its specification of the relevant causal chains determining reference. And efforts to make the view more precise must deal with counterexamples involving "deviant" causal chains. My concern, however, is not with the potential defects of the causal theory, but with an opportunity the causal theory offers those beleaguered Russellians trying desperately to come up with a definite description that they could view as synonymous with a name. To the extent to which Russellians find halfway plausible the causal theorists' story, why not simply wait for causal theorists to work out the details of their view and then just take the theory itself as providing the definite description that captures the meaning of a name? Causal theorists insist that the referent of "Dedefre" is *the individual whose being called by some name was the first link in a complex causal chain resulting in this use of the name*. Fine. After causal theorists are satisfied that there are no counterexamples to *their* theory, we Russellians can offer causal theorists the italicized definite description as the one that captures the meaning of "Dedefre."[9] The nice thing about this maneuver is that we will not have to worry about counterexamples from our foes the causal theorists. When the causal theorists offer us a view of what determines the referent of a name on a given occasion of its use, they are not describing some property of the referent it just happens to have. Causal theorists must surely admit that it is in virtue of certain *conventions* we follow that the name we use picks out the relevant first link in a causal chain leading to our present use of the name. Given the conventions of our language, a name will refer to the relevant constituent of its causal origin. But what is the difference between saying this and saying that as I use the term "Aristotle" it is analytic that Aristotle exists if and only if there is the appropriate first link in a causal chain resulting in this use of "Aristotle." One traditional characterization of analytic truth, after all, is simply truth determined by conventions of language.

There are two objections I want to address to the Russellians' attempt to capitalize on the causal theorists' insight. One is relatively easy to reply to, the other is more difficult.

First, causal theorists may well complain that it is surely a curious development that Russellians waited the good part of a century to come to the conclusion that it was the causal theorists' complex definite description that they "had in mind" as the meaning of ordinary names. It is even more absurd to suggest that the average person on the street had the causal theory "in mind" when he or she used, and understood others who used, ordinary proper names. The causal theory is an extremely sophisticated philosophical account of what determines the reference of ordinary names. The descriptions it makes available to Russellians for their use in analyzing the "meaning" of names as used by ordinary people are far too complex to ascribe plausibly to people as the intentions in mind that their use of names expresses.

Is there anything to this objection? The answer must surely be that there is not. Any philosopher who views meaning analysis as a central part of philosophy must come to grips with what is sometimes called the paradox of analysis. Whatever the explanation is, it must be acknowledged that people can use an expression meaningfully but in some sense, the sense relevant to providing a philosophical analysis, not know how it is that they are using the expression.

To be sure, causal theorists may well argue that the correct solution to the paradox of analysis is to recognize that *meaning* analysis is misguided. Philosophers who have searched over the millennia for the correct analyses of knowledge, goodness, causation, and the like have made, causal theorists might argue, a fundamental error in assuming that one should look to the thoughts of people using these terms to find meaning. Meaning is simply reference, and reference is determined by causal factors that lie outside human consciousness. This claim, however, obviously presupposes a causal account of reference, and my concern here is only to point out that there are alternative ways of trying to resolve the paradox of analysis.[10]

It is also useful to remember an observation made earlier. Causal theorists must surely in some sense recognize that language is governed by conventions. It is in part by virtue of certain rules we follow that the symbols we use have the referents they do. Causal theorists, then, must be claiming that the conventions *we follow now and always have followed* in using names involve that sophisticated philosophical story developed within the last couple of decades. But, causal theorists protest, following conventions does not involve knowing what the conventions are. Unsophisticated people follow extremely complex syntactical rules of sentence structure without knowing how to formulate these rules, and we can follow conventions that determine reference without knowing how to formulate those conventions. Fair enough. But one cannot deny Russellians a similar response. Meaning, Russellians should counter, is a matter of convention. To use a term with a certain meaning is to use it following certain rules, but there is a world of difference between following rules and being able to describe the rules one is following. There is nothing to prevent Russellians from crediting causal theorists with providing an insight into the nature of the *meaning* rules we have been implicitly following governing the use of at least some ordinary proper names. That such an insight has taken so long in coming is no more surprising than that linguists are still making informative discoveries about the underlying rules we follow in constructing sentences.

The second objection to "Russelling" the causal theory is more ingenious.[11] Classic causal theorists take the referent of a name *on a given occasion of its use* to be the individual whose being called by some name was the first link in the relevant causal chain leading to that use of the name. Russellians want to turn the tables on causal theorists by taking that description, "the individual whose being called by some name...," and using it in their analysis of the *meaning* of a name on a given occasion of its use. But something odd happens, causal theorists can charge, when Russellians attempt to make good this theft. I say "Dedefre was an Egyptian." Russellians bent on "Russelling" the causal theory suggest we view "Dedefre" as equivalent in meaning to the very description causal theorists use in identifying the referent of "Dedefre." To be successful, causal theorists will argue, Russellians must be able to substitute for "Dedefre" that definite description without changing the meaning of my statement "Dedefre was an Egyptian." But what would be the results of that substitution? We would get the following statement: "The man whose being called by some name was the first link in a causal chain resulting in this use of 'Dedefre' was an Egyptian." "What use of 'Dedefre'?!" causal theorists ask gleefully. The definite description *mentions* the word "Dedefre" but there is no longer any *use* of the word "Dedefre." In removing "Dedefre" to substitute for it the relevant definite description, we removed an essential element in the causal chain determining the reference of that expression, according to causal theorists. Russellians who made the substitution, as their theory should allow them, are left with a definite description that either fails to denote or is meaningless. This criticism, causal theorists might argue, illustrates a fundamental difference between the causal theory and Russell's view of names. Even if it is conventions that determine, in part, what language refers to, it is not something in the speaker's mind that determines what the speaker is referring to when he uses language.

How might Russellians recover from this difficulty in developing an analysis of proper names immune from attack by causal theorists? Note that the problem only arises for the attempt to "Russellize" that version of the causal theory that takes the referent of a name on a given occasion of its use to be the relevant constituent of the first link in a causal chain leading to *that use* of the name. Another causal theory might maintain that the referent of a name on a given occasion of its use is to be determined by the cause of the "linguistic community's" use of that name. Such a theory would seem to provide a relatively unproblematic definite description for use in a Russellian analysis of names as covert descriptions. "Dedefre" means "the man whose being called by some name is the first link in a causal chain leading to the present linguistic community's use of the name 'Dedefre.' " We could substitute this definite description for "Dedefre" in the sentence "Dedefre was an Egyptian" without losing its denotation. This view, however, encounters the difficulties mentioned before involving the attempt to construct a definite description whose denotation is parasitic upon the denotation of "the experts' " use of the name "Dedefre." The community using "Dedefre" might, unknown to everyone, be split into two groups whose use of the name can be causally traced to quite different first links. There may have been two Egyptian pharaohs each named "Dedefre" and each being the element in causal chains leading to the use of that name by different historians. But it is far from clear that such a circumstance would affect my ability successfully to use the name "Dedefre" to refer to some Egyptian. This just illustrates, causal theorists will argue, that the most plausible causal theory will hold that the referent of a name on a given occasion of its use is a function of the causal origin of *that use* of the token on that occasion. And this causal theory, for the reasons given earlier, will not provide Russellians with a synonymous definite description that they could have substituted for the name "Dedefre" in the sentence "Dedefre was an Egyptian."

The battle, of course, is not yet over. There are any number of machinations available to Russellians attempting to co-opt this causal theory. It is true that as soon as one eliminates the word "Dedefre" in my utterance "Dedefre was an Egyptian" one will be unable to substitute for it some successful description of *its* causal origin. But perhaps we can go counterfactual and substitute for the name a description of what would have caused me to use the name "Dedefre" had I used the name instead of the definite description. Thus for "Dedefre" in "Dedefre was an Egyptian" I can make the following substitution: the man whose being called by some name would have caused my use of "Dedefre" had I used that name instead of this description, was an Egyptian.

Now I am not sure this maneuver has any formal defects although it does introduce into the analysis all of the problems associated with counterfactuals, and, on some philosophers' views, it may violate prohibitions against self-reference designed to resolve the liar's paradox and Russell's paradox involving the class of all classes. I shall not pursue the issue here, however, for I think that there is a more elegant and interesting move that can handle the causal theorists' objection, a move entirely within the spirit of Russell's attempt to construe ordinary names as descriptions.

As so many others do, I have been discussing the debate between the causal theorists and Russell as to how names refer as though the issue is to be decided on the basis of whose view can best withstand counterexamples. As I noted in my introduction, however, there are a number of philosophical puzzles that a correct account of proper names must resolve. Causal theorists have a terrible time trying to explain how we can apparently understand and believe that which is expressed by sentences containing names that may not even refer (e.g., "Robin Hood"), and this is a major difficulty with the view. But even more fundamentally, Russellians, in proposing their analysis of proper names, are motivated by more basic views about language, mind, intentionality, and reference. Russellians are convinced (mistakenly, causal theorists may argue) that the ability of language to say something about the world is parasitic on the intentionality of thought. Words can represent individuals and states of affairs only because we can assign to them the intentional content of our thoughts, where the intentionality of thought is *not* to be assimilated to the intentionality of language. We who feel that names must be descriptions do so because we are convinced that names must have *meaning*, and names must have meaning because their representational character is parasitic upon the meaning or representational character of thought. "Russellians," as I have been using the term, do not all agree on the ontologically prior question of how thought represents,[12] but we are agreed that, in their absence, we can only think about particulars "clothed" in properties.[13] If I can think of Aristotle, it is only in terms of an individual exemplifying certain properties, and the ability of the term "Aristotle" to represent is parasitic upon the intentional content of my thought of the individual exemplifying those properties.

The preceding is not intended as an argument for Russell's conception of ordinary proper names. It is intended only as a very rough statement of some of the presuppositions of the view. These presuppositions, however, suggest a way to develop that analysis of ordinary names that will be immune from the causal theorists' objections. Let me explain.

We could not substitute for "Dedefre," "the man whose being called by some name eventually led to this use of 'Dedefre,' " for in making the substitution we would have lost the referent of "this use of 'Dedefre.' " Even as we use the term "Dedefre," however, we can be *thinking* of the individual whose being called by some name resulted in this use of the name, and we can hold that "Dedefre" has the intentional content of that thought. It is an interesting feature of *language*, one might argue, that one could not have used the definite description *instead* of "Dedefre" successfully to express that thought even though the thought expressed by the definite description *is* the thought expressed by "Dedefre." But it is no more than an interesting feature of language. One can still quite consistently hold that "Dedefre" has the meaning of the complex definite description. What we have here is simply an interesting counterexample to the claim that if two expressions have the same meaning, i.e., express the same thought, one could always have used the one instead of the other to express that thought. The ability of the one piece of language to express the relevant thought might itself depend on the use of the other piece of language.

This view about the meaning of proper names might strike some philosophers as particularly attractive by explaining away the intuition many have that there *is* something that makes names different from definite descriptions. One can always substitute one definite description for another synonymous definite description and preserve the meaning of the statement in which they occur. But if names express a thought in the way sketched earlier one cannot substitute for a name a definite description and preserve the meaning of the statement in which the name occurs even though the name will have the meaning of a definite description. We can accommodate the claim that there is something special about names, but do so within the spirit of a Russellian view about the meaning of names.

The distinctions made here have interest over and above their potential for undercutting causal theorists. One might hold, for example, that an expression such as "now" means "the time at which I am uttering this expression 'now.' " Note, however, that such a view would encounter the same alleged difficulties discussed previously in the Russellian attempt to steal the causal theorists' thunder. One could not have replaced "now" with "the time at which I am uttering the expression 'now' " in the sentence "The ballgame is starting now" without losing the denotation of the definite description. But again, I see no reason preventing one from holding that the *thought* expressed by "The ballgame is starting now" is simply the thought that the ballgame is starting at the same time I am uttering the word "now."

Before I conclude this essay let me emphasize and clarify a number of points. First, as I indicated earlier, I do not think that one should try to assess the plausibility of a theory of reference without placing that theory in the context of a more general account of intentionality and the puzzles an account of intentionality should solve. Second, I would not argue that one should construe all proper names as expressing thoughts about their causal origin. I am not at all convinced that one should not construe many ordinary names as equivalent in meaning to more straightforward descriptions. Why then have I spent so much effort trying to figure out how best the Russellians could incorporate the causal theorists' account of what determines reference into their own descriptivist theory of names? For two reasons. I suspect that at least *some* names should be construed as disguised descriptions of their causal origin, and it is useful to know how we should construe such descriptions. But more importantly, in the dialectic between the causal theorists and the Russellians, it is surely useful to make the causal theorists realize that we Russellians can always incorporate their intuitions in developing a descriptivist account of names, an account that will be impregnable to the causal theorists' criticisms. Since even most causal theorists acknowledge the power of Russell's view as a means of solving the philosophical puzzles mentioned at the start of this essay, they should surely find attractive a version of that view that can not only solve those puzzles but that can never be any less plausible than their own account of reference.

Notes

1. First set forth in "On Denoting" in *Logic and Knowledge*, ed. R. C. Marsh (New York: Macmillan, 1956), pp. 41–56.

2. One must make some crucial distinctions in specifying which intensional and modal statements are referentially opaque. It is *de dicto* reports of beliefs and *de dicto* modal claims that are referentially opaque where the definite descriptions, in the case of beliefs, occur in characterizing the object of the belief.

3. It is clear that Russell did try to construe ordinary proper names as disguised definite descriptions—see his discussion of the issue in chapter 5 of *The Problems of Philosophy* (Oxford: Oxford University Press, 1956). The question is complicated, however, by the fact that in a number of places, especially when he is explaining his views about definite descriptions, Russell seems to contrast the way in which definite descriptions denote with the way in which names refer. Presumably, the explanation is simply that Russell sometimes found it convenient to pretend that ordinary names were logically proper names for objects with which we can be directly acquainted. It is uncontroversial, however, that Russell believed that we cannot be directly acquainted with most of the things for which we have names.

In this essay I shall focus exclusively upon proper names. It is also tempting to extend the analysis to common nouns designating kinds of things. Thus one might analyze the meaning of a term such as "water" using the definite description "the kind of thing that presents a certain appearance, has a certain taste (or lack of taste), etc." Most of the comments I make about Russellian treatments of proper names would apply equally well to Russellian treatments of common nouns.

4. In *Semantics of Natural Language*, eds. D. Davidson and G. Harman (Dordrecht: Reidel, 1972), pp. 254–355.

5. Ibid, p. 279.

6. Howard Wettstein emphasizes this as a central problem for Russell's view of names and demonstratives in "Demonstrative Reference and Definite Descriptions," *Philosophical Studies*, 40 (1981), pp. 241–57.

7. Hilary Putnam, "The Meaning of 'Meaning' " in his *Philosophical Papers*, volume II, *Mind, Language and Reality* (Cambridge: Cambridge University Press, 1975), pp. 215–71.

8. The original introduction of the name could be construed as an act of mere "labeling" (as in Russell's conception of a logically proper name), as the act of assigning the name the meaning of a definite description (e.g., the person in front of me now), or as the act of "fixing the reference" of a name using a definite description. For a critique of the intelligibility of reference fixing see my *Metaphysical and Epistemological Problems of Perception* (Lincoln and London: University of Nebraska Press, 1985), pp. 121–29.

9. This suggestion was made by B. A. Brody in "Kripke on Proper Names," in P. French, T. Uehling and H. Wettstein (eds.), *Minnesota Studies in Philosophy*, vol. 2 (Minneapolis: University of Minnesota Press, 1977), 64–69 and has been discussed more recently by John Searle in *Intentionality* (Cambridge: Cambridge University Press, 1983), chapter 9. Searle certainly rejects the suggestion that it is always in terms of a description involving the causal origin of a name that we understand the name, but he admits that in certain limiting cases it may well be that this is the only sort of description we may have available. Searle stops short of claiming that names have the same meaning as definite descriptions although he does say that it is only by having thoughts of the sort expressed by

definite descriptions that one can have the intentional state necessary to assign to a name in order for that name to have a referent.

10. See my "The Paradox of Analysis," *Philosophy and Phenomenological Research*, 43 (1983), pp. 477-97.

11. This objection was first suggested to me by David Kaplan in informal discussion following a paper he delivered at the University of Iowa.

12. I have presented my own view on this issue in *Metaphysical and Epistemological Problems of Perception*, pp. 55-57.

13. It is not clear to me what Russell's view was about the possibility of being directly acquainted with *particulars*. He sometimes seemed to allow that we might use logically proper names to pick out particulars when we were directly acquainted with those particulars, and this suggests that he thought we could have access to particulars that are not parasitic upon our awareness of properties. (Otherwise, why would he not construe our thought of a particular, even in this case, as thought of the thing that exemplifies such and such properties?) Whatever Russell's view was, however, I am inclined to think that one can never be acquainted with, nor can one think of, a particular except in terms of the thing that bears certain properties.

Janet Farrell Smith

Russell on Indexicals and Scientific Knowledge

One major theme of Russell's treatment of indexicals in PLA[1] and HK is their indispensability to human knowledge. In IMT, apparently influenced by Carnap, Russell provides an analysis that claims to eliminate what he calls "egocentric particulars" ("I," "this," "here," "now"), and he concludes that they are "not needed in any part of the description of the world, whether physical or psychological" (IMT, 108).[2] In HK Russell still wishes to replace indexicals by objective spacetime coordinate descriptions. But he explicitly argues that this program can proceed only up to a certain point and that indexicals are not completely eliminable. They are indispensable, he claims, in stating the basis of empirical knowledge in immediate experience. Russell therefore finally rejects Carnap's claim in the *Aufbau* (1928) that "within any object domain a unique system of definite descriptions is in principle possible, even without the aid of ostensive definitions.... Any intersubjective, rational science presupposes this possibility."

A second major theme in Russell's treatment of indexicals in HK is their interdefinability, an attempt to reduce them to one basic type for inclusion in a "minimum vocabulary." All terms in a scientific language, on Russell's view, have either a nominal definition or an ostensive definition. A minimum vocabulary must meet these two conditions: (a) every other word used in science has a nominal definition in terms of the words of the minimum vocabulary, and (b) no one of the words in the minimum vocabulary has a nominal definition in terms of another within that vocabulary. In an empirical science, definitions of theoretical terms must ultimately be based upon ostensive definitions that utilize indexicals. Hence indexicals must be retained in a minimum vocabulary to express the "sensible origin" of knowledge.

In this essay I first sketch how Russell's epistemological and scientific views motivate his treatment of indexicals. Second, I examine Russell's arguments, contra Carnap, for the thesis that indexicals are indispensable. Third, I analyse Russell's thesis that indexicals are interdefinable, specifically that "I" is replaceable

©Copyright 1984 Janet Farrell Smith

with "the person attending to this." I consider some criticisms lodged by Bar-Hillel, then examine some aspects of the interdefinability thesis that are relevant to current work in philosophy of language and pragmatics. I conclude that although the indispensability thesis seems justified, Russell's attempt to establish interdefinability suffers from serious problems.

Following Bar-Hillel (1970), I use the term "indexical expression" to include the demonstratives "this" and "that," place-time indicator words such as "here," "now," and the first and second person pronouns "I" and "you." By the abbreviated term "indexical" used alone I will mean "indexical expression." The terms "indexical definite description" and "indexical sentence" mean, respectively, a definite description containing an indexical ("The person attending to this") and a sentence containing an indexical ("This is red").[3]

Russell maintains that each indexical expression "depends upon the relation of the user of the word to the object with which the word is concerned" (IMT, p. 120) and that the designatum of such an expression changes with each occasion of use. We normally assume that what is designated is directly sensed by the user of the word, in contemporary terms, the speaker. Indexical expressions are neither proper names ("Socrates," "Wales") nor words for qualities or relations ("hot," "is next to") nor logical words ("and," "or"). They appear to "escape the usual logical and semantical categories."[4] They are, rather, a species of what Russell calls "strict names," names that have no descriptive element in them.

I

Russell appears to have attributed the following five features to indexicals, from the logical atomist period of PLA (1918–19) to that of HK (1948).

(i) *The designatum of indexicals constantly changes according to speaker, time, place, and location* (PLA, p. 200; HK, p. 85). Because the designatum of "this" is continually changing it is not strictly classifiable as an ordinary proper name, such as "Socrates" (HK, p. 85). Ordinary proper names on Russell's view may be "ambiguous." Thus, the name "John Jones" simultaneously designates different men. In contrast, "this" is unambiguous when speaker, time, and location are specified. According to Russell, no other linguistic expression is context dependent in this manner and at the same time unambiguous in its designation.

(ii) *Indexicals designate without description.* The contrast between designation by a strict name and designation by a description holds constant in Russell's thought from OD (1905a) to HK (1948). Most ordinary proper names contain descriptions, a fact that "makes it difficult to get any instance of a name at all in the proper strict sense of the word" (PLA, p. 201). Russell takes "this" and "that" as "strict names" in PLA. These indexicals designate without descriptive content both in PLA and HK. Indexicals, in contrast to descriptions, do not depend on any internal structure or on any prior symbols for their designation.[5]

(iii) *The designatum of an indexical can be christened with a strict name.* Strict names can be stipulated to play a purely designating role that remains stable over several occasions of utterance. These names need not even be taken from ordinary expressions within natural language, but can be fabricated for the purpose at hand. Russell's "christening ceremony," described in PLA and mentioned again in HK, explains the method. The expression "this," used in the sentence "This is white" to designate a piece of chalk,

> will do very well while we are all here and can see it, but if I wanted to talk about it tomorrow it would be convenient to have christened it and called it "John." There is no other way in which you can mention it. You cannot really mention *it* itself except by means of a name. (PLA, p. 200)

In HK Russell says that once adopted, the fabricated "name" can function over multiple occasions of utterance. We say *"That* is the smell of a skunk" and *"that* is disagreeable", but

> Instead of "that," we might use a name, say "pfui," and should do so if we often wished to speak of the smell without mentioning skunks. But to anyone who had not had the requisite experience, the name would be an abbreviated description and not a name. (HK, p. 81)

In each of these cases, the "christening" name is devoid of description. In contrast, descriptive phrases draw upon the already fixed extensions of predicates embedded in them. Like strict naming, indexical designation does not depend on such prior fixed extensions of any internal terms.

(iv) *The designatum of an indexical is directly sensed*. Russell affirms in both PLA and HK that the designatum of an indexical or a strict name must be or have been directly sensed:

> It is only when you use the word "this" quite strictly, to stand for an object of sense, that it is really a proper name. (PLA, p. 201)

As noted above in HK, the expression "that" or "pfui" would be an "abbreviated description and not a name" to anyone who had not had the requisite experience.[6]

(v) *Indexicals designate particulars*. The role of indexicals in Russell's early and later work is to designate particulars. In the logical atomist period, "this" and "that" are defined as logical atoms or "words for particulars" (PLA, p. 200). In AMa (1927b), when Russell adopted a causal theory of perception and the theory that an event was a bundle of qualities, his notion of a particular changed. The particular is no longer a metaphysical absolute but something "relative to our knowledge" and capable of analysis. For example, electrons can be regarded as classes of events, and hence need not be taken as "ultimate particulars" (AMa, pp. 278, 319). Furthermore, the impossibility of unique designation of a particular changes from a logical to an empirical one. In AMa "this" or "here-now" designates a group of qualities simultaneously present ("compresent") with awareness.

When this "complex" of qualities is completely filled out so that nothing I experience is missing from it, Russell calls it a "complete complex of compresence" (HK, p. 294). Its exact recurrence in my experience is not *logically* impossible; it is merely "*empirically* so exceedingly improbable that we assume its nonoccurrence" (HK, p. 295).[7]

Russell concerns himself with the characteristics of indexicals because they play an important role in his theory of knowledge and later philosophy of science. He held that a central task for theory of knowledge, including scientific knowledge, is to answer the foundational question: How is knowledge based on experience? In answer Russell offers the principle of acquaintance: "Every proposition we can understand must be composed of constituents with which we are acquainted"; and in HK he argues that the definition of scientific concepts must ultimately terminate in ostensive definitions.[8] In his early period, the expression "this" designates an object of acquaintance, namely, that of which we are directly aware by sensory (or other) faculties. In his later period indexical sentences such as "This is red" or "redness here" tie the corpus of scientific knowledge to direct sensory experience.

Another central task of Russell's philosophy is to construct a "map of the physical world." In order to do this he must be able to proceed from the private subjective components of sensory experience to the public, intersubjective descriptions of knowledge (both common sense and scientific) that go beyond what we know in our immediate experience. How can this be done? Russell's solution involved a distinction between private, perceived space-time (here, now), and public, inferred space-time described by means of objective coordinate systems (Greenwich time, latitude and longitude). He then postulated that private space-time and public space-time are approximately correlated by means of "twofold locations."

> We construct a space containing both percipients and physical objects; but percepts have a twofold location in this space, namely that of the percipient and that of the physical object. Keeping one half of this location fixed, we obtain the view of the world from a given place; keeping the other half of this location fixed, we obtain the views of a given physical object from different places.... The physical world, I suggest, considered as perceptible, consists of occurrences having this twofold location. (AMa, p. 258)

Russell solves the problem of transition from private to public space-time by having indexicals represent the location of objects in these two space-times. He does not mean that an indexical represents two different locations, but that it represents the content of subjective experience in space-time, which is then correlated with a location in objectively constructed space-time. These correlations are made in the order of causation, not the order of knowledge. The percept is last in the order of causation, although first in the order of knowledge. The objective causal order contains the percept as an element of a causal chain.[9] Russell is thus able to distinguish proximate indexicals ("here") as representing a "minimal causal chain" and distal indexicals ("there") as representing a "longer" or "indirect" causal chain.[10]

Russell views scientific knowledge as knowledge of structure: "Wherever we infer from perception, it is only structure that we can validly infer; and structure is what can be expressed by mathematical logic, which includes mathematics" (AMa, p. 254). Space-time structures in scientific description "correspond with [perceptual structures] in a manner which preserves the logical (mathematical) properties" (AMa, p. 275). Indexicals are involved in these structural correlations. For example, Russell illustrates the transition from subjective experience to objective knowledge by replacing "Here I am" (called out to a friend in the night) with "At t_1, GMT, on date D_1, B.R. was at longitude $n_1 n_2$ and at latitude $n_3 n_4$." Indexicals are the focal point of these correlations: at first, they signify the subjective sensory experiences of the percipient; then they are replaced with coordinate descriptions. Of course they do not in themselves yield an explanation of how these correlations are made or why they can be made.

The four basic theses under scrutiny here are based on what Russell says in HK. They are:

1. *Coordinate replacement*: Indexicals, as well as strict names can be progressively replaced by coordinate descriptions, but only up to a certain point.
2. *Indispensability*. Indexical expressions cannot be entirely eliminated. They are indispensable to human discourse, including any science that requires human observation.
3. *Interdefinability*. Each indexical expression can be defined in terms of another (or combination of others).
4. *Reducibility*. All indexical expressions can be reduced to one basic type, although this basic type need not be one in particular.

Thus (1) and (2) are treated in section II; (3) and (4) in section III.

II

The coordinate replacement thesis, (1), takes its inspiration from Carnap's proposal in the *Logical Syntax of Language* (1937) to replace "name-languages" with "coordinate languages" (HK, p. 74). On this proposal, indexicals are eliminated in favor of descriptions by Carnap's method of uniquely designating structural descriptions, outlined in the *Aufbau* (1928, section 16). Carnap suggests in *Logical Syntax* that "the method of designation by proper names is the primitive one; that of positional designation corresponds to a more advanced stage of science and has considerable methodological advantages over the former" (p. 12). Designation by coordinates shows the place of objects in the system and in relation to one another by means of four real numbers signifying space-time coordinates. For example, in "Blue (*a*)," meaning "the object *a* is blue," we replace the name a with coordinates x_1, x_2, x_3, x_4. The result is "Blue(x_1, x_2, x_3, x_4)," meaning "the position (x_1, x_2, x_3, x_4) is blue." Names that designate a region of space-time are thus replaced by coordinates that eliminate any element of subjective reference.

Russell argued in HK that although Carnap's replacement of names, including indexicals, by coordinate descriptions was a useful and worthy goal, it could succeed only up to a certain point. Indexicals, he claimed, could never be completely dispensed with. In the following arguments Russell uses the term "names." What he claimed to be indispensable, however, were not ordinary proper names but names of the peculiar sort he called egocentric, i.e., indexicals. "This" and "that" are his prime examples.[11]

(i) Coordinates describe a point in space-time. They locate it by means of reference to axes and distance from the origin of axes. But, Russell asks, how do we designate the axes and the origin? We cannot go on indefinitely giving a description of the origin of each system in terms of another system. Ultimately we must be able to say, "*This* is the origin." In other words, we must be able to name the origin, in contrast to merely describing it. Names, as Russell points out, designate directly without depending on other terms in the language. They are in that sense rather arbitrary, whereas descriptions draw upon meaningful systems of predicates or numbers. "It is because coordinates are not arbitrary that they are not names." So, if we do not have a way of "knowing *some* places otherwise than by latitude and longitude, latitude and longitude become unmeaning" (HK, p. 77). Assignments of a finite number of coordinates might be done haphazardly; if so, these assignments would themselves be based on descriptions. But the origin and axes of a system themselves cannot be descriptively assigned or we will have a regress lacking an empirical basis. "We must have some method of identifying a place without mentioning the coordinates" (HK, p. 78). Indexicals can prevent such a regress by providing a nondescriptive means of identifying the origin of a system. Hence, Russell concludes, "We cannot wholly dispense with proper names [indexicals] by means of coordinates" (HK, p. 78).

(ii) Russell's second argument, in the chapter in HK on "Egocentric Particulars," maintains that some indexical element is necessary in a minimum vocabulary. He first questions whether names must be included in a minimum vocabulary that expresses our empirical knowledge (HK, p. 79). Ordinary proper names such as "Napoleon" may be replaced, following Carnap, with coordinate descriptions designating space-time regions. Then, since the assignment of coordinates requires assigning an origin and axes, the question arises as to whether the origin can be defined. He answers that it must be defined by reference to something observable. Theoretical constructs like the sun obviously will not do. Will the qualities and space-time relations used to define such constructs serve the purpose? Although these qualities are initially definable in purely physical terms not dependent on observation or needing immediate experience (e.g., color is defined in terms of wavelengths), eventually *some* quality or relation must be observed. To be observed is for someone to say, "So *that* is *Q*" where, e.g., "*Q*" is "blue." "That" is in some sense a name, though of the peculiar sort Russell calls egocentric. Hence, names of an egocentric sort (what we here call indexicals) are necessary in a minimum vocabulary.

(iii) Russell's third argument deals with the question of whether, by substituting descriptions for names, description will suffice in every instance instead of names, thus dispensing with the need for names (including indexicals) altogether. He considers replacing first and second person pronouns ("I," "you") with ordinary proper names ("Bertrand Russell"), which are then replaced by definite descriptions. But these latter descriptions ("The person identified by the passport as Bertrand Russell") are "known only through the sensible impressions of individuals, no two of which are exactly alike." When considering competing replacing descriptions ("the red-faced tramp," "the benign old gentleman in evening dress") we can secure "sets of closely similar occurrences." But in order to secure the precise and unique referent we must at some point revert to "*This* is his name." Hence we do not wholly escape from "this." Naming (in the sense of strict names or indexical designation) is at some point required (HK, p. 87).

(iv) In considering the attempt to replace all names with descriptions, Russell argues that every description or name that we can understand must ultimately be reducible to "something definable in terms of your experience," by which he means direct experience.

> For every word that you can understand must either have a nominal definition in terms of words having ostensive definitions, or must itself have an ostensive definition; and ostensive definitions, as appears from the process by which they are effected, are only possible in relation to events that have occurred to you. (HK, p. 87)

This principle, obviously a later version of the principle of acquaintance (OD, p. 56) stated in terms of ostensive definition, affirms the indispensability of indexicals as the designators of such direct experiences.

Bar-Hillel has raised an objection to Russell's indispensability arguments that will allow us, after analyzing it, to state Russell's position more clearly. While agreeing that indexicals are indispensable, Bar-Hillel nevertheless thinks that Russell's main argument in support of this thesis is wrong. Bar-Hillel interprets this argument as claiming that replacing "here" and "now" by coordinate descriptions does not eliminate indexicals because the origin of the system "can be taught and learned only with the help of indexical . . . signs." (Cf. arguments (i) and (ii).) Bar-Hillel calls this argument an obvious non-sequitur, "based on a confusion between using language and learning how to use language" (1979, p. 83).

In assessing this objection it is important to note first that Russell would have agreed with one major point Bar-Hillel makes on language use. Once learned, the use of a word such as "red" does not require the use of indexicals; its reference can be understood independently of the context of its production. He also would have agreed with Bar-Hillel's point that a token of the sentence, "The book at location l_1 and time t_1 is red," will be understood in exactly the same way as a token of the sentence, "This book is red" by "anybody having a certain knowledge." In fact, Russell made a point very much like this. From a practical point of view, he said, two competent persons (i.e., who have already learned the language in question) will both accept or reject a statement of the form "At time t, A was at longitude B and latitude C," as a replacement for "Here I am." The procedures for determining such coordinates lead "different people to the same result," and are important in legal as well as scientific contexts. These points of agreement, however, do not render arguments (i) and (ii) immune from Bar-Hillel's criticism.

To say that Russell confuses language use with language acquisition, however, misrepresents Russell's arguments and passes over some key epistemic and linguistic distinctions underlying his arguments. Arguments (i) and (ii) are misconstrued if interpreted as claiming that the origin of a coordinate system can only be taught and learned only with the help of indexicals. Russell did argue that indexicals were indispensable in language acquisition, but that is not his point in the preceding arguments.

To capture Russell's position we must distinguish: (a) direct sensory awareness (being aware of "this"); (b) the process of ostension (the linguistic or gestural process of pointing, signified by the word "this"); (c) the process of ostensive definition ("*This* is red" or "*That* is blue"). (a) can occur without (b) or (c). But (b) and (c) require (a). Furthermore, ostensive definition can be employed for various purposes, e.g., for language acquisition, or for tying down general concepts to a foundation in experience. Russell's argument (ii) points out that direct sensory awareness is required to tie general concepts to experience, and hence forms the basis of empirical knowledge. His point deals not with language acquisition but rather with the empirical basis, the foundation, of an entire language system. Argument (ii) thus deals with the epistemic foundation, or justification of language, not with its acquisition. Bar-Hillel fails to understand this, and misreads the argument.

Furthermore, Bar-Hillel's criticism conflates ostension for the purpose of identification with ostension for the purpose of ostensive definition and language acquisition. Ostension, or pointing, is one function of the indexical "this." To say that one has employed "this" in ostension or pointing (e.g., on what Kaplan (1979) has called "the demonstrative use of a demonstrative") is not to say that one has employed "this" in an ostensive definition for the purpose of language acquisition. One can use "this" for the purpose of identifying instances of terms one has already acquired (e.g., "*This* is the origin" as identifying the "center or origin of a coordinate system," or "*this* is 14 carat gold" and "*this* is electroplated gold").

Russell's argument (i) rests on the identifying function of "this" in defining the origin of coordinate systems, not on ostensive definition for the purpose of language acquisition. He assumes that the notion of a coordinate system is already established in the language, and then asks: "How is a certain coordinate system fixed?" His argument is that unless we already have some nondescriptive way of fixing this framework, i.e., some way of "naming" its origin, we face a regress that detaches scientific knowledge from its empirical basis. This, I take it, is what he means by saying that we must have a way of knowing "*some* places otherwise than by latitude and longitude or latitude and longitude become unmeaning" (HK, p. 77).

In arguments (i) and (ii) Russell hypothesizes an identification of designata in language akin to the physicist's choice of a certain coordinate system.[12] Acquiring the language of a coordinate system and fixing the origin of the system are theoretically distinct processes, even if in certain cases they are empirically coextensive (for example, in saying "*This* is the origin" to students learning the mathematical language of physics). Where the origin is fixed by the private sense experience of one individual speaker, the two processes indeed overlap. Failure to distinguish them has led to the misreading exemplified by Bar-Hillel.

What is indistinct at the level of subjective awareness, however, may be more clearly separated at the social level. The distinction between (a) acquiring a term (e.g., "gold") and (b) acquiring a method of recognizing its denotation is made quite sharply by Hilary Putnam's "sociolinguistic hypothesis" on the "division of linguistic labor" (Putnam, 1979). Ordinarily, lay people can do (a) without doing (b), at least without doing (b) in a technical scientific sense. But when a surefire method of recognizing gold is required, we enlist a special class of scientific speakers (goldsmiths, chemists). Whereas (a) requires an ostensive definition of "gold," (b) requires only the identification of gold. It is the identification requirement that figures in Russell's arguments (i) and (ii). Viewed from the standpoint of the solitary speaker of language, (a) and (b) may appear simultaneous and synonymous. But from the vantage point of the linguistic community they are distinct functions that make different uses of indexicals, when they use them at all.

Russell's argument for the indispensability of indexicals comes down to the indispensability of the sort of "naming" performed by indexicals. It is not only that such naming is accomplished nondescriptively. The indexical also expresses the relation between speaker and object. According to Russell, indexicals name complexes of compresence. A complex of compresence is a peculiar sort of construction, unlike a class.

> It is to be conceived...as something which can be known and named without having to know all it constituent qualities...in a way not reducible to all of its constituents. It is in fact the sort of object that is a "this" and that can have a proper name. (HK, p. 307)

(Presumably Russell uses "proper name" in the PLA sense of "strict name.") Since we normally do not know all the constituents of a complex of compresence, a uniquely referring description of the complex is normally not possible. It is in some sense our ignorance of the entire list of qualities "which makes names for complexes necessary" (HK, p. 308). If we can perceive it, we can name the complex — even if we do not know exactly *how* we know it. Since "we need a name for the complex to express what it is that we have discovered," and only a nondescriptive name will suffice in most instances, indexical designation is indispensable. "I-now" and "this" count as names (not *ordinary* names) by virtue of being "given to the whole or part of what the speaker is at the moment experiencing."

> When our verbal inventiveness fails, we fall back on "this" for the part of our total momentary experience to which we are specially attending, and upon "I-now" for the total momentary experience. (HK, p. 302)

"Private compresence" is Russell's term for the relation between those elements to which we are specially attending.

> The quality of centrality, for example, has "private compresence" with the color which is now occupying the center of my visual field. (HK, p. 305)

Indexicals do more than denote the compresent qualities, or even the privately compresent qualities. They express the momentary relation of awareness. They have a twofold semantic role of expressing the speaker's awareness of qualities and of designating the qualities. I suggest that this is part of what Russell means when he says that "the subjectivity which we sought to avoid [through scientific description] has not been wholly banished" (HK, p. 86). Russell's metaphor of the scientist in his "private world" may be most accurately grasped by exploring the role of indexicals in expressing relations of awareness. These relations cannot be *merely* denoted or designated because then the observer would have to be aware of the designatum, and so on, into a regress.

What precisely does Russell mean by his claim that indexicals are indispensable? Russell, like Frege, was not always clear about the level of language presupposed in his discussion.[13] His examples are taken from everyday usage in natural language, but his points are applied to scientific language as well. Surely, however, he is not to be taken as asserting literally that "this" or "here" is necessary to identify the origin of a coordinate system. This claim would sound preposterous to many practicing scientists. He may be claiming that some use of some indexical is required in the rational reconstruction of scientific and natural language. If so, his position still clearly diverges from that of Carnap, who explicitly excluded indexicals from his rationally reconstructed language.[14]

III

The theses of interdefinability, (3), and of reducibility, (4), are closely connected. For the indexicals under consideration ("I," "this," "here," "now") to be interdefinable on Russell's view means that each indexical can be replaced by another, or group of others. For the indexicals to be reducible means apparently that one indexical or combination thereof may be chosen as primitive and the others defined in terms of it. Russell does not assert that there is one indexical that is basic. He emphasizes, for example, that "here-now" would serve as the primitive just as well as "this," which is his usual choice for the defining indexical. Accordingly, on Russell's theory the first person "I" neither is necessarily primitive nor has special status. In this respect his view contrasts sharply with that of recent writers, such as John Perry (1980) and Roderick Chisholm (1982).[15]

In the chapter on "Egocentric Particulars" in HK, Russell gives an indication of how to use "this" as the primitive:

> "This" might be taken as the only egocentric word not having a nominal definition. We could say that "I" means "the person experiencing this," "now" means "the time of this," and "here" means "the place of this." (HK, p. 85)

Later in the chapter, he makes it clear that other reductions are possible:

> "This" denotes whatever, at the moment when the word is used, occupies the center of attention.... We may define "I" as "the person attending to this," and "here" as "the place of attending to this." We could equally well take "here-now" as fundamental: then "this" would be defined as "what is here-now," and "I" as "what experiences this." (HK, p. 92).

That these other reductions are possible implies that all the reductions are merely linguistic, not ontological. They make it possible to streamline language by adopting a relatively small "minimum vocabulary." Consequently, they make it easier to convert sentences containing indexicals into scientific language by replacing them with coordinate descriptions.[16]

The theses of interdefinability and reducibility of indexicals that are common to IMT and HK can be interpreted to mean that indexical expressions can be replaced one by another while preserving the epistemic import of the replaced expressions, that is, universally replaced without loss of information.[17] Although Russell does not explicitly endorse this interpretation, his strategies in IMT and HK suggest it. Let us examine whether Russell can consistently maintain his theses under this interpretation.

Bar-Hillel (1970) criticizes Russell for failing to recognize that the expression "this" has a variety of uses in natural language, and that replacing it with "I" results in a sentence that is ambiguous in a way that the original is not:

> Russell's statement, understood in the sense that "I" can always and without loss of information be replaced by "the person experiencing this," is false... because it is simply not the case that "given the speaker and the time, the meaning of 'this' is unambiguous." (p. 82)

He continues:

> Knowing *only* the speaker and the time of utterance of "The person experiencing this is hungry," we would not yet be justified in understanding that the speaker was hungry at the time of utterance of this token... whereas we could do so unhesitatingly on hearing "I am hungry" and knowing once again the speaker and the time of utterance only. (ibid.)

Bar-Hillel's point is that if Russell is correct, then "the person attending to this" should be replaceable with "I" and conversely without loss of information. For example, we should be able to replace

(1) I am hungry

with

(2) The person attending to (experiencing) this is hungry,

and conversely, without loss of information. But we cannot, since (2) is ambiguous in a way (1) is not. (1) clearly refers to me, but (2) may be referring to me or to someone else.

It might be supposed that the ambiguity in the preceding case can be eliminated by employing Russell's stipulation that "this" denotes "whatever, at the moment when the word is used, occupies the center of attention" (HK, p. 93), and taking the stipulation to mean that "this" designates whatever at that moment occupies the center of attention of *whoever (individually) understands the replacing sentence*. But even on this fortified interpretation, sentence (2) can still be read in two different ways. On reading A, "the person attending to this" is understood as designating whoever happens to fulfill the conditions of attending to "this" and being hungry. On reading B, the indexical definite description "the person attending to this" is understood to designate the speaker, regardless of whether the other conditions are satisfied. The ambiguity is located not in the lone indexical "this" but in the indexical definite description "the person attending to this." On reading A whoever satisfies the sentence (2) is the referent of the description; since it might not be me the speaker, replacement of (2) by (1) is not justified. On reading B "this" is taken to designate the speaker's awareness; consequently, replacement of (1) by (2) is justified. I conclude that (2) is indeed ambiguous and cannot replace (1) without loss of information.[18]

Several explanations can be given of the ambiguity in (2). The use of "the person attending to this" on reading A resembles what Donnellan (1966) calls the attributive use of a definite description. Its use on reading B resembles what he calls the referential use. In referential uses the internal structure of the definite description is less a factor than the intention of the speaker in securing reference. In this vein, we can say that on reading B the speaker's intention (or internal "christening ceremony") secures reference to *his or her* awareness.

Alternatively, we might regard reading B as rigid (Kripke) or *de re* (Putnam) designation. Kripke has argued that such ambiguities are best analyzed as ambiguities of scope, with "the 'rigid' reading equivalent to Russellian primary occurrence, the non-rigid to innermost scope."[19] Advantages of Kripke's approach include the possibility of using a set of technical devices (scope indicators) provided by Russell's own logical theory. It should be noted, however, that none of these explanations removes the ambiguity; they merely give us a way of understanding it.

The ambiguity in (2) appears to depend on the possibility that "this" has intersubjective reference. Russell considers the possibility when he raises the question whether "this" can have public meaning. He concludes that "two people are more likely to have the same 'this' if it is somewhat abstract rather than fully concrete," because of perspectival differences in concrete percepts (HK, p. 92). If "this" has some intersubjective reference, then a speaker could individually understand the replacing sentence (2) as true of him- or herself, or of others.[20] Thus, (2) would be ambiguous.

A close reading of Russell shows that he does not admit the possibility that "this" has intersubjective reference to concrete entities: he takes its concrete referent to be private, immediate experience. (In fact, he considers intersubjective reference of "this" only very briefly at the end of his chapter on "Egocentric Particulars" [HK].) So the preceding ambiguity requires an assumption that Russell does not make. If we deny the assumption, it does not make sense to give an attributive interpretation to the description "the person attending to this," because "this" does not then designate something that any person other than myself could attend to.

Further, the alleged ambiguity does not correspond exactly to the ambiguity produced by attributive and referential uses for definite descriptions. In "The person who stole my car is hungry," it makes sense on the attributive use to add "and I do not know who it is." But if "this" designates something private to the speaker, it makes no sense for the speaker to say "The person attending to this is hungry" and then add, "and I do not know who it is." If "this" is private then each person has his/her own experience of "this." It is absurd to call something private "this," and then to designate with the same word someone else's "this." Hence, the distinction between readings A and B collapses on the private interpretation of "this," and (2) is capable of replacing (1) without difficulty.

But if we adopt this solution, then the first person "I" or "my" is surreptitiously reintroduced into the replacing indexical definite description, "the person attending to this." In other words, (2) must implicitly be read as:

(2′) The person attending to the center of my awareness of this is hungry.

If the purpose of replacing sentences containing "I" and "my" with sentences containing "this" is to reduce the multiplicity of indexicals to one, for inclusion in

132 Janet Farrell Smith

a minimum vocabulary, then (2') does not accomplish the goal, since it contains "my." As a definition of sentences containing "my" and its cognates, (2') is circular.[21] (Russell does not, as noted earlier, claim that "this" must serve as the primitive indexical to which all others are reduced. He could revert to his alternative proposal to define "this" in terms of "I-now" and carry out another reduction.)

The interdefinability thesis as Russell first states it, defining "I" in terms of "the person attending to this," is thus open to objection on grounds of either ambiguity or circularity. A sympathetic critic might take these objections merely as evidence of the interrelated character of indexical expressions, a phenomenon Russell never denied but may in fact have (unwittingly) revealed in his attempt to make indexicals interdefinable. Such an interpretation would require taking Russell's interdefinability thesis in a weaker sense than he intended it.

Russell's problem, however, goes deeper than the difficulties noted so far. The root of these difficulties is the private-public split incorporated in the "two-fold meaning" of indexicals. The ambiguity in (2) is not an isolated counterexample but an indication of a dilemma in Russell's epistemological-scientific program.

Suppose Russell tries to avoid the ambiguity in indexical definite descriptions by restricting the designata of indexicals to private experience. He can then give an account of the role of subjective experience and direct awareness in the acquisition of empirical knowledge by means of indexicals. But then he faces enormous problems in explaining how connections between private and public objects can be made in the order of knowledge. That is, he faces great difficulty in bridging the gap between the two poles of "two-fold meaning." If, on the other hand, he does not restrict the designation of indexicals to private experience, he can then explain the correlations between perceptual space-time order and nonperspectival, public space-time order. But on this strategy he weakens and risks abandoning a central tenet of his empirical method, namely, that sensible experience is the basis of observational data.

Even if (1) and (2) can be understood only by a single individual (the speaker), Russell's dilemma persists. For the fact that an expression can be understood to refer to a single individual does not entail that its designatum is private. Solitary understanding need not presuppose private designata. Indeed, some philosophers argue that it presupposes the opposite, public designata (Frege, 1892; Wittgenstein, 1958, par. 38–47).

What is involved in being aware of something red is not only awareness of intrinsic qualities such as red, but awareness of structural properties involving space-time location, e.g., awareness that "this" is to my left, about a foot away from me, occurs now at a time two seconds later than when I first noticed it, etc. Awareness of these structural properties is required to understand such sentences as "The ball is red." But how is my awareness of the red ball correlated with its description in nonperspectival public coordinates? We may clarify the correlation as follows:

(a) Direct subjective awareness ("egocentric particulars")

(b) Event-structure in objective space-time within which consciousness occurs.

(a') Designations of (a) (Indexical expressions) (Perspectival description in subjective space-time)

(b') Description of (b) (Coordinate descriptions in nonperspectival public terms)

Russell's dilemma arises from locating expressions that designate private entities in (a'), the description of perspectival space-time. Whereas his coordinate replacement thesis requires a transition from (a') and (b') at the linguistic level, his epistemology requires a diagonal transition from (a) at the ontological level to (b') at the linguistic level. If Russell stipulates the designatum of "this" in (a') as private, he faces the problem of bridging the gap between private and public entities. If he stipulates in advance that the structure in (a) or (a') is correlative with (b'), he bridges the gap, but renders empirical discovery circular or vacuous.[22] He could have avoided the dilemma by allowing indexicals in (a') to have an intersubjective designatum. In this way he could accommodate both the fact that the expressions of (a') can be understood by single speakers, and for the fact that they can be correlated with nonperspectival public descriptions.

IV

Let us summarize our investigation into Russell's theses. The interdefinability thesis in its strong form, which holds that any indexical can be replaced by others without loss of information, must be regarded as doubtful. The thesis that indexicals can be reduced to a single primitive, for purposes of a minimum vocabulary, must therefore also be called into question. Partial replacement of indexicals by coordinate descriptions is possible, though this replacement faces difficulties on grounds not discussed here.

An assessment of Russell's indispensability thesis must be more complicated, since the role of indexicals changed with Russell's philosophical development. Indexicals become empirically more important in his later philosophy because they acquire a more refined role in designating the compresence of qualities in perceptual awareness. Logically speaking, they are just as important as they were in PLA, but in a different role. They do not designate "logical simples"; rather they correlate subjective space-time with objective space-time structure.

The difficulties in Russell's later philosophy elaborated in this essay were even more severe in his earlier philosophy. For the logical simples of PLA, though not defined as private, were known only through private sense-data. And the problems of transition from private awareness to public scientific description were more formidable prior to Russell's adoption of a causal theory of perception and a theory of twofold access to an ontology of event-structures.

Russell, throughout his career, took a position distinctive in twentieth century philosophy. He attempted both to recognize intersubjective scientific description and to connect with it an apparently ineliminable element of subjectivity. Unlike Frege, who starts with the notion that thoughts are public, communicable, objective entities, Russell begins the order of knowledge with the notion of a private sensory core. Yet both philosophers arrive at the position that there is an ineliminable core of "private" sense or meaning to indexical expressions and that this meaning cannot be conveyed in nonindexical description. Russell's "two-fold meaning" of indexicals bears some resemblance to Frege's dual senses of "I." Frege makes a fundamental distinction between the "primitive self-presentation" of "I" and its communicable, public use.[23] He tries without success to find a replacing description for the primitive self-representing use of "I." His affirmation of this use parallels Russell's arguments against Carnap's replacement program, namely that ultimately indexicals fail to be completely replaceable by descriptions.

Russell's problem derives from his conflation of the epistemological relation between perceiver and perceived with the linguistic relation between indexical expressions and their designata. To preserve the element of subjectivity in perspectival awareness, Russell emphasized its private nature. But if the designatum is private, then how is intersubjective understanding of indexicals possible? To avoid this problem, Russell could have taken the designata of indexicals as intersubjective or public, while simultaneously insisting on a unique, subjective, direct awareness of the compresent qualities in the perceived object. Russell does not adopt this solution, though it would be consistent with his insistence that indexicals are indispensable and that subjectivity "could not be wholly banished." Finally, Russell conflated an epistemic relation with the nature of what is designated. He tried to pack subjectivity (an epistemic relation between consciousness and the material of direct awareness) into "private meaning" (what is designated). But this was not necessary, especially in his later theory.

In answer to the question of whether indexicals are indispensable, then, one can answer: indexicals are not necessary from an ontological point of view because, in Russell's late philosophy, there are no simple particulars to designate. Indexicals are not necessary from a logical point of view because description can accomplish unique reference. Yet because they express the unique relation of awareness of sensory experience from an epistemological point of view, they are necessary to human discourse and communication.[24]

Notes

1. Abbreviations for the works by Russell cited in this essay are as follows: AMa, *Analysis of Matter* (1954 ed.), HK, *Human Knowledge*, IMT, *Inquiry into Meaning and Truth*, OD, "On Denoting," PLA, "Philosophy of Logical Atomism" (1956a ed.).

2. Russell's arguments in IMT for dispensing with "egocentric particulars" are not discussed here. David Kaplan criticizes these arguments in his "Demonstratives" (mimeograph, Dept. of Philosophy, UCLA 1977). Kaplan argues that Russell's replacement of indexicals by proper names (e.g., "I saw a table" is replaced by "Otto saw a table") is inadequate because (a) indexicals retain a kind of epistemic priority, and (b) for any prior collection of proper names, there will be things without a name (p. 91). Russell takes position (a) in HK, refuting his own former views. His arguments for the position are analyzed here in section II. See also David Kaplan, "Dthat" and "On the Logic of Demonstratives" both in *Contemporary Perspectives in the Philosophy of Language*, ed. P. French (Minneapolis: University of Minnesota Press, 1979).

3. The term "indexical" derives from Peirce, who classified signs as icons, indices, or symbols (see Burks "Icon, Index and Symbol," *Philosophy and Phenomenological Research*, 9(1949). The terms "indexical expression" and "indexical sentence" are used here in the sense defined by Bar-Hillel ("Indexical Expressions," in *Aspects of Language* [Jerusalem: Magnes Press, 1970], 1975).

4. Chisholm, "Russell on the Foundations of Empirical Knowledge," in *The Philosophy of Bertrand Russell*, ed. P. Schilpp (LaSalle, IL: Open Court, 1944), p. 438. The classification of indexicals is problematic, as Russell recognizes in IMT, 102–5.

5. Technically speaking, on Russell's theory, definite descriptions do not denote. For convenience of exposition I will speak here as if they do.

6. Russell is aware of how difficult it is to identify primitive noninferred, sensory material which is free of all interpretation. Nevertheless, Russell says we can progressively strip away interpretation from perception, and "approach asymptotically to the pure datum" (IMT, p. 155). The "pure" sensory datum is therefore a limit. See E. Nagel's discussion in "Russell's Philosophy of Science," in *The Philosophy of Bertrand Russell*, ed. P. Schilpp, pp. 334–35.

7. In IMT Russell attempts to abolish all particulars, including egocentric particulars: "Whatever is dated and located is complex and the notion of simple particulars is a mistake" (p. 303). "A complex of compresence which does not recur takes the place traditionally occupied by 'particulars' " (p. 307). In HK he reinterprets the notion of a particular, while still rejecting "ultimate" or "simple particulars."

8. See Russell's argument (iv) summarized in section II. Russell says, "For every word that you can understand must either have a nominal definition in terms of words having ostensive definitions, or must itself have an ostensive definition" (HK, p. 87).

9. The notion of "twofold location" of percepts in AMa becomes the "twofold meaning" (of "here") in HK. It is very difficult to give a precise exposition of the "twofold meaning" view that I criticize in section III. Russell is saying, roughly, that by their "twofold meaning" indexicals represent the "twofold location" he describes in *Analysis of Matter*. The terminology of "twofold location" or "twofold meaning" designates two different ways of naming (or describing) what is, ultimately, one and the same objective order. ("There is one public time, in which not only physical events, but mental events, also have their place" (HK, p. 91).)

10. See John Lyons's discussion of spatial deixis in *Semantics*, vol. 2 (Cambridge: Cambridge Univerisity Press, 1977), pp. 648ff., 669). Lyons suggests that " 'this' is roughly equivalent to 'the one near me' " (p. 648).

11. Russell is not arguing for the indispensability of ordinary proper names such as "Napoleon," because, as he notes, these can for the most part be replaced by words for qualities and complexes of compresent qualities. Proper names in the ordinary sense, he says, "are misleading and embody a false metaphysics," namely, that of substance (HK, p. 84).

12. The choice of a particular coordinate system has a pragmatic, i.e., context-dependent, element. Likewise, identification of designata generally has a pragmatic element. Russell affirms this pragmatic element by saying that indexicals are indispensable for identification both in natural and empirical scientific language. Identification may occur in, but is not identical with, language acquisition. Some identification is prior to language acquisition in the sense that language learning (e.g., within a culture) could not proceed without its having already been done. It is posterior to language acquisition in the sense that the identification of axes and origin of a particular coordinate system could not be accomplished without prior mastery of a mathematical language. The exact location of the origin might not matter, e.g., if we merely wanted to track motion of a particle through a system and we wanted simply to compare coordinates (x^1, y^1, z^1) with $(x^2, y^2, z^2), \ldots, (x^n, y^n, z^n)$. But the point

is that the physicist *chooses* a certain coordinate system for a certain purpose or because it is the most convenient, and that this choice has a pragmatic element that is expressed linguistically by indexicals. (My thanks to D. C. Carey and Stephen E. Smith for consultation on physics questions.)

13. See J. van Heijenoort, "Frege on Vagueness," *Synthese*, (1982) for a discussion of Frege, Russell, and Quine on this issue. The problem is compounded in Russell's case because he holds that in a logical language there are no names. Hence it is unclear how (or whether) indexical expressions would appear in a logical language, since they are names in one sense, i.e., "strict names."

14. Carnap explicitly restricted his discussion in *Logical Syntax* to nonindexical languages: "We shall deal only with languages which contain no expressions dependent upon extra-linguistic factors" (*The Logical Syntax of Language* [London: Routledge & Kegan Paul, 1937], p. 168). See discussion by Bar-Hillel in "Indexical Expressions," p. 75. Carnap also warned that his constructions in the *Aufbau* were intended to preserve only the logical, not the epistemological, value of the terms defined. He explicitly stated, as Nelson Goodman remarks, that "his system is not to be regarded as a portrayal of the process of acquiring knowledge. Nevertheless he considered the system to be a 'rational reconstruction' of that process, a demonstration of how the ideas dealt with 'could have been' derived from the original given." "The Significance of *Der logische Aufbau der Welt*," in *The Philosophy of Rudolf Carnap*, ed. P. Schilpp (LaSalle, IL: Open Court, 1963), p. 548. Russell's dissatisfaction may have to do with the latter claim.

15. On this topic see G. E. M. Anscombe, "The First Person," in *Mind and Language*, ed. S. Guttenplan (Oxford, 1975), and H. Castenada, *Thinking and Doing* (Dordrecht: Reidel, 1875) and "On the Philosophical Foundations of a Theory of Communications: Reference," in *Midwest Studies in Philosophy*, vol. 2 (Minneapolis: University of Minnesota Press, 1977), pp. 166-86.

16. Russell's analysis of "This is red" as "redness here" in IMT (p. 92) resembles Quine's later treatment in *Word and Object*, where demonstrative singular terms ("This river" are eliminated in a regimented language in favor of "indicator words" or indexical predicates (e.g. "x is a river and x is here") Quine, *Word and Object* [Cambridge, MA: MIT Press, 1960], pp. 162ff., 185). See my discussion in "Quine's Elimination of Demonstratives," unpublished paper.

17. The notion of interdefinability used here employs a relation of "informational equivalence" as suggested by A. W. Burks "Icon, Index and Symbol," and applied by John Perry in "Frege on Demonstratives," *Philosophical Review*, 86(1977), pp. 474-98.

18. Russell recognized a similar problem in the attempt to classify "this" as either a name or a concealed description. "If we treat it as a mere name, it cannot have in any sense a constant meaning, for a name means merely what it designates, and the designatum of 'this' is continually changing. If, on the other hand, we treat 'this' as a concealed description, e.g., 'the object of attention,' it will then *always apply to everything that is ever a 'this,'* whereas in fact it never applies to more than one thing at a time. Any attempt to avoid this undesired generality will involve *a surreptitious reintroduction of 'this' into the definiens*" (IMT, p. 103; emphasis added).

19. See Putnam (1977, p. 128). Kripke criticizes the *de re* interpretation in "Speaker's Reference and Semantic Reference," in *Contemporary Perspectives in the Philosophy of Language*, ed. P. French (Minneapolis: University of Minnesota Press, 1979), pp. 6-27; and *Naming and Necessity* (Cambridge, MA: Harvard University Press, 1980), pp. 7ff. and 10-14.

20. Further, the ambiguity can be taken to reside in sentence-tokens of (2) and not in the sentence-type, if we assume that all participants individually entertain (without uttering) the sentence-token "the person attending to this is hungry."

21. Roderick Chisholm suggested in conversation the following version of the circularity criticism: Taking "this" as Russell defines it to designate "whatever at the moment when the word is used, occupies the center of attention," what in Russell's theory prevents *my* center of attention from being *your* center of attention? To make it clear that I designate not your but my center of attention, we must add "my" as follows: "This" designates "whatever, at the moment when the word is used, occupies [my] center of attention." If we do not add "my" then the awareness and the object are indistinguishable, and solipsism follows. If we do add "my" then we presuppose, as Chisholm has argued (in *The First Person* [Minneapolis: University of Minnesota Press, 1981]), that the primary form of intentional reference is the first person. The present essay does not argue this latter position, but merely that the attempt to avoid the ambiguity between (2a) and (2b) by limiting designation of "this" to the speaker's private experience results in circularity.

22. See William Demopoulos and Michael Friedman, "The Concept of Structure in *The Analysis of Matter*," in this volume for a technical explanation of the problem.

23. John Perry, "Frege on Demonstratives," argues that the former, incommunicable sense, will not help Frege out of the problem he faces in accounting for indexical reference.

24. I am grateful to the following persons for helpful suggestions on an earlier draft: A. Anderson, R. Chisholm, W. Demopoulos, E. Eames, M. Friedman, W. Goldfarb, M. Sainsbury, W. Savage, and J. van Heijenoort.

C. Wade Savage

Sense-Data in Russell's Theories of Knowledge

Traditionally, sense-data are the ultimate data in a standard foundationalist account of empirical knowledge: the completely certain, immediate, precise data of experience from which all other empirical truths are inferred. During the first phase of his work in epistemology, Bertrand Russell subscribed to some version of this account. But, as he describes his evolution in *My Philosophical Development* (MPD), by 1921 his views on sense-data had undergone "a very important change" (p. 134); indeed, the "last substantial change" in "my philosophy" (p. 13). Previously he had "thought that sensation is a fundamentally relational occurrence in which a subject is 'aware' of an object," "had used the concept 'awareness' or 'acquaintance' to express the relation of subject to object," and had employed the term "sense-datum" to denote the object of sensory acquaintance. But then he "became convinced that William James had been right in denying the relational character of sensations," and in contending "that the supposed subject is the name of a non-entity [and that] those who still cling to it are clinging to a mere echo, the faint rumor left behind by the disappearing 'soul' upon the air of philosophy." Accordingly, Russell tells us, "In *The Analysis of Mind* (1921) I explicitly abandoned 'sense-data' " (pp. 134–35).

The reader must beware of this dramatic pronouncement. For, as we shall see, Russell goes on to describe an evolution of his views on sensation and perception that can easily seem to be, if not the reintroduction of sense-data under another name, at least the introduction of something very like them. The interpretive problem here is difficult, and far from solved. A few of Russell's commentators have argued that he completely abandoned sense-data; a few have argued that he retained sense-data in virtually their original form; many take his claim of abandonment at face value, without asking in what respects it is accurate and in which inaccurate; and many commentators completely avoid the issue. Russell's later philosophy cannot be fully understood without confronting and resolving the issue.

Neither of the extreme interpretations—that Russell completely abandoned sense-data, or that he virtually retained them—seems correct. As a first approximation to a correct interpretation, we may say that before abandonment sense-data were held to be the *absolutely* certain (indubitable, infallible), immediate (uninferred, self-evident), precise (analyzed, simple) data of empirical knowledge; and after abandonment were held to be only *relatively* certain, immediate, and precise, i.e. certain, immediate, and precise *to some degree*. We will seek an even more exact formulation. We shall find that the difference between the pre- and the postabandonment positions is exceedingly subtle, and less marked than the preceding formulation suggests. For there is evidence that even in the preabandonment phase Russell held that the actual data of sense are not absolutely certain, immediate, or precise; and that the sense-datum is an ideal that the actual data approximate more or less closely. Furthermore, in the postabandonment phase, Russell held that the actual data of sensation and perception admit of degrees, and that they converge toward an ideal limit as they become more and more certain, immediate, and precise. My suggestion will be that the original sense-datum becomes the ideal, practically unachievable limit of the actual data of sensation and perception.

The suggested view is of great importance. It is a sort of compromise between a pure foundationalist theory of knowledge and a pure coherence theory, and incorporates many of the best features of both. It may be some such view that is currently needed in philosophy of perception. For most workers in the field have been dissuaded from a pure foundationalist theory by the coherentist critics, and yet few can accept a pure coherence theory. It will emerge, however, that Russell's compromise is not without its difficulties.

Russell's Preabandonment Doctrine of Sense-Data

Russell defines "sense-data" in *The Problems of Philosophy* (PP) in a famous passage of chapter I (p. 12):

> Let us give the name of "sense-data" to the things that are immediately known in sensation: such things as colours, sounds, smells, hardnesses, roughnesses, and so on. We shall give the name "sensation" to the experience of being immediately aware of these things. . . . If we are to know anything about the table, it must be by means of the sense-data—brown colour, oblong shape, smoothness, etc.—which we associate with the table.

In chapter IV Russell introduces the term "acquaintance," and defines it as follows (pp. 46–47):

> We shall say that we have *acquaintance* with anything of which we are directly aware, without the intermediary of any process of inference or any knowledge of truths. Thus in the presence of my table I am acquainted with the sense-data that make up the appearance of my table—its colour, shape, hardness, smoothness, etc.

In this and the next few pages we learn that acquaintance is a general term for a relation with the following varieties: *sensation* of present sense-data (pp. 46–47), *memory* of past sense-data (pp. 48–49), *introspection*, or self-consciousness, of one's own mental activities, such as thoughts, feelings, and seeing the sun (pp. 49–50), and *conceiving* of universals, or general ideas, such as whiteness, brotherhood, and diversity (pp. 51–52).

Russell's list of examples of sense-data—"colours, sounds, smells, hardnesses, roughnesses, and so on"—seems to suggest that sense-data are particular instances of simple properties, and are in all cases simple. But a different suggestion emerges later in the book (PP, p. 114), when examples are given of judgments that arise "when the object of sense is complex." The two examples are "That patch of red is round," and "This is to the right of that," where "this" and "that" are seen simultaneously. These are contrasted with a judgment that "simply asserts the *existence* of the sense-datum, without in any way analyzing it": that expressed by "There is such-and-such a patch of red," or "There is that." The passage is puzzling. For unless "That patch of red is round" means "That patch is red and that patch is round," then the difference between it and the example of an apparently simple sense-datum is not clear. And if this is the meaning, then the sentence describes two sense-data and is not atomic. Furthermore, Russell notes that the two kinds of proposition "in the last analysis... may coalesce." As we shall see, the distinction between simple and complex sense-data is troublesome. In any case, the passage seems clearly to imply that there are complex sense-data, or objects of sense, which are objects of sensory acquaintance, and that not all sense-data are simple.

PP was a work designed for a general audience, and its standard of precision is occasionally below the high level Russell normally employed for professional audiences. In a brief paper entitled "The Nature of Sense-Data" (NSD), he gives his doctrine of sense-data a precise and terse formulation. First, he defines presentation and judgment (of sensation) (p. 76):

> Presentation (or acquaintance) is a two-term relation of a subject, or (better) an act, to a single (simple or complex) object, while judgment is a multiple relation of a subject or act to the several objects concerned in the judgment. From the fact that the presentation is a two-term relation, the question of truth or error cannot arise with regard to it: in any case of presentation there is a certain relation of an act to an object, and the question whether there is such an object cannot arise. In the case of judgment, error can arise; for although the several objects of the judgment cannot be illusory, they may not be related as the judgment believes that they are.

Next he defines "sensible presentations" as those having "objects simultaneous with the act of presentation," and finally defines "sense-data" as "objects of sensible presentations" (p. 77). He stipulates that the term "sensation" is to denote the "complex act-acquainted-with-object" (p. 77), and that the term "perception" is synonymous with "sensation" (p. 80). Thus "judgment of sensation" and "judgment of perception" (he normally prefers the latter) are synonyms in the paper. These definitions and explanations standardize the use of the ambiguous terms, "sensation" and "perception," during the preabandonment phase, and we will adopt them.

The preceding passage indicates that a subject can be acquainted with either a "simple" or a "complex object," from which it follows that sense-data can be either simple or complex. But examples are not provided. For these one must look elsewhere: in PP, and surprisingly, in volume 1 of *Principia Mathematica* (PM1). In PM1 (pp. 43–44) Russell carefully develops the logic of sensation, sense-data, and judgments of sensation, but under other labels: "perception" for "sensation" and "(perceived) object" for "sense-datum." He defines a complex object as follows (p. 44):

> We will give the name of "a *complex*" to any object such as "*a* in the relation *R* to *b*" or "*a* having the quality *q*" or "*a* and *b* and *c* standing in the relation *S*." Broadly speaking, a *complex* is anything which occurs in the universe and is not simple. We will call a judgment *elementary* when it merely asserts such things as "*a* has the relation *R* to *b*," "*a* has the quality *q*," or "*a* and *b* and *c* stand in the relation *S*." Then an *elementary* judgment is true when there is a corresponding complex, and false when there is no corresponding complex.

The types of complex objects mentioned here involve two-term and three-term — and by implication — *n*-term relations, and also qualities (properties). A specific example of an object involving a property can be found in an adjacent passage (pp. 43–44):

> A judgment does not have a single object, namely the proposition, but has several interrelated objects. That is to say, the relation which constitutes judgment is not a relation of two terms, namely the judging mind and the proposition, but is a relation of several terms, namely the mind and what are called the constituents of the proposition. That is, when we judge (say) "this is red," what occurs is a relation of three terms, the mind, and "this," and red. On the other hand, when we *perceive* "the redness of this," there is a relation of two terms, namely the mind and the complex object "the redness of this."

Specific examples of the relational type are not explicitly provided, but one is vividly suggested in the following passage (p. 43): "The complex object '*a*-in-the-relation-*R*-to-*b*' may be capable of being *perceived*; when perceived, it is perceived as one object. Attention may show that it is complex; we then *judge* that *a* and *b* stand in the relation *R*." An example of a complex object of this type is the fact described by the sentence "This is to the left of that."

The position in the preceding passages can be summarized as follows. A *sensa-*

tion (perception) is a two-term relation between a subject, S, and an object, which is called a sense-datum. Simple, or 0-term sense-data, are particulars, of which the most notable examples are instances of qualities, such as a particular instance of redness. Complex sense-data are n-term objects, where n is greater than or equal to 1, and may be called sensible facts. For the simplest complex sense-datum n = 1; e.g., this-having-the-quality-redness. For the next simplest, n = 2; e.g., this-being-to-the-left-of-that, or perhaps this-red-patch-being-to-the-left-of-that-blue-patch. And so on for any n. The *judgment of sensation* (perception) associated with a perception of a complex sense-datum is a multiple (more-than-two term) relation between a subject and (individually) the n constituents of the corresponding sense-datum. No judgment is associated with the perception of a simple sense-datum. The judgment is true if the corresponding sense-datum exists, false otherwise.

Sense-data are thus seen to be the basis and ground of our judgments of sensation. Simple sense-data are the constituent objects of our judgments, without which the judgments could not even exist. Complex sense-data are the facts that make the judgments true or false, the truth-conditions of the judgments. As Russell says in his pellucid essay, "On the Nature of Truth and Falsehood" (NTF, p. 157):

> We see that in the case of the judgment of perception there is, corresponding to the judgment, a certain complex which is perceived, as one complex, in the perception upon which the judgment is based. It is because there is such a complex object that the judgment is true. This complex object, in the cases where it is perceived, is the objective of the perception. Where it is not perceived, it is still the necessary and sufficient condition of the truth of the judgment.

The passages examined in the present section clearly suggest that sense-data are the *grounds* and *tests* for all our rational, conscious empirical knowledge. All such knowledge consists of well-founded, true judgments. The truth and falsity of every nonelementary empirical judgment is defined in terms of the truth and falsity of elementary judgments of sensation. And sense-data are the truth-conditions for every elementary judgment of sensation. Hence, sense-data are the *grounds* for all our empirical judgments. Furthermore, sense-data are the means by which our judgments are confirmed and disconfirmed. An elementary judgment of sensation is directly confirmed or disconfirmed as follows: the confirmer (who is the subject of the judgment, since sense-data are private) senses various sense-data and attends to their components and the relations between them. If attention reveals a sense-datum whose components correspond in type and number to the objects of the judgments, and whose relations are those which in the judgment are taken to obtain, then the judgment is confirmed. If no such sense-datum is perceived or noticed, then the judgment is, to some degree, disconfirmed. Nonelementary empirical judgments are indirectly confirmed or disconfirmed by determining (by means of inference) their agreement or disagreement with elementary empirical judgments. Hence, sense-data are the tests, or warrants, for all our empirical knowledge.

The Evolution of the Postabandonment Doctrine

Chapter XI of MPD contains Russell's own history of the development of his views on sensation and perception from abandonment until around 1959, when the book was published. Except for a few additional sentences scattered throughout the book, it constitutes his final published words on the subject. He describes his initial postabandonment position by quoting from AMi (MPD p. 136):

> When we do this [dispense with the subject as one of the actual ingredients of the world], the possibility of distinguishing the sensation from the sense-datum vanishes; at least I see no way of preserving the distinction. Accordingly the sensation that we have when we see a patch of colour simply *is* that patch of colour, an actual constituent of the physical world, and part of what physics is concerned with. A patch of colour certainly is not knowledge, and therefore we cannot say that pure sensation is cognitive. Through its psychological effects, it is the cause of cognitions, partly by being itself a sign of things that are correlated with it, as e.g., sensations of sight and touch are correlated, and partly by giving rise to images and memories after the sensation is faded.

It is tempting to interpret this passage as identifying the sense-datum with physical stimulation, for example, with the array of light at the retina in the case of vision. However, Russell may be using the word "physical" here to mean "nonmental," i.e., to refer to physical, physiological, or neurological processes. (It was this use that he made of the term in RSDP [section 4] in arguing that although sense-data are dependent on the body of the perceiver, they are not "mental.") The sensation, which is now held to be indistinguishable from the original sense-datum, is said to be the cause of the images and memories that are the psychological or cognitive ("mental") components of the causal process of perception. Now the most immediate such causes are neural excitations, so the best interpretation would seem to be this: sensing (acquaintance, awareness) is replaced by the having of a perceptual image, and the sense-datum is replaced by the neural excitation that causes the image, and is, confusingly, called a sensation.

If we assume that Russell uses "awareness" ("acquaintance") as roughly synonymous with "consciousness," then what he says in AMi (but does not allude to in MPD) about consciousness of sensation becomes clear. For, as with awareness, consciousness of a sensation (sense-datum) should consist in having an image of the sensation (sense-datum). And on pages 288–89 of AMi that is precisely what Russell says:

> When a sensation is followed by an image which is a "copy" of it, I think it may be said that the existence of the image constitutes consciousness of the sensation, provided it is accompanied by that sort of belief which, when we reflect upon it, makes us feel that the image is a "sign" of something other than itself. This is the sort of belief which, in the case of memory, we expressed in the words "this occurred."

The analysis suggested here can be stated as follows: S is conscious of X if and only if S has an image of X and a belief that refers the image to X. Where X is an image, consciousness of the image consists in having a second image and a belief referring it to the first. Here the one image can perhaps be a copy of the other. But where X is a sensation, consciousness of X consists, on our interpretation, in having an image of some neural excitation.

Since it is not clear in what respect an image can resemble or be a "copy" of neural excitation, Russell is right to put the word in quotation marks. An image can be said to be a copy of X in the sense of being referred by a belief to X. But it must be borne in mind that the referring belief, whose content is roughly "This occurred," does not imply that S was ever conscious of the "this" in any other sense than that of having an image of it. To be conscious of X in the sense of AMi is *not* to be conscious of it in the sense of awareness, the sense in which consciousness and its object are simultaneous. This point emerges in a passage three pages later (AMi, p. 292):

> A sensation which is remembered becomes an object of consciousness as soon as it begins to be remembered, which will normally be almost immediately after its occurrence (if at all); but while it exists it is not an object of consciousness.

Thus, from the perspective of the preabandonment position, in which S could be simultaneously aware of a sense-datum, the sensation is systematically elusive: S's attempt to grasp it while it occurs in an act of "consciousness" (awareness) necessarily fails. S can at best have an image of the sensation, and then only after it has occurred; and, to make matters worse, S can be conscious of the *image* of the sensation only in the sense of having another image of it, and so on ad infinitum. The sensation thus seems to remain forever out of S's cognitive grasp. In a moment I will suggest that it was this feature of his initial postabandonment view that made it ultimately unacceptable to Russell.

Russell's suggestion that he "dispense[s] with the subject" in AMi is a dramatic overstatement. His abandonment of sense-data accompanies his adoption of a position like that introduced by Hume and championed by James under the label *neutral monism*. On this doctrine both (mental) subjects and (physical) objects are analyzed into "neutral" elements that in themselves are neither mental or physical, and the difference between mental and physical objects is held to consist, not in their fundamental constituents, but in the way these are arranged. In Hume's version, the "neutral" elements are held to be ideas (images) and impressions (vivid ideas). Minds (selves, subjects) and bodies thus become "logical constructions formed out of materials not differing vitally and sometimes actually identical" (MPD, p. 139). Russell thus "dispenses with the subject" only in the sense that he replaces the simple subject by a complex subject composed of metaphysically neutral constituents.

In Russell's first version of his neutral monism (found in AMi), sensed and unsensed sensibilia are held to be the fundamental constituents of all things. In a later version (found in AMa) nonsensible events are added to sensibilia as fundamental constituents. In either version, acquaintance with sensibilia does not fit well into a neutral monist metaphysics, for acquaintance is assumed to be the act of a simple, unanalyzable ("pin point") subject. But an image caused by neural excitation fits in easily. The object called Russell is a collection of images, memories, and other events, whose subsets are arranged in causal chains. One such chain is Russell's memory of his pipe: the first event in this chain is a past impression of the pipe, and the last event is a present image resembling this impression. Another such chain is his visual perception of his pipe: the first event in this chain is light falling on the surface of the pipe, the next-to-last event is the neural excitation indirectly caused by the reflected light, and the last event is his present impression of a pipe.

The pipe itself is a collection of physical events, whose subsets are also arranged in causal chains. One of these chains ends with the optic array in the causal chain ending with Russell's visual impression of his pipe. The neural excitation produced by this optic array is clearly a part of Russell (though not necessarily a part of his conscious mind), and there may be reason for considering it part of the pipe as well. For when objects are analyzed into events, it is difficult to draw the boundaries between the perceiver and the perceived object. As Russell puts it in MPD (p. 139), "A sensation may be grouped with a number of other occurrences by a memory-chain, in which case it becomes part of a mind; or it may be grouped with its causal antecedents, in which case it appears as part of the physical world." (This use of "physical" is further evidence that the scope of the term is intended to include the neurophysiological, and that sensations are taken in MPD to be neurophysiological events—neural excitations, we have called them.)

To summarize, in AMi Russell replaced acquaintance with the having of an image and a feeling of belief, replaced the sense-datum with a neural event called a sensation, and, in neutral-monist fashion, replaced the simple subject with a complex subject composed of images, feelings, and other events arranged in the order that constitutes a mind. He retained the neutral-monist metaphysics throughout AMa, although he there added to it nonsensible events. But the theory ultimately failed to satisfy him, as he explains in MPD. For "new problems...arose as a consequence of the abandonment of sense-data," which required that "such words as 'awareness,' 'acquaintance,' and 'experience'...be redefined" (MPD, p. 136). The problems in question, Russell indicates, are concerned with how experience, or perception, provides knowledge of the external world (MPD, pp. 136-38), how empirical evidence—the evidence of the senses—is to be understood (MPD, pp. 136, 140). The difficulty, presumably, is that such knowledge seems ruled out by the new view that sensation is not cognitive, not knowledge. We saw that according to AMi the subject is not aware (simultaneously conscious) of the neural events that correspond to the original sense-datum. But if S is not aware of these neural events, then it would seem that he cannot have knowledge of them. And if he does not have knowledge of them, then it is difficult to understand how he can have knowledge of the external physical world, since the neural events in question comprise the causal interface between S and the external physical world. Whatever the precise nature of the difficulty, Russell says (MPD, p. 139) it forced him to the following conclusion:

> There is a duality...in any form of knowledge....We are aware of something, we have a recollection of something, and, generally, knowing is distinct from that which is known. This duality, after it has been banished from sensation, has to be somehow re-introduced.

Accordingly, he tells us, "In the *Inquiry into Meaning and Truth* ...I replaced 'acquaintance' by 'noticing,' which I accepted as an undefined term" (MPD, p. 140). He quotes three full pages of IMT (pp. 49-51) to describe the concept of noticing. We are warned that noticing is "very hard to define" and that "any very exact definition is likely to mislead," and are offered the following characterization (MPD, p. 142):

> "Noticing" is a matter of degree...[and] seems to consist mainly in isolating from the sensible environment. You may, for instance, in listening to a piece of music, deliberately notice only the part of the cello. You hear the rest, as is said, "unconsciously."...It seems then that the most immediate knowing of which we have experience [i.e., noticing] involves sensible presence plus something more....which may be called "attention"; this is partly a sharpening of the appropriate sense-organs, partly an emotional reaction. A sudden loud noise is almost sure to command attention, but so does a very faint sound that has emotional significance.

And then the following empiricist principle is laid down:

> Every empirical proposition is based upon one or more sensible occurrences that were noticed when they occurred, or immediately after, while they still formed part of the specious present. Such occurrences, we shall say, are "known" when they are noticed.

Thus knowing, or cognition—with its "duality" between the knowing and what is known—is reintroduced, and the basis of empirical knowledge is redescribed, as noticing.

Russell concludes his sketch of the view in IMT by summarizing various of its passages as follows (MPD, p. 143):

> "Perception" as opposed to "sensation" involves habit based upon past experience. We may distinguish sensation as that part of our total experience which is due to the stimulus alone, independently of past history. This is a theoretical core in the total occurrence. The total occurrence is always an interpretation in which the sensational core has accretions embodying habits. When you see a dog, the sensational core is a patch of colour stripped of all the adjuncts involved in recognizing it as a dog. You expect the patch of colour to move in the way that is characteristic of dogs, you expect that if it makes a noise it will bark or growl, and not crow like a cock. You are convinced that it could be touched and that it will not vanish into thin air, but has a future and a past. I do not mean that all this is "conscious," but its presence is shown by the astonishment that you would feel if things worked out otherwise. It is these accretions that turn a sensation into a perception.

Russell uses the sentence "There is a canoid patch of color" as a shorthand description of the pattern of colors constituting the sensational core of perception, intending no inference or implication whatever concerning the character of the object that has the pattern, in particular, no implication that it is anything like a canine (IMT, pp. 21, 139). We will use the phrase in the same way, i.e., as a convenient abbreviation for some such sentence as "There is an irregular, approximately oblong brown patch with a white spot at the upper end (the eye) and a long narrow bottom end (the tail) inside a green patch (the lawn on which the dog sits)."

These passages in MPD contain Russell's last published words on the postabandonment evolution of his theory of sensation and perception, but they are tantalizingly incomplete. For one expects, and yet fails, to find in them a definite answer to the question of whether Russell really did or did not abandon sense-data. The simple subject has definitely been abandoned, and replaced by the complex subject, analyzed as a collection of images, expectations, beliefs, and feelings. Sensing (acquaintance, awareness) has been replaced by noticing, and sense-data have apparently been replaced by experiences, or the sensational cores of experiences. Whether these replacements constitute "abandonment" of sensing and sense-data is not at all clear. Not surprisingly, then, answers to the question of whether Russell really abandoned sense-data have ranged over the entire spectrum from definite affirmative to definite negative. I now consider answers in each of these categories.

Some Interpretations of the Abandonment

A useful example of the definite affirmative answer can be found in Wesley Salmon's paper, "Memory and Perception in *Human Knowledge*" (1974). In brief, Salmon argues that Russell abandoned the infallible awareness or sensing of sense-data in favor of the fallible perceptual experience of external objects. I paraphrase passages in which he expounds what he takes to be Russell's postabandonment position:

> Sensations are unvarnished experiences, facts, which cannot in themselves be mistaken, and have a kind of incorrigibility. But they do not constitute knowledge, for there is no distinction between the knowing of a sensation and the sensation known. Sensations, though not premises, are causes of the judgments of perception and memory which are the premises of our knowledge. Perceptions, unlike sensations, involve interpretations which go far beyond what is immediately given in sensory experience. For example, when we see a canoid patch of color, we interpret it to be a dog; and this interpretation or inference may be false. Perceptions are therefore fallible. It is such fallible perceptions, not infallible sensations, which provide the premises for scientific inference.... Russell accepts neither sensations nor reports of sensations as premises of scientific inference.... Perceptual premises are comparable to premises provided by memory. Just as the putative object of my memory experience is a person, dog or table, and not some mythical sense-datum, so the putative object of my perceptual experience is a person, dog, or table. And in both cases the beliefs produced by the experience, and any statements corresponding to these beliefs, are about external objects. (pp. 140–141, 142 n. 1, 145–146)

This interpretation incorporates at least one central feature of Russell's initial preabandonment position in AMi, namely, the dictum that a sensation is not knowledge, not a cognition (premise), but rather a cause of cognition. But it is difficult to see how it can be a correct description of his final position in IMT and HK. For it entails that the canoid patch of color in Russell's example is not a datum for knowledge, and that the statement "There is a canoid patch of color" is not a premise; instead, the perception of a dog is the datum, and "There is a dog which has such and such visual properties" is the premise. And there are at least two objections to such an interpretation.

First, the only good reasons to hold that "There is a canoid patch of color" is not a premise are that (1) it is inferred, or (2) it does not describe a present experience; obviously neither of these conditions is built into the example. Russell imagines himself to be the perceiver and assumes that the perceiver notices a part or aspect of his perceptual experiences correctly described by "There is a canoid patch of color." How otherwise would he know how to describe the sensational

core? Consequently, the example provides us with one of those "differences that were noticed" on which "empirical propositions [are] based." Russell
sometimes seems to maintain that the sensational core of a percept is a theoretical, in-practice-unnoticeable feature of the perception [see below]. (Even if it did
follow from this doctrine that descriptions of sensational cores are not premises
of empirical knowledge, it does not follow that "There is a dog" is not such a
premise.)

Second, in IMT Russell virtually says that the sensational core of the perception is a datum (p. 139):

> The judgments that common sense bases upon perception, such as "there is a
> dog," usually go beyond the present datum, and may therefore be refuted by
> subsequent evidence.... That is why, in the search for data, we are driven to
> analysis: we are seeking a core which is logically independent of other occur-
> rences. When you think you see a dog, what is really given in perception may
> be expressed in the words "there is a canoid patch of colour." No previous or
> subsequent occurrence, and no experience of others can prove the falsehood
> of this proposition.

The search for data is a search for a sensational core that is logically independent
of other occurrences. Since no experience other than the patch of color can dis-
prove the proposition "There is a canoid patch of color" the patch is in this case
the datum sought; and the proposition describing it is a premise for empirical
knowledge—contrary to Salmon.

There is also a passage in HK (p. 167) where Russell describes inferences to
airplanes, birds, walls, houses, and roads from what he calls "the sensational datum," followed by a passage in which he says (pp. 170–71):

> We must exclude from our list of data not only the things that we consciously
> infer, but all that is obtained by animal [unconscious, spontaneous] infer-
> ence...for knowledge of things outside our own minds...it is necessary to
> regard only sensations as data.

These passages are further evidence that after the alleged abandonment, Russell
does not hold that ordinary, unanalyzed perceptions are data. And they raise additional doubts as to whether sense-data were ever abandoned, or at least doubts
as to whether they have not been reintroduced. For what is the difference between
the "sensational data" of which Russell speaks in HK, and the "sense-data" that
were allegedly abandoned, besides a difference in name? It is sufficiently difficult
to find a significant difference that it is not unreasonable to answer the question
whether Russell abandoned sense-data with a definite negative.

A close approximation to this answer is given by no less an authority than A.
J. Ayer. In his book, *Russell* (1972), we find the following passage (pp. 73–74):

. Wade Savage

Analysis of Mind... Russell gives up his belief in the existence of mental [sensations?]. This is partly because of his view that the subject, to which they are [ascrib]ed, is a logical fiction, and partly... because he has been persuaded that [no s]uch things are empirically detectable. No longer believing that there are [sen]sations, in the sense in which he had previously used the term, he cannot *a fortiori* believe that they have any objects; and he therefore also denies that [t]here are sense-data. But though he subsequently speaks of himself as having "emphatically abandoned" sense-data at this time [in MPD, p. 245], the change in his view is much less radical than this would suggest. He did cease to employ the term "sense-datum," but he continued to speak of percepts, to which he attributed the same properties as he had attributed to sense-data, except that of being correlative to sensory acts.

Before we assess this interpretation, a comment on terminology is in order. Russell usually uses "sensational datum," "sensational core," "sensible occurrence," and "sensible fact" where he once would have used "sense-datum." He frequently uses "percept" in the same way (especially in AMa), but he uses it equally often to denote the unanalyzed, unreduced perceptual experience (see IMT throughout, and HK, part III, book IV). Because of its ambiguity, we will avoid the term "percept."

Ayer's interpretation is dubious. He claims that, except for being correlative to a sensory act, all properties once attributed to sense-data are later attributed to sensational data, which suggests that Russell merely excised the offending subject and act of acquaintance, and left the original sense-datum — re-named — with all its other original properties to be used in the original way as a datum, as a certain, immediate, precise datum for empirical knowledge. And there are two objections to the suggestion.

First, it is difficult to understand why, if Ayer's suggestion is correct, Russell so consistently and adamantly maintained that he "abandoned" sense-data in AMi. Ayer himself calls attention to the fact that in a 1958 review of Ryle's *Concept of Mind* (reprinted in MPD) Russell says (MPD, p. 245):

> A second point upon which I am in agreement with him [Ryle] is the rejection of sense-data. I believed in these at one time, but emphatically abandoned them in 1921 [with a footnote to AMi, p. 141].

It is difficult to reconcile this emphatic statement with Ayer's suggestion that Russell retained the sense-datum, while merely stripping away the act of acquaintance.

Second, there is substantial evidence from a number of his writings that Russell replaced sense-data with entities having different properties. Earlier, we suggested the following description of the difference as a first approximation: before abandonment, sense-data were held to be *absolutely* certain (infallible, indubitable), immediate (uninferred, self-evident), and precise (analyzed, simple); after abandonment, they were held to be *relatively* certain, immediate, and precise. Let us turn to the texts to see whether they confirm this interpretation.

Are Sense-Data Certain, Infallible, Indubitable?

Several passages in PP state that sense-data are indubitable and completely certain. For example, "It is not possible to doubt the sense-data [associated with the table]" (p. 47); and also (p. 19):

> The certainty of our knowledge of our own experiences does not have to be limited in any way to allow for exceptional cases.... When I look at my table and see a brown colour, what is quite certain at once is... "a brown colour is being seen."

However, it must be borne in mind that the book was written for a popular audience and is occasionally imprecise. These statements seem to be cases in point, for they fail to take account of the distinction between and nature of sensation and judgment, and they are not informed by any analysis of doubt and certainty, which is plainly needed.

Such an analysis is provided in TK (part II, chapter IV). As previously noted, sensation is a two-term relation of acquaintance between a subject and a (simple or complex) object, and judgment is a multiple relation between a subject and the constituents of a complex. In TK Russell adds a new term to the relation—the logical form of the complex—and analyzes understanding, judgment, and belief and disbelief similarly. Since none of the points in this section turns on the inclusion or omission of this constituent, we will omit it for simplicity. Consider the case in which the complex associated with the judgment is a-to-the-left-of-b, or simply, a-L-b; and let s be the subject of the judgment. Then understanding can be symbolically represented as $U(s, a, L, b)$, judgment and belief (which are the same) as $J(s, a, L, b)$ or $B(s, a, L, b)$, and disbelief (which is not taken to be belief in the contradictory) as $D(s, a, L, b)$. (Russell does not use these symbols.) There are many "degrees of belief," or "degrees of uncertainty," ranging all the way from "complete suspense of judgment" to "full belief," or complete certainty; and there are many "degrees of disbelief," or "degrees of uncertainty," ranging all the way from "complete suspense of judgment" to "full disbelief," or "complete uncertainty" (pp. 142–43). Each such degree is a "different relation" (p. 143). By implication, Russell defines doubt, in one sense of the term, as a degree of certainty or uncertainty (considerably?) less than complete certainty or uncertainty; and, in another sense of the term, as an alternation, or vacillation, between belief and disbelief. For simplicity we will consider only doubt in the first sense, since all our points can be restated in terms of the second sense.

On the preceding analysis the following definitions of indubitability and certainty are natural. It is *psychologically indubitable to s* that aLb if and only if it is psychologically impossible that $D(s, a, L, b)$. It is *epistemologically indubitable to s* that aLb if and only if it is epistemologically inappropriate that $D(s, a, L, b)$. Certainty has a strong and a weak sense. In the strong sense it is *completely certain to s* that aLb if and only if it is indubitable to s that aLb. In the weak sense, it is *completely certain to s* that aLb if and only if $B_{max}(s, a, L, b)$, where B_{max} is full belief (complete certainty). We say "psychologically" impossible and "psychologically" necessary, since presumably any belief relation is logically possible. Accordingly, the statement that sense-data are indubitable, or completely certain in the strong sense, should mean that if a subject senses a sense-datum then the corresponding doubt is psychologically impossible, or epistemologically inappropriate. And the statement that sense-data are completely certain in the weak sense should mean that if a subject senses a sense-datum then the corresponding belief is maximal, or that it is epistemologically appropriate for it to be maximal. Are sense-data indubitable and completely certain in these senses? There is no direct answer in TK, or in any of Russell's other writings, to these questions. Indeed, the questions are never raised in this form. As we shall see, arriving at any answer requires both clarification of the question and considerable interpretation.

We turn now to *infallibility*. Because sensation is a two-term relation between a subject and an object, it is not capable of truth or error, and it is therefore misleading to say that sensation is infallible. For "infallible" may mean "true always" or even "true of necessity"; or it may mean "neither true nor false." And it is only in the latter, uninteresting sense that sensation is infallible in Russell's doctrine. It is only judgments, or beliefs (and propositions?), that can properly be said to be true or false, as Russell makes abundantly clear in chapter XII of PP and elsewhere; consequently, only judgments can properly be said to be infallible in any interesting sense. We will attempt to confine the discussion to the interesting senses.

It is clear that most of our judgments are fallible, and that many of them are or have been false. For example, my judgment that the table is to the left of the chair is fallible. The table and chair are known to me merely by description; consequently, I cannot base my judgment on acquaintance with either object. My judgment is obtained by inference from my sense-data, and such inferences are highly fallible. But consider judgments whose nonrelational objects are objects of acquaintance (by "objects" is meant terms other than the subject); for example, my judgment that a is to the left of b, where a and b are patches of color in my visual field. (Assume that the judgment is not linguistically or cognitively mediated, i.e., does not involve the words, "a," "b," "left of," or any others, nor any ideas, concepts, or representations of the objects of acquaintance.) Is this judgment infallible? Clearly not, for there may exist no corresponding sense-datum to make the judgment true. Consider, then, the same judgment where there does exist a corresponding sense-datum. It follows from the description of the case, together with Russell's definition of "true judgment," that the judgment is true.

To express this fact by saying that the judgment is infallible, or that it "must" be true, is to say something misleading and to employ an uninteresting sense of infallible. (As we will see, it appears that on occasion Russell makes this misleading statement.) The interesting question in this case is whether the process by which the judgment was produced is infallible, i.e., *completely reliable*.

We must distinguish between a *direct* process of this type and an *indirect* process. In a direct process, the judgment that aLb (to continue with our example) is produced by the sensation of a-L-b without any intermediate events that causally influence the judgment. Russell does not discuss this case. The explanation may be that he believes judgments of sensation are never directly produced, but are produced through the intermediate process of *analysis*. He discusses analysis in a passage of PM previously cited. He defines a judgment of perception (sensation) as a judgment derived by attention and analysis from a—presumably corresponding—perception (sensation), and then says (PMT, p. 43):

> A judgment of perception, according to the above definition, must be true. This does not mean that, in a judgment which *appears* to be one of perception, we are sure of not being in error, since we may err in thinking that our judgment has really been derived merely by analysis of what was perceived. But if our judgment has been so derived, it must be true.

(Only analysis is mentioned in the part of the passage quoted earlier, and only attention is mentioned in the statement of the definition of a judgment of perception. As we will discover, Russell's later treatment of analysis held it to be a complex process involving many acts of attention. Therefore we may refer to the process of deriving judgments from sensation simply as that of analysis.)

Now why does Russell assert that the judgment of sensation "must be true"? It is not because a judgment of sensation is by definition accompanied by a corresponding sensation, and is therefore true by definition, but rather because he believes that analysis is completely reliable. The process of deriving a judgment from a corresponding sensation includes, at a minimum: (a) sensing the corresponding sense-datum, (b) analyzing the sense-datum, and (c) forming the judgment. If (1) no extraneous process intervenes between (b) and (c), so that the judgment is formed on the basis of the analysis, and (2) no extraneous process intervenes between (a) and (b), so that the analysis is of the sense-datum in question, then, if analysis is reliable, the judgment of sensation is true—by definition: by definition of the terms, "on the basis of," "analysis of," and "reliable." Russell's statement that the judgment of sensation "must be true" is misleading, and possibly a little confused. It may in part be an expression of the definition just stated, but it is mainly an expression of his thesis that analysis is reliable. For suppose that conditions (1) and (2) are satisfied, and assume that analysis is reliable; then the judgment of sensation "must be true," in the sense that from these assumptions it follows logically that the judgment of sensation is true.

The reason the subject cannot be "sure" that the judgment is true is that some extraneous process may have intervened between (a) and (b), or between (b) and (c), with the effect that the analysis is not of the sense-datum in question, or is not the basis of the judgment. Either effect makes it to some degree likely that the judgment does not correspond to the sensation that led to it. But, one wants to interject, suppose the subject senses the sense-datum, a-to-the-left-of-b, and simultaneously judges that a is to the left of b: can't the subject then be sure, indeed absolutely certain, that the judgment is true? One reason for a negative answer is that the subject's belief that her judgment is true results from an inference based on analysis of the corresponding complexes, and the inference (if not the analysis) may be in error. We will return to this question under our discussion of self-evidence, after an examination of analysis.

Is Analysis of Sense-Data Reliable?

As we saw in the previous section, Russell implies in PM that the analysis involved in the production of judgments of sensation is completely reliable. In PP he appears to give up this doctrine. He distinguishes what he calls "absolute self-evidence" from a second sort, and defines the former as the property possessed by a "truth" when the corresponding fact is perceived. Then he says (p. 137):

> Although this sort of self-evidence is an absolute guarantee of truth, it does not enable us to be *absolutely* certain, in the case of any given judgment, that the judgment in question is true. Suppose we first perceive the sun shining, which is a complex fact, and thence proceed to make the judgment "the sun is shining." In passing from the perception to the judgment, it is necessary to analyse the given complex fact: we have to separate out "the sun" and "shining" as constituents of the fact. In this process it is possible to commit an error; hence even where a *fact* has the first or absolute kind of self-evidence, a judgment believed to correspond to the fact is not absolutely infallible, because it may not really correspond to the fact.

Whether Russell gives up his earlier doctrine in this passage depends on whether he intends "The sun is shining" to be compared with a sense-datum description. It seems that he does so intend it because he treats "the sun" and "shining" as components of the fact, just as he treats the referents of "this" and "white" as components of the sense-datum described by "This is white." Furthermore, the passage from the perception of the shining sun to the judgment that the sun is shining is comparable to the passage from the perception of a white patch to the judgment that the patch is white. If he thus intends the example, then "analysis" here denotes what it denoted in PM – the decomposition of a complex into its constituents, and he has abandoned his earlier doctrine that analysis is completely reliable.

Strictly speaking, however, the fact described by "The sun is shining" is not a fact that can be sensed; it is not a sense-datum. The term "sun" does not denote an object of acquaintance but is rather a covert description ("the blinding ball of light"); and the term "shining" does not denote a single universal but rather a complex of universals (casting of light). If the example is intended to be understood in this way, then analysis includes the process of translating the sentence "The sun is shining" into an equivalent sentence whose nonlogical terms denote only objects of acquaintance, by appropriate substitution of definition descriptions, variables, and quantifiers. For example, it might be translated into the sentence "There is one and only one x such that x is a great blinding ball of white light that periodically travels across the sky and x is casting light on the earth"; but this is not yet the final analysis, since it contains the covert descriptions "sky" and "earth." On this interpretation, the term "analysis" does not mean in PP what it means in PM. For in PM the process does not include the preceding process of translation; it is solely the process of decomposing a sense-datum into its components, For example, it is the process of decomposing the sense-datum described by "This is to the left of that," where "this" and "that" denote patches in the visual field, into the one patch, the other patch, and the relation of being-to-the-left-of. If "analysis" denotes different processes in the two works, then of course the unreliability of analysis in the sense of PP does not entail the unreliability of analysis in the sense of PM; and Russell may not have changed his view.

Obviously we need to distinguish two senses of "analysis," or types of analysis: *translational analysis*, which consists in translating a sentence into an equivalent whose nonlogical terms denote objects of acquaintance, and *decompositional analysis*, which consists in isolating the components of a complex fact with which one is acquainted, presumably by attending to the components. (There are still other types or senses of analysis in Russell: the analysis of a science required to discover its axioms; the philosophical analysis, or explication, of a concept; etc.). And then we need to examine Russell's views concerning the reliability of these two kinds of analysis one at a time.

Russell never explicitly discusses the reliability of translational analysis, unless it is in the immediately preceeding passage from PP. It seems obvious, however, that translational analysis is not completely reliable, given Russell's standards for reliability. For it is entirely possible that a person performing such an analysis will make any of a number of mistakes—employ an inappropriate description, insert an ordinary name rather than a logically proper name, make a mistake in logic (say, use the wrong quantifier or connective)—and consequently propose a translation that is not equivalent to the original. And it is not possible for the analyzer to be completely certain of not having made one of the possible mistakes.

Russell provides an extended treatment of decompositional analysis in TK (part II, chapter II), a treatment, however, that is confusing and apparently incomplete. He defines analysis as "the discovery of the constituents and the manner of combination of a given complex" (p. 119). His chief example is the analysis of a perceived capital letter T. The complex here consists of a horizontal stroke on top of a vertical stroke. He points out that "mere selective attention, which makes us aware of what is in fact part of a previously given complex, without making us aware of its being a part, is not analysis" (p. 123). He suggests that "the problem of analysis is the problem of transferring attention from the whole of a complex to the parts," and fleshes out this suggestion by distinguishing simple perception from complex perception of a complex. The former is defined as "attention to the whole combined with acquaintance with its parts," and the latter as "acquaintance with a whole combined with attention to its parts" (p. 125, italics omitted). (He clearly implies at the beginning of the book (pp. 8–9) that attention is a species of acquaintance, and at one point says: "attention is a kind of intensified acquaintance"; p. 162.) He then proposes that analysis of a complex consists in (a) simple perception of the complex, (b) complex perception of the complex at a later time, and (c) knowledge that the object of the one perception is identical with the object of the other (pp. 125–26). This knowledge is said to require attention to the object of the complex perception and, *simultaneously*, attention to the object of the (now past) simple perception (pp. 126, 127); and such attention is held to be possible (p. 126).

But Russell assesses his proposal as unsatisfactory: "Thus far nothing effective has been done in the way of analyzing analysis" (p. 127); and there he abruptly leaves the matter. Why he was dissatisfied is not at all clear, but the text provides good support for the following explanation. He believed that (1) a subject can simultaneously attend to a complex, C, and to its parts, c_1, c_2, etc., without perceiving c_i-part-of-C; and that (2) analysis of the complex requires perceiving c_i-part-of-C; and observed that (3) analysis of these complexes involving the part-whole relation is the original problem reappearing, still unsolved, in what is the beginning of a regress. If this is his objection, then a reply is possible. We can accept (1) and (2), incorporate them into the analysis of analysis, and deny (3). Although analysis of a perceived complex C, requires *perceptions* of the constituents as parts of the complex (of c_i-part-of-C), it does not require *analysis* of the objects (c_i-part-of-C) of these perceptions; hence there is no regress. (One difficulty that Russell does not mention, and we will not pursue, is whether it is psychologically possible for a subject to attend simultaneously to a complex and to each—or even one—of its parts.) Thus analysis consists of a sequence of perceptions each consisting of a sensation of c_i-part-of-C, attentive acquaintance with c_i, and attentive acquaintance with C. If the sequence contains a perception for each c_i, then the analysis is complete.

Analysis, thus analyzed, would seem to be completely reliable on Russell's view. For it is not possible for a subject to attend to a complex, C, or to a part, c_i, unless C and c_i exist; nor is it possible for a subject to perceive c_i-part-of-C unless c_i is a part of C. This conclusion will not seem correct unless it is understood that analysis involves only perceptions containing sensations of part-whole facts and acts of attentive acquaintance, and does not require any *judgments* corresponding to these. If, for example, a judgment corresponding to the subject's sensation of c_i-part-of-C were required, and the production of this judgment required analysis, an infinite regress of analysis would ensue. But no such judgment is required. Analysis then is completely reliable. However, if Russell's point in PM1 (p. 43; quoted earlier) is correct, then it does not follow that the subject can be (absolutely) certain, with regard to a given judgment produced by analysis, that it is true. For the subject cannot be (absolutely) certain that the judgment was produced by a process of analysis appropriate to that judgment. For example, the sequence of perceptions leading to the judgment that a is to the left of b might contain a sensation of some irrelevant part-whole fact: a-part-of-C', or b-part-of-C'', where C' is the complex a-left-of-c and C'' is the complex a-on-top-of-b.

Are Sense-Data Self-evident?

Russell introduces the term "self-evident" in chapter XI of PP to qualify "truths" (propositions, apparently) that either have not been inferred or cannot be inferred from others. In chapter XIII he sets out to distinguish two sorts of self-evident truths, one of which "ensures infallibility" (p. 135). Then, in a confusing passage (pp. 136–38) he distinguishes between "self-evidence of truths" and the "sort of self-evidence... which belongs to judgments in the first instance, and is not derived from direct perception of a fact as a single complex whole." The first sort of self-evidence is said to be "absolute." A serviceable interpretation of these definitions takes "truths" to mean either "propositions" or "judgments" (though in one place it seems to mean "facts"); and takes "direct perception" to mean "perception (sensation) unaccompanied by analysis of the sensed fact." Thus *absolute* self-evidence is a property of propositions, and *relative* self-evidence (as it seems appropriately called) is a property of judgments of perception (sensation) that have been obtained by analysis of a sensed fact. Absolute self-evidence is defined as follows (p. 137):

> In all cases where we know by acquaintance a complex fact consisting of certain terms in a certain relation, we say that the truth that these terms are so related has the first or absolute kind of self-evidence, and in these cases the judgment that the terms are so related *must* be true. Thus this sort of self-evidence is an absolute guarantee of truth.

Russell's remarks on the previous page make it clear that the truth in question is self-evident to the subject whose sensory acquaintance is directed upon the fact, or sense-datum. So the definition is this: a truth (proposition, judgment), P, is self-evident to a subject, S, if the fact that corresponds to P *is sensed by S*. The assertion that the judgment "must be true" is, on this reading, a misleading way of stating this definition. The assertion that self-evidence is an "absolute guarantee of truth" surely means that self-evidence provides absolute assurance, or certainty, of truth. More precisely, it should mean that if the fact which corresponds to P is sensed by S, then S can be absolutely certain that P.

In the passage immediately following the one just quoted Russell says: "But although this sort of self-evidence is an absolute guarantee of truth, it does not enable us to be *absolutely* certain, in the case of any given judgment, that the judgment in question is true," and he goes on to explain that in the analysis leading to the judgment "it is possible to commit an error." This passage seems blatantly to contradict its predecessor, and it is difficult to explain away the appearance. One possible explanation (among others) is that by "any given judgment" Russell refers to the case in which the judgment was obtained by analysis and the subject is no longer sensing the corresponding fact and does not remember whether one was sensed nor what it was. But why focus on cases where error is possible? Surely a subject can sense and analyze a fact and simultaneously judge that it obtains. In these cases isn't the judgment infallible and the subject absolutely certain that it is true?

This imprecise question can be precisely stated with the help of the analytic apparatus of doubt and certainty previously developed. The subject's judgment (belief) that aLb is the complex J-s-a-L-b, and the sensed complex is a-L-b. Let T denote the relation of correspondence, or truth. The statement that the subject doubts that her judgment corresponds to the sense-datum can then be expressed symbolically as (*) $D(s, J$-s-a-L-b, T, a-L-$b)$. And the statement that the subject is completely confident that her judgment corresponds to the sense-datum can be expressed as (**) $B_{\max}(s, J$-s-a-L-b, T, a-L-$b)$. To say that the subject can be certain in the weak sense that her judgment corresponds to the sense-datum can be taken to mean either that (1) (**) is psychologically possible, or that (2) (**) is epistemologically correct. Both (1) and (2) seem clearly true, since (**) agrees with the assumed data of s's acquaintance. To say that the subject can be certain in the strong sense that her judgment corresponds to the sense-datum can be taken to mean either that (3) (*) is psychologically impossible, or that (4) (*) is epistemologically incorrect. It may seem equally clear that (*) disagrees with the assumed data of s's acquaintance, and that therefore both (3) and (4) are true. However, although we assumed that s is acquainted with J-s-a-L-b and with a-L-b, we did not thereby assume that s is acquainted with the correspondence relation, T, or with the fact $(J$-s-a-L-$b)$-T-$(a$-L-$b)$, which would make (**) a true belief and (*) a false disbelief (doubt). And, indeed, there is a serious question as to whether this latter assumption could ever be true. For it may be that the relation of correspondence is not the sort of relation with which one can be acquainted; perhaps it is known only by description, and the belief in (**) is obtained by inference. If the latter assumption is never true, then judgments of sensation are not certain (infallible) in the strong, and interesting, sense.

Let us take stock. In the preabandonment period, a sense-datum is the (simple or complex) object in a two-term relation of sensation (acquaintance) with a subject. Thus defined, neither a *sense-datum* nor a *sensation* is meaningfully said to be certain, immediate, precise, or any of the opposites. A *judgment* based on a sensation is in some sense inferred from the sensation and mediated by its analysis; and no judgment of sensation is infallible, because even if analysis is infallible (which may be doubted) other errors of inference are possible. Consequently, the interpretation that preabandonment sense-data are certain, immediate, and precise and postabandonment sense-data only relatively so is unacceptable. It is tempting to advance the alternative interpretation that Russell abandoned sense-data and the sensations in which they are terms, and was left only with judgments of sensations (or their counterparts), which in both the pre- and postabandonment periods were neither absolutely certain, immediate, nor precise. But postabandonment texts do not support this interpretation either, as we shall see in what follows.

Russell's Final Theory of Empirical Knowledge

Russell's final theory of knowledge is contained in IMT and HK. The linguistic mode of speech is more evident in these than in earlier works, and the distinction between data and inference is often drawn as a distinction between propositions or statements. For example, in IMT data are defined as "propositions for which the evidence is not wholly derived from their logical relation to other propositions" (p. 125). But data are also defined nonlinguistically: in HK as "beliefs for which no further reason can be given" (p. 166), and in MPD as "all the things of which we are aware without inference" (p. 23). Furthermore, Russell makes it clear that beliefs of the datum variety do not require language, for example, the belief involved in "direct sensible knowledge" of a "sensible" fact, such as that expressed by "A loud bang is (or has been, or will be) taking place"; and the beliefs involved in immediate memory or immediate expectation of this sensible fact (HK, pp. 98-99). Remote memory is said to require "an auditory image accompanied by a feeling which could be (but need not be) expressed in the words 'that occurred' "; but he doubts that expectation of the distant future is possible without words (HK, p. 99). He remarks that "belief about something outside my own experience seems usually only possible through the help of language" (HK, p. 99). So he might claim that many inferences must be in the form of propositions or statements. But clearly data need not be.

The chief source for Russell's views on data in HK is part V, chapter VI, entitled "Degrees of Credibility," especially sections C and D. He distinguishes between the view that "premises," or "data," of knowledge "are certain in their own right," and the ("coherence") view that "since no knowledge is certain, there are no data, but our rational beliefs form a closed system in which each part lends support to every other part" (p. 391). His view, which is said to be a "compromise" between the other two, is "that a datum may be uncertain" (p. 391), "may be uncertain in a greater or lesser degree" (p. 395). Degrees of certainty, in one sense of the term, are identified with as degrees of credibility. Whether any datum or any belief or proposition is completely certain, completely credible, is left undecided (p. 381):

> Whether any degree of doubtfulness attaches to the least dubitable of our beliefs is a question with which we need not at present concern ourselves; it is enough that any proposition concerning which we have rational grounds for some degree of belief or disbelief can, in theory, be placed in a scale between certain truth and certain falsehood. Whether these limits are themselves to be included we may leave an open question.

We will return to this open question momentarily.

Russell holds that there is an important connection between mathematical probability and degree of credibility. "The connection is this: When, in relation to all the available evidence, a proposition has a certain mathematical probability, then this measures its degree of credibility" (p. 381). He believes, however, that the two notions are not equivalent, since degree of credibility has wider application than mathematical probability. For the class of cases in which mathematical probability given all the available evidence measures degree of credibility, the question of whether there are completely credible (certain) or completely incredible (doubtful) propositions is the question whether the probability of the propositions can take the value 1 or 0. The question thus becomes partly technical. Every reasonable probability function assigns 0 to contradictory statements and 1 to logically true statements. Whether these values can be assigned to other types of statements—and in particular to evidence statements—is controversial. So the technical considerations do not settle Russell's open question.

In accordance with his proposal that data may be uncertain, or not completely credible, Russell defines a datum as "a proposition which has some degree of rational credibility on its own account, independently of any argument derived from other propositions" (p. 392). Data are shown to have degrees by citing three cases: faint perception (examples: a departing airplane, a star dimming in the gathering light of dawn), uncertain memory, and dim awareness of logical connection. Rational credibility on its own account, or in its own right, as Russell often says, is what he calls "independent credibility" in IMT (p. 125) and "self-evidence" earlier in HK (pp. 156–57). It is what in PP (p. 138) he called "the second sort of self-evidence," and in TK (part II, chapter 7) "degrees of certainty."

The pervasiveness of the concept of self-evidence in his philosophy suggests that it is indispensable. And, indeed, Russell says after a critique of Descartes's criterion of clearness and distinctness: "This does not dispose of the concept of 'self-evidence'. . . I do not think we can entirely dispense with self-evidence" (p. 156). Self-evidence was held to be indispensable in the early epistemology of PP and TK because of the following consideration. Every proposition that is known to be true is one for which there is evidence itself known to be true, that is, one for which there is evidence for which there is evidence, and so on. Consequently, if a proposition, P, is known to be true, then one of the following must be true. (i) P is the last element of an infinite linear sequence of propositions, each nonterminal element of which is evidence for its immediate successor. (ii) P is the last element of a finite or infinite circular sequence of propositions with a circular initial segment, each nonterminal element of which is evidence for its immediate successor. (P may or may not be an element of the circular segment.) (iii) P is the last element of a finite sequence of propositions, the first element of which is self-evident. If (i) or (ii) is true, then the proposition is not known; hence (iii) is true. Therefore, if any proposition is known to be true, there are self-evident propositions.

In HK Russell offers an argument reminiscent of the preceding one above. Having defined a datum as a proposition with some degree of independent credibility, he reasons as follows (p. 392):

> It is obvious that the conclusion of an argument cannot derive from the argument a higher degree of credibility than that belonging to the premises: consequently, if there is such a thing as rational belief, there must be rational beliefs not wholly based on argument.

He notes that "it does not follow that there are propositions which owe *none* of their credibility to argument." The conclusion is rather that if there are rational beliefs then there are credible beliefs that do not owe all their credibility to inference. How does the conclusion follow? Assume that there are rational beliefs; and assume (the premise) that no conclusion can obtain from its premise a higher credibility; it is supposed to follow that there are independently credible beliefs. But how? Case (ii) — a circle of evidence — is possible given these assumptions if the members of the circular sequence all have the same credibility. Case (i) — an infinite sequence of evidence — is possible given these assumptions if every element of the sequence has no higher credibility than any predecessor. To rule out these subcases Russell must employ some additional, as yet unstated, premise.

The needed premise can be gleaned from his major objection to coherence theories, made as early as PP (p. 122). The objection is that there are indefinitely many coherent systems of belief, between which we cannot decide on the basis of their coherence alone. In other words there are indefinitely many sequences of premises and conclusions, between which we cannot decide except on the basis of independent credibility of their elements (first premises, or if there are none, important conclusions). A system of beliefs supported only by other beliefs in the system is not rational: it hangs in air, without support.

It is just such a metaphor that Russell uses to describe the manner in which a rational system of belief can be supported, or confirmed, by uncertain data having some independent credibility (HK, pp. 395-96):

Given a number of propositions, each having a fairly high degree of intrinsic credibility, and given a system of inferences by virtue of which these various propositions increase each other's credibility, it may be possible in the end to arrive at a body of interconnected propositions having, as a whole, a very high degree of credibility. Within this body, some are only inferred, but none are only premises, for those which are premises are also conclusions. The edifice of knowledge may be compared to a bridge resting on many piers, each of which not only supports the roadway but helps the other piers to stand firm owing to interconnecting girders. The piers are the analogues of the propositions having some intrinsic credibility, while the upper portions of the bridge are the analogues of what is only inferred. But although each pier may be strengthened by the other piers, it is the solid ground that supports the whole, and in like manner it is intrinsic credibility that supports the whole edifice of knowledge.

There must be piers (data) with some degree of independent grounding (some degree of independent credibility) if the bridge is to serve as a reliable basis for vehicular traffic (the system of propositions is to serve as a reliable basis for belief and action); otherwise the entire structure would collapse.

Must any of the piers be completely grounded? Must any of the data be completely credible, completely certain? The clear implication is that none need be for a usable bridge or system of knowledge to be erected. Are any of our data nonetheless completely certain? One can find evidence for the entire range of answers. First, the *positive* answer. "A clap of thunder is indubitable, but a very faint noise is not; that you are seeing the sun on a bright day is self-evident, but a vague blur in a fog may be imaginary" (HK, pp. 156–57). "My visual sensations, when I look in a mirror or see double, are exactly what I think they are" (HK, p. 167). "The physical world of my everyday experience... is indubitable, in a way in which the physical world of physics is not. The experience of seeing a chair is one that I cannot explain away. I certainly have this experience, even if I am dreaming" (PFM, p. 152). Now, the *negative* answer. "I do not claim *complete* certainty for anything" (MMD, p. 693). "I am prepared to concede that all data have *some* uncertainty... I shall not assume that the actual data which we can obtain are ever completely certain" (IMT, p. 125). "I am not contending that data are ever completely certain, nor is this contention necessary for their importance in theory of knowledge" (HK, p. 166). And finally the *non*answer. The evidence for it is that in part V, chapter VI of HK, examined in detail earlier, Russell leaves the question "open" and does not thereafter in the book close it.

These passages show that the question of Russell's final view on certainty, indubitability, and self-evidence of data cannot be decided directly, i.e., on the basis of passages dealing explicitly with the question. For his explicit statements on the topic form an inconsistent set. The question must be attacked indirectly, by marshaling other sorts of evidence. The examination of this indirect evidence will bring us to the more general question of what the admissible data are in Russell's final theory of knowledge.

Admissible Data for Knowledge

One argument that all data are held to be uncertain to some degree is that otherwise there would be no need for Russell to construct an epistemology in which knowledge based on uncertain data is possible. This argument is inconclusive. Russell might very well believe that one's own momentary sensational data are completely certain and yet hold that these do not by themselves provide a sufficient basis for a useful body of human knowledge. That they are not sufficient is the burden of Russell's critique of what he called the solipsist theory of knowledge: the theory that sense-data (or sensational data) together with suitable principles of demonstrative and/or nondemonstrative inference are a sufficient basis for knowledge. Russell subscribed to this theory in principle, though not in practice, in RSDP and KEW, and he later rejected it. The principles of inference are presumably those mentioned in PP: the laws of logic, and the probabilistic principle of induction.

In RSDP (section VI) Russell states that it is possible to construct material objects out of the sense-data of a single person, the observer, and he implies that the sense-data of the observer would, on such a construction, be an adequate data base for all correct inferences to the existence and character of material objects thus constructed. The implied reason is that on such a construction problematic inferences to unobservable objects become unnecessary. (This reason is insufficient, for an object constructed out of observable entities—say an infinity of these—may nonetheless be unobservable. It would appear that Russell later recognized the inadequacy. He says in HK [pp. 177–78]: "The principles required to justify inferences from mental states of which I am aware to others of which I am not aware are exactly the same as those required for inferences to physical objects and to other minds.") He concedes that such a construction is an "ideal, to be approached as nearly as possible, but to be reached, if at all, only after a long preliminary labour of which as yet we can only see the very beginning" (RSDP, p. 157). In the meantime he allows himself two types of inferred entity as part of the basis: (a) the sense-data of other people, for which there is evidence of testimony, and (b) unsensed sensibilia.

In AMa Russell gives up the attempt to construct material objects out of sensibilia alone: unobservable events are seen to be also required. In consequence, tables and chairs, and electrons and lightwaves cannot be regarded as entirely observable; and commonsense and scientific inferences to these again appear problematic. In HK (part III, chapter I) Russell concludes that if such inferences are to be justified, there must be principles of non-demonstrative inference among the "premises" of our knowledge, apart from the probabilistic principle of induction. The purpose of the last part of the book is to identify these principles. At the same time he officially concludes (HK part III, chapters II and III) that the solipsistic attempt to restrict the data for these inferences to "what I am now noticing" (p. 181) cannot succeed. His argument for this conclusion can be reconstructed as follows.

> It does not seem that any reasonable set of rules of nondemonstrative inference will make it possible for me to infer the existence and character of tables, electrons, and other minds from the fragmentary, transitory, constantly varying data of what I momentarily notice. For I do not at the moment notice the book I saw moments earlier: I notice only my memory image of it, or words in my present consciousness that suggest it. Nor do I notice the book even when I attentively look at it: at best what I notice is a certain spatial pattern of colors.

And so he concludes that "remembered facts must be included with perceived facts as part of our data, though we may as a rule assign a lower degree of credence to them than we do to facts of present perception" (HK, p. 189). Facts provided by testimony are not included among the data, but are regarded as the result of an inference justified by the principle of analogy (HK, pp. 190–95). All data are said to be "private" to the subject (HK, pp. 217, 225).

What, on the preceding suggestion, is the precise criterion for admissible data? Data are said to consist of "perceived facts" and "remembered facts." But exactly what class of facts is this? Given Russell's substitution of noticing for acquaintance, it might seem plausible to propose that datum facts are perceived or remembered facts that have been noticed. And indeed Russell at one point (HK, p. 178) seems to employ this criterion. But in doing so he says, "I notice my dog asleep," a use of "notice" that is inconsistent with the use made of it earlier in the reconstructed Russellian argument! There it was argued that one does not "momentarily notice" such things as books and dogs, much less dogs asleep, and that in consequence the class of "momentarily noticed" data is too restricted to comprise an adequate basis for knowledge. The problem, of course, is that Russell has used the word "notice" in the ordinary way, in which noticing may contain an inference. Thus used, it does not pick out the data of knowledge as opposed to the inferred items. And Russell has not provided us with any serviceable technical notion. As we found in MPD, he describes noticing as "attention," and as "partly a sharpening of the appropriate sense-organs, and partly an emotional reaction" (MPD, p. 142). This characterization does not enable us to decide whether Russell noticed his dog asleep in the technical sense.

In light of the familiar contrast between data and inference, the most natural criterion is that data are perceptions and memories that do not contain and are not products of inference. This criterion would exclude all but the sensational cores of perceptions and memories (strictly speaking, all but beliefs or propositions about sensational cores). And indeed such exclusion seems to be Russell's intent at one point in HK. He defines "animal inference" as "the process of spontaneous interpretation of sensations" (HK, p. 167), and says that what we ordinarily call "perception" is the "filling out of the sensational core by means of animal inferences" (HK, p. 169). And then follows a passage that has already been quoted in part (p. 170):

> From the above considerations it follows that we cannot admit as data all that an uncritical acceptance of common sense would take as given in perception. Only sensations and memories are truly data for our knowledge of the external world. We must exclude from our list of data not only the things that we consciously infer, but all that is obtained by animal inference, such as the imagined hardness of an object seen but not touched.

If Russell excludes from his data all but the sensational cores of his perceptions and memories, then it would seem that data must be independently credible to the highest degree; for they are credible and yet by definition are not the product of inference. And they must be certain in the highest degree, in the sense in which certainty and credibility are identical. This resulting view seems virtually indistinguishable from the preabandonment theory of knowledge that posited completely certain, completely immediate data, perhaps indistinguishable even from a return to the solipsistic theory of knowledge, whose data basis was at one point judged inadequate for knowledge. And it seems clearly to conflict with Russell's final theory of knowledge in part V of HK, which permits data having less than the highest degree of certainty and independent credibility, data that owe some of their credibility to inferences from other data.

One possible interpretation is that the passage is a lapse, a regression to an earlier view. But a more interesting one is available. The troublesome passage speaks of what are "truly data," implying that what is left after the removal of all conscious and unconscious inferences are "true data." The suggestion is that there are *grades of purity* in data, the purer having less admixture of inference than the less pure; the passage describes the process of purifying data to remove the inferential impurities. Perhaps Russell held, or was moving toward, the view that, although inferentially impure data may be used—indeed, may have to be used—in theory of knowledge, still the purer grades are to be preferred to the impure. This view can be supposed to incorporate the following rationale for using impure data. Although the purer the data, the better the theory of knowledge based on them, it is in practice impossible to obtain enough pure data to form the basis of a useful body of knowledge. Consequently, one must for the present make do with data of varying degrees of impurity and hope that in future purer data will be obtained and more adequate bodies of knowledge based on them.

Did Russell believe that pure data are possible? This question is addressed in the next section.

Pure Data

The groundwork for a notion of pure data is laid in IMT (chapters VIII, X, and XI), and various ingredients in the theory can be found in earlier works. In IMT Russell criticizes the coherence ("Hegelian") theorists of knowledge who "deny the distinction between data and inferences altogether," and "maintain that in all our knowledge there is an inferential element, . . . and that the test of truth is coherence rather than conformity with 'fact' " (IMT, p. 123). He objects that the view makes new knowledge—knowledge that could not have been inferred from existing knowledge—impossible. And he imagines the following reply on the part of the coherence theorist (p. 123):

> Any statement of the new knowledge obtained from perception is always an interpretation based upon accepted theories, and may need subsequent correction if these theories turn out to be unsuitable. If I say, for example, "Look, there is an eclipse of the moon," I use my knowledge of astronomy to interpret what I see. No words exist. . . which do not embody theories or hypotheses, and the crude fact of perception is therefore for ever ineffable.

The gist of this reply is that no datum is pure, in our sense of not containing or being the product of an inference. Russell's counter is as follows:

> I think that this view underestimates the powers of analysis. It is undeniable that our every-day interpretations of perceptive experiences, and even all our every-day words, embody theories. But it is not impossible to whittle away the element of interpretation, or to invent an artificial language involving a minimum of theory. By these methods we can approach asymptotically to the pure datum. That there must be a pure datum is, I think, a logically irrefutable consequence of the fact that perception gives rise to new knowledge.

A pure datum would presumably be reported in a proposition that obtains none of its credibility from other propositions. If such a proposition describing one's perception could be formulated, it would be an almost exact postabandonment replica of the original sense-datum proposition, or judgment of sensation. It would just as certain, self-evident, and independently credible as the original; it would be verified by noticing (attending to) and analyzing one's experience; it would be grounded, or made true, by the feature of one's perceptual experience it describes. It would thus lack only one property of the original: it would not describe (or be) the object term in a two-term relation called "acquaintance" between a subject and an object. And even this difference may be eliminable. For Russell sometimes describes acquaintance as a two-term relation between an *act* and an object; and noticing can be similarly described.

Are pure data obtainable (noticeable?), according to Russell? Or, to pose the linguistic version, are pure datum statements formulatable? The answer is that obviously they are, since "There is a red patch to the left of a blue patch" is an example and seems incorrect. For Russell says that by the method of analysis we can "approach asymptotically to the pure datum." If he is using the word "asymptotically" in its mathematical sense, which seems likely, then he means that we can by more and more analysis more and more closely approach a pure datum, though we cannot actually obtain (notice?) one. Or, to make the point in its linguistic version, we can by analysis and the development of an improved language approximate a pure datum statement, though we cannot actually formulate one. If this is Russell's meaning, then "There is a red patch to the left of a blue patch" is not a pure datum statement, since it has just been formulated.

What then are the next few items in the sequence of purer and purer datum statements? In what language are they written? Not ordinary English, presumably, since it seems impossible to devise a sentence of ordinary English that more accurately describes my perceptual datum than "There is a red patch to the left of a blue patch." In some places Russell suggests that the more accurate datum reports will be the product of psychological theorizing, and hence written in the technical language of psychology. For example (AMi, p. 140):

> In order...to arrive at what really is sensation in an occurrence...we have to pare away all that is due to habit or expectation or interpretation. This is a matter for the psychologist, and by no means an easy matter.

At one point Russell implies that these elements may not be conscious (not noticeable?). He says (AMa, p. 189): "Part [of the interpretation that usually accompanies a perception] can only be discovered by careful theory, and can never be made introspectively obvious [made conscious by mere attention]". If the interpretive component of a perception cannot be made conscious, then clearly the noninterpretative, sensational component cannot be made conscious either. The suggestion, then, is that psychology can formulate statements describing elements of our perceptual experience that are purer (less inferential) than those that are conscious and describable in ordinary language, and that there is a sequence of such experiences that "approach asymptotically to the pure datum."

Our question thus takes the following form: Are pure data obtainable by psychology? Or (linguistic version) are pure datum statements formulatable by psychology? Again one could argue that Russell's employment of the phrase "approach asymptotically" implies a negative answer, and that he regarded pure data as a useful but unobtainable ideal. But it is also possible that if he had fully developed his suggestion, he would have employed a different phrase and would have held that pure data are obtainable. In light of his remark (previously quoted from MPD, p. 143) that "sensation [is] that part of our total experience which is due to the stimulus alone," it seems reasonable to speculate that he might have adopted the following position. Pure data are comprised of stimulation at the receptors, and are unconsciously sensed by the receptors; and psychology is capable of describing the stimulation as initially sensed, without the layers of interpretation added to it by the rest of the perceptual-cognitive mechanism. On this view the original sense-datum rises phoenix-like from the ruins of Russell's abandonment, reincarnated at the level of unconscious sensation in the dress of cognitive psychology. Philosopher of science (including psychology) that he was, Russell might quite have liked the result.

Unfortunately there is a difficulty, whether pure data are held to be obtainable or unobtainable. Datum statements formulated in a psychological theory are supposed to be purer (less inferential, less theory-laden) than those available in ordinary language. But the language of psychology (and of every other science) is an extension of ordinary language, and psychological statements—including the allegedly purer datum statements—obtain some of their credibility from statements of the ordinary language they extend. In contrast, datum statements formulated in ordinary language obtain none of their credibility from psychological statements. Consequently, it is difficult to see how technical psychological datum statements can be purer than those formulatable in ordinary language. The psychological datum statements may be more accurate, and may describe features of experience that ordinary language cannot describe; but there is no reason to suppose that they will be inferentially purer. Consequently they do not seem to be members of any sequence of statements that "approach [asymptotically or otherwise] to the pure datum." Consequently, it would be hard to argue that they constitute a more adequate basis for our knowledge than do our ordinary perceptual propositions.

David Pears

Russell's 1913 Theory of Knowledge *Manuscript*

I

Russell's *Theory of Knowledge*[1] represents an important stage in the development of his philosophy, and it also throws a lot of light on Wittgenstein's *Tractatus Logico-Philosophicus*. I published an article about this in 1977,[2] but I want to add to it now, and especially to the account that I gave then of the place of the manuscript in Russell's oeuvre.

First, a few words are needed about the history of the manuscript. Russell wrote it in the spring of 1913. Wittgenstein read it, met Russell, and severely criticized it in May of that year. Russell then published the first six chapters as articles in *The Monist* in 1914 and 1915. Of these articles the best known are those reprinted by R.C. Marsh under the title "On the Nature of Acquaintance," in the Russell anthology that he edited in 1956, *Logic and Knowledge*.[3] Russell never published the rest of the manuscript, and the question why he refrained is interesting.

There is a letter written by him to Ottoline Morrell in 1913 that provides a partial answer to this question. He describes his meeting with Wittgenstein:

> We were both cross from the heat. I showed him a crucial part of what I had been writing. He said it was all wrong, not realizing the difficulties—that he had tried my view and knew it wouldn't work. I couldn't understand his objection—in fact he was very inarticulate—but I feel in my bones that he must be right, and that he has seen something that I have missed. If I could see it too I shouldn't mind, but as it is, it is worrying, and has rather destroyed the pleasure in my writing—I can only go on with what I see, and yet I feel it is probably all wrong and that Wittgenstein will think me a dishonest scoundrel for going on with it. Well, well—it is the younger generation knocking at the door—I must make room for him when I can, or I shall become an incubus. But at the moment I was rather cross.[4]

It is a ready conjecture that Russell refrained from publishing the parts of the manuscript that Wittgenstein criticized. There is a lot of evidence supporting this, but I shall only mention five points. First, we know that Russell had hoped that his manuscript would be the beginning of a long collaboration with Wittgenstein, who a few months later gave him his *Notes on Logic*, a work which he, Russell, rearranged for him.[5] Second, the first of the unpublished chapters of Russell's manuscript is "On the Acquaintance Involved in Our Knowledge of Relations," and at that time Wittgenstein held that relations are not objects but forms.[6] Third, most of Russell's subsequent chapters are concerned directly or indirectly with propositions and the understanding of propositions, and there is ample evidence that Wittgenstein rejected Russell's distinctive ideas on these topics. For example, in a letter to Russell dated July 2, 1913, he writes, "I am very sorry to hear that my objection to your theory of judgement paralyzes you,"[7] which suggests that Russell must have said (or written) that he could not answer the criticism or go on without answering it. There is also a clear reference in Wittgenstein's *Notebooks, 1914–16*[8] to his own earlier attempt to develop a theory of propositions like the one put forward by Russell in his manuscript, and this explains something in Russell's letter to Ottoline Morrell, namely, "He said...that he had tried my view and knew it wouldn't work." Fourth, the picture theory of propositions is, in large part, a reaction against Russell's 1913 theory.[9] Fifth, Russell's next major work, *The Philosophy of Logical Atomism*, contains conscious but incomplete moves away from his 1913 doctrines about qualities and relations and about propositional forms in the direction in which he believed Wittgenstein to have gone.[10]

It is highly probable that Wittgenstein's unanswered criticisms explain why Russell did not publish the second half of his manuscript. However, care is needed in specifying exactly what needs to be explained. The whole edifice of *Theory of Knowledge* is founded on Russell's doctrine of acquaintance, which he abandoned in 1919.[11] So after 1919 it is unnecessary to seek another explanation of nonpublication. The most that we can say about nonpublication after that date is that it was overdetermined. But how much was the other factor, Wittgenstein's unanswered criticism, operating during the preceding six years? Russell had to publish the first part first, and as the war continued he became increasingly preoccupied with pacifism. However, an examination of the contents of the manuscript will establish that Wittgenstein's unanswered criticism certainly gave Russell a sufficient reason not to publish the second part.

I shall begin with a general description of the contents of *Theory of Knowledge*. It deals with the epistemic basis of Russell's theory of language. The table of contents shows that he intended to cover the theory of logic too, but, though there are interesting remarks about logic in the text, there is no systematic treatment of it. The question that concerns him is, what sort of knowledge and what kinds of thought processes are sufficient for understanding contingent propositions and, if they are sense-datum propositions, for establishing their truth. His answer is that acquaintance takes us nearly all the way to both achievements.

He had given acquaintance a lot to do in *The Problems of Philosophy*, and arguably he had overworked it even there, but he goes further in *Theory of Knowledge*. There is in the later work a new explanation of the transition from acquaintance with the constituents of a proposition to understanding the proposition itself. This, of course, is a difficult transition to explain, as Wittgenstein must often have reminded him. Acquaintance always relates a subject to a single fixed object. So how can it be adapted to explain the relation to the shifting basis in the world that may make a proposition true or may make it false? Russell's answer was to introduce a new kind of acquaintance, acquaintance with forms. There is also another move that is difficult to explain, the move from acquaintance with a complex to apprehension of a truth about it. However, in *Theory of Knowledge* he does not add anything new to his earlier account of this move. He merely develops it in more detail.

The detailed examination of the contents of the manuscript, which now follows, falls into four sections. First, I shall briefly recapitulate the chapters that Russell published in *The Monist* in 1914 and 1915. Then I shall take a quick look at his treatment of acquaintance with predicates and relations in the first two chapters that he did not publish. The third section will deal with his account of understanding propositions and the fourth with his account of the apprehension of truths about sensed complexes. The third section will be the longest because it is concerned with the most difficult problem that Russell faced in the manuscript. I am, of course, forced by lack of space to omit certain topics, some of them important. The plan of my exposition is to follow Russell's attempt to push acquaintance as far as possible toward a solution of his two most difficult problems, and then to inquire what he thought was needed to solve them completely. This ought to yield a fairly clear picture of the relations between the ideas that he puts forward in the manuscript and his own earlier and later ideas.

II

In the chapters published by Russell in *The Monist* and reprinted as "On the Nature of Acquaintance" in *Logic and Knowledge* (1956), he defines acquaintance as an extensional relation between subject and object, argues for its existence against William James and other adversaries, and demonstrates its importance in cases in which the object is a particular. In the chapters published by him in *The Monist* but not reprinted, he deals with three kinds of acquaintance with particulars: sensation, memory, and imagination. In his own summary, in the unpublished part of the manuscripts, he writes: "These, we found, though their objects are usually somewhat different, are not essentially distinguished by their objects, but by the relations of subject and object. In sensation subject and object are simultaneous; in memory the subject is later than the object; while imagination does not essentially involve any time-relation of subject and object, though all time-relations are compatible with it."[12]

There are only two points that I want to make about this. First, the particular that is the object of acquaintance may be simple or complex, and this is especially important in the case of sensation. Second, Russell consistently held that acquaintance is an extensional relation not involving any knowledge of truths about its object. He concedes that it is usually accompanied by such knowledge, but holds that it never actually involves it.[13] It is surprising, but undeniable, that he maintains this thesis even about acquaintance with complex particulars.

Since this interpretation is important, it is worth pausing to deal with an objection to it. There are two passages in Russell's writings in which he says that acquaintance with the so-and-so requires not only acquaintance with *a* where *a* is in fact the so-and-so, but also knowledge that *a* is the so-and-so.[14] This might suggest the objection that in certain cases he believed acquaintance to be intensional.

However, the two passages do not really give this inference any support. For there is no reason to suppose that Russell takes the subject's original acquaintance with *a* to be intensional in the cases that he describes. The distinctive feature of his cases is that the subject has to achieve something more, either at the time or later, in order that, later still, a commentator may specify his acquaintance in a certain way, viz., as acquaintance with the so-and-so. We have to suppose that this commentator is asked, "Is the subject acquainted with the so-and-so?" Now one answer that he might give is, "He is, but he does not know that he is." That answer would be the one that we would expect Russell to allow in the light of everything else that he says about acquaintance; but in these two passages he imposes a special convention on the commentator: he must not say that the subject is acquainted with the so-and-so unless the subject knows that the object of his acquaintance is the so-and-so. However, this is not a point about the nature of the subject's acquaintance with the object but only a point about the way in which another person ought to report it later in response to a certain question.

If we do not impose Russell's convention on the commentator, but allow him to say "He is acquainted with the so-and-so but he does not know that he is," it might perhaps be best to treat the second conjunct as the cancellation of a cancelable implication of the first.[15] However, I do not need to go into that, nor do I need to deal with the rather different case in which the subject himself has to answer the same question. Enough has been said to show that the two passages do not imply that Russell thought that acquaintance is ever intrinsically intensional.

III

In the first two chapters that Russell never published, he argues that we are acquainted with predicates and relations as well as with particulars.[16] He had argued for the same conclusion in *The Problems of Philosophy*.[17] There is, however, an interesting difference in the way in which he now treats this topic. He is very concerned to specify the precise object of acquaintance when a relation is involved. This is because some dyadic relations are asymmetrical, and in such cases acquaintance with the relation itself without understanding of the different properties of its two slots for particulars would not be enough. The same is true of certain relations with more than two terms.

The general character of the difficulty with which he was contending is clear. If acquaintance is extensional it will not include any knowledge of truths about its objects. But acquaintance with an asymmetrical relation will be insufficient to explain its contribution to the sense of a proposition in which its name occurs unless that acquaintance involves the knowledge that it may link the same particulars in two different ways and the ability to discriminate between them. Similarly, acquaintance with any universal ought to involve knowledge of its type and therefore of the types of particulars with which it may combine to produce complexes (and, as I shall argue later, the same is true of acquaintance with particulars).

In January 1913 Wittgenstein wrote to Russell announcing his discovery that general words signify forms rather than objects.[18] It seems that he did not maintain this thesis for long and Russell never adopted it. Later, in *The Philosophy of Logical Atomism*, Russell says that, when someone is acquainted with a predicate, e.g., the color red, he knows a form, but he does not elaborate this and he certainly does not go so far as to imply that the color is a form.[19]

In *Theory of Knowledge* he clearly distinguishes universals from forms, and, as we shall see in a moment, he claims that we need acquaintance with both before we can understand a proposition. For example, he claims that, in order to understand the proposition "*a* is before *b*," we need (at least) acquaintance with the relation *precedes* and with the general form of dyadic relations. But did he think that acquaintance with this asymmetrical relation involves the knowledge that it may link the same particulars in two different ways and the ability to discriminate between them?

I cannot find a clear answer to this question in the text. He says that "sense" (sc., the sense of a relation) "is not in the relation alone, or in the complex alone, but in the relations of the particulars to the complex which constitute 'position' in the complex."[20] It would seem that the difference between these two positions must be grasped by anyone who understands the word "before," and so that knowledge of the difference would be included in acquaintance with this relation. However, Russell never says this. His next move is to suggest that the "word 'sequence' would be better than 'before' or 'after' as the name of the relation involved,"[21] and his conclusion is that we must be acquainted with the relation *sequence* itself; i.e., "that we have, in some cases, direct acquaintance with relations in the abstract signification which does not distinguish between the two senses of a relation."[22]

So his solution to the problem posed by acquaintance with asymmetrical relations is unclear. Understanding the difference between the two slots in the relation *before* is not included in acquaintance with the universal, because the universal is *sequence*. Nor is it included in acquaintance with the form of dyadic relations, which is entirely general. It therefore falls between two stools. This is not really surprising because the problem is part of a more general one, which extensional acquaintance is powerless to solve.

IV

My next task is to present the account of understanding propositions that Russell develops in *Theory of Knowledge*. It involves a dramatic extension of the scope of acquaintance, which now includes forms among its objects as well as particulars and universals. But first, the problem needs to be identified.

If acquaintance relates the subject to a single, fixed object, how can it explain his relation to the shifting basis in reality which may make a proposition true or may make it false? If the proposition is "*aRb*," it is obvious that understanding it does not require acquaintance with the complex *a-in-the-relation-R-to-b*. For the existence of this complex is sufficient to make the proposition true. So in 1910 Russell maintains that the only acquaintance needed by someone who understands the proposition is separate acquaintance with each of its elements, *a*, *R*, and *b*.[23]

However, that leaves two things unexplained. The subject still has to combine these constituents in thought, and when he does this, how does he know that the combination is meant for the possibility that *aRb* and not for the possibility that each of its constituents exists separately? And how does he know that *aRb* really is a possibility? It would be natural to answer the first question by bringing in his intention and the second by bringing in his knowledge of the types of the three constituents. But let us see how Russell answers them.

In 1910 he had assumed that the relation *judging*, which holds between the subject and all three constituents, secures both the desired results. However, that is little more than a solution by fiat. It does not even explain the difference discussed in the preceding section, between the two different ways in which an asymmetrical relation might be judged to relate the same particulars, still less the general difference between combining the constituents in thought and thinking of them one by one.

Let us begin with the question "What makes it possible to combine the three constituents in thought in a way that makes sense?" Russell's suggestion is that this is possible only for someone already acquainted with the general form of dyadic relational propositions, x ξ y.[24] He pictures this form as a kind of stencil with holes for any three suitable constituents. It is essential to his explanation that the subject already be acquainted with this form. He must have advance knowledge of it, knowledge that supports his understanding of logic.

This idea is best put in Russell's own words: "Every logical notion, in an important sense, is or involves a *summum genus*, and results from a process of generalization which has been carried to its utmost limit."[25] "Take, for example, the proposition 'Socrates precedes Plato.' This has the form of a dual complex: we may naturally symbolize the form by 'xRy' [better 'x ξ y'],[26] where we use a different sort of letter for the relation, because the difference between a relation and its terms is a *logical* difference. When we have reached the form 'xRy,' we have reached the utmost generalization that is possible starting from 'Socrates precedes Plato.' "[27] "It is clear that we have acquaintance (possibly in an extended sense of the word 'acquaintance') with something as abstract as the pure form, since otherwise we could not intelligibly use such a word as 'relation.' "[28] He goes further: "I think it may be shown that acquaintance with logical form is involved before explicit thought about logic begins, in fact as soon as we can understand a sentence. Let us suppose that we are acquainted with Socrates and with Plato and with the relation 'precedes,' but not with the complex 'Socrates precedes Plato.' Suppose now that someone tells us that Socrates precedes Plato. How do we know what he means? It is plain that his statement does not give us *acquaintance* with the complex 'Socrates precedes Plato.' What we understand is that Socrates and Plato and 'precedes' are united in a complex of the form 'xRy,' where Socrates has the *x*-place and Plato has the *y*-place. It is difficult to see how we could possibly understand how Socrates and Plato and 'precedes' are to be combined unless we had acquaintance with the form of the complex."[29] In general he holds that "there certainly is such a thing as 'logical experience,' by which I mean that kind of immediate knowledge, other than judgment, which is what enables us to understand logical terms."[30]

It might be thought that these passages do not make it absolutely clear that people who understand the proposition "Socrates precedes Plato" must be acquainted with the form in advance, just as many of Russell's remarks about their relation to the universal constituents of their propositions do not make it absolutely clear that it too must be advance acquaintance. This is because he often supposes that the people in question are being confronted with perceived complexes and are naming simple sense-data, and in such a situation the necessary acquaintance with the particular constituents of their propositions can only be achieved on the spot. However, since the propositions are contingent, the necessary acquaintance with the relation cannot be achieved on the spot even in perceptual situations.[31]

Now the form, like the relation, is general, and so it is at least possible for the necessary acquaintance with it too to be achieved before the subject finds himself in the perceptual situation. Moreover, even when he is in it, he will need advance acquaintance with the form, because what he judges is that it is contingently true at least that these two particulars stand in some dual relation to one another. This necessity is even clearer when the subject understands the proposition before he gets into the perceptual situation. So in all cases of understanding contingent propositions the subject needs advance acquaintance with the form.

In fact, this is the natural way to interpret many of Russell's remarks on this topic. He says: "In order to understand 'A and B are similar,' we must know what is supposed to be done with A and B and similarity; *i.e.* what it is for two terms to have a relation; that is, we must understand the form of the complex which must exist if the proposition is true,"[32] and "we must... regard the understanding of 'something has some relation to something' as logically preceding the understanding of any particular proposition asserting a particular case of dual relation."[33]

The next thing that Russell has to explain is how anyone achieves advance acquaintance with such a form. There is a risk of a vicious infinite regress here, because it is not easy to avoid the suggestion that he achieves the acquaintance when he establishes the truth of another proposition of the same form, and yet it is obvious that that proposition, in its turn, would first have to be understood by him. But let us see how Russell proceeds.

He identifies the form x ξ y with the fact that something has some relation to something. He writes: "We require of the form that there shall be one form, and only one, for every group of complexes which 'have the same form'; also, if possible, it would be convenient to take as the form something which is not a mere incomplete symbol. We may secure these *desiderata* by taking as the one form the fact that there are entities that make up complexes having the form in question.... For example, the form of all subject-predicate complexes will be the fact 'something has some predicate'; the form of all dual complexes will be 'something has some relation to something.' " This fact, he goes on to explain, "contains no constituent at all. It is, therefore, suitable to serve as the 'form' of dual complexes. In a sense, it is simple, since it cannot be analyzed. At first sight, it seems to have a structure, and therefore to be not simple; but it is more correct to say that it *is* a structure."[34]

At this point Russell has to face two questions. Are these entirely general facts contingent? And if they are, how does the subject establish them?

It is clear that, if they are contingent facts, Russell's explanation of understanding the sense of a proposition will slide into an infinite regress. For the only way to establish the fact that something has some relation to something would be to verify another singular proposition of that form, and before that could be done, it would be necessary to understand the sense of that proposition, and so on ad infinitum.

When Wittgenstein read Russell's manuscript, he took him to mean, or at least to be committed to the view, that the general facts are contingent. For in a passage in the *Tractatus*,[35] evidently intended as a criticism of Russell because it echoes his words, he writes:

> The "experience" that we need in order to understand logic is not that something or other is the state of things, but that something *is*: that, however, is *not* an experience.

If Russell replied that the general facts were not contingent, Wittgenstein had a ready answer in the *Tractatus*:

The mark of a logical proposition is *not* general validity. To be general means no more than to be accidentally valid for all things. An ungeneralized proposition can be tautological just as well as a generalized one.[36]

This could be directed not only against the thesis that true negative existential propositions are necessary but also against the extension of the thesis to true positive existential propositions.

It is even possible to conjecture more details of the criticisms of Russell's manuscript made by Wittgenstein in May 1913. For when Russell described the meeting to Ottoline Morrell, he said that Wittgenstein claimed to have tried his theory and to have found that it did not work,[37] and there is a passage in *Notebooks 1914–16* that almost certainly alludes to this failed attempt:

> I thought that the possibility of the truth of the proposition ϕa was tied up with the fact $(\exists x, \phi).\phi x$. But it is impossible to see why ϕa should only be possible if there is another proposition of the same form. ϕa surely does not need any precedent. (For suppose that there existed only the two elementary propositions, "ϕa" and "ψa" and that "ϕa" were false: why should this proposition only make sense if "ψa" is true?)[38]

However, Russell had another card to play. In *Theory of Knowledge* he says that the entirely general facts, with which he identifies the forms of propositions, are facts of a very special kind. He does not actually say that the corresponding propositions are self-evident, but he describes them in a way that implies that they are. "The importance of the understanding of pure form lies in its relation to the self-evidence of logical truth. For since understanding is here a direct relation of the subject to a single object the possibility of untruth does not exist, as it does when understanding is a multiple relation."[39]

If Russell's entirely general propositions are self-evident, the facts to which they correspond may not be contingent facts, and if they are not contingent facts there will be no need to verify singular propositions of the same form. In that case Wittgenstein's criticism will miss the mark. However, Russell's claim to detect self-evidence here is not reassuring, because he also makes the same claim about basic contingent propositions.[40] Wittgenstein, of course, believed that logic cannot be and does not need to be founded on self-evidence:

> Self-evidence, which Russell talked about so much, can become dispensable in logic, only because language itself prevents every logical mistake. What makes logic *a priori* is the impossibility of illogical thought.[41]

But if we want to understand why Russell thought that his entirely general propositions are self-evident, and what he took that to indicate about the nature of the facts to which they correspond, we need to look at his reasoning.

One of his arguments for the self-evidence of entirely general propositions is the traditional argument that in their case the transition from understanding to apprehension of truth is immediate. "In considering the understanding of propositions, a specially interesting case is afforded by the propositions of pure logic, which have no constituents: in their case understanding is a dual relation, the object-term having a pure form. This fact seems to be connected with the self-evidence of logical propositions."[42] "I do not think there is any difference between understanding and acquaintance in the case of 'something has some relation to something.' I base this view simply on the fact that I am unable introspectively to discover any difference. In regard to most propositions—*i.e.* to all such as contain any constants—it is easy to *prove* that understanding is different from acquaintance with the corresponding fact (if any): Understanding is neutral as regards truth and falsehood, whereas acquaintance with the fact is only possible when there is such a fact, *i.e.* in the case of truth; and understanding of any proposition other than a pure form cannot be, like acquaintance, a two-term relation. But both these proofs fail in the case of a pure form, and we are therefore compelled to rely on direct inspection, which, so far as I can discover, reveals no difference in this case between understanding and acquaintance."[43]

Introspection does not provide very strong support for the thesis that the transition from understanding to apprehension of truth is immediate in this case. However, there is an independent argument embedded in the end of this passage and set out more fully in three other passages that have already been quoted.[44] The argument is that entirely general propositions are simple, because they contain no constituents, and so understanding is in this case alone "a direct relation of the subject to a simple object," viz., the relation *acquaintance*.

However, at this point Russell really does face an unanswerable objection. He is trying to prove that entirely general propositions are self-evident. His conclusion is that their truth is apprehended as soon as they are understood. But when he tries to establish this conclusion by arguing that they are really simple objects of acquaintance, because they contain no constituents, he spoils his case by making their truth unintelligible. If they are simple, their truth is as unintelligible as their falsehood. Wittgenstein was surely right in thinking that the elimination of constituents does not make a proposition simple.

A fully generalized proposition, like every other proposition, is composite. (This is shown by the fact that in "$(\exists x, \phi).\phi x$" we have to mention "ϕ" and "x" separately. They both, independently, stand in signifying relations to the world, just as in the case of ungeneralized propositions.[45]

It is a conjecture that Wittgenstein made all these points in his conversation with Russell in May 1913. Possibly he thought of some of them later. But if we now turn to the second thing that Russell's theory was designed to explain, the subject's knowledge that *aRb* really is a possibility, we have independent evidence that an objection to this part of the theory was among the criticisms made by Wittgenstein at that meeting.

Wittgenstein wrote to Russell in June 1913:

> I can now express my objection to your theory of judgement exactly; I believe it is obvious that from the proposition "A judges that (say) a is in relation R to b," if correctly analyzed, the proposition "aRb ∨ −aRb" must follow directly without the use of any other premise. This condition is not fulfilled by your theory.[46]

On July 27, 1913, evidently after receiving a reply from Russell, he wrote:

> I am very sorry to hear that my objection to your theory of judgement paralyzes you. I think it can only be removed by a correct theory of propositions.[47]

Wittgenstein's point is that, if acquaintance with the constituents of a proposition is going to explain how the subject knows that he has put them together in a way that makes sense, then acquaintance must be intensional. For example, he must be acquainted with *a* and *b* as objects of the right kind to combine with *R* to produce *aRb*.

> If I know an object, I know all its possible occurrences in states of affairs. Every one of these possibilities must be part of the nature of the object. A new possibility cannot be discovered later.[48]

When Wittgenstein's point is put like this, it is a point against Russell's 1910 theory of judgment, and of course it does make an impact on that theory. However, it is clear that Wittgenstein actually made the point against the 1913 theory, which required acquaintance with the form of dyadic relations as well as acquaintance with the three constituents. It follows that Wittgenstein must have argued that, even when Russell had brought in acquaintance with the form, he had not made any progress toward a solution of the problem. For it remained unexplained how the subject knows that these constituents can be combined within this form. In short, if the form is treated as an object of acquaintance, it recreates the problem that it was designed to solve. This is the point of origin of Wittgenstein's picture theory of propositions.

V

My last topic is Russell's 1913 account of the apprehension of truths about sensed complexes. Since it does not contain any important additions to his earlier treatment of the subject,[49] I shall not describe it in great detail. My approach to it will be by way of the last topic, because I want to show how his failure to explain understanding the sense of propositions is connected with certain shortcomings in his explanation of the apprehension of perceptual truths.

It might be best to begin with a general description of the connection between the two faults. In all his theories of propositions Russell experienced difficulty in accounting for the fact that they have senses. How do we ever get these heavier-than-air machines off the ground? Acquaintance with their constituents certainly will not do the trick, because it will not explain the fact that, when they are combined, the combination immediately levitates in the way that we call "being true or false." Russell gives a sensible psychological account of the way in which the subject combines the constituents in thought, and his remarks on this topic are very like Wittgenstein's.[50] However, when he addresses himself to the question of how the subject knows that what he thinks is a real possibility, he spoils the explanation of the takeoff. For he introduces an entirely general proposition and immediately uses an acquaintance line to attach it to a single fixed point in the world, and that frustrates the enterprise.

The shortcomings of his account of the apprehension of truths about sensed complexes are similar, but they affect the point of arrival of the proposition rather than its point of departure. When the complex *a-in-the-relation-R-to-b* is presented to the subject and he judges that *aRb*, his understanding of the sense of this proposition must not be wholly derived from these two particulars and this instantiation of the relation. It must come, at least in part, from elsewhere. Otherwise, the proposition, in his understanding of it, will not be contingent. However, Russell's account does not include this requirement. He describes the situation in a way that does not allow the subject to make a sufficiently sharp distinction between the asserted combination of constituents and their actual combination, and so prevents him from watching the proposition land on or off target.

Let us take a brief look at some of the details. The subject senses and is therefore acquainted with the complex *a-in-the-relation-R-to-b*, and the question is how he arrives at the true judgment that *aRb*. Russell says that he must attend to the complex and analyze it in thought into its three constituents. This will give him acquaintance with the three constituents, if he did not already possess it. He then judges that this complex, sensed as a whole, is identical with the complex consisting of these three constituents.[51]

There are some differences between this account and Russell's earlier accounts[52] of the transition from acquaintance with a complex to a true judgment about it. One difference is that in his earlier accounts the doctrine of acquaintance with facts was used to make the transition look more foolproof than it is in reality,[53] and there is an interesting similarity between his treatment of acquaintance with the particular fact that *aRb* and his treatment of acquaintance with the entirely general fact that x ξ y, which is a form. Another difference is that in his earlier accounts Russell claimed that, if the subject confines his attention to the sensed complex and does not base his judgment on anything outside it, his judgment must be true, but he does not repeat that claim now. Perhaps he does not want to make acquaintance with the particular complex *aRb* too like acquaintance with the general form x ξ y.

However, the new account of the transition from acquaintance to judgment follows the same general lines as his earlier account, and it is flawed in the same fundamental way. When Russell construes the judgment that *aRb* as the identity-judgment, that this complex perceived as a whole is identical with the complex consisting of these three constituents, he makes it appear that the subject only has to make two simultaneous deictic references to the complex, one with a phrase not reflecting its composition. It then seems that he does not run any risk of falsehood in his judgment. However, this is an illusion produced by packing all the risks of falsehood into the referential phrase reflecting the composition of the complex. If he knows that the complex is really composed of the three constituents, and if he knows that the relation really is *R*, these pieces of knowledge must have come, at least in part, from points outside the complex. To put the criticism the other way, the sense of the proposition, as he understands it, must not be wholly derived from the composition of this complex and this instantiation of the relation.

Notes

1. *The Collected Papers of Bertrand Russell*, vol. 7, ed. Elizabeth Eames in collaboration with Kenneth Blackwell (London: Allen & Unwin, 1984).
2. "The Relation between Wittgenstein's Picture Theory of Propositions and Russell's Theories of Judgement," *Philosophical Review* (April 1977), pp. 177-96.
3. In *Logic and Knowledge*, ed. R. C. Marsh (London: Allen & Unwin, 1956), pp. 127-74.
4. See R. W. Clark, *The Life of Bertrand Russell* (London: Jonathan Cape and Weidenfeld & Nicolson, 1975), pp. 204-5.
5. Brian McGuinness, "The Grundgedanke of the *Tractatus*," in *Understanding Wittgenstein*. Royal Institute of Philosophy Lectures, vol. VII (1974), pp. 32-55.
6. See his letter to Russell dated January 16, 1913 in *Notebooks 1914-16*, ed. G. H. von Wright and G. E. M. Anscombe, (Oxford: Blackwell, 1961), p. 120. See also *Notes on Logic*, Ibid., p. 98.
7. *Notebooks 1914-16*, p. 121.
8. *Notebooks 1914-16*, entry for October 21, 1914, paragraph 4.
9. See my article in *Philosophical Review*, cited in note 2.
10. See "The Philosophy of Logical Atomism," in *Logic and Knowledge*, ed. Marsh, p. 205, discussed in section III.
11. See "On Propositions," in Logic and Knowledge, ed. Marsh, pp. 305-6.
12. *Theory of Knowledge* (London: Allen & Unwin, 1984), p. 100.
13. See *The Problems of Philosophy*, p. 46, and "On the Nature of Acquaintance," in *Logic and Knowledge*, pp. 127, 130, and 168.
14. *The Problems of Philosophy*, p. 53, and "Knowledge by Acquaintance and Knowledge by Description," in *Mysticism and Logic* (London: Longmans, 1918), pp. 214-15.
15. See H. P. Grice, "The Causal Theory of Perception," *Proceedings of the Aristotelian Society*, supp., 35 (1961).
16. *Theory of Knowledge*, part I, Chapters 7 and 8.
17. Ch. 10.
18. See note 6, this chapter.
19. See note 10, this chapter.
20. *Theory of Knowledge*, p. 88.
21. Ibid.
22. Ibid. p. 89.
23. "On the Nature of Truth and Falsehood" (1910), in *Philosophical Essays* (New York: Simon & Schuster, 1968), pp. 147-59.

24. He says that the form is xRy, but it is necessary to indicate that the second term is a variable like the first and the third. See *Theory of Knowledge*, pp. 98–99.
25. *Theory of Knowledge*, p. 97.
26. See note 24, this chapter.
27. *Theory of Knowledge*, p. 98.
28. Ibid., pp. 98–99.
29. Ibid., p. 99.
30. Ibid., p. 97.
31. See section I of this essay.
32. *Theory of Knowledge*, p. 116.
33. Ibid., p. 130.
34. Ibid., p. 114.
35. *Tractatus Logico-Philosophicus*, trans. D. F. Pears and B. F. Mc Guiness (London: Routledge & Kegan Paul, 1961), 5.552.
36. Ibid., 6.1231. Cf. *Notebooks 1914–16*, entries for October 14–29, 1914. In most of the entries on these days Wittgenstein is struggling with the problem of completely general propositions and there are many echoes of Russell's ideas in *Theory of Knowledge*, which in the end he rejects.
37. Clark, *Life of Bertrand Russell*, pp. 204–5.
38. *Notebooks 1914–16*, October 21, 1914, last entry.
39. *Theory of Knowledge*, p. 132.
40. See *The Problems of Philosophy*, pp. 113–15.
41. *Tractatus Logico-Philosophicus*, 5.552.
42. *Theory of Knowledge*, p. 177.
43. Ibid., pp. 130–31.
44. Ibid., pp. 114, 132, 177.
45. *Tractatus Logico-Philosophicus*, 5.5261. Cf. 4.0411.
46. See *Notebooks 1914–16*, p. 121.
47. Ibid.
48. *Tractatus Logico-Philosophicus*, 2.0123. Cf. *Notebooks 1914–16*, November 4, 1914, last entry.
49. *Principia Mathematica*, vol. I, chapter 2, p. 43 (1910 edition), and *The Problems of Philosophy*, pp. 136–38.
50. *Theory of Knowledge*, p. 116. Cf. *Tractatus Logico-Philosophicus*, 4.031.
51. *Theory of Knowledge*, pp. 124–28.
52. See note 49, this chapter.
53. See my "The Function of Acquaintance in Russell's Philosophy," *Synthèse*, 46 (1981), pp. 149–66.

William Demopoulos and Michael Friedman

The Concept of Structure in The Analysis of Matter

The Analysis of Matter (1927) is perhaps best known for marking Russell's rejection of phenomenalism (in both its classical and methodological forms) and his development of a variety of Lockean Representationalism—Russell's causal theory of perception. This occupies part 2 of the work. Part 1, which is certainly less well known, contains many observations on twentieth-century physics. Unfortunately, Russell's discussion of relativity and the foundations of physical geometry is carried out in apparent ignorance of Reichenbach's and Carnap's investigations of the same period. The issue of conventionalism in its then contemporary form is simply not discussed. The only writers of the period who appear to have had any influence on Russell's conception of the philosophical issues raised by relativity were Whitehead and Eddington. Even the work of A. A. Robb fails to receive any extended discussion,[1] although Robb's causal theory is certainly relevant to many of Russell's concerns, especially those voiced in part 3, regarding the construction of points and the topology of space-time. In the case of quantum mechanics, the idiosyncrasy of Russell's selection of topics is more understandable, since the Heisenberg and Schrödinger theories were only just put forth. Nevertheless, it seems bizarre to a contemporary reader that Russell should have given such emphasis[2] to G. N. Lewis's suggestion that an atom emits light only when there is another atom to receive it—a suggestion reminiscent of Leibniz, and one to which Russell frequently returns. In short, the philosophical problems of modern physics with which Russell deals seem remote from the perspective of postpositivist philosophy of physics.

But if the observations on philosophy of physics seem dated, this is not true of the theory of theories that the book develops. As Grover Maxwell emphasized,[3] it is possible to extract from the book a theory of theories that anticipates in several respects the Ramsey sentence reconstruction of physical theories articulated by Carnap and others many decades later.

I

The heart of the theory of *The Analysis of Matter* is the claim that our knowledge of the external world is purely structural. For Russell, this thesis was based on the contention that we are not "directly acquainted" with physical objects. On a more neutral reading, the basis for the thesis is the belief that the reference of the class of theoretical predicates has an explanation in terms of the reference of another family of predicates. Such an explanation, if it could be given, would be highly nontrivial since no definitional or reductive relation between the two classes of predicates is claimed, although there is for Russell something like a reductive relation between our knowledge of theoretical properties and our knowledge of perceptual properties. In this respect the theory of *The Analysis of Matter* stands in marked contrast to the phenomenalism of Russell's 1914 external world program.[4] The point of the latter, of course, is to assume only perceptual objects (sensibilia, or actual and possible sense-data), and perceptual relations (especially perceptual similarity relations), and to *explicitly define* all other objects and relations from these. In *The Analysis of Matter*, Russell wishes to exploit the notion of logical form or structure to introduce scientific objects and relations by means of so-called *axiomatic* or *implicit definitions*. Thus, if we represent a scientific theory by

(1) $\theta(O_1, \ldots, O_n; T_1, \ldots, T_m)$,

say, where $O_1, \ldots, O_n$ are observational or perceptual terms and $T_1, \ldots, T_m$ are theoretical terms, then Russell in 1927 is prepared to accept the Ramsey sentence

(2) $\exists \tau_1, \ldots \exists \tau_m \theta(O_1, \ldots, O_n; \tau_1, \ldots, \tau_m)$

as the proper statement of our scientific knowledge. And (2) is legitimate whether or not the theoretical terms in (1) are explicitly definable from the observational terms; indeed, the whole tenor of Russell's discussion in *The Analysis of Matter* is that theoretical terms will not be explicitly definable in purely observational terms.[5]

It is not entirely clear why Russell abandoned his earlier phenomenalism. His explicit discussion of the issue in chapter XX of *The Analysis of Matter* is rather inconclusive. Postulating nonperceptible events allows us to maintain a very desirable continuity in stating the laws of nature,[6] but it appears that "ideal" perceptible events (the sensibilia of 1914) would serve equally well.[7] A perhaps more interesting reason for Russell's shift emerges from his discussion of the then current physics in part 1. Briefly, the point is that a phenomenalist reduction in the style of the 1914 program does not do justice to the novel "abstractness" of modern physics. Compared with the knowledge expressed in classical physics or common sense, for example, the knowledge conveyed by twentieth-century physics appears to be on a higher level of abstraction: it is "structural" or "mathe-

THE CONCEPT OF STRUCTURE   185

matical" in an important new sense. For Russell, this leads to a partial skepticism regarding our knowledge of the physical world:

> Whatever we infer from perceptions it is only structure that we can validly infer; and structure is what can be expressed by mathematical logic.[8]

> The only legitimate attitude about the physical world seems to be one of complete agnosticism as regards all but its mathematical properties.[9]

The view expressed in these passages is very strongly anticipated in Russell's *Introduction to Mathematical Philosophy* (1919), where its Kantian motivation is quite evident:

> There has been a great deal of speculation in traditional philosophy which might have been avoided if the importance of structure, and the difficulty of getting behind it, had been realized. For example, it is often said that space and time are subjective, but they have objective counterparts; or that phenomena are subjective, but are caused by things in themselves, which must have differences *inter se* corresponding with the differences in the phenomena to which they give rise. Where such hypotheses are made, it is generally supposed that we can know very little about the objective counterparts. In actual fact, however, if the hypotheses as stated were correct, the objective counterparts would form a world having the same structure as the phenomenal world, and allowing us to infer from phenomena the truth of all propositions that can be stated in abstract terms and are known to be true of phenomena. If the phenomenal world has three dimensions, so must the world behind phenomena; if the phenomenal world is Euclidean, so must the other be; and so on. In short, every proposition having a communicable significance must be true of both worlds or of neither: the only difference must lie in just that essence of individuality which always eludes words and baffles description, but which, for that very reason is irrelevant to science. Now the only purpose that philosophers have in view in condemning phenomena is in order to persuade themselves and others that the real world is very different from the world of appearance. We can all sympathize with their wish to prove such a very desirable proposition, but we cannot congratulate them on their success. It is true that many of them do not assert objective counterparts to phenomena, and these escape from the above argument. Those who do assert counterparts are, as a rule, very reticent on the subject, probably because they feel instinctively that, if pursued, it will bring about too much of a *rapprochement* between the real and the phenomenal world. If they were to pursue the topic, they could hardly avoid the conclusions which we have been suggesting. In such ways, as well as in many others, the notion of structure...is important. (pp. 61-62)

To sum up, on Russell's "structuralism" or "structural realism," of "percepts" we know *both* their quality and structure (where Russell's use of the term "quality" includes relations), while of external events we know only their structure. The distinction is, in the first instance, between properties and relations of individuals and properties and relations of properties and relations. Structural properties are thus a particular subclass of properties and relations: they are marked by the fact that they are expressible only in the language of higher-order logic. Unlike Locke's distinction between primary and secondary qualities, the structure/quality distinction does not mark a difference in ontological status: external events have both structure and qualities—indeed when we speak of the structure of external events, this is elliptical for the structural properties of their qualities. Neither is it the case that one is "more fundamental" than the other or that qualities are "occurrent" while structure is a power. What is claimed is a deficiency in our knowledge: of external events we know only the structural properties of their properties and relations, but we do not know the properties and relations themselves. Of course physical knowledge falls within the scope of this claim, so that the theory of perception immediately yields the consequence that physical theories give knowledge of structure and *only* knowledge of structure.

Russell's emphasis on structure in *The Analysis of Matter* has close affinities with much other work of the period, especially with the two classics of early (pre-1930) positivism: Schlick's *General Theory of Knowledge* (1918, second edition 1925) and Carnap's *Aufbau* (1928). Indeed, the "critical realism" of *General Theory of Knowledge* is identical in almost every respect to Russell's structural realism of 1927. Schlick argues that modern physics deals with real unobservable entities (atoms, electrons, the electromagnetic field) which cannot be understood as logical constructions out of sense-data in the manner of Mach's *Analysis of Sensations* (1897) or Russell's 1914 external world program (§26). Such entities are not experienceable, intuitable, or even picturable; accordingly, Schlick goes so far as to call them "transcendent" entities and "things-in-themselves" (25). Nevertheless, this "transcendent" presents no obstacle to our knowledge or cognition, for *knowledge relates always to purely formal or structural properties*—not to intuitive qualities or content. Thus, while we cannot experience or intuit the entities of modern physics, we can grasp their formal or structural features by means of axiomatic or implicit definitions in the style of Hilbert's *Foundations of Geometry* (1899)—and this is all that knowledge or cognition requires (§§5–7). The similarities with Russell's view of 1927 are patent. However, there is one significant difference: Schlick draws a sharp contrast between knowledge (*erkennen*) and acquaintance (*kennen*). On his account *knowledge* by acquaintance is a contradiction in terms, for only structural features are ever knowable (§12). We are acquainted with or experience (*erleben*) *some* qualities (content), but we have knowledge or cognition of none. As we have seen, for Russell we know both the form and the content of percepts.

Carnap's *Aufbau* does not embrace structural realism. *All* concepts of science are to be explicitly defined within a single "constructional system" whose only

THE CONCEPT OF STRUCTURE   *187*

nonlogical primitive is a "phenomenalistic" relation R_s of *recollected similarity*. Yet the form/content distinction and the notion of logical structure are equally important. To be sure, all concepts of science are to be constructed from a basis in the given, or "my experience," but the *objectivity* of science is captured in a restriction to purely structural statements about this given basis. Although the "matter" or content of Carnap's constructional system is indeed subjective or "autopsychological"—and therefore private and inexpressible—what is really important is the logical form or structure of the system. For it is logical form and logical form alone that makes objective knowledge and communication possible:[10]

> Science wants to speak about what is objective, and whatever does not belong to the structure but to the material (i.e. anything that can be pointed out in a concrete ostensive definition) is, in the final analysis, subjective. One can easily see that physics is almost altogether desubjectivized, since almost all physical concepts have been transformed into purely structural concepts.... From the point of view of construction theory, this state of affairs is to be described in the following way. The series of experiences is different for each subject. If we want to achieve, in spite of this, agreement in the names for the entities which are constructed on the basis of these experiences, then this cannot be done by reference to the completely divergent content, but only through the formal description of the structure of these entities.[11]

Characteristically, Carnap does not rest content with a simple reference to logical form or structure, he turns his "objectivity requirement" into a definite technical program: the program of defining all scientific concepts in terms of what he calls *purely structural definite descriptions* (§§11–15). Such a definition explains a particular empirical object as the unique entity satisfying certain purely formal or logical conditions: the *visual field*, for example, is defined as the unique five-dimensional "sense class" (§§86–91). The point is that purely structural descriptions contain no nonlogical vocabulary; ultimately, we will need only variables and the logical machinery of *Principia Mathematica* (or set theory).[12] Thus, while Russell in *The Analysis of Matter* would formulate our physical knowledge in the manner of (2) (i.e., by turning all theoretical terms into variables), Carnap in the *Aufbau* goes much further: all terms whatsoever are to be replaced by variables. (The reader might very well wonder how Carnap's one nonlogical primitive R_s is to be itself eliminated in favor of variables. We shall return to this later.)

II

We believe there are insurmountable difficulties with the theory of theoretical knowledge just outlined. So far as we are aware these difficulties were first raised by M. H. A. Newman in an article published in *Mind* in 1928. Newman's paper—the only philosophical paper he ever published—is not as well known as it deserves to be. (The prose is quite delightful, and for that reason alone, it deserves a wider readership.) This paper contains much that is of interest today, and so we propose to discuss the structuralism of Russell's *Analysis of Matter* from the perspective of Newman's paper.

Newman begins his discussion with the observation that on any theory of scientific knowledge, the question of the truth of at least some propositions of physics should turn out to be nontrivial. Consider, for example, the question whether matter is atomic. Newman observes that on any account "this is a real question to be answered by consideration of the evidence, not a matter of definition."[13] In fact, whether matter is atomic is a question that concerns the holding of various "structural properties," although they are of a fairly high level of abstraction. (It entails, for example, that physical objects have isolable constituents, and that these constituents have a certain theoretically characterizable autonomy.) Newman's point is that whether the world exhibits such properties is a matter to be discovered, not stipulated, and we may demand of a theory of theories that it preserve this fact. The gist of his criticism of Russell is that (with one exception) Russell's theory does not satisfy this constraint. Let us see how the argument goes.

The difficulty is with the claim that *only* structure is known. On this view, "the world consists of objects, forming an aggregate whose structure with regard to a certain relation R is known, say [it has structure] W; but of...R nothing is known...but its existence;...all we can say is, *There is* a relation R such that the structure of the external world with reference to R is W" (Newman, p. 144). But "*any* collection of things can be organized so as to have the structure W, provided there are the right number of them" (p. 144). Thus on this view, only cardinality questions are open to discovery! Every other claim about the world that can be known at all can be known a priori as a logical consequence of the existence of a set of α-many objects. For, given a set A of cardinality α, we can, with a minimal amount of set theory or second-order logic, establish the existence of a relation having the structure W, provided that W is compatible with the cardinality constraint that $|A| = \alpha$. (The relevant theorem from set theory or second-order logic is the proposition that every set A determines a full structure, i.e., one that contains every relation [in extension] of every arity on A; such a structure forms the basis for a [standard] model for the language of second [or higher] order logic.)

It is important to be clear on the nature of the difficulty Newman has uncovered. The problem is *not* a failure of the theory to specify the domain of objects on which a model of our theories of the world is to be defined. The difficulty is not the one of Pythagoreanism raised by Quine[14] and John Winnie[15]; that is to say, it is not that Russell cannot rule out abstract models. Indeed Russell himself raises this problem in the introduction to *The Analysis of Matter*:

It frequently happens that we have a deductive mathematical system, starting from hypotheses concerning undefined objects, and that we have reason to believe that there are objects fulfilling these hypotheses, although, initially, we are unable to point out any such objects with certainty. Usually, in such cases, although many different sets of objects are abstractly available as fulfilling the hypotheses, there is one such set which is much more important than the others.... The substitution of such a set for the undefined objects is "interpretation." This process is essential in discovering the philosophical import of physics.

The difference between an important and an unimportant interpretation may be made clear by the case of geometry. Any geometry, Euclidean or non-euclidean, in which every point has co-ordinates which are real numbers, can be interpreted as applying to a system of sets of real numbers—i.e., a point can be taken to *be* the series of its co-ordinates. This interpretation is legitimate, and is convenient when we are studying geometry as a branch of pure mathematics. But it is not the important interpretation. Geometry is important, unlike arithmetic and analysis, because it can be interpreted so as to be part of applied mathematics—in fact, so as to be part of physics. It is this interpretation which is the really interesting one, and we cannot therefore rest content with the interpretation which makes geometry part of the study of real numbers, and so, ultimately, part of the study of finite integers. (pp. 4–5)

In this case we have a simple criterion for separating important from unimportant interpretations: the important interpretations are connected with our observations, the unimportant ones are *not*. Newman's problem arises *after* the domain has been fixed: in the case of abstract versus physical geometry we have to distinguish different relations on different domains. The problem is made easier by the fact that we can exclude one of the domains *and therefore* one class of relations. When the domain of the model is *given*, we must "distinguish between systems of relations that hold among the members of a given aggregate" (Newman, p. 147). This is a difficulty because there is *always* a relation with the structure W. Russell cannot avoid trivialization by claiming that the relation with structure W that exists as a matter of logic is not necessarily the *important* relation with structure W (as the interpretation in R^3 is not the important interpretation of geometry). That is to say, one cannot avoid trivialization in this way without some means of distinguishing important from unimportant relations on a given domain. But the notion of importance that must be appealed to is one for which Russell can give no explanation, and in fact, his own theory precludes giving any explanation of the notion.

Newman's summary is well worth quoting in full:

In the present case [i.e., in the case where we must choose among relations on a given domain rather than choose among different relations on different domains] we should have to compare the importance of relations of which nothing is known save their incidence (the same for all of them) in a certain aggregate. For this comparison there is no possible criterion, so that "importance" would have to be reckoned among the prime unanalyzable qualities of the constituents of the world, which is, I think, absurd. The statement that there is an *important* relation which sets up the structure W among the unperceived events of the world cannot, then, be accepted as a true interpretation of our beliefs about these events, and it seems necessary to give up the "structure/quality" division of knowledge in its strict form. (p. 147)

Recall that giving up the structure/quality division in its strict form means giving up the idea that we do not know the qualities of unperceived objects. This of course would rob Russell's theory of its distinctive character, and so far as we can tell, Russell remained equivocal on this issue for the remainder of his philosophical career.

It might be thought that Newman's objection depends on too extensional an interpretation of relations, and that once this is given up, a way out of the difficulty is available. The idea is that logic (or logic plus set theory) only guarantees what Newman calls *fictitious* relations—relations whose only extrinsic property is that they hold between specified pairs of individuals—e.g., binary relations whose associated propositional functions are of the form "x is a and y is b, or x is a and y is c, etc.," where a, b, and c are elements of A. But in fact this is not so. Given some means of identifying the individuals of the domain A, we can always find an isomorphic structure W' which holds of a nonfictitious relation R' on domain A'. We may now define a nonfictitious relation S whose field is included in A: S is just the image of R' under the inverse of the isomorphism that correlates A and A'. Newman's example is a simple combinatorial one. Consider a graph $\Gamma(R)$ of a relation R on $A \times A$, where $A = \{a, \alpha, \beta, \gamma\}$

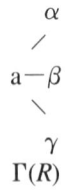

$$
\begin{array}{c}
\alpha \\
\diagup \\
a - \beta \\
\diagdown \\
\gamma
\end{array}
$$
$\Gamma(R)$

Define a *new* relation S on A by letting S hold of (x, y) if $f(x)$ and $f(y)$ belong to different alphabets where "a" $= f(a)$, "α" $= f(\alpha)$, "β" $= f(\beta)$, "γ" $= f(\gamma)$. Then S is nonfictitious. It is clear that this strategy is perfectly general. Following Newman, call a nonfictitious relation *real*. Then reality in this sense is "preserved under isomorphism"; i.e., any extensionally specified relation may be regarded as the image of a real (nonfictitious) relation. And this real relation exists if the fictitious one does. Thus a claim of the form "There exists a *real* relation R such

THE CONCEPT OF STRUCTURE   *191*

that..." will be true given a claim of the form "There exists a relation R such that..." Of course S may nonetheless be *trivial* or *unimportant*. But this just shows that eliminating extensionalism does not solve our problem.

We might try to add further constraints on the notion "R is a real relation." But then we move away from the relatively clear intuition that motivated its original characterization, viz., that a relation with only a purely extensional characterization is fictitious. (Notice that certain obvious candidates such as "projectability" cannot be appealed to since it is precisely the class of relations and properties which enter into laws that we are attempting to delimit.)

The conclusion Newman draws from this analysis is, we think, the right one: since it is indisputably true that our knowledge of structure is nontrivial—we clearly do not stipulate the holding of the structural properties our theories postulate—it cannot be the case that our knowledge of the unperceived parts of the world is *purely* structural. The unobservable/observable dichotomy is not explicable in terms of the structure/quality division of knowledge without giving up the idea that our knowledge of the unobservable parts of the world is discovered rather than stipulated. Of course it is also possible to give up the naïve intuition on which Newman's conclusion from his analysis depends. In this case one would *accept* the stipulative character of the theoretical components of our knowledge, and indeed much of the philosophy of science that immediately preceded and subsequently followed *The Analysis of Matter* did just this. Russell is unique in wanting to preserve a nonconventionalist view of the world's structure, while retaining a structure/quality or form/content division of knowledge that is intended to more or less correspond to the division between theoretical and observational knowledge.

By the way, Newman's objection also explains the intuition that despite its intention, Russell's structuralism collapses into phenomenalism. The difficulty is that every assertion about unperceived events is trivially true, i.e., true as a matter of logic plus an empirical assumption concerning cardinality. Now the phenominalist claims that statements about the external world are "reducible" to statements about perception. Whatever *else* this may mean, it requires that, given the appropriate reductive definitions, statements about the physical world are entailed by statements about perception. But if Russell's view is accepted, this characteristic consequence of phenomenalism is almost guaranteed: if statements about the physical world are true as a matter of logic, then they are implied by every proposition, and, in particular, they are implied by the statements of perception. Thus *modulo* the single nonlogical assumption concerning the cardinality of the external world, Russell's structuralism guarantees the truth of this phenomenalist thesis!

The only reference to Newman's paper of which we are aware is in the second volume of Russell's autobiography. Russell very graciously acknowledges Newman's criticism in a letter he reprints without comment. The letter is worth quoting at length. Dated April 24, 1928, it is identified simply as "To Max Newman, the distinguished mathematician."

Dear Newman,
Many thanks for sending me the off-print of your article about me in *Mind*. I read it with great interest and some dismay. You make it entirely obvious that my statements to the effect that nothing is known about the physical world except its structure are either false or trivial, and I am somewhat ashamed at not having noticed the point for myself.

It is of course obvious, as you point out, that the only effective assertion about the physical world involved in saying that it is susceptible to such and such a structure is an assertion about its cardinal number. (This by the way is not quite so trivial an assertion as it would seem to be, if, as is not improbable, the cardinal number involved is finite. This, however, is not a point upon which I wish to lay stress.) It was quite clear to me, as I read your article, that I had not really intended to say what in fact I did say, that *nothing* is known about the physical world except its structure. I had always assumed spaciotemporal continuity with the world of percepts, that is to say, I had assumed that there might be co-punctuality between percepts and non-percepts, and even that one could pass by a finite number of steps from one event to another compresent with it, from one end of the universe to the other. And co-punctuality I regarded as a relation which might exist among percepts and is itself perceptible.[16]

To our knowledge, Russell never discusses the puzzle in any of his later work. He seems to give up the idea that our knowledge of the physical world is purely structural, but there is no account of how, on his theory of knowledge (e.g., the theory developed in *Human Knowledge: Its Scope and Limits* [1948]), such non-structural knowledge can arise. Yet all the elements of the earlier and later theories are the same—the only difference is in the conclusion drawn. Thus either the original claim (that we are restricted to purely structural knowledge) was theoretically unmotivated or the argument of the later theory contains a lacuna. The difficulty in adjudicating between these alternatives is that the theoretical development is made to depend on what we regard as falling within "acquaintance." And this makes the resolution quite artificial: in the earlier theory we could not assume acquaintance with (what Maxwell used to call) a cross category notion such as spatiotemporal contiguity or causality, but in light of the difficulties of that theory we now find that we *can* assume this![17] We are not saying that one *cannot* resolve the issue in this way. But it seems quite clear that without a considerable advance in the theoretical articulation of this rather elusive Russellian concept, no such resolution of the difficulty can be very compelling.

III

There is another consequence that Newman draws, although it is much less explicit in the article. Russell's structuralism can be viewed as a theory of how the reference of the theoretical vocabulary is fixed. On this view the reference of a T-predicate is fixed by two things: (1) its connection with observation, and (2) its structural properties. As we have seen, the connection with observation fixes the domain (or at least, establishes that very many sets are *not* the domain of interpretation). Structure is supposed to complete the task while preserving the nonstipulative character of the truth of our theoretical knowledge. As we saw, Newman observes that within Russell's theory, there is no analogue for relations of the important/unimportant criterion for domains. From a contemporary, model-theoretic standpoint, this is just the problem of intended versus unintended interpretations: Newman shows that there is always some relation, R (on the intended domain) with structure W. But if the only constraints on something's being the intended referent of "R" are observational and structural constraints, no such criterion for distinguishing the intended referent of "R" can be given; so that the notion of an intended interpretation is, in Quine's phrase, provided by our background theory and hence cannot be a formal or structural notion in Russell's sense. Now, in fact, something strikingly similar to this argument has recently been rediscovered by Hilary Putnam, and it has been used by him to pose a puzzle for certain "realist" views of reference and truth.

Putnam's formulation of the argument is model theoretic and general rather than informal and illustrative: suppose we are given a theory T all of whose observational consequences are true. We assume, for the sake of the argument, that the observational consequences are true. We assume, for the sake of the argument, that the observational consequences of T may be characterized as a subset of the sentences generated from a given "O-vocabulary." It is assumed that the interpretation of the language $L(T)$ of T is specified for its O-vocabulary, so that T is "partially interpreted" in the sense that the interpretation function is a partial function. Assume that T is consistent and that M is an abstract model of the uninterpreted sentences of T of the same cardinality as T's intended domain. Following Putnam we let "THE WORLD" denote the intended domain of T. Now extend the interpretation to the theoretical vocabulary of T by letting each predicate of the theoretical vocabulary of T denote the image in THE WORLD of its interpretation in m under any one-to-one correspondence between M and THE WORLD. Call this interpretation (which extends the partial interpretation) "SAT." Clearly SAT is completely arbitrary, and should be an utterly unacceptable extension since it trivializes the question whether T is true. Any theory of knowledge and reference that is incapable of rejecting SAT, i.e., any theory that is incapable of distinguishing truth from truth under SAT−TRUTH (SAT)−is committed to the implication, T is true if T is TRUE (SAT). But T is TRUE (SAT) as a matter of logic! That is,

"*T* is TRUE (SAT)" follows, via the completeness theorem, from "*T* is consistent." So any theory that cannot exclude SAT as an intended interpretation of *L*(*T*) cannot account for our naive confidence in the belief that our theories, if true, are "significantly true."[18].

Except for its metalogical flavor, this argument parallels Newman's. Where Putman argues from the consistency of a set of sentences, Newman argues directly from the existence of a relational structure satisfying the intuitive conditions of a model. (Recall that Newman was writing in 1928 and in the logicist tradition of Russell and Whitehead—a tradition to which the metalogical turn in mathematical logic was quite alien.)[19]

The chief difference between Putman and Newman is in the use made of the argument. Putman, as we have said, employs the argument against a certain form of realism—one which is rather difficult to isolate, although there are some suggestions. For example, Putman says it is that form of realism which holds that even an epistemically ideal theory might be false; or any view which regards truth as radically nonepistemic; or any theory of truth and reference which "treats language as a 'mirror of the world,' rather than one which supposes merely that 'speakers mirror the world'—i.e. their environment—in the sense of constructing a symbolic representation of that environment."[20] All these remarks, though certainly suggestive, are vague and elusive.

In a recent book, Putman expresses the significance of the result slightly differently.[21] There he characterizes the argument as supporting Quine's observation[22] that fixing the set of true observation sentences together with the set of accepted theoretical sentences will not determine the reference of the theoretical vocabulary. Putman shows that the indeterminacy affects the reference of the T-vocabulary in every possible world, and in this respect extends Quine's observation.[23] The formal connection with Newman's argument is this. Newman shows that fixing the domain and models up to isomorphism does not fix the intended reference of the *T*-vocabulary. Putman shows that fixing the domain and models up to elementary equivalence does not fix the intended reference of the *T*-vocabulary. (Thus formally Newman's argument is stronger than Putman's, since isomorphism strictly implies equivalence, although we do not wish to lay much stress on this fact.)

It may be that Newman's argument contains an important observation about realism in *general*—not merely about *structural* realism. The recent work of Putman, to which we have drawn attention, is intended to suggest that it does. But we have been unable to find or construct a clear statement of the connection. Certainly the argument poses difficulties for partial interpretation accounts of theories that exactly parallel the difficulties confronted by Russell's theory: both accounts of theoretical knowledge and reference fail to square with our naive beliefs regarding the nature of the truth of theoretical claims. The conclusion we have suggested is a conservative one: the argument shows that neither Russell nor the neopositivist doctrine of partial interpretation has gotten the analysis of theoretical knowledge and reference quite right. A satisfactory account of these notions must do justice to such "obvious facts" as that the world's structure is discovered rather than stipulated. We are skeptical of our ability to do this on any view of reference and truth that does not take the language of physical theory as the "ultimate parameter" within which reference is fixed.

IV

The difficulty Newman raises for Russell's use of the notion of structure can be clarified and deepened if we look at an analogous difficulty that arises for Carnap in the *Aufbau* and then take a brief glance at Wittgenstein's *Tractatus*. Newman's problem can be put this way. Russell wishes to turn theoretical terms into variables by Ramsification; accordingly, physics becomes the assertion that there *exist* properties and relations having certain logical features, satisfying certain implicit definitions. The problem is that this procedure trivializes physics: it threatens to turn the *empirical* claims of science into mere *mathematical* truths. More precisely, if our theory is consistent, and if all its purely observational consequences are true, then the truth of the Ramsey sentence *follows* as a theorem of set theory or second-order logic, provided our initial domain has the right cardinality — if it does not, then the consistency of our theory again implies the existence of a domain that does. Hence, the truth of physical theory reduces to the truth of its observational consequences, and as we saw earlier, Russell's realism collapses into a version of phenomenalism or strict empiricism after all: *all* theories with the same observational consequences will be equally true.

We have observed that Carnap attempts to go Russell one better in the Aufbau by turning *all* scientific terms into variables by means of purely structural definite descriptions. So Carnap's program is faced with a closely analogous difficulty, a difficulty he himself articulates with characteristic honesty and precision in §§153–155. Up to this point in the *Aufbau*, all scientific concepts have been introduced via structural definite descriptions containing the single nonlogical relation R_s of recollected similarity: the visual field, for example, is the unique five-dimensional "sense class" *based on* R_s. However, the goal of "complete formalization" — converting all definitions into *purely* structural definite descriptions — can only be achieved if the basic relation R_s is itself eliminated (§153). How is this to be done? Well, R_s also has a logical form or structure: it has a *graph* $\Gamma(R_s)$. For example, R_s is asymmetrical (§108), and there is one and only one "sense class" based on R_s that is five-dimensional (§§117–119). To be sure, we can know these formal properties of R_s only empirically, but once we know them, we can express them in a purely formal schema $\gamma(R_s)$, where R is now a *relation variable*. The idea, then, is to define R_s as the unique relation with this graph:

(3) $R_s = (\iota R)\Gamma(R)$.

However, as Carnap immediately points out, there is a serious problem with this procedure. Since $\Gamma(R)$ is now a purely formal schema containing no nonlogical primitives, the *uniqueness* claim implicit in (3) will never be satisfied. As long as the condition Γ is consistent, there will always be infinitely many distinct relations with this graph, even if we confine ourselves to relations on the field of R_s:

> Our assumption is justified only if the new relation extensions are not arbitrary, unconnected pair lists, but if we require of them that they correspond to some experienceable, "natural" relations (to give a preliminary, vague expression).
>
> If no such requirement is made, then there are certainly other relation extensions [besides R_s itself] for which all constructional formulas can be produced.... All we have to do is carry out a one-to-one transformation of the set of basic elements into itself and determine as the new basic relations those relation extensions whose inventory is the transformed inventory of the original basic relations. In this case, the new relation extensions have the same structure as the original ones (they are "isomorphic"). (154)

The analogy with the Newman problem is evident.

How does Carnap handle the problem? He introduces the notion of *foundedness* to characterize those relation extensions that are "experienceable and 'natural,' " and argues that one can view this notion as a primitive concept of logic:

> [Foundedness] does not belong to any definite extralogical object domain, as all other non-logical objects do. Our considerations concerning the characterization of the basic relations of a constructional system as founded relation extensions of a certain kind hold for every constructional system of every domain whatever. It is perhaps permissible, because of this generality, to envisage the concept of foundedness as a concept of logic and to introduce it, since it is undefinable, as a *basic concept of logic*... let us introduce the class of founded relation extensions as a basic concept of logic (logistic symbol: *found*) without considering the problem as already solved. (§154)

In other words, Carnap proposes to do precisely what we saw Newman recoil from: he wants to reckon "importance" (foundedness) as "among the prime unanalyzable qualities of the constituents of the world"! Once this is done, the problem of defining R_s is easily solved. We replace (3) with

(4) $R_s = (\iota R)(found(R)$ and $\Gamma(R))$.

(See §155.) It is clear, however, that we must side with Newman here: the idea that (4) is a purely logical formula *is* absurd.

Actually, it is not entirely obvious why Carnap needs a definition like (3); it is not clear why he needs to make a *uniqueness* claim. He could express our empirical knowledge, as Russell does, with a purely existential claim

(5) $\exists R\ \Gamma(R)$,

and (5) fulfills the goal of "complete formalization" just as well as (3): both contain no nonlogical vocabulary. Of course (5) is vulnerable to the Newman objection in precisely its original form – it again threatens to turn empirical truth into mathematical truth – but let us slow down and reflect for a moment. For, when applied to our current physical theories, the assumptions needed to prove (5) turn out to be rather strong. In particular, we will need some version of the axiom of infinity and some version of the power set axiom applied to infinite sets (that is, we will need the continuum). Contemporary model theory for second-order logic makes both these assumptions, and that is why (5) is a *theorem*. Suppose, however, that we are transported back into the 1920s. The line between logic and mathematics is much less clear, and it is equally unclear whether strong existence assumptions like the axiom of infinity and the power set axiom are to be counted as part of logic *or* mathematics.[24] (In *Principia Mathematica*, for example, Russell carries along the axiom of infinity as an undischarged hypothesis.) Accordingly, the status of (5) is much less clear-cut.

To see some of the issues here, consider the strictest and most rigorous version of logicism devised in this period, namely, Wittgenstein's *Tractatus* (1921). The *Tractatus* is clear and emphatic about the axiom of infinity and set theory: neither is part of logic (5.535, 6.031). In fact, logic makes no cardinality claims whatsoever: there are no privileged numbers (5.453). By the same token, however, such cardinality claims are not part of mathematics either, for mathematics is a "logical method" involving only the simplest forms of combinatorial equations (6.2–6.241). Although Wittgenstein is not very explicit in the *Tractatus* about the precise scope of mathematics, it is apparently exhausted by a rather small fragment of elementary arithmetic. On this kind of conception, then, formulas like (5) will *not* be theorems of logic or mathematics; if true at all they can only be empirically (synthetically) true. Hence, on a Tractarian conception of logic and mathematics, we could perhaps make sense of Carnap's program of "complete formalization" after all. And, for all we know, Wittgenstein could have had something very much like this in mind. (See *Tractatus* 5.526–5.526, for example, where Wittgenstein says that we can describe the world completely by means of *fully generalized* propositions. See also 6.343–6.3432.) In any case, whether or not these considerations have any connection with Wittgenstein's intentions in the *Tractatus*, they do illustrate some of the intellectual tensions produced by logicism's attempt to account simultaneously for both pure mathematics and applied mathematics (mathematical physics). In general, it appears that we can account for the distinctive character of one only at the expense of the other. This is perhaps the final lesson of the Newman problem.

Notes

1. Cf. J. Winnie, "The Causal Theory of Space-Time," *Minnesota Studies in the Philosophy of Science*, Vol. VIII (Minneapolis: University of Minnesota Press, 1977), pp. 156ff. for a discussion of Russell's remarks on Minkowski space-time, and their relation to Robb's theory.
2. See *Analysis of Mind*, specially pp. 125ff.
3. See especially "Scientific Methodology and the Causal Theory of Perception," in I. Lakatos and A. Musgrave (eds.), *Problems in the Philosophy of Science* (Amsterdam: North Holland, 1968), and "Structural Realism and the Meaning of Theoretical Terms," *Minnesota Studies in the Philosophy of Science*, Vol. IV (Minneapolis: University of Minnesota Press, 1971).
4. As articulated in "The Relation of Sense-Data to Physics," *Scientia* (1914) and *Our Knowledge of the External World* (1914).
5. Notice that whether the terms are implicitly or explicitly definable depends on the logical framework within which the definitions are to be constructed. Is (1) a first-order theory with identity? An extension of first-order set theory? A formulation in some higher-order logic? These differences matter because, if one is working in a sufficiently strong background language, one can often *transform* axiomatic or implicit definitions into explicit definitions (cf. Quine, "Implicit Definition Sustained," *Journal of Philosophy*, 61 [1964], pp. 71–73, for one such strategy). Of course this way of expressing the issue is anachronistic, since these distinctions were not available to Russell. Consequently the distinction between implicit and explicit definition is not so clearcut for Russell. Thus, for example, Russell appears willing to allow implicit definitions even in 1914 when, in section IX of "The Relation of Sense-Data to Physics," he defines physical things as "those series of appearances whose matter obeys the laws of physics."
6. *The Analysis of Matter* (1927), pp. 216f.
7. Ibid., pp. 210–13.
8. Ibid., p. 254.
9. Ibid., p. 270. See also Chapter 14, especially the discussion of Eddington on pp. 136f.
10. I.e., one finds the form/content distinction drawn in such a way that form is objective and communicable, whereas content is neither. Schlick came to view the form/content distinction in much the same way in his later writings, while Russell came to place much less stress on this (somewhat romantic) view of the distinction. (For Schlick's view see "Experience, Cognition and Metaphysics" [1926] and *Lectures on Form and Content* [1932], in vol. 2 of his *Collected Papers* [Dordrecht: Reidel, 1979].) Schlick explicitly acknowledges the influence of the *Aufbau* and of Wittgenstein's *Tractatus*.
11. *Aufbau*, §16. In the explanatory references to this section, Carnap refers to the passage from Russell's *Introduction to Mathematical Philosophy* quoted earlier. Immediately before this section, he refers to Schlick's doctrine of implicit definition in *General Theory of Knowledge*.
12. As Carnap himself emphasized, this kind of program for individuating concepts by means of purely formal properties only begins to make sense in the context of modern, *polyadic* logic. Monadic concepts correspond to unstructured sets whose only formal property is their cardinality. Polyadic concepts have such diverse formal properties as transitivity, reflexivity, connectedness, dimensionality, and so on. In Russell's terminology from *Introduction to Mathematical Philosophy* and *The Analysis of Matter*, only polyadic concepts have "relation-numbers."
13. Newman, "Mr. Russell's Causal Theory of perception," *Mind* (1928), p. 143. All references to Newman are to this article.
14. Quine, "Implicit Definition Sustained."
15. John A. Winnie, "The Implicit Definition of Theoretical Terms," *British Journal for the Philosophy of Science*, 18 (1967), theorem 2, pp. 227ff.
16. *The Autobiography of Bertrand Russell, Volume 2* (London: Allen & Unwin, 1968), p. 176.
17. Maxwell opted for this solution. (See the papers cited in note 3.) Unlike Russell, Maxwell was quite explicit about the nature of the problem.
18. John Winnie, in the paper cited in note 15, employs an argument of this form in the proof of his theorem 1. Winnie's discussion focuses on formal features of the puzzle: that there is not a unique interpretation of the theory and that there is always an arithmetical interpretation. Newman and (we believe) Putman emphasize a different point, viz., that *mere consistency* seems to be sufficient

for *truth*; i.e. since *T* has an arithmetical interpretation it has a true interpretation *in the world* (i.e., in THE WORLD).

19. See Warren Goldfarb, "Logic in the Twenties: The Nature of the Quantifier," *Journal of Symbolic Logic*, 44 (1979), pp. 351–68.

20. Putnam, *Meaning and the Moral Sciences* (Boston: Routledge & Kegan Paul, 1978), p. 123. The other suggestions may also be found in this chapter, which is a reprint of Putnam's 1978 APA presidential address.

21. *Reason, Truth and History* (Cambridge: Cambridge University Press, 1981), pp. 33f.

22. W. V. Quine, "Ontological Relativity," in *Ontological Relativity and Other Essays* (New York: Columbia University Press, 1969).

23. See the appendix to *Reason, Truth and History*.

24. Carnap, for one, seems remarkably sanguine about this. He is apparently willing to count both *AxInf* and *PowerSet* as logical. In §125, for example, he introduces and n-dimensional real number space with a completely innocent air. Apparently, then, he is willing to count virtually all of set theory as logic (see also §107). This is why (5) could not possibly serve as an expression of our *empirical* knowledge of Carnap.

R. M. Sainsbury

On Induction and Russell's Postulates

Russell's later epistemology, dominated by his *Human Knowledge: Its Scope and Limits* (1948),[1] has received relatively little attention. Yet it contains plenty to interest a contemporary audience. There is a version of foundationalism that subtly avoids many difficulties standardly held to beset such a position. There is a naturalistic approach to various aspects of knowledge, a naturalism which both regards evolutionary facts as relevant to problems about induction, and also singles out the purely descriptive task of locating knowledge as a phenomenon within the natural order, a task that turns its back on traditional skeptical problems. There is a discussion of what would nowadays be called "Goodman's paradox," on the basis of which Russell draws the conclusion that a correct system of inductive reasoning could not be purely formal.[2] And there is more besides.

I want to look above all at Russell's "postulates of scientific inference." He held that unless these are known independently of experience, "science is moonshine" (p. 524). Yet he also held that postulates state contingent facts about the way the actual world happens to be. This may not strike us as a very comfortable position, but Russell offers solace in the form of a combination of modified foundationalism and a species of naturalism. The nature of this foundationalism, as presented in *Human Knowledge*, will set the background to the issues.

1. A Minimal Foundationalism

Foundationalism must entail that there is a distinction between (as I shall put it) *data*, which form the foundations of knowledge, and *hypotheses*, which form its superstructure and are justified, if at all, by, and ultimately only by, data. This much, Russell accepted. But this much has often been coupled with the following further doctrines, all of which Russell rejected:

(a) The data are certain.
(b) No proposition can contribute to the justification of a datum.
(c) A datum has a distinctive content.

Russell defined a datum as:

a proposition which has some degree of rational credibility on its own account, independently of any argument derived from other propositions. (p. 409; cf. p. 401)

This is consistent with the degree of rational credibility of a datum being less than maximal, and thus makes room for Russell's view that "a datum may be uncertain." He argues for this from such phenomena as faint perceptions, uncertain memories, and the dim awareness of logical connections: these may give us grounds, however inconclusive, for believing hypotheses. They serve as data, despite being uncertain.

The denial of (b) is closely connected with the denial of (a):

I may have a faint memory of dining with Mr So-and-So sometime last year, and may find that my diary for last year has an entry which corroborates my recollection. It follows that every one of my beliefs may be strengthened or weakened by being brought into relation with other beliefs.(p. 401)

In Russell's foundationalism, unlike some traditional versions, one cannot identify the data on a purely structural basis. In some traditional versions, if one sets out a person's body of knowledge as a flow diagram, with arrows indicating the flow of justification, his data would be identifiable as beliefs having no incoming, but at most outgoing, arrows. Consider a sub-structure like this:

In some traditional systems that permit such a substructure (and not all do), one could infer that neither A nor B is a datum. For Russell, one cannot infer anything about whether or not A and B are data. The diagram is consistent with either or both being data. (Unless some other arrows enter A or B, however, at least one must be a datum.) To display Russell's system in this fashion, one would have to attach numbers to the arrows to show how much credibility was being transmitted, and numbers to the propositions to indicate their total degree of credibility from all sources. A datum could then be defined as a proposition whose total degree of credibility exceeded the sum of the degrees associated with the inflowing arrows.

A traditional doctrine is that the source of the "intrinsic" credibility of a datum is the subject matter of the proposition. For example, the proposition concerns the subject's sense experience, so it is intrinsically credible for him. This is the sort of doctrine I intend to subsume under (c). Although he is not completely explicit, Russell seems to have rejected this. There are plenty of examples, like the one quoted about dining with Mr. So-and-So, in which it is obvious that it is not some feature of the proposition itself that gives rise to its "intrinsic" credibility, but rather something about how the believer is related to it. One could believe "I dined last year with Mr So-and-So" in circumstances under which it has no intrinsic credibility at all. But under other circumstances the proposition can have some intrinsic credibility, for example, when it is the content of an apparent memory. This shows that having some special subject matter, for example, being about sense experience, is not necessary for being a datum.

Subject matter should also not be held to be sufficient for being a datum, as is established by examples of illusion or hallucination when the subject is aware that his experience is nonveridical. I have not found this point in *Human Knowledge*, but nor have I found anything inconsistent with it.

The first of these points, that a special subject matter is not necessary for being a datum, suggests that in Russell's definition of a datum we should not understand the phrase "independently of any argument derived from other propositions" to entail "independently of any other fact about the person for whom it is a datum." Rather, the "intrinsic" credibility of a person's datum consists in its having some credibility not owed to other of his *beliefs*. Its credibility may well be owed to facts about him other than what he believes. For example, placed in full view of a walnut tree, the belief "There's a walnut tree" may not owe any credibility to the perceiver's other beliefs, though its credibility is dependent on such facts as that his senses are working normally.[3] This latter sort of dependence should not be allowed to rule the belief a nondatum.

This concession is important, for it renders highly implausible the iteration principle (If X knows that p, then X knows that X knows that p), which has characterized traditional foundationalism. It is much easier for "There's a walnut tree" to *be* intrinsically credible for you, thanks to the fact that your senses are working normally, than for you to *know* that it is intrinsically credible for you. In order that "There's a walnut tree" should *be* intrinsically credible for you, there is no need for you to defeat Descartes's demon; but, arguably, you do have to defeat the demon to know that your senses are working normally, and thus to *know* that "There's a walnut tree" is intrinsically credible for you.

So once you allow, as there is evidence that Russell does, that the intrinsic credibility of a proposition can be affected by the believer's circumstances, you should come to have serious qualms about the iteration principle. I have not found any explicit statement of such qualms in *Human Knowledge*. However, Russell had a quite different reason for having them, at least with respect to some kinds of knowledge. He stressed the importance of the kind of knowledge, not necessarily conceptual in character, that animal behavior may be held to manifest. The conditions for this kind of knowledge, summarized on page 450, clearly permit knowledge that the knower does not know he has, and so defeat the iteration principle.

The significance of the iteration principle is that it determines a project for epistemology: Descartes's project. The Cartesian idea is that the knowing subject should be able to sift through his beliefs, distinguishing knowledge (or justified belief) from unsatisfactory belief. The project requires that the knower be able to identify his knowledge. That is, it requires the iteration principle. If one takes seriously the falsehood of the iteration principle, one will not suppose that one who genuinely possesses knowledge is thereby assured of success in Descartes's project. Russell's shift of perspective toward knowledge as an evolutionarily adaptive natural process is a move away from Descartes's project. Whether his emancipation from the Cartesian style of epistemology is complete is another matter.

Russell summarizes his foundationalism in the following passage:

> The edifice of knowledge may be compared to a bridge resting on many piers, each of which not only supports the roadway but helps the other piers to stand firm owing to interconnecting girders. The piers are the analogues of the propositions having some intrinsic credibility, while the upper portions of the bridge are the analogues of what is only inferred. But although each pier may be strengthened by the other piers, it is the solid ground that supports the whole, and in like manner it is intrinsic credibility that supports the whole edifice of knowledge. (p. 413)

Only a datum can be a primary source of credibility. The credibility of any nondatum is ultimately owed only to data. The question that will be my concern in this essay is the one to which Russell devotes part VI of *Human Knowledge*: how do data transmit credibility to hypotheses? It is in answering this question that Russell introduces his "postulates of scientific inference," postulates that are contingent, not knowable through experience, yet that have to be known if science is to be known.

2. The Transmission of Credibility: Russell's Doctrines Concerning Principles of Evidence

Consider a hypothesis, H, which is made credible by some body of data, D. Let us call this relation between H and D the C-relation. Russell appears to hold the following theses:

1. Particular facts of the form $C(H, D)$ hold in virtue of some general features of H and D. Hence there are general principles—I shall call them *principles of evidence*—determining the conditions for the obtaining of the C-relation.
2. Principles of evidence are true in virtue of contingent facts about the actual world. Russell refers to these facts as the *postulates of scientific inference*.
3. Principles of evidence must be known, if any hypotheses can be known.

4. Principles of evidence cannot be known from experience.
5. Principles of evidence are known.

In this section I simply present the evidence that these are Russell's views. In subsequent sections I evaluate some of them.

Evidence for (1) can be found in many places. His treatment of the principle of induction makes it plain that it has the kind of generality he thinks is appropriate, though he also thinks that, unless stated with some "hitherto undiscovered limitation" (p. 436), it will give the wrong results. As he says later:

> Induction, we have seen, is not quite the universal proposition that we need to justify scientific inference. But we most certainly do need *some* universal proposition or propositions. (p. 524)[4]

This need is based on the fact, as I would put it, that it is the nature of the *C*-relation itself that requires characterization, if we are to understand and validate scientific inference.

Further evidence for (1) comes from his discussion of animal expectation. He envisages a dog's expectation of *B*, triggered by a perception of *A*. Suppose, further, that *A* is always, or nearly always, followed by *B*. Does this justify the dog's expectation? He argues that it is not enough.

> Suppose that, although A is in fact always followed by B, this generalization only happens to be right, and most logically similar generalizations are wrong. In that case we must regard it as a stroke of luck for the dog that she has hit on a case in which a fallacious process, by chance, leads to a true result. (p. 446)

Notice here that where some would have looked to natural necessity in the generalization, Russell looks to whether data and hypothesis instantiate the *C*-relation. The quotation assumes that data and hypothesis could not be thus related if most logically similar generalizations are wrong.

The following quotations are evidence that Russell holds (2):

> Any principle which will justify inference from the particular to the general must be a law of nature, i.e. a statement that the actual universe has a certain character which it would be possible for it not to have....
>
> Scientific inferences, if they are in general valid, must be so in virtue of some law or laws of nature, stating a synthetic property of the actual world, or several such properties. (pp. 354, 436)

Russell does not distinguish between synthetic and contingent.

One of the most explicit assertions of (3) is:

> We need, among the premises of science, not only data derived from perception and memory, but also certain principles of synthetic inference. (p. 355)

He is prepared to count these principles of evidence among our data.

> I am here including among data the principles used in any inferences that may be involved [in getting to hypotheses]. (p. 401)

Bearing in mind that a datum is a belief, this quotation again makes plain that it is not merely that principles of evidence have to be true, they also have to be known (or at least justifiably believed):

> When an argument is stated as simply a possible, the connection asserted in every step has to be a datum. (p. 412)

However, there is one moment when he shows some hesitation:

> It is more necessary [for the justification of inferences] that there should *be* laws than that they should be known. (p. 354)

Thesis (4) is a doctrine familiar from Hume, and also familiar from Russell's own earlier writings. A clear statement of it, along with a hint of an argument, is:

> The truth of [the postulates] cannot be made even probable by any argument from experience, since such arguments, when they go beyond hitherto recorded experience, depend for their validity upon the very principles in question. (p. 436)

Russell is quite tentative in his affirmation of (5). For one thing, he thinks that the only way to prove it is by accepting (3) and rejecting skepticism: since we do have knowledge of hypotheses, we must have whatever other knowledge this knowledge requires. For another thing, when he comes to say what this knowledge is like, he finds it resembles animal expectation—a kind of nonconceptual knowledge. Thus we find:

> Our knowledge of these principles—if it can be called "knowledge"—exists at first solely in the form of a propensity to inferences of the kind that they justify. It is by reflecting upon such inferences that we make the principles explicit. (p. 526)

Russell warns that he will depart from tradition in his use of the term "knowledge." He more or less identifies knowing with having a reasonable degree of credibility in belief (p. 444–45), and I shall throughout consider only the latter.

In the following three sections, I shall discuss in detail the theses (2), (3), and (4).

3. The Contingency Thesis

A *principle of evidence*, as I shall use the phrase, is a conditional statement. Typically, the antecedent will set out conditions satisfiable by data, and the consequent will state that such data confer rational credibility on a hypothesis whose content is related in a certain way to that of the data. In short, a canonical form would be: For any D, if they satisfy . . ., then D confer rational credibility on any H satisfying ____. We would have to allow for credibility to be a matter of degree, though this refinement will be needless for our purpose. Strictly speaking, both antecedent and consequent of a principle of evidence can be any proposition, whether a datum or a hypothesis. For Russell's view is that a credible hypothesis can add credibility to a datum, and it can certainly do this to another hypothesis. However, the basic case is one in which the antecedent specifies a condition on data, and the consequent specifies a condition on a hypothesis, and it will make the exposition easier to couch the principles in terms of the basic case. A further qualification is that a principle of evidence should allow for relativization to a person: if D are data *for x* and satisfy . . ., then if H satisfies ____ it is rationally credible *for x*. I shall not always make this relativization explicit.

It is important to be clear about exactly what such principles deliver. Is it conclusions of the form specified in the C-relation: H is credible relative to D? Or is it an absolute assignment of credibility to H? The point is that some H might be credible relative to one set of data but not relative to another, so if we had only conclusions of the form $C(H, D)$ we still would not know what it is rational to believe, for we would not have been told what set of data it is best to use.[5] One way around part of this difficulty is to stipulate that the antecedent of a principle of evidence requires that the data be the total of one's data, and it is on these data that the condition is placed. We can then see the consequent as assigning (a degree of) credibility absolutely to a hypothesis. One would still need a justification for thinking that it is a good thing to try to expand one's total body of data (see note 5); and it would remain an open question, and one concerning which some initial skepticism is appropriate, whether any plausible principles of this form can be formulated. But I leave these problems to one side.

Russell presents some of his postulates explicitly as empirical generalizations, rather than as principles of evidence, for example, postulate I:

> *Given any event A, it happens very frequently that, at any neighbouring time, there is at some neighbouring place an event very similar to A.* (p. 506)[6]

But he presents other postulates as principles of evidence themselves. Postulate II, for example, is (approximately)[7] a principle of evidence.

> It is frequently possible to form a series of events such that, from one or two members of the series, something can be inferred as to all the other members. (p. 508)

Russell feels able to move freely between these two very different kinds of postulates in virtue of his thesis that a principle of evidence (properly speaking) is made true, if it is true, just by contingent features of the world, and so is itself contingent. This is what I call the *contingency thesis*. To avoid confusion, I shall use

Russell's term "postulates" to refer to the particular propositions he calls postulates, and will always regard the contingency thesis as stated with respect to principles of evidence, and not postulates. As we have seen, some of the postulates are obviously contingent. With respect to these, what is of interest is whether some corresponding principle of evidence is necessary or contingent. Thus, corresponding to postulate I would be a principle of evidence along the lines:

> If it is a datum that an event α occurred at a place p, time t, and that α has a value v for some parameter Φ, then the hypothesis that an event occurs near p and near t and with a value for Φ near v is rationally credible.[8]

Russell argues against the view that principles of evidence are necessary, notably on pages 387 and 420 of *Human Knowledge*. I quote the latter passage in full:

> If "probability" is taken as an indefinable, we are obliged to admit that the improbable may happen and that, therefore, a probability-proposition tells us nothing about the course of nature. If this view is adopted, the inductive principle may be valid, and yet every inference made in accordance with it *may* turn out to be false; this is improbable but not impossible. Consequently a world in which induction is true is empirically indistinguishable from one in which it is false. It follows that there can never be any evidence for or against the principle, and that it cannot help us to infer what will happen. If the principle is to serve its purpose, we must interpret "probable" as meaning "what in fact usually happens"; that is to say, we must interpret a probability as a frequency.

Russell distinguishes two senses of "probable." One makes "is highly probable" equivalent to "is highly credible," and it is this sense that is at issue in the passage quoted. The only principle of evidence mentioned in the passage is the inductive principle, which, as we have mentioned, Russell took to be invalid in its standard formulations. But it seems clear that the argument, if good at all, would be good against any principle of evidence. It trades on no special feature of the inductive principle.

The main thrust of the passage, adapted to the terminology I have introduced, seems to me to be this: if principles of evidence were necessary, then they would hold regardless of the actual course of events. But then there would be no connection between forming one's beliefs in accordance with good principles of evidence and being right. So there would be no *point* in forming one's beliefs in accordance with good principles of evidence. Being a *good* principle would be an empty honor.

There is a subsidiary argument to the effect that if the principles were necessary there could never be any evidence for or against them. Given that some necessary truths are knowable but not knowable a priori, it would not follow immediately from the necessity of principles of evidence that there is no evidence for them.[9] In any case it is odd that Russell should regard this as a defect in the necessity thesis, since he is, as we have seen, at pains to point out that, on his version of the thesis that principles of evidence are contingent, there can be no evidence for the principles themselves. I postpone all discussion of the epistemic status of principles of evidence until section 4, and return now to the main argument for contingency: that it is needed to connect credibility to being right.

Russell, in the passage, merely asserts this need. But it has to be argued for. An opponent might deny it, and perhaps lend color to his denial by asking us to consider a universe in which the evil genius presents Descartes with a facsimile of his veridical experience, yet nothing exists other than these two spirits. The opponent might claim that while this makes all the difference to the *truth* of Descartes's beliefs, it makes no difference to their degree of credibility. Once one has accepted that a falsehood can be credible, it is tempting to say that credibility imposes no requirement of truth, however indirect. Let us examine the clash between these positions more closely.

An initial point is that it ought not to be controversial that *some* principles of evidence are contingent. For suppose we know a contingent truth of the form "Most Φs are Ψs." Then (ceteris paribus) if it is a datum that α is a Φ, the hypothesis that α is a Ψ is rationally credible. This is a principle of evidence, but it is contingent. Russell took this as the model for all principles of evidence. The controversial issue is not whether there are some principles of evidence having this status, but whether all do.

It may be objected that the real principle of evidence at work in the preceding example is one that assimilates "Most Φs are Ψs" to the data. It is then unclear whether the "real" principle is contingent. Certainly, it is not contingent upon most Φs being Ψs.[10] The most this could show, however, is that contingent principles like the one given in the preceding paragraph are derivable from necessary principles together with contingent facts about the course of nature. The point fails to show that there are no contingent principles.

The contingency thesis, then, is best formulated as the thesis that *all* principles of evidence are contingent. The main argument at which Russell hints in the passage quoted is directed at the necessity of any principles of evidence. If any were necessary, one might form one's beliefs in accordance with them, yet be wrong more often than not. Is this true? Would its truth damage the view that there are necessary principles of evidence? One can analyze Russell's argument as having two parts, corresponding to these two questions.

(i) Necessary principles of evidence could award credibility to no end of false conclusions. There is a sense in which it is true, as Russell says in the passage quoted, that if a principle of evidence is necessarily true, it "tells us nothing about the course of nature." The sense is that a necessary proposition does not entail any contingent proposition, so there is nothing to be inferred from it about the special nature of our world, the special features of the actual course of nature. But does it follow from this that it is possible for every inference made in accor-

dance with a necessary principle to have a false conclusion, while having true premises? It might seem that it does not. For are not decent principles of inference self-correcting? Will not the very content of the principle ensure that the falsity of its conclusions disables it for future use? So as soon as the principle starts yielding false conclusions, will it not cease to be applicable, in virtue of the total data no longer being of the sort that can transmit credibility to related hypotheses?

Here is a simple example of a form of principle that allows all conclusions to which it assigns credibility to be false: for all F, G, if the data entail that more of the observed Fs are G than non-G, then any hypothesis is rationally credible if of the form: the next (hitherto unobserved) F to be observed is G.[11] Suppose that the sum of your current data entails that more of the observed Φs are Ψ than non-Ψ. Let us also suppose that these are *only* data, and in particular that the principle of evidence has not been used to transmit any credibility to them. But now you start using the principle and you infer that the unobserved Φ, α, is Ψ, the unobserved Φ, β, is Ψ, and so on. Plainly, it could be that all of these conclusions are false.[12] As their falsehood becomes a datum, there will come a time when you will not have data that can be used to extract, by modus ponens from the *current instance* of the principle, an attribution of credibility to "the next Φ is Ψ." In this modest sense the principle is self-correcting. But at this stage,[13] you will have the data needed to apply another instance of the principle, in which non-Ψ replaces Ψ: if the data entail that more of the observed Φs are non-Ψ than Ψ, then any hypothesis is rationally credible if of the form: the next (hitherto unobserved) Φ to be observed is non-Ψ. Every application of this fresh instance of the principle might yield a false conclusion: the next run of observed Φs might be Ψs. What Russell is asking us to find paradoxical is that, if the principle is necessary, such a series of false predictions does not impugn its correctness.

The basis of Russell's case is that data do not entail hypotheses, not even when they lend them credibility. This does not lead at once to the conclusion that a principle of evidence could yield none but false hypotheses. Perhaps the same principle could at one time confer credibility upon H, given data D, and also later confer credibility on not-H, given subsequent augmentation of D. Then it obviously could not be that all the hypotheses upon which the principle confers credibility, in the history of a single world, are false. But there is no necessity that the hypotheses delivered by a growing body of data should be thus related. They could all be false together. Russell wants us to say that the realization of this possibility would be a refutation of the principle: the truth of a principle ought to guarantee that the possibility is not realized, and so should tell us something about the course of events in the actual world.

I think we must accept the possibility. But must we draw Russell's conclusion from it?

(ii) Does it matter that (i) is true? I think not. But consider the opposite view. A principle of evidence is supposed to confer rational credibility. But what is ra-

tional about believing something unless there is at least a good chance that it is true? One does not expect *every* credible proposition to be true. But one has a right to expect that if one follows the strategy of forming one's beliefs in accordance with correct principles of evidence, one should end up with more truths than falsehoods. If a principle could be true while, from now on, conferring credibility only upon falsehoods, one would be denied this right. It is not that one is looking for some absolute guarantee that some principle of evidence that one takes to be true is really true. Nor is one looking for a guarantee of the truth of any inductive belief. The point is, rather, that if one *does* follow a true principle, that ought to ensure that one believes a *reasonable proportion* of truths. To deny this connection is to prevent inquiry from being a search after truth. It becomes merely a search for "rational" belief: a goal that, shorn of its link with truth, is of no value.

It is trivial that a proposition that is awarded credibility by a correct principle of evidence on the strength of some data, D, is probable, relative to D, in the sense of being credible, relative to D. What the preceding argument claims is that it must also be probable in a frequency sense, echoing Russell's claim already quoted.[14] The frequency in question is a decent ratio (say exceeding 1/2) between true and false beliefs among those formed in accordance with the principle of evidence. It would certainly be very pleasant to be able to show that this frequency in fact obtains for the principles of evidence we use.

To undermine this line of thought, to show that a principle can be true even if there is no such frequency, consider the fact that principles of evidence can but reflect the nature of our cognitive powers. If we were omniscient we would need no such principles. The facts themselves would be, so to speak, laid out before us. We would not need to grope our way toward them from the evidence. If we found rather little correlation between written records of past events and our apparent memories of them, we could not use the principles of evidence we do use. Principles of evidence, if correct, must reflect the best we can do. But, unless we make a sharp turn toward idealism, we cannot *stipulate* that the best we can do will lead to a preponderance of truth. Perhaps truth is beyond us. So it is wrong to say that, *by definition*, a correct principle of evidence will award rational credibility to more truths than falsehoods.

This does not entail that an empty, because no longer truth-connected, ideal of rationality must replace that of truth. We cannot aim higher than to do the best we can. *Best* is the best we can do in the search for truth. But to search is not necessarily to find.

What my argument purports to show is that a realist will not find anything especially disconcerting in the possibility, established under (i), of a correct principle of evidence leading us badly astray. For a realist, this is just the way we relate to truth. The argument does not, of course, purport to establish realism. But, in the context of *Human Knowledge*, realism can be taken for granted. Part of the overall aim of the book is to reject the method of construction, characteristic of Russell's idealism in, for example, "The Relation of Sense-Data to Physics."[15] In its place is the method of inference, involving the intelligibility of objects lying beyond acquaintance, and of which our knowledge cannot be certain.

If I am right, Russell's realism ought to have undermined his argument for the contingency thesis. How can we explain this tension? Part of the explanation lies in his failure to give due attention to the distinction between saying how things must be if our scientific beliefs are to be, by and large, justified, and saying how things must be if our scientific beliefs are to be, by and large, true. The reason for this assimilation, in turn, is that he had enumerative induction before his mind as the main model for a principle of evidence. Faced with the problem of what regularities should be extrapolated, he sought an answer in terms of the *content* of the regularities, in terms, for example, of whether they instantiated postulate I.[16] And so the natural conclusion was that the inferences are justified only if regularities of the relevant kind obtain. And, if they do, it is not merely that scientific beliefs will be, by and large, justified; they will also be, by and large, true. Had Russell had before his mind a quite different kind of principle of evidence, for example, one that attributes credibility to a hypothesis in virtue of its explaining the data, it seems unlikely that his thinking would have followed this route.

There is also a deeper explanation, which I elaborate in section 6, of why Russell should have thought that the possibility of conferring credibility on none but false hypotheses matters: Russell *does* have to confront the skepticism to which realism is inevitably subject, but he confronts it in a different form.

The upshot is that the claim that some principles of evidence are necessary survives Russell's attack, but that is not to say that it is true.

4. Must Principles of Evidence Be Known?

If it were in general correct that, if one's reasoning is to lead from knowledge to knowledge (or credibility to credibility), one needs to know any principles of inference involved in one's reasoning, as well as the premises to which the principles apply, then one would do well to include the principles among one's premises: they would be among the things knowledge of which is required for knowledge of the conclusion. So should one who argues from P and if P then Q to Q include modus ponens among his premises? Suppose modus ponens is formulated: for all propositions A, B, and C, if A is true, and so is *if A then B*, then B is also true. As Lewis Carroll showed,[17] adding this premise does not obviate the need for an application of modus ponens. So the propounder of the original argument gains nothing by including it, explicitly or implicitly, among his premises. This establishes either that one cannot include all one needs to know, in order to know a conclusion, among one's premises, or that one does not need to know the principles of inference one uses. The unattractiveness of the first disjunct is an argument for the second.

It is even clearer that it is wrong to hold that a principle of evidence needs to be known, in order to confer credibility. A principle linking D and H entails that one who believes D is rational to believe H. If the principle does not include itself among D (and we certainly assume that principles of evidence do not normally do this), then the credibility of H is independent of knowledge of the principle. So it seems as if Russell has simply made a mistake in saying that the principles of evidence must be known, if the hypotheses to which they relate are to be rationally credible.

In one who believed in the iteration principle, this mistake would be fairly easy to explain. The principle, applied to credibility, makes it impossible for H to be credible for someone without it also being credible for him that H is credible. It is hard to see how we are to have a decent basis for the stronger (iterated) claim without the principle that confers the first credibility being itself credible.[18] But Russell, I have suggested, eschews the iteration principle. So how can his mistake be explained?

The answer lies in Russell's very low key conception of knowledge, a conception that in effect robs his claim that the principles of evidence must be known of any significance – and thus, indeed, saves him from a mistake. The conditions for the kind of knowledge that Russell says we have of principles of evidence are set out on page 450 (the last page of part VI, chapter 1). In effect, the upshot is that you know a principle if it is true, you reach hypotheses that it licenses, and you do so as a causal consequence of the impact on you of the data that it specifies. This does not entail knowledge, or rational belief, or even belief, as the terms are normally used. I do not say this in criticism of Russell. Rather, abstracting from Russell's special conception of knowledge, in *Human Knowledge*, it would be less misleading to say that he held that we do *not* have to know the principles of evidence.

To leave it at that would be to miss something important. As Russell clearly states at the very beginning of part VI (p. 439), the principles are involved in two philosophical tasks: the descriptive task, of saying what the principles are that adequately describe what is generally accepted as good inductive reasoning; and the justificatory task, of saying whether this reasoning is *really* good. It is the latter task, rather than the former, which creates *for the philosophical inquirer* the need to know the principles of evidence. While a person who reasons in accordance with a true principle ends up with a rationally credible conclusion, we want to know whether the principles we implicitly invoke, the ones specified in discharge of the descriptive task, are true. There is no nonskeptical answer to that question, it would seem, except one that shows that we know the principles, and know them, moreover, in the ordinary sense of the term. Showing this would, in Russell's framework, be the way to provide a solution to the traditional problem of justifying induction.

5. Can Principles of Evidence Be Known from Experience?

In the most naive view, it is observed cases of $\Phi\alpha$ and $\Psi\alpha$ that support generalizations of the form "For all x, if Φx then Ψx." But if the consequent of a principle of evidence has the form that we have supposed—"H is rationally credible for x"—it is not clear what sort of evidence would support it because it is not clear what it would be to "observe" that we had a true instance of the consequent. What observations are supposed to establish that H was, or was not, credible for x?

Russell's view is that a principle would be supported, if it could be shown that most of the hypotheses upon which it confers rational credibility are true. For Russell, the problem is that showing this itself requires a principle of evidence, so we seem caught in a circle.

Before looking at this supposed circle, it is worth pointing out that a presupposition has already been made concerning the proper analysis of what it is for a principle of evidence to be correct. It must have the property I shall call that of being *truth yielding*, where a principle is truth yielding if and only if most of the hypotheses upon which it confers credibility are true. The circle for Russell consists in the fact that we cannot move from the datum that a principle has been truth yielding up to now to the hypothesis that it is in general truth yielding without invoking *another* principle of evidence.

We ought not to accept without question this analysis of what it is for a principle of evidence to be true. If the argument of section 3 is correct, truth yieldingness is not a necessary condition of the truth of a principle of evidence. Moreover, it is not obvious that is is sufficient. Might not a principle of evidence, like a person, fortuitously light upon truth more often than falsehood, without thereby delivering rational credibility? Russell says that what is needed to prevent this fortuitous correctness is that the principle will confer credibility on a *class* of hypotheses.[19] But if the class is a "manufactured" (grue-like) class, there is still the possibility of fortuitousness. Russell remained too much a Humean even to consider a notion of natural law involving necessity.

Let us return to Russell's alleged circle. He cannot mean that no principle of evidence could be justified empirically. Some data, D, and a principle, P_1, might confer credibility on another principle, P_2. What he must mean is that they cannot *all* owe all their support to being established empirically. If they are to owe all their support to being established empirically, they cannot be data, by definition, since a datum has some credibility on its own account. So one has a picture of a collection of principle-free data, and one asks oneself: how can I get anywhere? The answer, clearly, is that one can make no acceptable progress without moving to a hypothesis that is C-related to the data. One cannot infer from this alone that it is impossible for all the principles of evidence to receive empirical support. For example, consider the following structure:

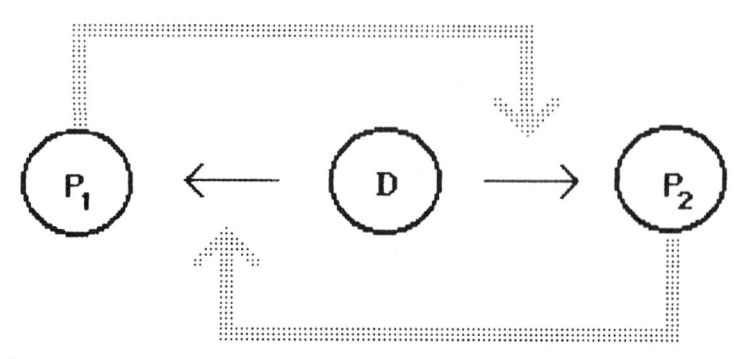

The circles represent propositions or sets thereof. The thin black arrows connect the premises of some inductive reasoning to the conclusion. The shaded arrows are principles entailing that such premises lend rational credibility to such conclusions. In virtue of principle P_1, data D support P_2 (or support the proposition that P_1 is truth yielding). Every principle is supported empirically, yet there is no *straightforward* circle: no principle is the one in virtue of which the data that support it do so.

To introduce a charge of circularity, we have to introduce a foundationalist notion: that of a *total* justification. In a total justification, there will be a justification for every proposition mentioned, unless that proposition is a datum; and every principle of inference must be mentioned. The possibility of a total justification, in this sense, appears to be a consequence of the view that data alone are the ultimate source of credibility. There can be no total justification of all the principles of inference, unless either some principle is a datum or some principle occurs in its own justification. In the preceding simple structure, the justification of P_2 by D and P_1 is not a datum; for totality, one has to extend the justification to include a justification of P_1, and this reintroduces P_2. This circularity defeats the aim of showing that every proposition ultimately owes its credibility to, and only to, data.

If this argument is accepted, and it is granted that some principle of evidence is credible, then some principle is a datum. There are theoretically two possibilities. Some principle could be a sensory datum, like an apparent memory or a perception; but this seems absurd. Alternatively, some principle is known a priori. This is the alternative that Russell adopts.

I suspect that the most controversial aspect of this part of Russell's position is his reliance on the notion of total justification. We are often told that *in practice* justifications are not, and need not be, total, that justification is relative to context, and that the "philosophical" notion of total justification is too radically unlike our ordinary notion to derive its title to coherence from the ordinary one. I shall not present any such criticisms in detail. But I will draw attention to three points, which may arm Russell against this kind of criticism. The first is that we must bear in mind that Russell's overall objective is not to argue for skepticism but rather correctly to identify the epistemological status of principles of evidence. The second is that he is not in the position of one who insists on justification while being prepared to take nothing for granted. On the contrary, he is rather liberal about what he will take for granted: all the data. The third is that he is not claiming that we need total justifications in practice. However, he rightly does not let practical concerns inhibit his philosophical curiosity. Practical concerns no doubt do not often require the explicit articulation of principles of evidence. But if we could succeed in articulating them, we would certainly be right to ask what their epistemic status is.

6. The Challenge of Skepticism

Russell's official discussion of skepticism in *Human Knowledge* is brief:

Skepticism, while logically impeccable, is psychologically impossible. (p. 9)

But the next sentence makes it plain that the skepticism Russell has in mind is what one might call a *first-order atheistic* skepticism: for example, one involving "the denial of physical events experienced by no one." This skepticism is atheistic in that it involves *denying* some commonly held beliefs, rather than merely *doubting* them. It is first-order in that the beliefs in question do not say anything about knowledge, credibility, or justification. Russell is no doubt right to dismiss such a skepticism in a couple of sentences. But the real enemy is a skepticism of a different kind: a *second-order agnostic* skepticism, as I shall call it. Russell does not acknowledge this skepticism, but I believe that it exerts an influence on his thought.

This influential skepticism is agnostic in that it adopts the attitude of doubt rather than denial, and second-order in that the propositions it doubts have the form: it is credible that *p* (where *p* is first-order). This is the serious form of skepticism about induction. Such skeptics believe as stoutly as the rest of us that bread will nourish and the sun rise. No doubt it would be psychologically impossible for them to rid themselves of these beliefs. What they doubt, however, is whether any such beliefs — any hypotheses, in the sense of this essay — are really worthy of credence; equivalently, whether there are any true principles of evidence. It seems psychologically possible genuinely to have this doubt. These skeptics cannot be dismissed in Russell's laconic way.

If there are necessary principles of evidence, their truth might be evident to us a priori. This is certainly what Mackie hopes with respect to his indifference principle, and what might reasonably be hoped for the principle that what best explains one's data is credible: *if* these are true at all, it would be a reasonable ambition to make their truth manifest a priori. But we have learned from Russell's attack on necessary principles that this will not quell every form of skepticism. To the extent that one of skeptical leanings will accept a necessary principle of evidence, one will so interpret it that it remains an open question whether there is any real value in believing what is credible. For, the skeptic will complain, it is an open question whether having credible beliefs will guarantee even a preponderance of true beliefs. This form of skepticism, I said in section 3, was one we would expect to be associated with a realist metaphysics, with the view that how the world is can totally outrun our powers of discovery.

Let us compare this with the form of skepticism that lurks close to the surface of *Human Knowledge*. This consists simply in doubting whether the principles of evidence that we in fact use, principles identified in accomplishing what I have called the descriptive task, are true; equivalently, in doubting whether any hypothesis is credible. But what does being credible amount to here? By the contingency thesis, credibility will be connected to truth: having only credible beliefs will ensure having a preponderance of true ones. This skeptic has to accept that *if* there were any credible beliefs, his skepticism would be at an end, at least with respect to those beliefs.

It is apparent that what is in effect the same skepticism can emerge in two different forms. Suppose we have a truth-yielding conception of credibility, as could issue, and in Russell's system does issue, from contingent principles of evidence: a conception, that is, according to which believing a preponderance of truths is constitutive of having none but credible beliefs. No skepticism can arise about whether the beliefs upon which any such true principles confer "credibility" deserve to be believed. But there is room for skepticism about whether any such principles are true. Now suppose we have a conception of credibility that is not, constitutively, truth yielding, a conception that, Russell has shown, is forced on us if we have necessary principles of evidence. Then there may be no room for skepticism about whether such principles are true, but there is room for skepticism about whether the "credibility" they deliver is anything worth taking seriously. The skeptic will say it is not to be taken seriously, if it is not truth yielding.[20]

The underlying skepticism is essentially the same in each case, so we can choose in which form we will confront it. Russell made credibility truth yielding and is faced with the skeptic who doubts whether any principles of evidence are true. There is no explicit confrontation, since Russell thinks, wrongly, that he has already dismissed skepticism. But Russell makes it plain that the question of whether we know the postulates is problematic.

> There is the difficulty that there is, *prima facie*, little reason to suppose these principles [of evidence] true, and still less to suppose them *known* to be true. (p. 439)

We have seen that he hopes to overcome the difficulty by using a very modest conception of knowledge, one that, as I have said, does not even involve belief, and makes the knowledge in question of a kind with animal expectation. While it is an important fact that there is a continuity between animal expectation and more explicit and conceptual predictions, it is not one that can carry any weight against the skeptic. No doubt there is a connection between a way of forming expectations being evolutionarily adaptive, and it being one that yields a preponderance of truths. Skeptics can accept this. What they will doubt is whether ways of forming expectations or principles of evidence, which have been truth yielding up to now, will continue to be so. Perhaps they must be if we are to survive. But then the doubt is whether we will.

In section 3, I said that the skepticism that addresses necessary principles of evidence is only what one should expect within a realist perspective. In this section I have said that it is really the same skepticism that addresses contingent principles of evidence. The claims taken together entail that this latter skepticism, too, is no less than what a realist should expect. And this is, I think, the correct conclusion. If the course of nature is independent of our knowledge, or possibility of knowledge, then there is a possibility, which the skeptic will argue to be an epistemic one, that principles that have been truth yielding up to now will cease to be so.

The equivalence of these forms of skepticism I think establishes something else: that there is no substantial issue over whether or not the contingency thesis is correct. Necessary principles will not yield all we need because of skepticism about whether they are truth yielding. Contingent principles will not yield all we need because of skepticism about whether they are true. It does not matter whether we formulate principles of evidence as necessary, if true at all, and then confront the challenge of skepticism in the first form; or whether we formulate principles of evidence as contingent, if true at all, and then confront the challenge of skepticism in the second form.

In the formulation Russell prefers, he sees that meeting the skeptical challenge head-on involves showing that we have knowledge of contingent principles of evidence that is not derived from experience. He also sees that it is no easier to meet the challenge in its other form, as addressed to necessary principles of evidence. We can, indeed, criticize him for thinking that this possibility of skepticism refutes the necessity of principles of evidence, since it tells as much against the contingency thesis. And it has to be admitted that Russell does not succeed, or even seriously engage, in showing that we have the knowledge we need to refute the skeptic. But success in this project is something that, I suggest, no realist has achieved.[21]

Notes

1. All page references in what follows are to this book, unless otherwise indicated. American readers are warned that the pagination of this British edition differs from that of American editions.

2. Page 422 (part IV, chapter 7). Russell had drawn attention to this problem of induction, much later made famous by Nelson Goodman in his *Fact, Fiction and Forecast*, 2nd ed. (Indianapolis: Bobbs-Merrill, 1965), as early as 1912: "On the Notion of Cause," *Proceedings of the Aristotelian*

Society, 13 (1912/13), reprinted in Russell's *Mysticism and Logic* (1918, paperback edition, 1963), at pp. 147–49. I interpret Russell's postulates of scientific inference as an attempt to overcome the problem. They do not succeed, for they invoke an unrestricted notion of similarity—one that does not exclude the similarity possessed by two grue things, one of which is green, the other blue. But this problem is not my concern here.

3. At least, this could be argued. The opposing case is that the belief would still be credible, though false, if the subject were the unwitting victim of an illusion.

4. Compare also: "If we are justified in believing that all men are mortal, that must be because, as a general principle, certain kinds of particular facts are evidence of general laws" (p. 354).

5. A. J. Ayer used this point in an attempt to discredit necessary principles of evidence: "The Concept of Probability as a Logical Relation," in Stephan Körner (ed.), *Observation and Interpretation* (New York: Dover Press, 1957). The strongest form of the objection is this: why strive officiously to increase the quantity and variety of one's data? The natural answer is: because this will make it more likely that one will attain the truth. Ayer's claim that this answer is not available to one who holds that principles of evidence are necessary (that there are necessary 'probability'-relations) parallels Russell's attack on the contingency thesis, discussed in this section.

6. The ontology of *Human Knowledge* is founded on events. This postulate is Russell's transposition into his favored ontology of the traditional doctrine that there exist substances.

7. More exactly, it is a *form* of a principle of evidence. Further work should provide an intrinsic specification of a kind, K, of series, and a type, T, of property that can be inferred, which would make the following principle of evidence (in the strict sense) true: "If the total data entail that one or two things belong to a K-series and have a T-type property, Φ, and nothing in the data counts against the hypothesis that all members of the series have Φ, then this hypothesis is rationally credible." (The qualification "nothing in the data *counts against* the hypothesis..." might seem to introduce a circularity. However, there need not be anything vicious here. A relational predicate "counts against" could be defined in terms of some set of principles of evidence. It *could* be quite noncircular [depending on the content of the other principles] whether or not any principles in a given set tell against a hypothesis. There must certainly be a question, not to be pursued here, whether any such set of principles would be plausible.)

8. Henceforth I shall usually abstract from complications to do with totality of data. See note 7 above.

9. There can be empirical evidence (e.g., authority) even for an a priori necessary truth. Examples of necessary truths that are not knowable a priori are given by Saul Kripke, "Naming and Necessity," in G. Harman and D. Davidson (eds.), *Semantics of Natural Language* (Dordrecht: Reidel, 1972).

10. For example, J. L. Mackie suggests that a similar principle is "logical or quasi-logical," and so, presumably, necessary. See his "A Defence of Induction," in G. F. Macdonald (ed.), *Perception and Identity: Essays Presented to A. J. Ayer* (London: Macmillan, 1979), pp. 113–28, at p. 118–19.

11. Whatever the inadequacies of such principle, it is of a kind with Russell's postulates. Plausible candidates for necessary principles of evidence would include Mackie's indifference principle (see note 10) and the principle that a hypothesis can acquire credibility by explaining the data.

It is surprising that Russell, in *Human Knowledge*, paid so little attention, indeed no attention at all, to the concept of explanation. This bypasses an interesting possibility: perhaps the fundamental kind of nondeductive reasoning is inference to the best explanation. Then the restriction on the principle of induction for which Russell was looking might be this: extrapolation of regularities is justified only when it follows from an explanation of them. This idea was briefly discussed in the original version of this essay, as presented at the Conference on the Philosophy of Bertrand Russell (Minnesota, 1982). It has been excellently presented and defended by John Foster: "Induction, Explanation and Natural Necessity," *Proceedings of the Aristotelian Society*, 82 (1982/83), pp. 87–101.

12. Strictly speaking, the conclusion of an application of a principle of evidence has the form: it is rationally credible that H. However, I shall in this discussion speak of H itself as the conclusion. It is plainly the falsehood of the propositions upon which credibility is conferred that Russell takes to be objectionable.

13. More exactly, after one more non-Ψ Φ has been observed.

14. From p. 420. See p. 207, this essay.

15. *Scientia*, 4 (1914); reprinted in *Mysticism and Logic* (1917).

16. "Given any event A, it happens very frequently that, at any neighboring time, there is at some neighboring place an event very similar to A" (p. 506).

17. "What the Tortoise Said to Achilles," *Mind* 4, (1895), pp. 278-80.

18. Let us use "K_x" as the epistemic operator (knowledge or credibility, as preferred), with the x subscript representing a relativization to a person. Suppose P is: for all x, if D is x's total data, K_xH. Suppose D are α's total data. Then $K_\alpha H$. Iteration requires that if $K_\alpha H$, then $K_\alpha K_\alpha H$. This cuts both ways: if you know that $K_\alpha H$ you can use it to establish $K_\alpha K_\alpha H$; if $K_\alpha K_\alpha H$ appears doubtful, it casts doubt on $K_\alpha H$. If $K_\alpha P$, one could use this plus K_α (D are α's total data) to establish $K_\alpha K_\alpha H$.

19. Page 446 (quoted in section 2). Cf. p. 387: "If I say that an inductive argument makes a conclusion probable, I mean that it is one of a class of arguments most of which have conclusions that are true."

20. P. F. Strawson, in *Introduction to Logical Theory* (London: Methuen, 1953), part II, chapter 9, failed to give this point due weight. It may be conceptually true that it is rational to reason in accordance with accepted standards of inductive argument. But this does not knock out skeptics who ask why one ought to be rational. They will accept the value of rationality only if it can be shown to make true belief more likely (in a frequency sense) than false belief.

21. I am grateful to the editors of this volume for their comments on an earlier draft.

John Earman

Concepts of Projectability and the Problems of Induction

Projectability is most often discussed in connection with the distinction between "genuine" and "Goodmanized" predicates. But questions about projectability arise for the most mundane of hypotheses and predicates where not the slightest hint of Goodmanian trickery is present. And there are a number of different concepts of projectability, each corresponding to a different problem of induction. Some of these problems are not only solvable but have actually been solved, solved in the sense that interesting sets of sufficient and/or necessary conditions for projectability have been found. In some cases the conditions are so mild that a coherent inductive skepticism is hard to maintain, whereas in other cases the conditions are so demanding that skepticism seems to be the only attractive alternative. Again, in some of the cases Goodmanian considerations are the key; in others they are irrelevant.

The purpose of this note is to provide a classification scheme for the various senses of projectability that will reveal what is at stake in the corresponding problems of induction. A useful beginning can be made by recalling the twofold classification Russell offered in *Human Knowledge*:

> Induction by simple enumeration is the following principle: "given any number of α's which have been found to be β's, and no α which has been found to be not a β, then the two statements: (a) 'the next α will be a β,' (b) 'all α's are β's,' both have a probability which increases as n increases and approaches certainty as a limit as n approaches infinity." I shall call (a) "particular induction" and (b) "general induction."[1]

Each of Russell's categories needs to be refined. Under particular or instance induction I will recommend a fourfold partition, first distinguishing weak and strong senses according as the induction is on the next instance or the next m instances, and second distinguishing two ways of taking the limit as the number n of instances increases toward infinity according as we march into the future with the accumulating instances or stand pat in the present and reach further and further back into the past for more instances. Under general or hypothesis induction

I will recommend a twofold partition depending on whether the hypothesis is a simple generalization on observed instances or a theoretical hypothesis that outruns the data. The upshot is a collection of six problems of induction with six rather different solutions.

1. Instance Induction: Marching into the Future

Only nonstatistical hypotheses will be considered. Further, it is assumed that the "instances" E_i, $i = 1, 2, 3, \ldots$, of the hypothesis H are deductive consequences of H and the "background evidence" B (i.e., $H, B \vdash E_i$). If you want H to be a universal conditional, e.g., $(\forall x)(Px \supset Qx)$, take instances to be ($Pa \supset Qa$) and the like; or else let B state that all the objects examined are P's and take instances to be (Pa & Qa) and the like.

DEFINITION 1. Relative to B, H is *weakly projectable in the future-moving-instance sense* for the instances $E_1, E_2, \ldots$ *iff*
$$\lim_{n \to \infty} Pr(E_{n+1}/E_1 \& \ldots \& E_n \& B) = 1.$$

DEFINITION 2. Relative to B, H is *strongly projectable in the future-moving instance* for the instances $E_1, E_2, \ldots$ *iff*
$$\lim_{m, n \to \infty} Pr(E_{n+1} \& \ldots E_{n+m}/E_1 \& \ldots \& E_n \& B) = 1.$$

Claim: A sufficient condition for both weak and strong future-moving-instance projectability is that $Pr(H/B) > 0$.

Proof: (a) Weak projectability (Jeffreys).[2] By Bayes's theorem and the assumption that $H, B \vdash E_i$,

(1) $Pr(H/E_1 \& \ldots \& E_{n+1} \& B) =$
$$\frac{Pr(H/B)}{Pr(E_1/B) \times Pr(E_2/E_1 \& B) \times \ldots \times Pr(E_{n+1}/E_1 \& \ldots \& E_n \& B)}$$

If $Pr(H/B) > 0$, the denominator on the right-hand side of (1) will eventually become smaller than the numerator, contradicting an axiom of probability, unless $Pr(E_{n+1}/E_1 \& \ldots \& E_n \& B) \to 1$ as $n \to \infty$. (b) Strong projectability (Huzurbazar).[3] Rearrange Bayes's theorem to read

(2) $Pr(E_1 \& \ldots \& E_n/B) = \dfrac{Pr(H/B)}{Pr(H/E_1 \& \ldots \& E_n \& B)}.$

Setting $u_n \equiv Pr(E_1 \& \ldots \& E_n/B)$, (2) shows that $u_n \geq Pr(H/B) > 0$. Since $u_{n+1} = u_n Pr(E_{n+1}/E_1 \& \ldots \& E_n \& B)$, $u_1, u_2, \ldots$, is a monotone decreasing sequence that tends to limit $L \geq Pr(H/B) > 0$. So

(3) $\lim\limits_{m, n \to \infty} \dfrac{u_{n+m}}{u_n} = \dfrac{L}{L} = 1$

There is an immediate application to the projectability of predicates.[4]

DEFINITION 3. Relative to B, the predicate "P" is *weakly projectable in the future-moving sense* over the sequence of individuals $a_1, a_2, \ldots$ iff
$$\lim_{n \to \infty} Pr(Pa_{n+1}/Pa_1 \& \ldots \& Pa_n \& B) = 1.$$

DEFINITION 4. Relative to B, the predicate "P" is *strongly projectable in the future-moving sense* over the sequence of individuals $a_1, a_2, \ldots$ iff
$$\lim_{m, n \to \infty} Pr(Pa_{n+1} \& \ldots \& Pa_{n+m}/Pa_1 \& \ldots \& Pa_n \& B) = 1.$$

From the previous results we know that a sufficient condition for both weak and strong projectability of "P" in the future-moving sense is that

(C) $Pr((\forall i)Pa_i/B) > 0$.

Thus, contrary to what is sometimes suggested, definitions 3 and 4 do not serve to separate "grue" from "green,"[5] except on what I take to be the wholly implausible assumption that the universal generalization of the one but not the other receives a zero prior.

When is (C) necessary as well as sufficient for future-moving instance induction? The limit of $Pr(Pa_1 \& \ldots \& Pa_n/B)$ as n goes to infinity exists and is independent of the order in which the instances are taken. Further, we know that

(4) $\lim_{n \to \infty} Pr(Pa_1 \& \ldots \& Pa_n/B) \geq Pr((\forall i)Pa_i/B).$

But to assure that

(A) $\lim_{n \to \infty} Pr(Pa_1 \& \ldots \& Pa_n/B) = Pr((\forall i)Pa_i/B)$

we need to assume what Kolmogorov calls an axiom of continuity.[6] Then (C) is a necessary condition for strong projectability of "P" in the future-moving sense; for

(5) $\lim_{m, n \to \infty} Pr(Pa_{n+1} \& \ldots \& Pa_{n+m}/Pa_1 \& \ldots \& Pa_n \& B) =$
$\lim_{m, n \to \infty} [Pr(Pa_1 \& \ldots \& Pa_{n+m}/B)/Pr(Pa_1 \& \ldots \& Pa_n/B)],$

and if (A) but $\neg$(C), this limit is not 1 independently of how m and m go to infinity; e.g., first taking the limit as $m \to \infty$ gives 0.

(C) is not a necessary condition for weak future-moving projectability of "P." Carnap's systems of inductive logic provide examples where (C) and strong future-moving projectability fail but weak future-moving projectability holds. However, the point can be illustrated in a more general way, independently of

Carnap's c-function apparatus.[7] Suppose that Pr is *exchangeable* for "P" over the a_is, i.e., for every m

(E) $\quad Pr(\pm Pa_1 \& \ldots \& \pm Pa_m/B) = Pr(\pm Pa_1' \& \ldots \& \pm Pa_m'/B)$

where $\pm P$ indicates that either P or $\neg P$ may be chosen and $\{a_i'\}$ is any permutation of the a_is in which all but a finite number are left fixed. If (E) holds, De Finetti's representation theorem gives

(D) $\quad Pr(Pa_1 \& \ldots \& Pa_n/B) = \int_0^1 \Theta^n \, d\mu(\Theta)$

where μ is a normed probability measure on the unit interval $0 \leq \Theta \leq 1$.[8] Choosing μ to be the uniform measure gives

(6) $\quad Pr(Pa_1 \& \ldots \& Pa_n/B) = 1/n + 1$.

Thus, (C) fails. But

(7) $\quad Pr(Pa_{n+1}/Pa_1 \& \ldots \& Pa_n \& B) = (n + 1)/(n + 2)$,

which is Laplace's rule of succession, so that "P" is weakly projectable in the future-moving sense. Under (E) the necessary and sufficient condition for the failure of weak future-moving projectability is that

(CM) $\quad \lim_{n \to \infty} \dfrac{\int_0^1 \Theta^{n+1} \, d\mu(\Theta)}{\int_0^1 \Theta^n \, d\mu(\Theta)} \neq 1$.

The label (CM) is supposed to indicate a closed-minded attitude, for (CM) is equivalent to the condition that $\mu([0, \Theta^*]) = 1$ for some $\Theta^* < 1$, ruling out the possibility that an instance of "P" can have a probability greater than Θ^*. The extreme case of closed-mindedness is represented by a μ concentrated on a point; for example, if $\mu(\{1/2\}) = 1$, then each instance of "P" is assigned a probability of $1/2$ independently of all other instances, so that the user of the resulting Pr function is certain (in the sense of second order probability) of the probability of an instance of "P," so certain that no number of other instances of "P" will ever change her mind. The probability measure in Wittgenstein's *Tractatus* had this character.[9]

To summarize: Suppose that you give a nonzero prior probability to the hypothesis that the sun always rises. Then the rising of the sun is strongly future-moving projectable over the series of days. On the other hand, suppose that you are absolutely certain that the sun won't always rise. It is still possible for your belief that the sun will rise tomorrow to approach certainty as your experience of new dawns increases without bound. But, assuming (A), it is not possible for your belief that the sun will rise on any number of tomorrows to approach certainty as your experience of new dawns increases without bound.

Another sense of projectability for predicates sometimes used in the literature[10] is codified in

DEFINITION 5. Relative to B, "P" is *somewhat future-moving projectable* over the sequence of individuals $a_1, a_2, \ldots$ *iff* for each $n > 0$, $Pr(Pa_{n+1}/Pa_1\&\ldots\&Pa_n\&B) > Pr(Pa_n/Pa_1\&\ldots\&Pa_{n-1}\&B)$.

Under exchangeability (E), "P" is somewhat future-moving projectable unless the measure $\mu(\Theta)$ is completely concentrated on some value of Θ, as can be seen by applying the Cauchy-Schwartz inequality. Thus, the case of a closed-minded μ which is not completely closed-minded provides an example where "P" is somewhat but not weakly future-moving projectable. And in general there is no guarantee that projectability in the sense of definition 5 will have the limiting properties postulated in definitions 3 and 4.

Humean skepticism with respect to future-moving instance induction, weak or strong, stands on unstable ground. If $Pr((\forall i)Pa_i/B)$ is any positive real number, no matter how small, future-moving instance induction must take place, like it or not. Setting $Pr((\forall i)Pa_i/B) = 0$ avoids strong future-moving instance induction, but if past experience, as codified in B, does not record a negative instance, then $Pr((\exists i)\neg Pa_i/B) = 1$ says that there is absolute certainty that the future will produce a negative instance, a not very Humean result.

Humeans can escape between the horns of this dilemma either by refusing to conform their degrees of belief to the axioms of probability or else by refusing to assign degrees of belief at all. The first tack is unattractive in view of the 'Dutch book' and other arguments that promote the axioms of probability as rationality constraints on degrees of belief.[11] The second tack seems to lead to something closer to catatonia than to active skepticism.

2. Instance Induction: Standing Pat in the Present While Reaching into the Past

There is a second way of taking the limit as the number of instances accumulates without bound, a way that is, perhaps, more directly relevant to Hume's classic problem of induction. To explain it, suppose as before that $H, B \vdash E_i$, but now let i range over all the integers so that we have a doubly infinite sequence of instances $\ldots E_{-2}, E_{-1}, E_0, E_1, E_2, \ldots$

DEFINITION 6. Relative to B, H is *weakly projectable in the past-reaching instance sense* for the sequence $\{E_i\}$ *iff* $\forall n$
$$\lim_{j\to +\infty} Pr(E_{n+1}/E_n\&E_{n-1}\&\ldots\&E_{n-j}\&B) = 1.$$

DEFINITION 7. Relative to B, H is *strongly projectable in the past-reaching instance sense* for the sequence $\{E_i\}$ *iff* $\forall n$

$$\lim_{m,\ j \to +\infty} Pr(E_{n+1}\&\ldots\&E_{n+m}/E_n\&E_{n-1}\&\ldots\&E_{n-j}\&B) = 1.$$

Corresponding senses of projectability apply to predicates. (Of course, the future versus the past direction of time is not the issue here; rather the point concerns whether the "next instance" lies in the direction in which the limit of accumulating evidence is taken.)

For the future-moving sense of instance induction to be valid it was sufficient that the prior probability of the universal generalization be nonzero. But not so for past-reaching instance induction. Consider the predicates "P" and "$P*$," where the latter is defined by

$$P*a_i \equiv (Pa_i \ \&\ i \leq 1990) \lor (\neg Pa_i \ \&\ i > 1990).$$

We can assign nonzero priors to both H: $(\forall i)Pa_i$ and to H^*: $(\forall i)P*a_i$ but obviously not even weak past-reaching projectability is possible for both "P" and "$P*$." For $P*a_n$ is logically equivalent to Pa_n for $n \leq 1990$ and to $\neg Pa_n$ for $n > 1990$, so that if

(8) $\lim_{j \to +\infty} Pr(Pa_{1991}/Pa_{1990}\&\ldots\&Pa_{1990-j}\&B) = 1$

then

(9) $\lim_{j \to +\infty} Pr(P*a_{1991}/P*a_{1990}\&\ldots\&P*a_{1990-j}\&B) = 0.$

Thus, unlike definitions 3 and 4, definitions 6 and 7 do distinguish between "grue" and "green" in the sense that both cannot be projectable in the past-reaching sense. But the cut between past-reaching nonprojectable versus projectable predicates does not necessarily correspond to the cut between Goodmanlike versus non-Goodmanlike predicates (see sec. 5 below).

If exchangeability (E) holds for "P" then past-reaching projectability for "P" is equivalent to future-moving projectability. Thus, if we assign nonzero priors to both $(\forall i)Pa_i$ and $(\forall i)P*a_i$, exchangeability cannot hold for both "P" and for "$P*$." Or if exchangeability does hold for both, then for at least one of them the measure μ in De Finetti's representation must be closed-minded.

This is more or less what one would have expected since in the present setting exchangeability functions as one expression of the principle of the uniformity of nature.[12] What is interesting is that there is a principle of induction—weak and strong future-moving instance induction—whose validity does not depend on a uniformity of nature postulate. Furthermore, uniformity of nature in the guise of exchangeability is precisely what one does *not* want in order to make true some of the truisms of confirmation theory, such as that variety of evidence can be more important that sheer amount of evidence. Return to formula (1) used to prove Jeffreys's theorem and note that the more slowly for given n the factor

226   John Earman

$Pr(E_{n+1}/E_1\&\ldots\&E_n\&B)$ goes to 1, the smaller the denominator on the right-hand side of (1) and, thus, the larger the posterior probability of H. Intuitively, the more various (and nonexchangeable) the E_is, the slower the approach to 1 is. Perhaps this intuition can be turned round to yield an analysis of variety of evidence, but I will not pursue the matter here.

Crudely put, the problem of future-moving instance induction concerns whether the future will resemble the future, while the problem of past-reaching instance induction concerns whether the future will resemble the past. The former problem can be posed and solved without much attention to the form the resemblance is supposed to take; for *any* predicate, "genuine" or "Goodmanized," will, irresistibly, lend itself to future-moving projectability as long as a nonzero prior is assigned to the universal generalization on the predicate, and there is no danger of being led into inconsistency as long as the initial probability assignments are coherent. But the latter problem, as Goodman's examples have taught us, requires scrupulous attention to the form of resemblance if inconsistencies are to be avoided. Future-moving instance induction leaves only narrow and unstable ground for the skeptic to stand on. By contrast, past-reaching instance induction provides the grounds for but does not require a blanket skepticism, while the strongest form of general induction virtually begs for skepticism. It is to general induction that I now turn.

3. General Induction

Still assuming that $H, B \vdash E_i$, $i = 1, 2, 3, \ldots$, we can say that

DEFINITION 8. Relative to B, the hypothesis H is *weakly projectable* on the basis of instances $E_1, E_2, \ldots$ *iff* the probability of H is increased by each new instance, i.e.,
$Pr(H/E_1\&\ldots E_{n+1}\&B) > Pr(H/E_1\&\ldots\&E_n\&B)$ for each $n > 0$.
Claim: The necessary and sufficient conditions for H to be weakly projectable are that $Pr(H/B) > 0$ and that $Pr(E_{n+1}/E_1\&\ldots\&E_n\&B) < 1$.
Proof: Write out Bayes's theorem.

The price for weak projectability of H is low; but what we buy may be unexciting since there is no guarantee that the increases that come with increasing instances will boost the probability toward 1. Thus, we also formulate

DEFINITION 9. Relative to B, the hypothesis H is *strongly projectable* on the basis of the instance $E_1, E_2, \ldots$ *iff*
$\lim_{n\to\infty} Pr(H/E_1\&\ldots\&E_n\&B) = 1.$

Claim: H is *not* strongly projectable if there is an alternative hypothesis H' such that (i) $B \vdash \neg(H\&H')$, (ii)$H', B \vdash E_i$ for all i and (iii) $Pr(H'/B) > 0$.

Proof: Assume that H is strongly projectable and assume that there is an H' satisfying (i) and (ii) and show that (iii) is violated. By Bayes's theorem and (ii),

(10) $\dfrac{Pr(H/E_1\&\ldots\&E_n\&B)}{Pr(H'/E_1\&\ldots\&E_n\&B)} = \dfrac{Pr(H/B)}{Pr(H'/B)}$

By (i), $Pr(H/X\&B) + Pr(H'/X\&B) \leq 1$. So if H is strongly projectable, the limit as $n \to \infty$ of $Pr(H'/E_1\&\ldots\&E_n\&B)$ is 0. Thus, taking the limit in (10) gives

(11) $+\infty = \dfrac{Pr(H/B)}{Pr(H'/B)} \Rightarrow Pr(H'/B) = 0.$

Philosophers of science routinely claim that any amount of data can be covered by many, possibly an infinite, number of hypotheses. Strictly speaking, this is not so if it means that there are many H's satisfying (i) and (ii) above. Take the E_i to be Pa_i and take H to be $(\forall i)Pa_i$. Then H admits of no logically consistent alternatives satisfying (i) and (ii) and, hence, no alternatives satisfying (i)-(iii). Such lowly empirical generalizations escape the above negative result, and if (A) and (C) hold, so does strong projectability. For if (A) and (C), then

(12) $\lim\limits_{n\to\infty} Pr((\forall i)Pa_i/Pa_1\&\ldots\&P_n\&B) =$

$\lim\limits_{n\to\infty} [Pr((\forall i)Pa_i/B)/Pr(Pa_1\&\ldots\&Pa_n/B)] = 1.$

We can also consider a doubly infinite sequence of individuals $\ldots a_{-2}, a_{-1}, a_0, a_1, a_2, \ldots$ and demand strong projectability in the past-reaching sense, i.e.,

DEFINITION 10. Relative to B, $(\forall i)Pa_i$ is *strongly projectable in the past-reaching sense iff* for all n
$\lim\limits_{j\to +\infty} Pr((\forall i)Pa_i/Pa_n\&Pa_{n-1}\&\ldots\&Pa_{n-j}\&B) = 1.$

If (C) holds along with exchangeability and the natural generalization of (A), viz., for all n

(A') $\lim\limits_{j\to +\infty} Pr(Pa_{n+j}\&Pa_{n+j-1}\&\ldots\&Pa_n\&Pa_{n-1}\&\ldots\&Pa_{n-j}/B)$
$= Pr((\forall i)Pa_i/B),$

then definition 10 is satisfied. In effect, exchangeability has the flavor of "If you've seen an infinite number of them, you've seen them all."

Once we move beyond direct observational generalizations to theories that outrun the data, it is surely true that there are many rival theories that cover the same data. For such a theory strong projectability on the basis of its instances is impossible unless the dice have been completely loaded against all the alternatives.

We might then hope for a more modest form of projectability, as given in

DEFINITION 11. Relative to B, H is (r, s) *projectable* on the basis of its instances E_1, E_2,... *iff* $Pr(H/B) = r < .5$, but there is a sufficiently large N such that $Pr(H/E_1\&...\&E_N\&B) = s > .5$.

Claim. H is *not* (r, s) projectable for any r and s if there is an H' such that (i) $B \vdash \neg(H\&H')$, (ii) H', $B \vdash -E_i$ for all i, and (iii) $Pr(H'/B) \geq Pr(H/B)$.

Proof. Use (10) with $n = N$. If H is (r, s) projectable and there is an H' satisfying (i) and (ii), the left side of (10) is greater than 1. But if (iii) holds, the right-hand side is less than or equal to 1.

For this more modest form of general induction to work we don't have to load the dice completely against all rivals covering the same instances, but we still need to load them.

Although the Bayesian apparatus has shown itself to be very useful in clarifying issues about confirmation and induction, it proves to be idle machinery when it comes to testing nonstatistical scientific theories. Such a theory can have its probability boosted above .5 and toward 1 by finding evidence that falsifies rival theories. But in such cases simple eliminative induction suffices; and when eliminative induction does not work, then neither does Bayesianism, unless the dice have been loaded against all rival theories.

4. Russell on Induction

Having begun with Russell's formulation of the problem of induction, I now want to return to *Human Knowledge* to see what progress Russell made on the problem. Given that the book is the product of one of the great minds of Western philosophy, the results are more than a little disappointing. Here are four interrelated reasons for disappointment.

First, Russell did not distinguish between the past-reaching and future-moving senses of instance induction. When he gets specific about what instance induction means he tends to make it sound like the future-moving variety, as in "Let a_1, a_2,..., a_n be the hitherto observed member of α, all of which have been found to be β, and let a_{n+1} be the next member of α."[13] This is the easiest and most neatly "solvable" case, but Russell makes little progress toward its "solution," despite the fact that some of his reasoning is close to that later used by Jeffreys[14] to prove that the probability of the next instance approaches 1 (see the third comment below). One can speculate that Russell, having already decided that the validity of induction requires an extralogical principle not justified by experience, was not on the lookout for the kind of result provided by Jeffreys and Huzurbazar.

Second, Russell recognized Goodman's "new problem" of induction; and then again he didn't. He did because he used examples of Goodmanized hypotheses (see the fourth comment) and because he says that β

> must not be what might be called a "manufactured" class, i.e., one defined partly by extension. In the sort of cases contemplated in inductive inference, β is always a class known by intension, but not in extension except as regards observed members . . . and such other members of β, not members of α as may happen to have been observed.[15]

But then again he didn't because he didn't recognize that there is a distinction to be drawn between past-reaching and future-moving instance induction and that it is only for the former that Goodman's "new problem" arises.[16]

Third, Russell formulated the problem of induction in part V. Part VI discusses Keynes's attack on general induction. Assuming as before that $H, B \vdash E_i$, we can apply a result from Keynes's *Treatise on Probability*[17] to conclude that

(13) $Pr(H/E_1\&\ldots\&E_n\&B) =$
$$\frac{1}{1+[Pr(\neg H/B)/Pr(H/B)] \times [Pr(E_1/B\&\neg H)x\ldots xPr(E_n/E_1\&\ldots\&E_{n-1}\&B\&\neg H)]}.$$

Set $Q_n \equiv Pr(E_n/E_1\&\ldots\&E_{n-1}\&B\&\neg H)$ and $q_n \equiv Q_1x\ldots xQ_n$. Then if $Pr(H/B) \neq 0$, the posterior probability of H will go to 1 in the limit as $n \to \infty$ if $q_n \to 0$. Russell comments:

> If there is any number less than 1 such that all the Q's are less than this number, then the product of n Q's is less than the nth power of this number, and therefore tends to zero as n increases.[18]

The reasoning here is similar to that used to prove Jeffreys's theorem on future-moving instance induction, but Russell does not make the connection. When H is a simple empirical generalization, e.g., $(\forall i)Pa_i$, and the E_i's are Pa_i, Russell says that "it is difficult to see how this condition [as quoted above] can fail for empirical material."[19] When i runs from 1 to $+\infty$ and the continuity axiom (A) holds, the factor $Pr(Pa_1\&\ldots\&Pa_n/B\&\neg(\forall i)Pa_i)$ in the denominator of the Keynes formula (13) must go to 0. But when i ranges from $-\infty$ to $+\infty$ and the instances accumulate in the past-reaching sense, this factor cannot be shown to go to 1, unless by "empirical material" Russell means material for which exchangeability or the like holds.

Fourth, the difficulty with general induction to theoretical hypotheses can be seen from a simplified version of Keynes's formula, viz.,

(14) $Pr(H/E\&B) = \dfrac{1}{1 + [Pr(\neg H/B)/Pr(H/B)] \times Pr(E/\neg H\&B)}.$

Suppose that $Pr(H/B)$ is nonzero but small. Then in order for $Pr(H/E\&B)$ to be large, E must be such that it would be improbable if H were false ($Pr(E/\neg H\&B)$ small). But as Russell notes, it may be hard to find such evidence. Take, for sake of illustration, H to be Newton's theory of gravitation and E to be the discovery of Neptune. Then there are many alternatives to H "which would lead to the expectation of Neptune being where it was"; for example, take H' to be the hypothesis that Newton's law of gravitation holds up to the time of discovery of Neptune but not afterward.[20] Russell scores a point with his Goodmanian illustration, but the point obscures the fact that the general problem arises even when Goodmanian alternatives are not at issue.

5. Prospects for a Theory of Projectability

From the perspective of the preceding approach some philosophical theories of projectability appear to be confused as to purpose, or false, or both. Consider the most ambitious and widely discussed philosophical theory of projectability, Goodman's entrenchment theory.[21] Conditions couched in terms of relative entrenchment of predicates seem irrelevant to some of the questions of projectability distinguished here and inadequate to others. For example, any hypothesis, no matter how ill entrenched its predicates, is weakly projectable on the basis of its positive instances if it has a nonzero prior—that is, a theorem of probability. To claim that H gets a zero prior if it conflicts with an H' that is supported, unviolated, and unexhausted, that uses better-entrenched predicates than those of H, and that conflicts with no still better entrenched hypothesis, is to make a claim that is constantly belied by actual scientific practice where new hypotheses using new predicates are given a "fighting chance" of a nonnegligible prior. On the other hand, strong projectability of a hypothesis, even if all of its predicates are supremely well entrenched, may be provably impossible if rival hypotheses are given a fighting chance, even when the rivals use ill-entrenched predicates. The most obvious application of the entrenchment notion is to what I called the problem of past-reaching instance induction. Of course, the general problem is independent of the direction of time and, more importantly, of the time dimension, for parallel problems arise for projecting from one side of a division of the range of a nontemporal parameter into the other side (say, from cases where $(v/c) <$ < 1 to cases where v is near c). But as Rosenkrantz[22] has emphasized, there are numerous cases in the history of science where scientists project predicates that are unentrenched and that, from the perspective of entrenched theory, appear to be Goodmanized because they agree with the old entrenched predicates to a good degree of approximation in the well-sampled side of the division but diverge on the other side.

It is time to pause to ask what can be expected from a "theory of projectability." A minimalist theory would be established by finding sharp and interesting necessary and sufficient conditions for the various notions of projectability. The results reported here take us only part of the way toward this minimalist goal. But once the goal is reached, what more remains to be done? A more grandiose theory of projectability would, presumably, consist of descriptive and/or normative rules for determining when the conditions developed in the minimalist theory are or ought to be met. The prospects for constructing such a theory with the tools of analytic philosophy seem to me dim.

To make this skeptical conclusion plausible it suffices to focus on cases where we found that projectability turns largely on prior probability considerations. Objectivist accounts of prior probability assignments have been offered by Reichenbach,[23] in terms of frequency counts, by Jaynes,[24] in terms of maximum entropy calculations, and by others. But in every instance there are serious if not crippling difficulties with the proposed method of assignment.[25] Without assigning specific prior probabilities we could seek a theory to justify assigning some nonzero priors to a class of favored hypotheses. Keynes's "principle of limited variety" was designed for just this purpose. In *Human Knowledge* Russell attacks Keynes's theory (and rightly so, I think). But Russell's own five 'postulates of induction,' designed he says to "provide the antecedent probabilities required to justify induction,"[26] are just as unattractive. Separability and continuity of causal lines, common causes for similar structures ranged around a center, etc., have a certain intuitive appeal, but they involve contingent assumptions that may not hold in the actual world if it is anything like what the quantum theory says it is like. For the subjectivist school of probability, as represented by De Finetti and followers, the envisioned theory of projectability would consist of a psychological account of how people in fact distribute initial degrees of belief consistent (hopefully) with the axioms of probability. This is a task for cognitive psychology, not armchair philosophy. Of course, I expect that psychology will find that entrenchment and other considerations suggested by philosophers will play some role in the account, but I do not expect that the account will consist of a neat set of rules of the type envisioned in the philosophical literature.

Goodman has charged that the problem of induction and its solution have been misconceived. I agree, but I think the misconception extends further than Goodman would allow. In any case, it is curious that philosophers have reached for more grandiose theories of projectability before getting a firm grip on minimalist theories. In addition to filling in the gaps in the results reported here, it would be nice to have results based on alternatives to exchangeability.[27] One would also like to have information about how fast the posterior probability increases and whether, as Keynes worried, we are all dead before the value gets anywhere near 1.[28]

Notes

1. Russell, *Human Knowledge: Its Scope and Limitations* (New York: Simon and Schuster, 1948), p. 401. See also Russell's *A History of Western Philosophy* (New York: Simon and Schuster, 1945),

chapter 17 ("Hume"), and *Problems of Philosophy* (Oxford: Oxford University Press, 1956), chapter 6 ("On Induction").

2. H. Jeffreys, *Scientific Inference*, 2nd ed. (Cambridge: Cambridge University Press, 1957).

3. V. S. Huzurbazar, "On the Certainty of Inductive Inference," *Proceeding of the Cambridge Philosophical Society*, 51 (1955), pp. 761–62.

4. Paul Horwich, *Probability and Evidence* (Cambridge: Cambridge University Press, 1982), gives an interpretation of Russell's principle of particular induction that corresponds to our definition 3. However, since Russell's discussion was directed toward Hume's problem, definition 6 (given later) may provide a better interpretation.

5. Or "goy" from "boy" as in R. C. Jeffrey, *The Logic of Decision*, (New York: McGraw-Hill, 1965), pp. 175–77. But see Jeffrey's later discussion in the second edition of *The Logic of Decision* (Chicago: University of Chicago Press, 1983), pp. 188–90. See also sec. 2 below. And compare with the confused discussion in K. Popper, *The Logic of Discovery* (New York: Scientific Editions, 1961), appendix vii.

6. A. Kolmogorov, *Foundations of Probability* (New York: Chelsea, 1956). In measure-theoretic terms, continuity requires that if $A_1 \supseteq A_2 \supseteq \ldots$ is a sequence of μ-measurable sets and $A = \bigcap_{n=1}^{\infty} A_n$, then $\mu(A) = \lim_{n \to \infty} \mu(A_n)$. In the presence of finite additivity, continuity is equivalent to countable additivity, requiring that if $\{B_i\}$ is a sequence of pairwise disjoint sets, then

$$\mu(\bigcup_{i=1}^{\infty} B_i) = \sum_{i=1}^{\infty} \mu(B_i).$$

7. R. Carnap, *Logical Foundations of Probability* (Chicago: University of Chicago Press, 1950), and *The Continuum of Inductive Methods* (Chicago: University of Chicago Press, 1952).

8. B. De Finetti, "Foresight: Its Logical Laws, Its Subjective Sources," in H. Kyburg and H. Smokler (eds.), *Studies in Subjective Probability* (New York: Wiley, 1964). μ is uniquely determined by the *Pr* values if, as we are assuming, there are an infinite number of individuals. Instead of exchangeability, Carnap speaks of "symmetric *c*-functions."

9. L. Wittgenstein, *Tractatus Logico-Philosophicus*, trans. D. F. Pears and B. F. McGuiness (London: Routledge & Kegan Paul, 1961), 5.15–5.152.

10. See Horwich, *Probability and Evidence*, and Jeffrey, *The Logic of Decision*.

11. See De Finetti, "Foresight," and A. Shimony, "Scientific Inference," in R. G. Colodny (ed.), *The Nature and Function of Scientific Theories* (Pittsburgh, University of Pittsburgh Press, 1970). These Dutch book arguments are based on a finite series of bets and do not suffice to justify countable additivity or continuity. Extensions to an infinite series of bets are studied in E. Adams, "On Rational Betting Systems," *Archiv für mathematische Logik und Grundlagenforschung*, 6 (1961), pp. 7–29, 112–28.

12. Carnap did not interpret exchangeability (or symmetry of *c*-funtions) in this way since he specified that the subscripts on the individuals are to have no spatiotemporal significance.

13. Russell, *Human Knowledge*, p. 404.

14. Jeffreys's result was not available when Russell was writing *Human Knowledge*. Or at least the result did not appear in the first edition (1931) of *Scientific Inference* or the 1937 reissue; it is in the 1948 second edition.

15. Russell, *Human Knowledge*, p. 404.

16. In fairness to Russell it should be noted that it is not clear that Goodman himself passed this test.

17. J. M. Keynes, *A Treatise on Probability* (New York: Harper & Row, 1962), pp. 235–37.

18. Russell, *Human Knowledge*, p. 424.

19. Ibid.

20. Ibid., p. 411.

21. N. Goodman, *Fact, Fiction and Forecast*, 3rd ed. (Indianapolis: Hackett, 1979).

22. R. Rosenkrantz, "Why Glymour Is a Bayesian," in J. Earman (ed.), *Minnesota Studies in the Philosophy of Science*, vol. X (Minneapolis: University of Minnesota Press, 1983), pp. 69–97.

23. H. Reichenbach, *Theory of Probability* (Berkeley: University of California Press, 1971).

24. E. T. Jaynes, "Prior Probabilities," *IEEE Transactions on Systems Science and Cybernetics*, SSC-4, no. 3 (1968), pp. 227–41.

25. Difficulties with Reichenbach's approach are well known. For criticisms of Jaynes's approach,

see K. Friedman and A. Shimony, "Jaynes' Maximum Entropy Prescription and Probability Theory," *Journal of Statistical Physics*, 3 (1971), pp. 381–84, and T. Seidenfeld, "Why I Am Not an Objective Bayesian: Some Reflections Prompted by Rosenkrantz," *Theory and Decision*, 11 (1979), pp. 413–40.

26. Russell, *Human Knowledge*, p. 487.

27. Generalizations of De Finetti's representation theorem are discussed in B. Skyrms, *Pragmatics and Empiricism* (New Haven, Conn.: Yale University Press, 1984), and J. von Plato, "The Significance of the Ergodic Decomposition of Stationary Measures for the Interpretation of Probability," *Synthese*, 53 (1982) pp. 419–32.

28. I am grateful to C. A. Anderson, G. Hellman, P. Kitcher, B. Skyrms, and W. Sudderth for helpful comments on an earlier draft of this paper.

James Hawthorne

Giving up Judgment Empiricism: The Bayesian Epistemology of Bertrand Russell and Grover Maxwell

Human Knowledge: Its Scope and Limits was first published in 1948.[1] The view on inductive inference that Russell develops there has received relatively little careful study and, I believe, has been largely misunderstood. Grover Maxwell was one of the few philosophers who understood and carried forward the program of Russell's later work. Maxwell considered *Human Knowledge* to be one of Russell's most significant works for its treatment of perception, the event ontology, the theory of space-time, the philosophy of mind, and especially for its solution of the mind-body problem. Furthermore, Maxwell wholly agreed with Russell's rejection there of judgment empiricism (the doctrine that all contingent knowledge can be validated on the basis of experience and [noncontingent] logic alone). But with regard to a positive account of inductive inference Maxwell, with his Bayesian version of inductive logic, parted ways with Russell, or so he believed. Of Russell's positive account Maxwell says:

> He takes the untested, untestable, and, in this sense, non-empirical (though nevertheless, contingent) assumptions upon which our significant knowledge of the world and ourselves rest to be his notorious six "Postulates of Scientific Inference." But, in spite of my boundless admiration for Russell's later work, I do not think that he ever used these postulates significantly or ever showed how they could do much for anyone, be he scientist, philosopher, or man-in-the-street.[2]

Maxwell's comment is typical of how Russell's positive account of induction is usually understood. Everyone knows that Russell's account involves the contingent postulates, but there is little understanding of the precise role they are supposed to play.

This essay is an attempt to gain better insight into Russell's positive account of inductive inference. I contend that Russell's postulates play only a supporting role in his overall account. At the center of Russell's positive view is a probabilistic, Bayesian model of inductive inference. Indeed, Russell and Maxwell actually held very similar Bayesian views. But the Bayesian component of Russell's view in *Human Knowledge* is sparse and easily overlooked.[3] Maxwell was not aware of it when he developed his own view, and I believe he was never fully aware of the extent to which Russell's account anticipates his own. The primary focus of this paper will be the explication of the Bayesian component of the Russell-Maxwell view, and the way in which it undermines judgment empiricism.

Bayes's theorem is an equality derivable in probability theory. By a Bayesian inductive logic I mean any view of theory confirmation that takes Bayes's theorem as expressing the essential features of the logic of theory confirmation. Bayes' Theorem may be written as follows:

$$P(T_1/E) = \frac{P(E/T_1) \, P(T_1)}{\Sigma_i P E/T_i) \, P(T_i)}$$

where $\Sigma_i P(T_i) = 1$, and where for each pair T_i and T_j, $i \neq j$, $P(T_i \cdot T_j) = 0$. If we think of $T_1, T_2, \ldots$, as an exhaustive list of mutually incompatible theories and E as a statement of the evidence, then Bayes's theorem says that the probability of a theory, say T_1, on the evidence E is determined by the likelihood which each T_i assigns to E, $P(E/T_i)$, and the probability of each T_i prior to the evidence, $P(T_i)$. The terms $P(T_i)$ are often called the prior (or a priori) probabilities of the T_i's.

By my criteria many probabilistic accounts of inductive logic are Bayesian, but not all. Among Bayesian views are subjectivist and personalist versions (see, e.g., Frank P. Ramsey, Bruno De Finetti, and L. J. Savage),[4] logicist accounts (e.g., John Maynard Keynes, Harold Jeffreys, Rudolf Carnap),[5] and frequentist views (e.g., Hans Reichenbach, Wesley Salmon, and Grover Maxwell).[6] Maxwell's Bayesian views derive chiefly from Salmon. Russell's account comes from Keynes. Among the non-Bayesian probabilistic models of inductive inference are the classical statistical accounts of R. A. Fisher, J. Neyman and E. S. Pearson, and the logicist account of Henry Kyburg.[7]

What I call the Russell-Maxwell view on inductive inference may be expressed as steps in an enthymematic argument. The view takes the major premise to be fairly obvious:

1. Inductive inference is probabilistic.

A corollary of this premise is:

1a. Any adequate logic of inductive inference must be formally expressible in probability theory and justified with an account of its soundness (i.e., of how and why it may be expected to lead from true premises to probably true conclusions). In particular, the logic should give an account of how the confirmation of scientific theories by collections of singular evident events is possible.

Next an investigation of the logic of probability theory leads to an intermediate conclusion:

2. The theory of probabilistic inference, and Bayes's theorem in particular, shows that valid inductive inference may be formulated in terms of a purely logical component (i.e., the logic of probability theory) and an appropriate assignment of values for prior probabilities.

Russell and Maxwell investigate non-Bayesian inductive methods as well (e.g., induction by simple enumeration). They conclude that the success of any inductive method must depend for its soundness on contingent presuppositions. But both of them see Bayes's theorem as expressing the most comprehensive account of the logic of the confirmation of scientific theories. If purely logical considerations could furnish the right kind of prior probabilities, judgment empiricism might be saved. This leads to the next step in the view. A minor premise is argued for:

3. Logic alone neither guides nor justifies assigning the kinds of values for prior probabilities that are required for the soundness of inductive inferences.

This leads to the conclusion:

4. The valid application of the logic of inductive inference must presuppose some contingent principles to guide and justify the right kinds of prior probabilities. And, on pain of circularity, these principles cannot be justified inductively.

Russell formulated his postulates as an attempt to state the principles presupposed by inductive inference. Maxwell fills the role of the postulates with a different contingent principle, which I will briefly describe later. Their disagreement over the form of the contingent principles is the only major difference in their views. There are, of course, relatively minor differences in the details of their arguments (e.g., they have different accounts of the interpretation of probability). In this essay I will primarily follow Russell's version.

The first hint at the Bayesian flavor of Russell's view, and the role his postulates will play in it, surfaces in the introduction to *Human Knowledge*. The final paragraph of the introduction begins:

That scientific inference requires, for its validity, principles which experience cannot render even probable is, I believe, an inescapable conclusion from the logic of probability. (HK, p. xv)

How does the logic of probability require that inductive inference depend on unconfirmable contingent principles? Russell's answer comes in two parts. The first part claims that inductive inference must be probabilistic; the second claims that probabilistic inference, where valid, depends on an appropriate selection of prior probabilities, and logic alone cannot suffice for this selection.

Regarding the first part Russell writes:

> It is generally recognized that the inferences of science and common sense differ from those of deductive logic and mathematics in a very important respect, namely, that when the premises are true and the reasoning correct, the conclusion is only probable. (HK, p. 335)

He then proceeds to investigate various accounts of what probability *is*. He concludes that there are two kinds: *mathematical probability* and *degree of credibility*. Mathematical probabilities assert the relative frequency with which members of one class occur in another class. Degree of credibility, Russell says, is much more widely applicable than mathematical probability:

> Any proposition concerning which we have rational grounds for some degree of belief or disbelief can, in theory, be placed in a scale between certain truth and certain falsehood. (HK, p. 381)

Probability as degree of credibility represents this scale of *rational* belief. It is a logical tool that should guide our degree of subjective (i.e., psychological) certainty in the truth of propositions. The totality of a person's actual beliefs may not be logically consistent. A logic is a normative standard of rationality, not a description of one's actual belief set. A person falls short of the standard for, among other reasons, lack of logical omniscience. Russell sees the relationship between subjective certainty (which he also calls psychological probability) and degrees of credibility to be strictly analogous to this relationship between actual belief and logical consistency. Just as two sets of beliefs may be inconsistent with each other but internally consistent, so two rational credibility functions may assign different, but internally consistent (with the laws of probability theory), degrees of credibility to propositions. The logic of credibility functions, as expressed by the laws of probability, describes necessary conditions for one's subjective degree of certainty in various propositions to hang together in a coherent way.

Modern Bayesians bolster the view that a notion like degree of credibility is a rational guide to belief and action by arguing that any betting system that violates probabilistic laws can be "Dutch booked" (i.e., the system will accept as fair a system of bets that logically cannot win, no matter what the outcome of the gamble). If one's subjective degree of certainty is to guide one's actions in a rational way, then one may only be certain of avoiding Dutch book by bringing one's subjective degrees of certainty into line with some rational credibility function. In this way Dutch book arguments tie together the ideas of probabilistic credibility as a logic and a guide to life. But Russell seems unaware of such arguments.

Russell finds a certain connection between mathematical probability and degree of credibility:

> The connection is this: When, in relation to all available evidence, a proposition has a certain mathematical probability, then this measures its degree of credibility. For instance, if you are about to throw dice, the proposition "Double sixes will be thrown" has only one thirty-fifth of the credibility attaching to the proposition "Double sixes will not be thrown." Thus the rational man, who attaches to each proposition the right degree of credibility, will be guided by the mathematical theory of probability *when it is applicable*. (HK, p. 381)

This connection is an important one. Carnap calls it *direct inference*. A direct inference is an inference from a statistical description of a whole population to the likelihood that a sample from the population exhibits some specified attributes. The relationship is expressed in terms of conditional credibility functions.

In Russell's example the population is the set of (possible) throws of the dice, and the statistical description says that the relative frequency of double sixes among throws is one thirty-sixth. Let T be the set of throws of the dice, and let D be the subset of T which consists of all double sixes. The statistical description may be represented by "$F(D, T) = 1/36$" (i.e., the frequency of D's among T's is 1/36). Then, where P is a rational credibility function and n is the next toss, "$P(n \in D / n \in T \cdot F(D, T) = 1/36) = 1/36$" expresses a direct inference. It says that the rational degree of credibility of the next throw, n, being a double six, given the statistical hypothesis, $F(D, T) = 1/36$ (along with the fact that n is a throw, i.e., $n \in T$) is 1/36. There are, of course, more complex cases of direct inference. For example, let m be another toss of the dice: $P(n \in D \cdot m \notin D / n \neq m \cdot n \in T \cdot m \in T \cdot F(D, T) = 1/36) = 1/36 \times 35/36 = .027$.

Direct inference is sometimes called statistical syllogism. It is a straightforward extension of the deductive entailment relation. It is a relation of partial entailment of an instance (or conjunction of instances) by a more general hypothesis.

There are a multitude of differing rational credibility functions. Given two arbitrary sentences A and B, in general there will be rational credibility functions P_α and P_β such that $P_\alpha (A/B) \neq P_\beta (A/B)$. In general the degree to which one sentence makes another credible is not logically determinate. Two rational people can honestly disagree on the degree to which a sentence is credible without either being internally inconsistent. The logic of probability only supplies constraints that must be satisfied for a credibility function to be internally consistent. But all rational credibility functions should agree in cases of direct inference. For, supposing the truth of a statistical hypothesis, H, about a population and given an event description, E, which describes an instance of the statistical population, the only rational way to assign E credibility on the basis of H is to assign it the value H specifies.

Recent work on the logic of statistical inference largely consists of attempts to supplement the standard probabilistic axioms for credibility functions with axioms that would require all credibility functions to agree on direct inferences. In these investigations a precise syntactic system (like the language of first-order logic, or an extension of it) is constructed so that statistical statements have a perspicuous syntactic structure. Then the direct inferences are specified in terms of the logical structure of the sentences involved. For our purposes it is not important whether such formal attempts succeed. What is important is that any statistical scientific theory worth its salt plays the role of premises (on the right-hand side of conditional credibility functions) in direct inferences about the evidence. All rational credibility functions should agree on the degree of credibility afforded the evidence by a given statistical theory or hypothesis. For nonstatistical theories the only direct inferences come from logical entailments, and the degree of credibility (in a direct inference) afforded evidence by a theory is either 1 or 0 (depending on whether the theory entails the evidence or its negation, respectively).

In this essay I will express credibility functions as a subscripted letter "P" (e.g., P_α, P_β, P_γ,...). The subscript is to remind us that credibility functions may differ on the degree of credibility they assign a sentence. But since all credibility functions agree on the degree of credibility for a direct inference, I will mark direct inferences by dropping the subscript. So if $P_\alpha (E/H)$ is a direct inference I will write "$P(E/H)$."

We are now prepared to see how the theory of probability shows that inductive inference may be formulated so as to depend for its soundness only on logic and appropriate values for prior probabilities. I will explicate two Bayesian arguments investigated by Russell. Russell draws the first from Keynes.[8] I will generalize it slightly, and employ a more readable notation (see HK, pp. 408–10 and 435–37).

Let T_1 be a theory that taken together with initial condition statements a_1, a_2,..., and other relevant background knowledge g, logically entails the observable evidential statements e_1, e_2,..., respectively. After n observations Bayes's formula for the credibility function P_α yields

$$P_\alpha(T_1/e^n \cdot a^n \cdot g) = \frac{P(e^n/a^n \cdot g \cdot T_1) \, P_\alpha(T_1/a^n \cdot g)}{P(e^n/a^n \cdot g \cdot T_1) \, P_\alpha(T_1/a^n \cdot g) + P_\alpha(e^n/a^n \cdot g \cdot -T_1) \, P_\alpha(-T_1/a^n \cdot g)}$$

Here "e^n" represents the conjunction "$(e_1 \cdot e_2 \ldots e_n)$," and the same convention applies to "a^n."

Taking the initial condition statements as irrelevant to T_1 on g alone (i.e., $P_\alpha(T_1/a^n \cdot g) = P_\alpha(T_1/g)$, since the initial conditions should only be relevant to T_1 in light of the outcome of the test), noting that the value of the direct inferences

$P(e^n/a^n \cdot g \cdot T_1) = 1$ (since $T_1 \cdot g \cdot a^n$ entails e^n), and dividing numerator and denominator by the prior probability of T_1 (i.e., $P(T_1/g)$) we have

$$P_\alpha(T_1/e^n \cdot a^n \cdot g) = \frac{1}{1 + \dfrac{P_\alpha(e^n/a^n \cdot g \cdot -T_1)}{P_\alpha(T_1/g)} \times (1 - P_\alpha(T_1/g))}$$

Note that the term $(1 - P_\alpha(T_1/g))$ is equal to $P_\alpha(-T_1/g)$. So, as evidence increases (i.e., as n increases), T_1 becomes highly confirmed (i.e., $P_\alpha(T_1/e^n \cdot a^n \cdot g)$ goes to 1) if and only if two conditions are met: $P_\alpha(T_1/g) > 0$, and $P_\alpha(e^n/a^n \cdot g \cdot -T_1)$ goes to 0 as evidence (i.e., n) increases. If these conditions can be satisfied, then a whole class of inductive inferences will be justified.

Russell finds the second condition unproblematic in many cases dealing with empirical material. He notes (following Keynes) that

$P_\alpha(e^n/a^n \cdot g \cdot -T_1) = P_\alpha(e_n/a_n \cdot e^{n-1} \cdot a^{n-1} \cdot g \cdot -T_1)$ X
$P_\alpha(e_{n-1}/a_{n-1} \cdot e^{n-2} \cdot a^{n-2} \cdot g \cdot -T_1)$ X...X
$P_\alpha(e_1/a_1 \cdot g \cdot -T_1)$.

If each of the terms on the right is less than some fixed value $q < 1$ *for arbitrarily large n*, then $P_\alpha(e^n/a^n \cdot g \cdot -T_1) < q^n$, which goes to 0 as n increases. This satisfies Russell that the second condition can often be met.

Russell finds the first condition, the question of which theories should get nonzero prior probabilities, to be the primary problem. He finds it difficult to see how any empirical hypothesis can be found initially credible (or incredible) independent of experience. And there is an additional difficulty. If the prior probability for a true theory, say T_1, is too low (but nonzero) on credibility function P_α, then the whole lifespan of the human race may not be of sufficient length to gather the amount of evidence needed to make $P_\alpha(T_1/e^n \cdot a^n \cdot g)$ appreciably large (i.e., by making n large enough for

$$\frac{P_\alpha(e^n/a^n \cdot g \cdot -T_1)}{P_\alpha(T_1/g)}$$

to become appreciably small).

We will return to difficulties with prior probabilities. But first I want to consider another, more general Bayesian analysis that arises in *Human Knowledge* (see pp. 406–7) in a section on induction by simple enumeration. I am going to generalize the analysis substantially, but the seeds of it are clearly there, in the text (see also pp. 410–12). This analysis leads back to the same kind of problem with prior probabilities. Let $T_1, T_2, \ldots,$ be a (possibly infinite) list of competing theories such that $P_\alpha(T_i \cdot T_j/g) = 0$ whenever $i \neq j$ and $\Sigma_i P_\alpha(T_i/g) = 1$. Let e be a possible outcome of initial condition a (taken together with background g). Induction by simple enumeration is the process of determining the probability of

e on an accumulating body of relevant evidence $e^n \cdot a^n$ (where superscripts are understood as before). The following is a theorem of probability theory:

$$P_\alpha(e/a \cdot e^n \cdot a^n \cdot g) = \Sigma_i\, P_\alpha(e/a \cdot e^n \cdot a^n \cdot g \cdot T_i)\, P_\alpha(T_i/a \cdot e^n \cdot a^n \cdot g)$$
$$= \Sigma_i\, P_\alpha(e/a \cdot g \cdot T_i)\, P_\alpha(T_i/e^n \cdot a^n \cdot g).$$

(Note that $\Sigma_i\, P_\alpha(T_i/e^n \cdot a^n \cdot g) = 1$.) The second line of the equality depends only on two additional assumptions: each T_i, together with background knowledge g and initial condition a, bears a direct inference relation to e independent of the other data ($e^n \cdot a^n$); initial conditions are relevant to the T_i, given g, only in light of their associated outcomes. This formula expresses a kind of inductive systematization that theories impose on simple inductions. Notice that if increasing evidence (for large n) drives the posterior probability of one of the theories toward 1, then the simple induction takes on the logical value imposed by that theory in direct inference (i.e., if (as n increases) $P_\alpha(T_1/e^n \cdot a^n \cdot g) \to 1$, then (as n increases) $P_\alpha(e/a \cdot e^n \cdot a^n \cdot g) \to P(e/a \cdot g \cdot T_1)$). Thus, the probability of the next event given by simple induction depends entirely on the probability various theories assign it and the credibility of each theory on past evidence.

The degree of credibility of each theory is given by Bayes's theorem. For example, the credibility of T_1 is given by

$$P_\alpha(T_1/e^n \cdot a^n \cdot g) = \frac{P(e^n/a^n \cdot g \cdot T_1)\, P_\alpha(T_1/g)}{\Sigma_i\, P(e^n/a^n \cdot g \cdot T_i)\, P_\alpha(T_i/g)}$$

where $\Sigma_i\, P_\alpha(T_i/g) = 1$. Notice that the posterior probability of T_1 on $e^n \cdot a^n \cdot g$ depends only on the logically determined values $P(e^n/a^n \cdot g \cdot T_i)$ *and* on the values of the prior probabilities of the various possible theories. In general the T_i may be statistical theories, yielding values for $P(e^n/a^n \cdot g \cdot T_i)$ other than 1 or 0. But they are direct logical inferences on which all rational credibility functions agree.

To get a clearer picture of what Bayes's formula does, consider the case where the T_i are all deterministic theories. That is, suppose for each T_i, $T_i \cdot g \cdot a^n$ either entails e^n or it entails $-(e^n)$. Then for each T_i and each outcome e^n, either $P(e^n/a^n \cdot g \cdot T_i) = 1$ or 0. If every theory entails the evidence, then it follows from Bayes's theorem that $P_\alpha(T_i/e^n \cdot a^n \cdot g) = P_\alpha(T_i/g)$. The only way evidence can change the credibility of a particular theory, say T_1, is either by making $P(e^n/a^n \cdot g \cdot T_1) = 0$ so that $P_\alpha(T_1/e^n \cdot a^n \cdot g) = 0$ and T_1 is falsified, or by making $P(e^n/a^n \cdot g \cdot T_i) = 0$ for some T_i other than T_1. In the latter case

$$P(T_1/e^n \cdot a^n \cdot g) = \frac{P_\alpha(T_{1/g})}{\Sigma_j\, P_\alpha(T_{j/g})}$$

where j ranges only over those theories not falsified by $e^n \cdot a^n \cdot g$. This is just hypothetico-deductive theory confirmation with weights assigned to the various alternative theories. The prior probabilities assign each theory a weight, and the weights all add to 1. Imagine these theories lined up in the order of magnitude of their prior probabilities. When some theories are falsified by the evidence, eliminate them from the line and renormalize the weights of the remaining theories to 1. The true theory, represented here by T_1, can become highly confirmed only if all theories with greater weight and the most substantial of the less weighty theories are falsified. Bayes's formula measures the relative size of a theory's prior probability to the collective size of the priors of all as yet unrefuted theories.

Cases in which the T_i's include statistical theories are only a little more complicated. Dividing out the numerator from the earlier Bayes equation we have

$$P(T_1/e^n \cdot a^n \cdot g) = \frac{1}{1 + \Sigma_{i \neq 1} \frac{P(e^n/a^n \cdot g \cdot T_i)}{P(e^n/a^n \cdot g \cdot T_1)} \frac{P_\alpha(T_i/g)}{P_\alpha(T_1/g)}}$$

The ratios

$$\frac{P(e^n/a^n \cdot g \cdot T_i)}{P(e^n/a^n \cdot g \cdot T_1)}$$

are called the likelihood ratios. $P_\alpha(T_1/e^n \cdot a^n \cdot g)$ goes to 1 if and only if the likelihood ratios all go to 0 (with increasing evidence). And $P_\alpha(T_1/e^n \cdot a^n \cdot g)$ goes to 0 just in case at least one of the likelihood ratios blows up to infinity (with increasing evidence).

In both the case of purely deterministic alternative theories and in the more general case involving statistical theories, the logic of probability leads to the same conclusion: probabilistic inference will assign a high degree of credibility to a true theory if and only if that theory is assigned a nonzero prior degree of credibility and, in addition, all of its competitors that have prior credibility of any appreciable size in comparison can be refuted (relative to it) by the evidence. If two theories agree on the evidence, then the relative size of their posterior probabilities remains proportional to the relative size of their priors. This establishes the second step of the Russell-Maxwell view, and we've specified what formal condition prior probabilities must satisfy if inductive logic is to make true theories highly confirmed.

The Bayesian analysis establishes this claim: inductive logic succeeds in making a true theory highly probable on the evidence within a reasonably short segment of human history *just in case* the prior probability assigned to it is not too low and the prior probabilities assigned to evidentially indistinguishable false competitors are significantly lower than the prior of the true theory.

I don't pretend that Russell had in mind the precise details of the second Bayesian analysis when he wrote *Human Knowledge*, but closely related arguments drawn from Keynes are sketched there. The preceding version above has evolved into its present form through the work of more recent Bayesians. I became aware of much of it through working with Grover Maxwell.

We now approach step 3 of the Russell-Maxwell view. If judgment empiricism is to be saved, then logical considerations alone must provide that prior credibilities are assigned to hypotheses in the right way. Can any noncontingent, purely logical principle guide the assignments of prior credibilities so as to determine that true hypotheses are assigned large enough values and their evidentially indistinguishable competitors are assigned small enough values?

Both Russell and Maxwell come to this issue already fairly convinced by more general Humean considerations that logic alone cannot justify any inductive method. The Bayesian analysis promises to surmount the Humean obstacles if purely logical considerations can furnish prior probabilities of the required sort. So both philosophers expect to find deficiencies in purely logical accounts. Russell investigates attempts related to Keynes's analysis.[9] Maxwell considers Carnap's attempt.[10] Rather than reconstructing the details of particular logicist attempts and their failures, I will outline a more general critique. It is closely related to issues raised by Russell and Maxwell.

First, then, consider that no purely logical account should assign a prior probability of zero to any contingent hypothesis. For every contingent hypothesis is true in some possible world, and prior to the evidence our world could be any one of those worlds. The logic of probability theory (and the Bayesian analyses in particular) shows that if a contingent hypothesis has a zero prior probability, then no evidence can give it a nonzero posterior probability. If logic alone is to provide priors that give a true hypothesis any chance at confirmation it must assign to it and all its contingent competitors nonzero priors.

Any reasonably sophisticated hypothesis has an infinite number of contingent competitors. They cannot all have the same nonzero prior probability, for then they would sum to infinity rather than 1. Indeed, since the sum of these priors must be 1, for any positive real number ϵ (as close to zero as you wish) there must be an infinite number of these hypotheses with prior probabilities less than ϵ. If inductive logic is to highly confirm the true hypothesis, then purely logical considerations must assign all but a relative few of its competitors arbitrarily small prior credibilities, priors so small that all the evidence obtainable in human history would not suffice to confirm the true hypothesis were it among them. How could purely logical considerations determine which subset of contingent hypotheses is so sure to contain the true one that only its members receive high enough priors to have a chance at confirmation? And how could these considerations eliminate those competitors to the true hypothesis that agree on all possible evidence? After all, they are contingent too.

Logical considerations cannot assign priors to hypotheses on the basis of their empirical content, for logical consideration alone cannot play favorites among competing contingent claims. So logicist accounts usually make their assignments of priors on the basis of the syntactic structure of the hypotheses. The idea seems to be that ad hoc, implausible, and silly competitors will have syntactic logical structures that will expose them (in some precise way) as ad hoc, implausible, and silly. But, isn't it logically possible that some such hypotheses are true? That nature does not in fact instantiate such hypothesis would be a contingent (not a purely logical) assumption. Besides, examples a la Nelson Goodman's[11] grue-predicates show how the logician's bag of tricks can always furnish an infinite number of seemingly silly competitors with the same logical structure as the true hypothesis. This move, calling on Goodmanesque predicates, can be countered only by some sort of restriction to hypotheses formulated in a preferred vocabulary, a vocabulary in which predicate terms pick out the real properties and relations (natural kinds?) rather than hokey Goodmanesque composites. Maxwell, commenting on Carnap's system, points out the trouble with such a restriction[12]:

> In order to apply Carnap's system, given any instance of evidence to be used, we must already know what are the relevant individuals and properties in the universe (as well as the cardinality of the relevant classes of individuals). In other words, we must already have the universe "carved at the joints" and spread out before us (otherwise we could not perform the necessary counting of stated descriptions, etc.). But just how to "carve at the joints," just what are the important relevant properties, and just which segments of the world are to be designated as individuals are all contingent questions—or, at least, they have crucial contingent components—and, moreover, are often the most important questions that arise in scientific inquiry. Before any application of Carnap's system can begin, we must assume that a great deal—perhaps most—of that for which a confirmation theory is needed has already been accomplished. We may, as might have been expected, put the objection in a form that, by now, is familiar ad nauseum: Given any body of evidence, there is an infinite number of mutually incompatible ways of "carving the world" (setting up state-descriptions, structure descriptions, etc.) each of which will give different results for predictions, "instance confirmations," etc.

Such considerations lead Russell and Maxwell to the conclusion of their argument. Logic and evidence alone cannot eliminate the myriad competing hypotheses (some of them evidentially indistinguishable) which vie with the true one for inductive confirmation. Science avoids them only because scientists find them silly and implausible (if they find them at all). If these hypotheses are false, they are only contingently false. Only contingent principles can rule them out. Inductive logic is sound only if some contingent principles guide and justify the assignment of prior degrees of credibility (assigning sufficiently large priors to true theories and sufficiently small priors to evidentially indistinguishable competitors) so that the evidence available to us in a reasonable stretch of human history can eliminate initially plausible false competitors and confirm true ones.

In an earlier chapter of *Human Knowledge* on causal laws Russell summarizes the conclusions he will draw from his later Keynesian analysis. Here he makes it abundantly clear that the role of his Postulates of Scientific Inference is to guide the assignment of prior probabilities to theories. I will quote at some length:

> In the establishment of scientific laws experience plays a twofold part. There is the obvious confirming or confuting of a hypothesis by observing whether its calculated consequences take place, and there is the previous experience which determines what hypotheses we shall think antecedently probable. But behind these influences of experience there are certain vague general expectations, and unless these confer a finite a priori probability on certain kinds of hypotheses, scientific inferences are not valid. In clarifying scientific method it is essential to give as much precision as possible to these expectations, and to examine whether the success of science in any degree confirms their validity. After being made precise the expectations are, of course, no longer quite what they were while they remained vague, but so long as they remain vague the question whether they are true or false is also vague.
>
> It seems to me that what may be called the "faith" of science is more or less of the following sort: There are formulas (causal laws) connecting events, both perceived and unperceived; these formulas exhibit spatio-temporal continuity; i.e., involve no direct unmediated relation between events at a finite distance from each other. A suggested formula having the above characteristics becomes highly probable if, in addition to fitting in with all past observations, it enables us to predict others which are subsequently confirmed and which would be very improbable if the formula were false. (p. 314)

I won't take time for a careful treatment of Russell's postulates here. I only want to suggest that the five postulates he sets down seem to be an attempt to state the basic assumptions underlying a version of a scientific realist view of the world. They state a metaphysical view that characterizes the world as composed of mind-independent events and spatiotemporally continuous causal sequences. After listing the five postulates at the beginning of a chapter that summarizes them, Russell clearly states their purpose:

> The postulates collectively are intended to provide the antecedent probabilities required to justify inductions. (HK, p. 487)

The postulates seem to provide Russell with the required antecedent probabilities in two senses. They explain how it is that we can have relatively accurate knowledge of the (mostly distant) events that make up the world, i.e., through the mediation of spatiotemporally continuous causal processes. The relative constancy, stability, and similarity inherent in many of these processes together with our vast experience at the perceiving end of them account for our exceptionally good luck at discovering credible hypotheses that are true or nearly true. Second, the postulates function as a guide in assessing the rational credibility of (other) contingent hypotheses. A hypothesis or theory is totally incredible (has probability 0) if it is inconsistent with the causal makeup of the world as described by the postulates. If a hypothesis is at all credible, its prior degree of credibility should be assessed, it seems, on the basis of how coherently (as compared with credible competitors) it fits together the postulated causal structure of the world.

The postulates are metaphysical in that they express basic contingent facts about the makeup of the world, they must be known if any empirical knowledge beyond immediate experience is possible, and they cannot themselves be known empirically (i.e., on the basis of experience and logic alone).

But although experience of barking dogs suffices to *cause* belief in the generalization "Dogs bark," it does not, by itself, give any grounds for believing this is true in untested cases. If experience is to give such a ground, it must be supplemented by causal principles such as will make certain kinds of generalization antecedently plausible. These principles, if assumed, lead to results which are in conformity with experience, but this fact does not logically suffice to make the principles even probable. (HK, p. 507)

Maxwell was unaware of Russell's Bayesian leanings, but he acknowledges his agreement with Russell that inductive inference needs a boost from some preinductive, contingently true postulate. He comments that Russell's postulates may reflect an important part of our commonsense knowledge, but he finds them neither necessary nor sufficient for a viable theory of induction. Maxwell (like most other philosophers) seems to have missed the Bayesian component of Russell's inductive logic. He (and others) finds the postulates perplexing because it is difficult to see how the postulates, standing alone, can furnish anything like inductive rules of inference. The postulates seem to suggest what kinds of theories to search for, but they furnish no machinery for testing or confirming theories with evidence. I think this is the main thrust of Maxwell's criticism of Russell's approach. But Maxwell found fault with the postulates on other grounds, too. He found them inadequate as a guide to the assignment of prior probabilities.

Maxwell's arguments suggest that even if the version of scientific realism expressed by Russell's postulates is true (as it may well be) there are a multitude of incompatible, but evidentially indistinguishable, theories that satisfy them. Given one such theory, the logician can easily concoct the rest. Appeals to *simplicity* will only help narrow the field if it is contingently true that nature favors simpler theories. This would be an additional contingent postulate. And, again, Goodman's grue-predicates illustrate that the logician can often get the desired syntactic simplicity by drawing on his bag of tricks. ("Theories gotten without tricks are more likely a priori" would be another plausible, but contingent, *assumption*.)

Maxwell's method for assigning prior probabilities to theories is simply this:

a person should assign prior probabilities by ordering and weighting the alternatives in accordance with his best carefully considered intuitive judgment of their respective credibilities (actually Maxwell used a frequency theory of probability instead of degree of credibility, so his version explicates "credibilities" in terms of "relative frequencies of truth among similar hypotheses"). Maxwell backs this recommendation with a contingent but (on pain of circularity) unconfirmable postulate. It says, roughly, that we have the innate (perhaps, naturally selected) capacities to develop the following abilities: first, to propose hypotheses such that a nonvanishing proportion of them are true; and second, to rank these hypotheses, by means of subjective estimates, in such a way that the evidence will pare away the initially most credible competitors of a true hypothesis. This is a rational reconstruction of how we actually proceed both in science and in daily life, and, Maxwell argued, no inductive logic can improve on it.[13]

I will conclude with a long quotation from the last two paragraphs of *Human Knowledge*. Maxwell believed that the view it expresses was one of Russell's most significant contributions.

As mankind have advanced in intelligence, their inferential habits have come gradually nearer to agreement with the laws of nature which have made these habits, throughout, more often a source of true expectations than of false ones. The forming of inferential habits which lead to true expectations is part of the adaptation to the environment upon which biological survival depends.

But although our postulates can, in this way, be fitted into a framework which has what we may call an empiricist "flavor," it remains undeniable that our knowledge of them, in so far as we do know them, cannot be based upon experience, though all their verifiable consequences are such as experience will confirm. In this sense, it must be admitted, empiricism as a theory of knowledge has proved inadequate, though less so than any other previous theory of knowledge. Indeed, such inadequacies as we have seemed to find in empiricism have been discovered by strict adherence to a doctrine by which empiricist philosophy has been inspired: that all human knowledge is uncertain, inexact, and partial. To this doctrine we have not found any limitation whatever. (p. 507)

Notes

1. Bertrand Russell, *Human Knowledge: Its Scope and Limits* (New York: Simon & Schuster, 1948).
2. Grover Maxwell, "The Later Russell: Philosophical Revolutionary," in *Russell's Philosophy*, ed. George Nakhnikian (London: Duckworth, 1974), pp. 169–82.
3. Kenneth Blackwell, Archivist of the Bertrand Russell Archives at McMaster University, reports that the Archives has a two foot stack of manuscripts related to *Human Knowledge*, and that much of this material is devoted to various probabilistic investigations and derivations. Perhaps more detail from Russell's Bayesian investigations can be found there.
4. Frank P. Ramsey, "Truth and Probability" (1926), in Henry E. Kyburg and Howard E. Smokler

(eds.), *Studies in Subjective Probability* (New York: Wiley, 1964), pp. 61-92; Bruno De Finetti, "La Prévision: ses lois logiques, ses sources subjectives" (1937), translated in Kyburg and Smokler, *Studies in Subjective Probability*, pp. 93-158; L. J. Savage, *The Foundations of Statistics* (New York: Wiley, 1954).

5. John Maynard Keynes, *A Treatise on Probability* (London and New York: Macmillan, 1921; 2nd ed., 1929); Harold Jeffreys, *Theory of Probability*, 2nd ed. (Oxford: Clarendon Press, 1948); Rudolf Carnap, *Logical Foundations of Probability* (Chicago: University of Chicago Press, 1950).

6. Hans Reichenbach, *The Theory of Probability* (Berkeley: University of California Press, 1949); Wesley Salmon, *The Foundations of Scientific Inference* (Pittsburgh: University of Pittsburgh Press, 1966 & 1967); Grover Maxwell, "Induction and Empiricism: A Bayesian Frequentist Alternative," in Grover Maxwell & Robert Anderson, Jr. (eds.), *Minnesota Studies in the Philosophy of Science*, vol. 3 (Minneapolis: University of Minnesota Press, 1975), pp. 106-65.

7. R. A. Fisher, *Statistical Methods for Research Workers* (Edinburgh and London: Oliver & Boyd, 1925); J. Neyman and E. S. Pearson, *Joint Statistical Papers* (Berkeley: University of California Press, 1967); Henry E. Kyburg, Jr., *The Logical Foundations of Statistical Inference* (Boston: Reidel, 1974).

8. John Maynard Keynes, *Treatise on Probability*.

9. See HK, pp. 408-12 and 433-44.

10. See Maxwell, "Induction and Empiricism," pp. 161-62.

11. Nelson Goodman, *Fact, Fiction and Forecast*, 2nd ed. (New York: Bobbs-Merrill, 1965).

12. Maxwell, "Induction and Empiricism."

13. Grover Maxwell, "Induction and Empiricism," and "Corroboration without Demarcation," in P. A. Schlipp (ed.), *The Philosophy of Karl Popper: The Library of Living Philosophers* (LaSalle, IL: Open Court, 1974), pp. 292-321.

C. Anthony Anderson

Russell on Order in Time

After a brief flirtation with instants of time as primitive entities, Russell proceeded to construct instants out of classes of events. His most vigorous and rigorous analysis of the construction appears in a little-discussed paper "On Order in Time" (*Proceedings of the Cambridge Philosophical Society*, vol. 32 [1936], pp. 216–28; hereafter: OT). Small wonder that the paper is little discussed. It utilizes the intricate logical notation of *Principia Mathematica* throughout, and if you attempt to work through the details, you will discover that Russell's powers of deduction had not waned. (He was sixty-three.) That such a mind thought the matter worthy of such concentration is a sufficient justification for reopening the case. In the present essay I explain what Russell accomplished in "On Order in Time," with some consideration of similar ideas in the earlier works *Our Knowledge of the External World* and *The Analysis of Matter*. I find some flaws and suggest repairs and improvements. Proceeding from the precise and uncontroversial to the vague and perennially debatable, I consider philosophical objections, some due to Russell's earlier self, to constructing instants out of events. Finally, I take on the most general question in the immediate neighborhood: "Why construct anything out of anything?" Russell's enthusiasm for the epistemic power of logical constructions diminished over the years. But I think his own appraisal of the upshot of his paper underestimates what can be established and overestimates what has been established:

> It is shown that the existence of instants requires hypotheses which there is no reason to suppose true. (OT, p. 216)

The Postulates

In *Our Knowledge of the External World* (KEW) Russell had constructed the time series of instants on the basis of the following primitive concepts, definitions, and postulates. (I have formalized these for comparison with OT.)

Primitives: $S(x,y)$ — "x and y are events and the times at which x exists coincide (in part or whole) with the times at which y exists." $P(x,y)$ — "x and y are events and x temporally wholly precedes y, i.e., every time at which x exists is temporally precedent to any time at which y exists." I have added the English paraphrases as an aid to intuition. Russell just says of the first relation that it holds between two events if they overlap or are contemporaries or are (at least partially) simultaneous. And $P(x,y)$ if x and y are events and x wholly precedes y. The notions of an event and of a time are not really permissible in the explanation of these relations—both are defined (in KEW). The relations are known by acquaintance in experience.

DEFINITION: $Evt(x) \rightarrow (\exists y)S(x,y)$.

"x is an event" means "x overlaps something or other."

POSTULATES:

I. (a) $Evt(x) \supset \sim P(x,x)$.

"If x is an event, then x does not wholly precede x."

(b) $Evt(x) \supset .Evt(y) \supset .Evt(z) \supset .P(x,y) \supset .P(y,z)$
$\supset .P(x,z)$.[1]

"If x, y, and z are events and x wholly precedes y and y wholly precedes z, then x wholly precedes z."

(c) $Evt(x) \supset .Evt(y) \supset .P(x,y) \supset \sim S(x,y)$.

"If x and y are events and x wholly precedes y, then x does not overlap y."

(d) $Evt(x) \supset .Evt(y) \supset . \sim S(x,y) \supset .P(x,y) \vee P(y,x)$.

"If x and y are events and x does not overlap y, then either x wholly precedes y or y wholly precedes x."

To these four, which give the fundamental properties of overlapping and precedence (with an exception to be noted later), Russell adds the definition:

DEFINITION: $Init\ (x,y) \rightarrow S(x,y). \sim (\exists z)[P(z,x).S(z,y)]$.

"x is an initial contemporary of y" means "x overlaps y but there is no z that wholly precedes x and that overlaps y." In terms of this, he adopts the postulate:

II. $Evt(x) \supset Evt(y) \supset .S(z,x) \supset .P(z,y)$
$\supset (\exists w)[Init(w,x).P(w,y)]$.

"If x and y are events and a contemporary of x, say z, wholly precedes y, then an *initial* contemporary of x, w, wholly precedes y." This postulate guarantees, given the others, that events shall have first instants. I'm agin it. The Big Bang, I am told, was an event that likely did not have a first instant—the initial singularity is outside of the space-time manifold.

Finally, to ensure that the instants of the construction are compact (there is another between any two), Russell adopts:

III. $Evt(x) \supset . Evt(y) \supset . P(x,y)$
$\supset (\exists z)(\exists w)[Evt(z).P(x,z).S(z,w).P(w,y)]$.

"If x and y are events and x wholly precedes y, then there is an event z wholly preceded by x and overlapping a w wholly preceding y."

The proof of compactness using postulates II and III is neat, but we shouldn't get carried away. Russell didn't. He listed II and III as *assumptions* in KEW, but his statements concerning their truth is cautious. *Provided* II is true, he says, events will have first instants. *If* III, then the series of instants is compact. But if our project is epistemological, and it is, these last postulates cannot be taken as data. Things brighten in OT, where we find:

DEFINITION: $S(x,y) \rightarrow \sim P(x,y). \sim P(y,x)$.

"x overlaps y" means "x does not wholly precede y and y does not wholly precede x."

I(c) and I(d) become logical truths. II and III are dropped *as postulates* and Russell adopts:

A. $\sim P(x,x)$.
B. $P(x,y) \supset . P(y,z) \supset P(x,z)$.

from which I(a) and I(b) follow. The construction also requires:

C. $R(x,y) \supset . R(y,z) \supset . R(x,z)$

where:

DEFINITION: $R(x,y) \rightarrow (\exists z)[S(x,z).P(z,y)]$.

("$R(x,y)$" may be read "x begins to exist before y begins to exist.")

Quine has complained, in his review of OT, that Russell's definition of overlapping ($S(x,y)$) misses the mark if the type of individuals includes nonevents.[2] For in that case two individuals, if nonevents, will overlap if neither temporally precedes the other (which they won't). Quine suggests defining events as entities in the field of P and confining S to events. Russell would respond, I think, that all his individuals are events. Everything else is constructed. Quine's suggestion won't do anyway since it rules out a priori, what should be left open, namely, that there should be one great event that persists from the beginning of time to the end.

Well, things are getting nice and tidy. We are left with only A, B, and C and a definition. Postulate C, if you don't cheat and use the informal reading, is not self-evident. It really reads:

$(\exists u)[S(x,u).P(u,y)] \supset .(\exists v)[S(y,v).P(v,z)]$
$\supset (\exists w)[S(x,w).P(w,z)]$.

Now write out S in terms of its definition and contemplate the result. The thing is not self-evident. (It is evident if you think about it.) Imagine, then, my delight at finding that *both* B and C follow from:

D. $Q(x,y) \supset .P(y,z) \supset P(x,z)$,

where

DEFINITION: $Q(x,y) \to (\exists z)[P(x,z).S(z,y)]$.

(Read "$Q(x,y)$" as "x ends before y ends.") This reads, with no cheating, "If x wholly precedes something which overlaps y, and y wholly precedes z, then x wholly precedes z." Now *that* really *is* self-evident. And imagine my disappointment at finding out that Norbert Wiener has already discovered this in 1914 (as Russell at one time knew—Wiener is cited in KEW, 2nd ed., p. 97, note).[3]

Enough tinkering with the postulates. We should adopt A and D; the rest that is required for the construction follows.

Instants as Classes of Events

According to Russell, an instant is a class of events such that (1) everything in the class overlaps everything else in the class, and (2) nothing outside the class overlaps everything in the class. Using *Principia* notation, the simplest expression of this is that a class of events α is an instant if and only if:

$\alpha = \hat{x}(y)[y \in \alpha \supset S(x,y)]$.

"The class α consists of exactly those events x such that if y is anything in α, then x overlaps y."

Russell credits the idea of this *sort* of construction to Whitehead.[4] But Whitehead had constructed instants as "enclosure series,"[5] roughly as infinite sequences of events, each containing another that converges to... well, they may not converge *to* anything. Whitehead just took the infinite series of Chinese-box-like events to *be* the instants. To this Russell objects in *The Analysis of Matter* (AMa):

> Let us begin with the absence of a lower limit or minimum. Here we are confronted with a question of fact, which might conceivably be decided against Dr. Whitehead, but could not conceivably be decided in his favour. The events which we can perceive all have a certain duration, i.e. they are simultaneous with events which are not simultaneous with each other. Not only are they all, in this sense, finite, but they are all above an assignable limit. I do not know what is the shortest perceptible event, but this is the sort of question which a psychological laboratory could answer. We have not, therefore, direct empirical evidence that there is no minimum to events. Nor can we have indirect empirical evidence, since a process which proceeds by very small finite differences is sensibly indistinguishable from a continuous process, as the cinema shows. *Per contra*, there might be empirical evidence, as in the quantum the-

ory, that events could not have less than a certain minimum spatio-temporal extent....

I conclude that there is at present no means of knowing whether events have a minimum or not; that there never can be conclusive evidence against their having a minimum; but that conceivably evidence may hereafter be found in favour of a minimum. It remains to consider the question of a maximum. (pp. 292, 293).

Russell is a bit harsh here. It might turn out that our best theory of the external world postulates the infinite divisibility of events. In such a case, probability anyway would be with Whitehead. Still, if we are building from the bottom, it is better not to have such assumptions at the beginning (I think we shall need the assumption that there are infinitely many events *later*).

In Russell's construction there is no need to assume that events are nested one within the other without end. They need only overlap—we collect them together into "maximal" overlapping classes and call the results "instants." The relation of *temporal precedence* for instants thus constructed is defined:

DEFINITION: $T(\alpha,\beta) \rightarrow (\exists x)(\exists y)[x \in \alpha . y \in \beta . P(x,y)].In(\alpha).In(\beta)$.

One instant α temporally precedes another β if and only if some $x \in \alpha$ and some $y \in \beta$ are such that $P(x,y)$, i.e., x wholly precedes y.[6] But Russell was worried that still there might not *be* any such maximal classes of events. So there might not be any instants.

Russell also defines, which may be independently interesting, the *duration* of an event as the class of all the events that overlap the event. And he proves that durations can be arranged in a series according to the following plan: if two durations do not begin together, put first the one with the earlier beginning; if they begin together, put first the one with the earlier end. I have not been able to figure out why anyone would want to prove such a thing.

The Existence of Instants

Russell begins and ends OT with discouraging comments about the existence of instants. On the first page, he says that their existence "requires hypotheses which there is no reason to suppose true." And on the last page he says, "But in the absence of such possibilities[7] [to be discussed later in this section] I do not know of any way of proving the existence of instants anywhere if it is possible that all events existing at the beginning of some event (or at the end) continue during a period when others begin and cease (or have previously existed during such a period)" (p. 228). And about the conditions that he proves sufficient for the existence of instants, Russell says in the middle of the essay, "There is, however, no reason, either logical or empirical, for supposing these assumptions to be true" (p. 219).

254   C. Anthony Anderson

But there is a clear, distinct, and sufficient reason for the existence of instants. Russell himself noted it and proved informally in *The Analysis of Matter* (chapter 27) that there are instants. But first, the condition he develops in OT:

$$\exists \, !S \stackrel{\cdot}{-} S|P|S$$

is a sufficient condition for the existence of at least one instant. This guarantees that there are two events a and b, such that the last instant of a is the first instant of b. Yes, but what does the condition mean? $S|P|S$ is the *relative product* of S, P, and S, in that order, so that $x(S|P|S)y$ if and only if for some u, v, x overlaps u and u precedes v and v overlaps y. The condition states that for some x and y, x overlaps y but not-$x(S|P|S)y$.

And Russell develops a condition sufficient for *every* event having a *first* instant. Adopt this definition:

DEFINITION: $U(x,y) \to (\exists z)[Init(z,x).P(z,y)]$.

Then the sufficient condition is:

$R(x,y) \supset U(x,y)$,

where R is defined earlier. This is the condition that is taken in KEW as postulate II.

A condition sufficient for every event having a last instant is given thus:

DEFINITION: $Fin(x,y) \to S(x,y). \sim (\exists z)[S(z,y).P(x,z)]$.

"x is a final contemporary of y" means "x overlaps y but nothing overlapping y is wholly preceded by x."

Then the sufficient condition for events having last instants is as follows: anything wholly preceding something overlapping the event, wholly precedes a final contemporary of the event. Given:

DEFINITION: $V(x,y) \to (\exists z)[Fin(z,x).P(y,z)]$,

the desired condition is

$Q(y,x) \supset V(x,y)$,

where Q is defined earlier. This one is, I suppose, as reasonable as the other.

So there you have it and I must agree that these conditions are neither evident to the senses, self-evident, nor likely to be deducible from such by the rules of reason.

But *the* condition only mentioned by Russell in OT and actually used by him in AMa is that the set of events overlapping a given event can be well ordered. The principle that any set can be well ordered is better known nowadays as an equivalent of the axiom of choice. My favorite version is this:

(AC_1) For any relation there is a function that is a subset of it and that has the same domain.

Indeed, it suffices to confine our attention to binary relations. The relation, R, say, is any definite set of ordered pairs $<x,y>$. The function, F, let's say, is to be a subset of R with just one such pair $<x,y_1>$ for each x such that a pair $<x,y>$ belongs to R. If R is a definite such multitude, then *surely* there *is* such a subcollection as F! This is, as Gödel remarked,[8] almost as evident as any of the other principles of set theory. And Russell says in AMa that he had been persuaded of its truth (in another formulation) by Frank P. Ramsey and Henry M. Sheffer. He then proceeds to give (in AMa) a perfectly cogent, if slightly informal, proof that there are instants (pp. 299-302). Sometime between 1926 and 1936 Russell changed his mind about the axiom of choice. In his reviews of Ramsey's essays[9] Russell seems optimistic about the extensionalized and simplified theory of types advocated by Ramsey. But by the time of *My Philosophical Development* he advocates intensionalism again. The R and F in AC_1 are *not*, for Russell, sets of ordered pairs; they are *attributes*—relations-in-intension. (Strictly, talk of functions, for Russell, reduces to talk of propositional functions.) Or, worse, perhaps they are expressions. But in any case, the thing loses its appearance of truth in either its intensionalistic or nominalistic versions. (Not that it looks false on the attribute reading. One just can't tell.) This is, I suppose, why Russell rejected the axiom of choice (or its equivalent) and the proof of the existence of instants based on it.

But we need not follow him in this. If we don't, and I won't, instants come easily. Take one of the least evident equivalents of (AC_1), *Zorn's lemma*:

(Z) If A is a nonempty set of sets and if for any chain B that is a subset of A, UB, the union of B, is an element of A, then A contains a maximal element.

A *chain* of sets is a collection B such that for any sets C and D belonging to B, either C is a subset of D or D is a subset of C. A *maximal* element of a set of sets A is an element of A that is not a subset of any other element of A.

THEOREM. If z is any event, then there exists an instant containing z, i.e., a set $\alpha = \hat{x}(y)[y \in \alpha \supset S(x,y)]$, such that $z \in \alpha$.

Proof: Let α be the set of all sets A containing z and such that every element of A overlaps every other element of A. This is a subset of the power set of $\mathscr{E}$, the set of events, and hence exists. α is nonempty since $\{z\} \in \alpha$. Let B be a subchain of α. Consider UB. Since z belongs to every element of B, z belongs to UB. Let x,y be two elements of UB. Then at worst for some sets C and D, say, $x \in C$ and $y \in D$, where C and D are elements of the chain B. Then $C \subseteq D$ or $D \subseteq C$, and x and y belong to some element of α and hence overlap. Thus UB belongs to α and, by Zorn's lemma, α has a maximal element M. Now M contains z and is an instant—for anything in it overlaps everything else in it. And if some event x overlapped everything in M and was not in M, then $M \cup \{x\}$ would be an element of α. But then M would not be maximal.

Q.E.D.

Of course, this proof is in Zermelo-Fraenkel set theory, something that Russell did not accept. But we might. So the axiom of choice, which implies Zorn's lemma (that would be the epistemic order), implies the existence of an instant containing any given event. Since events exist, instants exist. That is about as close to a proof as anything ever gets in philosophy.

Let me sum up. Russell's construction can be based on some pretty evident axioms about S and P, and the existence of instants can then be proved using the axiom of choice. From an extensional point of view the latter looks quite evident, though Russell himself rejects it. Further, Russell has given some interesting and correct sufficient conditions for events having first and last instants. These might be independently important in the detailed development of the theory. So far, pretty good.

Compactness

When you think about it, instants *are* quite strange. They do not appear often in everyday talk at all. They are of use to the scientist who needs, apparently, instantaneous slices of reality matched with real numbers in order to formulate mathematical laws of nature. Given this reflection, the Russellian conquests so far begin to pale a bit. If instants of time are to be of much, perhaps any, use, they must form a *compact* series; there must be an instant between any two instants. In KEW Russell adopts postulates II and III, which entail the compactness of the series of instants (see Wiener, notes this chapter, for details). But these postulates are seriously a posteriori. I agree with the Russell of OT that there are no obvious reasons for accepting either as epistemically basic. So we should seek more evident sufficient conditions for compactness. True to form, Russell does exactly that. In OT he claims to prove that the two conditions:

(a) No event lasts only for an instant,

(b) Any two overlapping events have at least one instant in common,

guarantee compactness. The second of these follows from Zorn's lemma. Just go through the construction of the theorem proved earlier but begin with *two* overlapping events x and y instead of one event z. This would leave us with only (a), which, though debatable, is certainly plausible.

Unfortunately, there's an error in Russell's proof.[10] The two conditions are not sufficient for compactness. In the accompanying diagram, let *being to the left of* represent temporal precedence. And let temporal overlapping be represented by a line segment being over or under (or identical with) another.

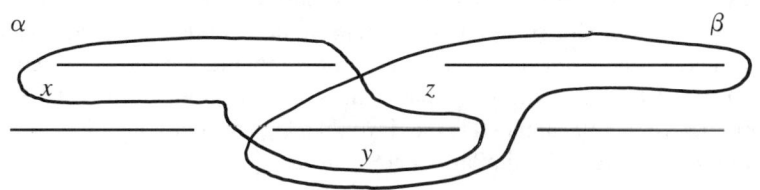

[Diagram: line segments labeled α, β, x, y, z with overlapping enclosures]

Then the event y lasts only for two instants α (the set consisting of x and y) and β (consisting of y and z). And if the diagram is imagined to continue in the same way, all events last for two instants and any two overlapping events have an instant in common. But the series of instants is not compact (please verify that the postulates A and D obtain). Alas, the best condition I can think of that entails compactness is just:

E. $P(x,y) \supset (\exists z)[P(x,z).P(z,y)]$,

i.e., there is an event between x and y if x wholly precedes y. As far as I can see, Russell's two postulates from KEW (which Wiener, by the way, also uses) are no better epistemically than this. Worse, I think.

Well, then, what about *continuity?* If we get this far, I see no obstacle to using the ideas of Russell's construction of real numbers to construct a continuum of hyperinstants—segments of instants so far constructed. Then we will have what we need. Or almost.

Should Instants be Constructed out of Events?

I want now to consider some detailed objections to the project. I reserve general objections to the very idea of construction until the next section.

Recurrence

In another little-noticed paper "Is Position in Time and Space Absolute or Relative?" (*Mind*, n.s., no. 39 [1901], pp. 293–317), Russell attempts to refute his future theory. He claims that it is "difficult, if not impossible, to free the relational theory from contradiction" (p. 293).

In this paper he takes an event to be just a compound consisting of a quality together with a time. Events are incapable of recurring. Qualities are inherently capable of recurring. Therein lies the problem for the relational theory. If you begin with qualities, which can recur, how can you obtain events, which cannot recur, with using times? I quote:

> Whatever can, in ordinary language, recur or persist, is not an event; but it is difficult to find anything logically incapable of recurrence or persistence, except by including temporal position in the definition. When we think of the

things that occur in time—pleasure, toothache, sunshine, etc.—we find that all of them persist and recur. In order to find something which does not do so, we shall be forced to render our events more complex. The death of Caesar or the birth of Christ, it may be said, were unique: they happened once, but will never happen again. Now it is no doubt probable that nothing exactly similar to these events will recur; but, unless the date is included in the event, it is impossible to maintain that there would a logical contradiction in the occurrence, of a precisely similar event. (p. 295)

A possible answer occurs to Russell. Why not take time to be the entire state of the universe? Or, as we might put it, take instants to be maximal sets of contemporaneous events. Sound familiar? But early Russell has objections to later Russell:

Perhaps it may be said that the whole state of the universe has the required uniqueness: we may be told that it is logically impossible for the universe to be twice in the same state. But let us examine this opinion. In the first place, it receives no countenance from science, which, though it admits such recurrence to be improbable, regards it as by no means impossible. In the second place, the present state of the universe is a complex, of which it is admitted that every part may recur. But if every part may recur, it seems to follow that the whole may recur. In the third place, this theory, when developed so as to meet the second objection, becomes really indistinguishable from that of absolute position. There is no longer an unanalyzable relation of simultaneity: there are a series of states of the universe, each of which, as a whole and only as a whole, has to each other a simple relation of before and after; an event is any part of a state of the universe, and is simultaneous with any other part of the same state, simultaneity meaning merely the being parts of some one state; before and after do not hold between events directly, but only by correlation. Thus the theory in question, except for the fact that it is no longer simple, is merely the absolute theory with states of the whole universe identified with moments. The reasons against such an identification are, first, that events seem to have an order which does not, in its very meaning, involve reference to the whole universe, and secondly, that immediate inspection seems to show that recurrence of the whole state of the universe is not logically absurd. (pp. 295–296)

The first of these objections to constructing moments of time is easily answered on Russell's OT theory. Events, in the OT sense, stand in the relation of precedence to one another independently of any reference to moments of time—events in this new sense do not involve instants in their very structure. It's the other way around.

The second objection, that it appears to be logically possible for the entire state of the universe to recur, should just be allowed as correct. And in *Inquiry into Meaning and Truth*, much later, Russell did admit this (pp. 126–27). Perhaps this is not quite directly incompatible with his construction, but it's pretty close. The relation of temporal precedence T is irreflexive. *Instants* cannot therefore recur. But isn't it possible for the time series to close on itself?

One possible line is this. We should admit that we are not entirely justified in taking temporal precedence to be irreflexive. An instant might precede itself if the loop closes somehow beyond our ken. But temporal precedence is *locally* irreflexive, and we can just regard our construction as dealing with a nonrepetitive stretch.

Another approach would be to attempt to avoid the consequence that T is irreflexive by altering the postulates. Oddly, it doesn't help to drop the postulate that P is irreflexive. If α is an instant, then $\sim T(\alpha,\alpha)$ holds independently of this property of P. This is actually momentarily slightly puzzling. It looks as if logic has taken the upper hand and demanded that the series of instants be ordered by an irreflexive relation. Suppose $T(\alpha,\alpha)$. Then $(\exists x)(\exists y)[x\in\alpha.y\in\alpha.P(x,y)]$. If α is an instant, for all $x,y\in\alpha$, $S(x,y)$, i.e., $\sim P(x,y)$. $\sim P(y,x)$ — which contradicts the last clause of the quantified sentence just noted. The catch is that the definition of $S(x,y)$ is no longer adequate if we have allowed that we might have $P(x,x)$. The correction along this line is to restore S as a separate primitive and to revert to a longer list of axioms in the manner of KEW. But probably I am seriously taxing your tolerance for technicalities.

One way then, and perhaps the simplest to state, is just to narrow the scope of the construction. If someone complains that this amounts to limiting the application of the temporal series to apply where it applies, we reply: Yes, it applies where it applies and not in another place. So what?

Relativity

It will be said that the construction is a mistake because the clear teaching of the general theory of relativity is that time is *not* a single linear continuum. Russell's reply, or one of them, is that since the construction concerns psychological time (AMa, p. 294), all the events concerned are in your head. Since local time is a single linear continuum even according to the theory of relativity, all is well.

I fear that I am ill qualified to do combat with the issues here, given my quite superficial understanding of relativity. Still, Russell's reply seems odd on any theory. Surely he supposes that the postulates governing events apply also to (local) events that are not experienced? Indeed, in OT he mentions physics as the discipline to which his construction is relevant.

But the reply seems to be along the right lines. If the theory of relativity has been confirmed by experiments and observations, and it has, then these processes and the events involved in them will have to be supposed to obey some simple postulates about order in time. And the resulting theory had better be consistent with the (local) validity of those temporal assumptions. And I gather that it is.[11]

In chapters 28 and 29 of *The Analysis of Matter*, Russell applies his method of construction directly to space-time using a five-termed relation of *compresence* between space-time volumes. This involves new complications and, for me, new puzzles. A complete analysis would require another paper (by somebody else). But, as presently advised, relativity does not seem to invalidate Russell's linear construction locally applied.

Epistemology

Some will complain that Russell's postulates are insufficient or dubious. The objection, hinted at earlier, is that the assumptions that are really obvious or subject to very little doubt, A and D (on my reconstruction), are not sufficient to endow instants with many of the properties required for their principal use — in the theory and application of science. The postulate (or postulates) that guarantees compactness, for example, is not clearly and distinctly true. Certainly we do not experience events between any two events we experience.

Some will say that we must simply drop the dubious epistemological project implied by the objection and revert to a modest branch of natural science: naturalized epistemology. Perhaps there are hints of this in Russell himself — in *Human Knowledge, Its Scope and Limits*. (I think they are only hints.) I would argue against such a line. Rational reconstruction, with the emphasis on the "rational," is the name of the game. If we are to replace the rotting planks of the ship by something more solid, there had better be some objective sense of "more solid." As far as I can see, this pretty much constrains the principles of rationality to be necessary (not contingent) and normative (and not merely descriptive). Of course I cannot argue this large issue in such an essay as this. Russell saw the task (usually) as one of rational reconstruction — and not simply as the job of describing what we take ourselves to know.

A better reply is this. The evident postulates are to be taken as given. *Additional* assumptions, such as are required to ensure the compactness or even continuity of the series of instants, are taken as hypotheses that are confirmed according as their consequences are verified or not. Of course, the verification will be through the application of the constructed theory of instants as used in science. Or, if this is not the correct analysis of scientific inference, the additional assumptions must be found to be part of the best explanation of the observed facts.

If we proceed in that way, you may say, why not just take *instants* as primitive, postulate *their* properties, deduce, and confirm (or whatever one does in nondeductive inference)? Partly this involves a more general question: why construct anything out of anything if inductive inference is ultimately going to be used? I discuss this general matter later. The remainder of the objection is answered thus: events are better known than instants. Some of the assumptions about events are quite evident; the remainder are as well confirmed — by the same evidence — as the corresponding assumptions about instants. The postulates about instants just contemplated would *all* involve the unobserved and the nonevident.

In summary, then, the problem of recurrence is handled by narrowing the scope of the analysis to nonrecurring times, relativity is appeased by considering only local time, and uncertainty is minimized by leaving dubious postulates to be made probable by a posteriori methods. A great deal of contraction! Well, what did you expect? We are seeking the hard center.

General Considerations on Constructionalism

The Russellian approach to the Problem of the External World is not very popular in some quarters. Indeed, constructional systems generally, except in certain parts of mathematics, are quite unpopular. I want to consider, last of all, some extremely general criticisms of the idea of attempting to "construct" some things out of others.

Arbitrariness

One can extract from Paul Benacerraf's seductive paper, "What Numbers Could Not Be,"[12] a criticism of constructions generally. It is roughly this: there are many constructions, any of which fulfills whatever role we require the constructed entity to play. These different constructions will sometimes involve necessarily distinct entities; e.g., in the case of numbers, $2 = \{\{\varnothing\}\}$ or $2 = \{\varnothing, \{\varnothing\}\}$, hence they cannot all be correct. But we have and can have no nonarbitrary way of choosing one of them. Hence, we must choose none. Or, perhaps, all the constructions are incorrect.

Whatever may be the case with numbers, it is not obviously true that in all cases there are alternative constructions that are just as good. Whitehead's construction is epistemically inferior. And sheer isomorphism is not sufficient to ensure identity of goodness. Suppose we take the first instant at which an event exists to be the set of all events that precede it. Incorrect. For then it would be possible for the first instant at which an event exists to exist even if the event itself never exists. (Actually, this observation bodes ill for the construction of hyperinstants mentioned earlier. Perhaps the best plan is just to postulate more events and properties thereof as needed.)

Suppose that the worst comes and we cannot find arguments based on any reasonable criteria for ruling out the remaining competing constructions. Then it still may be that any of the constructions is better than the reconstructed theory. So one distributes reasonable belief equally among the constructions. Just because one cannot choose, nonarbitrarily, between four men, say, all equally strong, but stronger than Jones, does not imply that none is better than him if one wants some lifting done.

But, you may ask, *are* any of the reconstructed theories really any better than the original? This brings me to: the next point.

Rationality

I have already confessed my allegiance to old-fashioned epistemology. Now I would like to do something more to justify (epistemically, of course—we are not merely describing here) that faith. Some have argued[13] that we are no better off *after* the constructing is done than before. How, exactly, is the claim to be made out that we are more justified in believing in instants, say, as collections of events, than in instants sui genera?

Let T_1 and T_2 be theories consisting of sets of propositions (not sentences) and closed under entailment. And suppose that with respect to all the known relevant observational facts, they both entail or fail to entail, explain or fail to explain (N.B.), the same propositions. Still T_1 might be more probable than T_2. I speak here of comparative probability—the idea of assigning numerical probabilities to arbitrary propositions seems highly doubtful (to me). If T_1 is the theory of events together with the set theory needed for Russell's construction and T_2 is this *plus* an independent theory of instants, then T_1 is a priori more probable than T_2. For T_1 consists of propositions true in every possible world in which all the propositions of T_2 are true, but not conversely. So T_1 has less chance of being wrong. If the two theories otherwise have the same explanatory power (and aren't we dealing with a case where that is so?), then T_1 is to be preferred. Of course, T_1 still may not be the only theory left in the field.

Aesthetics

A final word on theory construction and acceptance. William James was right when he urged that it is entirely sensible to accept theories on the basis of nonrational criteria.[14] This is, as I construe it, not so shocking as it sounds. We have all been instructed by philosophers of science that theories are badly underdetermined by the data. I take this to mean that given the rules of deductive logic, the formulas of probability theory, the necessary truths of epistemology, and the facts of experience, alternative theories that are incompatible are still justified to the same degree. We are then free to turn to other marks of goodness. I would urge that aesthetic criteria may be applied. Indeed, it is clear that they already are. Economy, cited as a good-making feature of theories, is basically an aesthetic matter when applied to ideology—i.e., to the primitive concepts adopted. I suggest that if we give the Beautiful its rightful place as Judge next after the Good and the True, Russell's theory of instants defeats its nearest competitors.

Notes

1. Our use of dots as punctuation in logical formulas follows Alonzo Church, *Introduction to Mathematical Logic I* (Princeton, N.J.: Princeton University Press, 1956); see p. 75. Roughly, the

dot replaces a left bracket whose mate is as far right as possible consistent with the formula being well formed.

2. W. V. O. Quine, Review of "On Order in Time," *Journal of Symbolic Logic*, 1 (June 1936), pp. 72-73.

3. N. Wiener, "A Contribution to the Theory of Relative Position," *Proceedings of the Cambridge Philosophical Society*, 17 (1914), pp. 441-49.

4. In *Our Knowledge of the External World* (Chicago and London: Allen & Unwin, 1914). See the preface and Lecture IV, p. 91.

5. A. N. Whitehead, *The Concept of Nature* (Cambridge: Cambridge University Press, 1920), especially chapter 4.

6. It is then not excessively difficult to prove, using A and D (and as Russell does in OT using A, B, and C) and a modicum of set theory, that instants of time form a simply ordered series. Formally one uses the definitions:

DEFINITION: $In(\alpha) \rightarrow \alpha = \hat{x}(y)[y\in\alpha \supset S(x,y)]$.
DEFINITION: $T(\alpha, \beta) \rightarrow (\exists x)(\exists y)[x\in\alpha.y\in\beta P(x, y).].In(\alpha).In(\beta)$.

It follows, using A and D, that:
(i) $\sim T(\alpha, \alpha) - T$ is irreflexive.
(ii) $T(\alpha, \beta) \supset .T(\beta, \gamma) \supset T(\alpha, \gamma) - T$ is transitive.
(iii) $In(\alpha) \supset .In(\beta) \supset .T(\alpha, \beta) \vee (\alpha = \beta) \vee T(\beta, \alpha) - T$ is connected in its field. That is to say, T is a *simple ordering*. I omit the proof; Russell's is entirely valid.

7. The possibilities mentioned here both require the use of the axiom of choice or its equivalent, the well-ordering principle.

8. Kurt Gödel, "What Is Cantor's Continuum Problem?" *American Mathematical Monthly*, 54 (1947), pp. 515-25.

9. Reviews of *Foundations of Mathematics and other Logical Essays* by F. P. Ramsey. *Mind*, n.s., 49 (Oct. 1931), pp. 476-82, and in *Philosophy*, 7 (1932), pp. 84-86.

10. The error occurs on line 10 from the bottom, p. 219 (line 7 from the bottom of p. 351 of the reprint of OT in *Logic and Knowledge*, ed. Robert C. Marsh [London: Allen & Unwin, 1956]). The stated further condition is not sufficient as claimed.

11. See, for example, C. W. Misner, K. S. Thorne, and J. A. Wheeler, *Gravitation* (San Francisco: Freeman, 1973), p. 19, section 1.3, cited in Major L. Johnson, Jr., "Events as Recurrables," in *Analysis and Metaphysics*, ed. K. Lehrer (D. Reidel, Dordrecht, 1975).

12. Paul Benacerraf, "What Numbers Could Not Be," *Philosophical Review*, 74 (1965), pp. 47-73.

13. For example, Ernest Nagel, "Russell's Philosophy of Science," in *The Philosophy of Bertrand Russell* ed. P. A. Schilpp (New York: Tudor, 1944).

14. William James, "The Will to Believe," in *The Will to Believe and other Essays in Popular Philosophy* (New York: Dover, 1956).

Elizabeth R. Eames

Cause in the Later Russell

Throughout his career, Russell sought to bring common sense, science, and perception into one consistent logical scheme.[1] His methodological project was to do this completely by means of logical constructions. If this could be achieved, he would be able, on the one hand, to show how the familiar objects, relations, and persons of common sense were logically constructible from some kind of purified data of perception. On the other hand, he would be able to analyze the concepts and entities of science so as to reveal them as logical constructions from the same purified data.[2] Although Russell did not succeed in his early attempts to "exhibit matter wholly in terms of sense-data...of a single person,"[3] he was able, in his later work, to construct a systematic picture of the world in which perception and physics each had a place and in which they were related to one another through events. It is this theoretical achievement of Russell that attracted the interest and effort of Grover Maxwell, and formed the foundation of a just appraisal of Russell's work and of a development and extension of the perspective of physical realism.

Physical realism, as understood by Maxwell, is a broader and less restricted empiricism than that of logical empiricism. This view accords reality to a world that is there and that can be understood in terms of an event ontology consistent with science. Physical realism incorporates a causal theory of perception to connect our experience with the real world, and employs a principle of acquaintance by which this experience is linked by logical constructions to the entities of science.[4] This essay addresses two questions: What is the concept of cause that plays a vital role in this picture of the world as the later Russell frames it? And, are there aspects of the concept of cause that may prove troubling to Russell's position or, possibly, to that of the physical realism which Maxwell builds on the later Russell?

Science: Particulars, Events, Causes

We may take *The Analysis of Matter* to represent Russell's mature approach to the problem of constructing a philosophical framework for science. In this work Russell asks what the logical structure of physics, considered as a deductive system, is (i.e., the problem of the logical analysis of physics). He inquires what facts and entities we know that are relevant to physics, and may serve as its empirical foundation (i.e., the epistemological problem). Finally, Russell asks what the ultimate existents are in terms of which physics is true, what their structure is, and what their relations are to space-time, causality, and qualitative series (i.e., the ontological problem).[5]

In the order of exposition of *The Analysis of Matter* the logical analysis of the formal system of physics comes first before the discussion of the epistemological or ontological problems. The logical systematization is to a large extent prior to, and, initially, independent of, the formulation of the empirical basis of science and the choice of the epistemological and ontological units of analysis. Accordingly the ground-level unit of analysis for the logical system is called by Russell a "particular"; such a unit is said to be irreducible in the relative sense that for a given area at a given point in inquiry no further analysis is called for. Russell also tells us that such hypothesized particulars cannot be asserted to exist without qualification.[6] But, since physics is an empirical science, there must be a bridge between the point-instants and particles that are the result of the logical construction and the realm of experience. Such a bridge, however, is not between material units of analysis and subjective or mental data, since Russell's neutral monism requires that both the bridge and the entities bridged be neutral as to mind and matter.[7] The bridge between theoretical construction and experience turns out to be composed of events. Russell says, "I shall therefore assume henceforth that the physical world is to be constructed out of 'events,' by which I mean practically, as already explained, entities or structures occupying a region of space-time which is small in all four dimensions."[8]

The work of the construction of point-instants and of electrons that is carried out in the text shows that the requirements of the constructions of physics can be met by the use of events. As far as physics is concerned, the correlations of electrons, of quanta of energy, and so forth, can be stated in the form of differential equations, as is appropriate for causal laws.[9] But in the world of common sense in which objects, and relations between objects, and laws expressing generalizations concerning objects and relations are concerned, causal concepts not statable as differential equations are of great importance. It is in the commonsense world of objects that perception occurs. "Objects" are inferred as the common causal ancestors of groups of events "grouped about a center." A continuity of events in a single perspective, separated out from contemporaneous events, forms the causal line of a persistent object. A continuity of percepts from the different perspective of the observer constitutes another causal line, that of the persistent observer. In supporting such causal inferences Russell employs the principles of same cause-same effect, and different effects-different causes.[10]

But even with such causal inferences, certain problems appear in linking the causal lines and causal centeredness used to frame objects and relations with the elegant apparatus of point-instants and electrons used in the constructions of space-time and particles required by physics. In relativity, space and time and its points and instants have become the four-dimensional manifold of space-time.

In this world causality is defined "in its broadest sense as embracing all laws which connect events at different times, or, to adapt our phraseology to modern needs, events the intervals between which are time-like."[11] But, as this would lead to the "inextricable intertwining" of geometry and causation, Russell proceeds to "distinguish time-like and space-like intervals by saying that the former occur when there is some direct causal relation, while the latter occur where both events are related to a common ancestor or a common descendant."[12]

Space and time, on the one hand, and cause, on the other, are thus reciprocally defined; if events are simultaneous but separated in space, there is no causal connection between them, but when they are successive there may be a causal connection between them. Causal lines occur where events occur one after another in time, and are similar to one another; these are called semi-independent causal lines. Copunctual events are defined as simultaneous events not separated by a space interval such as occur in a percipient when different causal lines converge and make a total effect that is causally related both to each separable causal line and to the convergence itself. "It is these two opposite laws, of approximately separable causal lines on the one hand, and interactions of co-punctual events on the other, which make the warp and woof of the world, both physical and mental."[13]

It seems that as long as the discussion is on the level of space-time no means of differentiating causal from noncausal groups of events is available, but that when space and time are considered, the ordering of simultaneity and succession and the use of similarity can provide such a causal order. Does this mean that the "warp and woof" of the world belong to the world of space and time, the commonsense world? Or can causal ordering be read back into the world of space-time, the world of physics?

Since the constructions of space-time, point-instants, and particles (electrons) are said to be artificial and to be defined logically in terms of events and their compresence, we can assume that the fundamental units of analysis are events. Events include both inferred and perceived events, but the latter are epistemologically prior. Such perceived events are not to be conceived in terms of a mind or self or subject, since Russell holds a neutral-monist position. The importance of perceived events in the analysis follows from the fact that it is from them that all events are inferred, from the fact that the objects and relations of common sense are constructed from them, and from the fact that, ultimately, the point-instants and electrons of physics are constructed from them also. These perceived events require the status of "reals" if the analysis is to escape the perils of phenomenalism and solipsism. Russell views such perceived events as real, ordered by the abstract laws of physics, as qualitatively part of an observer's experience, and as events in the brain of the percipient.[14] Without the brain-electron-percept-event linkage Russell's constructions threaten to fall apart into what he calls "the concrete but disjointed knowledge of percepts" and "the abstract but systematic knowledge of the physical world."[15]

However, this linkage is a difficult one to maintain. Russell argues that an electron can be shown to be a construction from events. As a preliminary to this argument he states that we know in an intimate fashion our own percepts, thoughts, and feelings, and that, given the causal theory of perception, we can conclude that "percepts are in our heads, for they come at the end of a causal chain of physical events leading, spatially, from the object to the brain of the percipient."[16] Given the theory of space and time structures that he has developed, "a percept is an event or a group of events, each of which belongs to one or more of the groups constituting the electrons in the brain."[17] Leaving aside the discussion of the causal theory of perception for the present, we can conclude that the brain-electron-percept-event linkage is central to the argument of *The Analysis of Matter* and depends on the concept of cause.

> A percept, at any rate when it is visual, will be a steady event, or system of steady events, following upon a transaction. Percepts are the only part of the physical world that we know otherwise than abstractly. As regards the world in general, both physical and mental, everything that we know of its intrinsic character is derived from the mental side, and almost everything that we know of its causal laws is derived from the physical side. But from the standpoint of philosophy the distinction between physical and mental is superficial and unreal.[18]

The Analysis of Matter contains the picture of the scientific realism that Maxwell and others have admired. What Russell has done is to combine a logical and mathematically constructed theory to fit the current needs of physics (and to a lesser degree those of the other sciences) with an event ontology and an empiricism as free as possible from the limitations of the subjective. The picture of the world that emerges is saturated with causality: causality that allows the construction of continuities and transactions, the separation of spacelike and timelike intervals, and especially the causal theory of perception on the basis of which events perceived are there — in the brain of the perceiver. There is a circularity involved here, for how can we know that the causal line is from the star to the brain event, which is the visual percept referred to the star, except on the basis of earlier percepts? But the circularity by which science explains how and what we perceive on the basis of what has been perceived is perhaps neither vicious nor avoidable. We will return to a discussion of this aspect of Russell's treatment of causality later.

Russell admits that the causal theory of perception has been assumed, and that he can find no way of resolving Hume's doubts concerning causality. Without an analysis that justifies inductive generalizations there can be no conclusive escape from solipsism or phenomenalism, both of which are unacceptable. Russell says, "Since, however, all science rests upon induction and causality, it seems justifiable, at least pragmatically, to assume that, when properly employed, they can give at least a probability.... I have made this assumption baldly, without attempting to justify it."[19] Russell acknowledges that these problems have been left unresolved in *The Analysis of Matter*, and, as we shall see, he returns to them in *Human Knowledge*.

As far as the treatment of events, point-instants, and electrons is concerned, *Human Knowledge* is not substantially different in terms of the constructions involved. There is a difference in the relation between events and qualities of the "complete complex of compresence," the bundle of qualities that constitute the event as experienced. The ontological effect of the shift is that "mental events" are said to have qualities directly given in experience, whereas the qualities of "physical events" are unknown, except in terms of their space-time structure. It thus seems that while the space-time structure and the causal laws of the earlier work are constructed from events, both perceived and inferred, the physical events of *Human Knowledge* are constructed from the space and time structure, and hence depend on causal laws that order this structure.

Russell here states explicitly a reciprocity between the space-time of physics and the causal laws of physics. Physical space-time is inferred from perceptual space and time. Events are located in space-time by means of the correlation of physical space-time and perceptual space and time, and by means of causal laws of physics that assign them an order. On the other hand, causal laws when expressed as differential equations assume an order in terms of space-time. The assigning of coordinates is itself dependent on the use of causal laws; that is, "the relation of causal laws to space-time order is a reciprocal one."[20]

Here again is a circularity involved in the definition of cause, space and time, and space-time. Essentially, the difference between this position and that of *The Analysis of Matter* is that the anomalous status of events is more marked in relation to compresent qualities, and that the circularity of the relations between events and space and time is more obvious. In the case of *Human Knowledge* each complex of compresent qualities is said to be unique by virtue of the improbability of the recurrence of such complexes. The qualities that together constitute the complex of compresence are each held to occur in scattered times and places, hence no assumption of events or qualities as universals is necessary in Russell's view.[21] In the light of the current discussion of event ontologists as to the identity of events[22] seen as particulars, as instantiation of qualities, or as space-time units, it appears that Russell held events to be all three: particulars insofar as the event is the terminus of the analysis in any given case; qualities (though not as the instantiation of universal qualities); and minimal spans of space and time, according to the definition provided in *The Analysis of Matter* as the basis for the construction of point-instants.

My argument is that in one sense Russell's later work on space, time, matter, and causality is a resounding success. It is this work that has attracted current philosophers of science to Russell's philosophy, and it is this work that Russell himself felt to have been his most important contribution to philosophy. It consists in giving events a time span and a spatial location in some sense in our experience, and in showing how the space-time points can be logically and mathematically constructed from events.

The question of the real location of events is then resolved by placing perceived events in the physical brain, for which scientific evidence of causal connections can be offered, and by using such events as the basis for the rest of both the scientific and commonsense "objects" and "relations" inferred from them on the basis of causal lines and structures arranged about centers. This is not to say that no questions concerning events and time-series are left unresolved. The status of events that are percepts is left unclear. The connection of causal relations to space and time relations is also left ambiguous; sometimes causes are seen to be inferred from invariable sequences, in other passages space and time relations are discriminated in terms of causal laws.

Science: Induction and Causal Postulates

As we have noticed, Russell acknowledges the problem of providing a basis for inductive reasoning in *The Analysis of Matter*, judging it to be intimately connected with the topic of causality, and part of the problem bequeathed by Hume that he does not directly tackle. This is the new and major topic of *Human Knowledge*, called in this book "non-demonstrative inference." Russell considers the various views of probability that might provide a basis for inferences from specific observations to generalizations, reviewing such proposals as Mill's "uniformity of nature," and Keynes's "limited varieties." He finds that none of these is sufficient to fill the gaps between the given complexes of compresent qualities, the commonsense ordering of events, and the structures of physical theories required to complete his survey of human knowledge. At the end of the book he puts forth a set of five postulates that he believes sufficient for this purpose, and it is no surprise that causality figures intimately in all five of them. They include concepts that had been used in his earlier work without their being treated explicitly as postulates.

In discussing causality with respect to the need for postulates justifying induction, Russell considers the commonsense concept of cause and effect, and accepts a modified version of this concept for his principles. He explicitly rejects the idea that causality is invariable sequence, at least insofar as common sense understands it. Belief in an external cause of perception is embedded in animal behavior and in the very idea of perception, as it is implied in common language.[23]

Russell identifies three kinds of laws in science – laws of differential equations, which express the correlation of changes; laws of quasi-permanence, and laws of statistical regularity; only the second is problematic. Laws of quasi-permanence bring us to the enunciation of a causal principle to the effect that "given an event at a certain time, then at any slightly earlier or slightly later time there is, at some neighboring place, a closely similar event."[24] The postulate of quasi-permanence allows us our commonsense belief in things, and in the identity of a thing through changes. But this also involves "causal lines," a term defined as "a temporal series of events so related that, given some of them, something can be inferred about the others whatever may be happening elsewhere." Such "more or less self-determined causal processes" involve, as he says, constancy of quality, of structure, or gradual change in either.[25] Russell does not regard laws of statistical regularity as a postulate and dismisses it with the remark that it is useful in some areas of physics but need not be treated as a postulate. Russell discusses the "structural postulate" that has to do with the grounding of our belief in a common world that we share as perceivers; it refers to similarity or identity of structure that is shared by different perspectives "ranged about a center." His examples have to do with the different sounds that are similar in structure that different auditors hear when they are all listening to a broadcast. There, as in his early work, he refers to the imputation of a common causal ancestor for these differently positioned, but closely similar, observed structures. The common structures may be, he says, event-structures or material-structures, for example, a piece of music or a house; but, of course, since, as soon as we move away from common sense, all structures turn out to be event-structures, this is not an important distinction.[26] Russell also refers to "interaction" where causal lines intersect, and he employs a structural postulate to show that probable inferences can be made about what will ensue following such interactions, depending on the complexity of the causal lines involved and the accessibility of past observations that may allow us to make predictions.

The only other postulate discussed is that of "analogy," and this is specifically introduced to solve the problem of the necessity of supposing that others' perceptions are as valid a basis of evidence as one's own. If, using the causal postulates already accessible to you, you consider the probability that when you hear another person report an experience in words that, if you uttered them, would mean that you had had such and such an experience, and you are having the experience the other's words report, it is likely that you and the other observer are observing the same thing. The argument is based on employing analogy in supporting a similarity of another person's experience with one's own.[27]

The postulates meet the conditions of being true, of being believed in, of leading to no conclusion that experience confutes, and of being logically necessary if any occurrence or set of occurrences is ever to afford evidence in favor of any other occurrence. There may be some epistemological problems with these criteria, but for Russell this is the solution for the support of nondemonstrative inference. This use of the concept of causality involved in them is striking and raises some questions about what that concept becomes in his later philosophy. The causal concepts, which were to have been replaceable within a fully developed physics by differential equations, but which seem indigenous to every other domain of knowledge, thus come back as solutions to the problem of induction, itself a postulate of physics. The three problems *The Analysis of Matter* leaves unsolved are (1) a kind of circularity in the use of causal concepts in the constructions in which cause itself is defined, (2) the need for some basis for the validation of inferences going beyond observations (the problem of induction), and (3) the viability of epistemological assumptions involved in the position of scientific realism in the later work of Russell. The first two problems find a joint answer in *Human Knowledge* that at least appears to legitimize the circularity by giving it a name and an explicit recognition as postulated. The third concern, which is epistemological, will be addressed in our next section, in the course of which the full picture of this shift in his concept of cause will be seen and its problems exposed.

Experience: Percepts and Causes

In order for Russell's scientific realism to be viable it must include an empiricist principle that enables the basic propositions, from which the event descriptions, point-instants, and so forth are constructed, to have a basis in experience. This basis is provided by the principle of acquaintance: "every proposition which we can understand must be composed wholly of constituents with which we are acquainted."[28] Maxwell adds to the principle of the doctrine of ramification and says that with the aid of Ramsey sentences, all the rest of the position is constructible. Hence, this Maxwell principle of acquaintance, and whatever causal assumptions may go along with it, demands our attention.

We must remind ourselves that in *Our Knowledge of the External World* sense-data and universal entities are held to be given in the direct two-term relation of acquaintance between subject and object. During this period, Russell holds a dualism of subject and object, mind and matter, particular and universal. But in 1921 in *The Analysis of Mind* he abandons the direct two-term relation of acquaintance, admits that all perceptual experience involves "encrustations of habit, memory, and expectation," and adopts neutral monism, which precludes the dualism of subject and object, mind and matter, and particular and universal.[29] In this book, the principle of acquaintance is seriously eroded. Russell maintains that he adopted neutral monism in 1920 and did not change his views after, which implies that *The Analysis of Mind* and *The Analysis of Matter* represent the same position. Since the former is a more detailed treatment of perception, memory, and belief, it is more appropriate as the basis for the consideration of cause in the context of epistemology.

Russell begins his discussion of cause in *The Analysis of Mind* with a criticism of the traditional notion, and he concludes that "cause in the only sense in which it can be practically applied, means 'nearly invariable antecedent.' "[30] He then goes on to apply the concept of invariable sequence in an examination of the so-called causal laws of physics and psychology. Physics is said to be concerned with changes in physical objects or pieces of matter; psychology with changes in what are called the appearances of the object at different places.[31] Perceptions are analyzed as the successive appearances of an object in one place. Physics, then, is distinguished from psychology in being interested in systems of particulars, that is, in objects or pieces of matter, or the correlations of changes in different places. Psychology is concerned with actual particulars, rather than systems of particulars, that is, with correlations of successive particulars at one place.

If we replace the term "cause" with "correlation," then causal relations of pieces of matter become correlations of changes of systems of particulars, and the causal relations of perception become the correlations of changes of particulars from one time to another. Moreover, the causal theory of perception, which says that one piece of matter is the cause of the perception of the piece of matter, becomes the doctrine that certain sequences of changes in the "appearance of an object" from different places are correlated with certain sequences of changes in "the appearance of the object" from one place at different times. The phrase "appearance of an object" is put in quotation marks because it refers to the particular, or, in earlier terms, the sense-datum, from which the "object" is constructed.

Russell describes the correlation of changes in appearances from one perspective by means of the analogue of a photographic plate.

> A photographic plate exposed on a clear night reproduces the appearance of the portion of the sky concerned, with more or fewer stars according to the power of the telescope that is being used. Each separate star which is photographed produces its separate effect on the plate, just as it would upon ourselves if we were looking at the sky.... All that we need say is that *something* happens which is specially connected with the star in question... since that star produces its own special effect upon the plate.[32]

Russell uses phrases that suggest the traditional conception of cause as something operative or productive of effects. He refers to the "active" place where the star is, and the "passive" place where the perception of the star is. It is true that the reference is qualified by saying that these terms are "only names," and that he does not intend to introduce any notion of activity.[33] However, it may be asked why Russell uses such terms and refers, as he does, to the "production" of effects, and of a process "radiating outward" from a star.

Further examples of the same embarrassment occur in the description of perceptions: "The appearances of objects" are distinguished in that "they *give rise to* mnemic phenomena," and they are themselves "*affected by* mnemic phenomena."[34] In distinguishing between those mental occurrences that have an external stimulus, and those that are "centrally excited," Russell holds that the former may be regarded as an appearance of an object external to the brain; however, if the mental occurrence has not sufficient connection with objects external to the brain to be regarded as an appearance of such an object, "then its physical causation (if any) will have to be sought in the brain."[35] Thus Russell shifts from treating causal laws as statements about sequences of events, to treating them as statements about "action," "production," and "effects."

There is a similar shift involved in the formulation of his causal theory of perception. This theory is assumed in *The Analysis of Mind*, as it is in *The Analysis of Matter*. In the distinction between the "sensational core" of perception and the associations that memory and habit add to this, Russell says:

> For our purposes, it is not important to determine what exactly is the sensational core in any case; it is only important to notice that there certainly is a sensational core, since habit, expectation and interpretation are diversely aroused on diverse occasions, and the diversity is clearly due to differences in what is presented to the senses.... Thus, although it may be difficult to determine what exactly is sensation in any given experience, it is clear that there is sensation, unless, like Leibniz, we deny all action of the outer world upon us.[36]

Similarly, in the attempt to distinguish between images and sensations, Russell says that the only valid means is by their causes and effects. "Sensations come through sense-organs, while images do not.... We could distinguish images from sensations as having mnemic causes, though they may also have physical causes."[37]

Is Russell guilty of shifting from one meaning of causation to another? Or can all that is said of causation be interpreted by taking cause to be a regular sequence of events? It might be claimed that when Russell speaks of causes "producing" effects, he is using these terms only for convenience, and intends that "cause" should be defined as "invariable sequence." But even if this claim is allowed, a further difficulty arises.

Consider Russell's description of the star: its production of light, the transmission of light, and the resultant occurrence of a perception of light mean, he says, that the system of particulars called the appearance of the star is connected with other particulars called the "intervening medium," and with still other particulars called the "sensations of the star." Further, he distinguishes what may be called the regular appearances of the star, which are associated with the star itself, from the irregular appearances due to the intervening medium. The former are defined as "consisting of all those appearances which it presents *in vacuo*, together with those which, according to the laws of perspective, it would present elsewhere if its appearances elsewhere were regular."[38] In order for any particular to be counted as the "irregular appearance of a certain object" all that is necessary is "that it should be derivable from the regular appearances by the laws which express the distorting influence of the medium. When it is so derivable, the particular in question may be regarded as caused by the regular appearances, and therefore by the object itself, together with the modifications resulting from the medium."[39]

The causal explanation for activity of the star can therefore be interpreted as the correlations between the sets of changes in star appearances, in the emission of light, and in the subsequent sensations of the star; and the different roles of the medium, the original source of the light, and the events in the nervous system are compatible with this interpretation. However, when one thinks of the star, the medium, and the nervous system as systems of particulars, and of these particulars as perceptions, the explanation becomes complicated. For the physical objects in question, which are discussed by physics, physiology, and psychology, are really "systems of appearances," and, in fact, the explanations of those sciences are constructed from percepts that are themselves the particulars of which the whole world is constructed. With respect to causation this means that we begin with sequences of percepts, that these percepts are formed into systems, some of them called physical objects and some correlated in what are called causal laws. Therefore, the physical object, the star itself, the light, the intervening medium, the eye, and the nervous system are all sequences of percepts. How is it possible, then, without circularity, to talk of sequences of changes in which physical objects, intervening media, organic stimulations, and reactions in the nervous systems are all sequential events? Only the final stage, the percept itself, is experienced, and the so-called earlier events of the sequence are not themselves observed nor can they be observed. These other events are inferred as causes *from* the sequences of percepts. How can they at the same time be the ground *from which* the causal connections are inferred?

The epistemological problem of causation, then, in this period of *The Analysis of Mind* and *The Analysis of Matter*, may be stated in this way: if the sequences of events which are empirically observed and on the basis of which the terms "cause" and "effect" are used, are percepts, then to support the inference to the causal theory of perception it would be necessary to have observed repeated sequences of events in which, for instance, the emission of light from objects was followed by the occurrence of visual experience. It would never be possible, however, to observe whether sequences of objects or physical conditions followed percepts, since by definition only percepts are observable. It would then be possible to observe only percepts followed by percepts; the effect but not the causes would be observed. In this case, by Russell's own criteria, the concept of cause would not be applicable. The problem is one of circularity, and it appears to be involved in all of Russell's discussions of the causes of perception. If we now recall that the "events" of *The Analysis of Matter* are percepts and events inferred from percepts, it is clear that the epistemological circle of *The Analysis of Mind* also infects *The Analysis of Matter*, calling in question the sequences of events in continuities of causal lines, and the similarities of events ranged about a center that is causally ancestral to those events. Only a limited number of those events are percepts, and the causal lines involved in the causal theory of perception are assumed before the lines of causality themselves can be traced.

In a passage in *Human Knowledge* Russell seems to admit the problematic status of causal inferences:

> Everything that we believe ourselves to know about the physical world depends entirely upon the assumption that there are causal laws. Sensations, and what we optimistically call "perceptions," are events in us. We do not actually see physical objects, any more than we hear electromagnetic waves when we listen to the wireless. What we directly experience might be all that exists, if we did not have reason to believe that our sensations have external causes. It is important, therefore, to inquire into our belief in causation. Is it a mere superstition, or has it a solid foundation?[40]

Here Russell seems to recognize the very problem we have been considering in relation to his earlier treatment of cause. He seems also to assume that it is necessary to have a concept of cause that is more than the observation of regular sequences in order that a solipsistic kind of phenomenalism be avoided.

It would not be relevant to inquire whether it is possible to believe that certain regular sequences of events are observed and do give a basis for probable inference. It is evident, and Russell has already pointed out, that such sequences *are* observed, and that it *is* possible, with a minimum of faith in the future being like the past, to make probable predictions on that basis. To believe in an external cause for one's experience requires a greater commitment than the adoption of the view of causal laws as observed sequences of changes, and in this passage Russell seems to recognize that this is the case.

This emphasis on the necessity of certain assumptions about the nature of the world being made in order that any empirical knowledge be possible is the chief theme of *Human Knowledge*, as we have seen in our discussion of the postulate of nondemonstrative inference. It may be maintained that the difficulties that have emerged with respect to the circularity of the causal theory of perception could be overcome with the aid of the postulates that may provide the assumptions necessary as a foundation for the inferences to the unobserved causes of perception. In one passage, Russell, in discussing the postulate of structure with respect to causal laws, constructs a situation in which one sees a number of books of the same printing, all bearing the author's name; one is told a certain man is the author; one is introduced to him; and he says he is the author. When it occurs to you that the author may be the cause of the facts you have before you, Russell writes, this will cease to be astonishing if there is a law: "Any complex event tends to be followed by other complex events identical, or approximately identical, with it in structure, and distributing themselves from next to next throughout a certain region of space-time."[41]

However when one attempts to apply this modest description of the causal law of nature to the example given by Russell, a difficulty arises. If the description of a causal law as involving the distribution of identical events in space-time is applied to the example of the alleged author and the copies of his book, one wonders why this book's immediate predecessor in the presses would not be linked as a cause of the second book, rather than the remote and unlike fountain pen with its human manipulator? Or why would the home activities of the typesetters not be as relevant as the activities of the author? In the case of the causal chain allegedly selected on the basis of the persistence or continuity of qualities or structures, the example of broadcasting is given. Why would other atmospheric waves not be linked with sound waves rather than the activities in the studio? It seems that the description of causal chains and laws given in *Human Knowledge* would be consistent with considering night the cause of day. But it is difficult to believe that this would satisfy the epistemological or metaphysical needs of Russell's theory. It seems, then, that in *Human Knowledge*, Russell has been led to give a much more important role to this principle in his philosophy and that the principle itself involves a good deal more than the bare assertion of the occurrence of sequences of events.

The same considerations apply to the circularity of perception. If we return to the star, the light, the eye, the perceived star, we find that tracing this complicated causal chain would involve more than identical events next to next through space-time, or the persistence or gradual change of qualities and structures. It is only when we are already in command of the scientific explanations that we can read persistence of structure or identity of events into this situation. Moreover, only the "sensational core" of the perceptual experience is connected with what is perceived, and the disentangling of the effects of habit, memory, and anticipations from this core requires the use of causal inferences concerning perception, memory, and imagination. The given experience in Russell's analysis with its commonsense objects and relations demands an analysis, but that analysis is itself the outcome of a set of inferences that derive their authority from the given perceived events, which are what is being investigated.

Conclusion

Thus far we have seen that the development of the later concept of cause, in its ontological role in the construction of orders of events, and in its epistemological role in the causal theory of perception, demands more of a basis than Russell provides in the percepts-events of his mature work. On the one hand, the units of analysis that link percepts with the construction of point-instants and particles constructed from them (i.e., events) are defined only in terms of minimum volumes of space and time. On the other hand, the given experiential qualitative complexes of compresence, when stripped of the accretions of memory, habits, and linguistic expression, are ordered only as relations of experienced space and time. It seems that substantive causal assumptions are needed before the event-structures and qualitative complexes can be brought together in any systematic way, and certainly in any way that meets the needs of common sense.

From my perspective, it seems to be the case that the circle within which events and the perception of events are thus constricted could be broken, if the given structure of experience were allowed to include causal connection from which further causal inferences could be derived. If, as Russell said, our human perceptions, habits, actions, and speech are naturally saturated with causality, it may be that this is a good reason to recognize experience as itself ordered causally as well as spatially and temporally. Such enriched perceived structures could support, on the one hand, a causal theory of perception in which the eye-light connection is given rather than inferred. On the other hand, causal givenness might allow the discrimination of causal lines and structures from contiguously and contemporaneously given causally irrelevant happenings. Whether such a view of experience would be compatible with an event ontology is another question.

If we look back at the complicated role played by the concept of cause in the later philosophy of Russell we find a major philosophical advance, and some major philosophical difficulties. The advance comes by way of the explicitness with which Russell spells out the role of causal lines and causal centeredness with respect to the construction of the concepts of physics in terms of events, intervals, point-instants, and electrons. In this sense the construction of *The Analysis of Matter*, supplemented by *Human Knowledge*, fulfills the promise of the plan of constructing the concepts of space, time, matter, and cause by logical techniques, and justifies both Russell's own judgment and the high opinion of contemporary philosophers of science such as Grover Maxwell. It seems also to be part of that advance that Russell, stretching the scope of empiricism and probing its limits, uncovered in *Human Knowledge* the limits of this empiricism and put forth a set of postulates involving causality as necessary if common sense and scientific knowledge are to be possible. In this sense it would be true to say of Russell's later work that if it was a "retreat from Pythagoras," it could also be considered "an advance from Hume." On the other hand, certain major problems emerge in the study of Russell's later work, and most of them turn up in the discussion of cause.

In 1912 Russell had called for a purified concept of cause with no implication of compulsion, operation, necessary connection, or universality. In this view causes are to be inferred only when the connection is observed, and without excluding the possibility of action at a distance and without requiring that there be a resemblance of cause and effect.[42] As we have seen in his later philosophy, Russell needs and employs an "operational" concept of cause, inferred where it cannot be observed on the basis of the principle of same cause-same effect, and different effect-different cause, and hence, based both on similarity and contiguity in space and time. Therefore, in having been forced to give a stronger metaphysical meaning to cause, he found it even more difficult to provide an empirical warrant for it. Especially is that true in the light of Russell's more and more limited claims for some direct, incorrigible, or unmediated empirical base, such as his principle of acquaintance had once provided. If Maxwell is to follow Russell's lead with respect to acquaintance, he may give an analysis of acquaintance similar to that of the 1914 quotation of that principle. (And Russell had excellent reasons for abandoning the view of direct, immediate, indubitable two-term acquaintance with the accompanying realist view of propositional constituents.) Or, more likely, Maxwell may follow Russell into a modified "acquaintance principle" as is suggested by the adoption of the causal theory of perception, and, in that case, he faces difficulties with the necessity for extensive psychological and linguistic analysis required to uncover what Russell calls the "sensational core" that warrants the "basic perceptual proposition," the perceptive premise of his empiricism. It goes beyond the scope of the present discussion to analyze the problems of this kind of analysis, which, for Russell, would require a careful consideration of *An Inquiry into Meaning and Truth*,[43] and, for Maxwell, an extensive study of his work on perception, and the way this would tie in with his version of the logical construction that parallels Russell's. But whatever the outcome of a revised "principle of acquaintance," and whether either of the two Russellian alternatives or some other be adopted, we cannot view the circularity of the causal theory of perception as entirely innocent, although admitted. In conjunction with the circularity involved in the reciprocal definitions of causal laws and space-time locations in which events themselves are caught, we find real conceptual difficulties for a physical realism on a basis of an empiricism founded on the causal theory of perception.

Notes

1. For a full discussion of this theme see my *Bertrand Russell's Theory of Knowledge* (London: Allen & Unwin, 1969).

2. Bertrand Russell, *My Philosophical Development* (New York: Simon and Schuster, 1959), pp. 205-7.

3. Bertrand Russell, "The Relation of Sense-Data to Physics" (1914) in *Mysticism and Logic* (London: Allen & Unwin, 1917), p. 157.

4. Grover Maxwell, "Structural Realism and the Meaning of Theoretical Terms," *Analyses of Theories and Methods of Physics and Psychology*, Minnesota Studies in the Philosophy of Science, vol. IV, ed. S. Winokur and M. Radner (Minneapolis: University of Minnesota Press, 1970); Grover Maxwell, "Theories, Perception and Structural Realism," *Pittsburgh Studies in the Philosophy of Science*, vol. IV, ed. R. Colodny (Pittsburgh: University of Pittsburgh Press, 1971); Grover Maxwell, "Russell on Perception: A Study in Philosophic Method," in David Pears (ed.), *Bertrand Russell: A Collection of Critical Essays* (New York: Doubleday [Anchor], 1972); Grover Maxwell, "Corroboration without Demarcation," in *The Philosophy of Karl Popper*, vol. I, Library of Living Philosophers, ed. Paul Arthur Schilpp (LaSalle, IL: Open Court, 1974), pp. 292-321; Grover Max-

well, "The Later Bertrand Russell: Philosophical Revolutionary," in *Bertrand Russell's Philosophy*, ed. George Nakhnikian (London: Duckworth, 1974), pp. 169–82.

5. Bertrand Russell, *The Analysis of Matter* (New York: Harcourt, Brace, 1927), pp. 1–10.

6. Ibid., pp. 8–9.

7. Some writers have argued that there is a difference between the "phenomenalism" of *The Analysis of Mind* of 1921 and the realism of *The Analysis of Matter* of 1927. It is for this reason, perhaps, that the "later Russell" has been dated from the latter book. However, both books state the causal theory of perception, and Russell himself refers to his having adopted the position of neutral monism in 1920 and retaining it ever since. See *My Philosophical Development*, p. 13. Also see Elizabeth R. Eames, "The Consistency of Russell's Realism," *Philosophy and Phenomenological Research*, 27 (June 1967), pp. 502–11. Russell, commenting on this article, wrote: "I have read your article with much pleasure and profit. I am glad that you find my philosophy less incoherent than most people do. I think also that your interpretation of my philosophy is more correct than most people's" (Russell to Eames, Sept. 30, 1967).

8. Russell, *Analysis of Matter*, p. 286.

9. Ibid., pp. 245–46.

10. Ibid., p. 282. Defending the view that "all our percepts are composed of imperceptible parts," Russell cites two premises: that "exact similarity is transitive," and that "indistinguishability is not transitive." In addition, he writes, there is another source, "derived from causal arguments"; we argue, he writes: "Different effects, different causes."

11. Ibid., p. 313.

12. Ibid., pp. 313–14.

13. Ibid., p. 315.

14. Ibid., pp. 382ff.

15. Ibid., p. 275.

16. Ibid., p. 320.

17. Ibid.

18. Ibid., p. 402.

19. Ibid., pp. 398–99.

20. Bertrand Russell, *Human Knowledge: Its Scope and Limits* (New York: Simon and Schuster, 1948), p. 326.

21. Ibid., pp. 294ff.

22. Reference to current discussions of issues concerning the definition of "event," "event-individuation," and "event-identity" is beyond the scope of this essay. Let the following references to different positions on the issue suffice: Roderick M. Chisholm, "Events and Propositions," *Noûs* (Fall 1970), pp. 15–24; Donald Davidson, "The Individuation of Events," in *Essays in Honor of Carl G. Hempel*, ed. Nicholas Rescher (Dordrecht: Reidel, 1970); Jaegwon Kim, "Causation, Nomic Subsumption, and the Concept of Event," *Journal of Philosophy*, 70 (1972), pp. 217–36.

23. Russell, *Human Knowledge*; for the difficulties of invariable sequence as a causal concept, see p. 315; for the role of cause in animal behavior, perception, and language, see p. 456.

24. Ibid., p. 458.

25. Ibid., p. 459.

26. Ibid., p. 464.

27. Ibid., pp. 493–94.

28. Russell, *Mysticism and Logic*, p. 219. Quoted by Maxwell in "Structural Realism and the Meaning of Theoretical Terms" (Note 4, this chapter).

29. Bertrand Russell, *The Analysis of Mind* (London: Allen and Unwin, 1921), Lecture I.

30. Ibid., p. 99.

31. Ibid., p. 99.

32. Ibid., pp. 99–100.

33. Ibid., p. 130, note 2.

34. Ibid., p. 131 (italics mine).

35. Ibid., p. 136.

36. Ibid., pp. 140–41.

37. Ibid., pp. 149–51.

38. Ibid., p. 136.
39. Ibid., p. 136.
40. Russell, *Human Knowledge*, p. 311.
41. Ibid., p. 467.
42. Bertrand Russell, "On the Notion of Cause," *Proceedings of the Aristotelian Society*, 13 (1912–13); reprinted in *Mysticism and Logic and Other Essays*.
43. Bertrand Russell, *An Inquiry into Meaning and Truth* (London: Allen & Unwin, 1940).

Kenneth Blackwell

Portrait of a Philosopher of Science

I

Since the present volume directs critical attention to Bertrand Russell's work and also honors the memory of Grover Maxwell, whose published writings on Russell's philosophy of science are a vigorous defense of some rarely shared views on perception and empiricism, I will quote a paragraph from the only letter from Maxwell to Russell in the Russell Archives. This letter will serve to illustrate the ties between these two philosophers of science. Maxwell's letter begins with a little-known quotation from a letter in volume 1 of Russell's *Autobiography* (1967), so I will provide the context of that quotation. Russell is writing to Lucy Martin Donnelly in 1906 about the joys of philosophical research:

> [A] thing I greatly value is the kind of communion with past and future discoverers. I often have imaginary conversations with Leibniz, in which I tell him how fruitful his ideas have proved, and how much more beautiful the result is than he could have foreseen; and in moments of self-confidence, I imagine students hereafter having similar thoughts about me. There is a "communion of philosophers" as well as a "communion of saints," and it is largely that that keeps me from feeling lonely. (pp. 183–84)

The result Russell refers to is the developing science of mathematical logic, as embodied in the then growing manuscript of *Principia Mathematica*.

Maxwell writes from the Minnesota Center of Philosophy of Science on January 25, 1968:

> Dear Lord Russell:
>
> The moving passage in your autobiography about the "communion of philosophers" has moved me to write you that my attitude toward you and many of your views is the same as the one you express there towards Leibniz – with the *exception* of the portion beginning, "and how much more . . ." and ending ". . . have foreseen." I should also like to say that there is at least one exception

to your comment on p. 15 of *My Philosophical Development* to the effect that no one has accepted the theory [of perception] that you outline in the following chapter, "My Present View of the World," and develop in detail in *Human Knowledge*.... I must admit that, with the exception of a few of my better students, I have not been able wholly to persuade any other philosopher of its truth, in spite of prolonged and vigorous attempts. But there are encouraging signs that the current fads and fashions that comprise what passes as philosophy today and which I believe to be responsible for my failure in this enterprise are beginning to lose some of their hold. For my part I am at least as firmly convinced that your views on these matters are, in general, the closest thing we have to the truth today as I am that quantum mechanics and other current physical theories are today the closest things to the truth in their respective domains.

Although no reply is extant in the Archives, I imagine that Russell liked Maxwell's letter, which continues with a paragraph on confirmation theory in relation to Russell's postulates of scientific inference and then offers a word of praise for his "admirable efforts in behalf of world peace."[1] In the last sentence quoted from his letter, Maxwell expresses exactly the attitude of tentativeness that Russell both held and recommended toward current scientific theories and his own theories in the philosophy of science, and which he called the scientific method in philosophy. In this essay I shall focus on the value of science for Russell's philosophizing, with reference to his career as a philosopher of science, and to the ethic that he found exemplified in the best science and that he adopted in a general way.

II

In his 1914 paper, "On Scientific Method in Philosophy," Russell outlines the motivation of the most outstanding philosophers toward work in philosophy. "Plato, Spinoza, and Hegel," he says, "may be taken as typical of the philosophers whose interests are mainly religious and ethical, while Leibniz, Locke, and Hume may be taken as representatives of the scientific wing. In Aristotle, Descartes, Berkeley, and Kant we find both groups of motives strongly present" (1918a, p. 97). To this latter group we may add Russell's collaborator Whitehead, and Russell elsewhere recognized that, in coming to philosophy, he himself sought both religious satisfaction and knowledge (1956b, p. 19). In philosophy he wished to find justification for the religious and ethical views he could not (at the time) discard; and he also hoped to discover the certain basis for knowledge that his education so far had failed to provide him.

Russell's education was unusual for its time. Instead of an emphasis upon the classical languages and literatures, the focus was on science (including mathematics), with peripheral attention to history and modern languages and literatures. He records his youthful fascination with "billiard-ball" determinism and what he called "the technological view of the road to human welfare" (1961, p. 45). Yet philosophy soon claimed him, through the dual routes of his work in the foundations of mathematics and his worry about religious beliefs.

There are many relevant comments on mathematics and religion in his early writings. Presenting them in a critical edition is the object of an editing program at McMaster (Griffin, 1981; Blackwell, 1983). The *Collected Papers* project aims to collect and annotate as definitively and reliably as possible all the shorter writings of Russell, published and unpublished, including his diaries but excluding his letters. Five of us, with the help of a considerable staff funded by the Social Sciences and Humanities Research Council of Canada, finished editing the first volume in 1983. Volume 1 includes the first complete (and correct) text of the famous "Greek Exercises," and also a newly discovered journal that Russell kept from 1890 to 1894. We christened the new journal "A Locked Diary" because Russell said he kept such a diary at this time (1967, vol. I, p. 82), and this one has a locked clasp. As an example of an early comment, it contains an entry from 1890 written probably within days of reading James Mill's refutation of the first-cause argument for God's necessary existence:

August 31st. Alas! the only shred of faith I had left in me is, for the time at least, gone. I did believe in a Deity, and if I did have to close my eyes to the fact that His moral qualities did not manifest themselves with the same clearness as His intellectual, still I derived immense comfort from the belief, and from the necessary deduction that a world governed by an all-wise and all-powerful Being must be tending to good always. But now! – I have begun to feel that the reasoning which always convinced me before, for a long time so as to preclude even comprehension of doubt, has lost its cogency. I began by seeing that the existence of evil really cannot, at least in the present state of knowledge, be reconciled by any straight-forward reasoning with the government of a perfectly beneficent and perfectly wise God; I was finally overturned by some passages in Mill's *Autobiography*, in which he puts this argument very clearly. With regard to my old argument, a necessary prime Cause and Lawgiver, I see that it affords no explanation of the mystery but merely offers one permanent unchangeable Mystery in the place of the many which Science now is unable to answer. This argument Mill puts clearly in speaking of the education he got from his father: "He told me that the question, Who made me? cannot be answered, because it immediately suggests the further question, Who made God?" I still think that the hypothesis of an almighty First Cause affords a consistent explanation of the Universe, and therefore has the same kind of probability as the theory of the Ether, but the degree of its probability must depend upon its explanation of a large number of particular facts, on which I am not qualified to give an opinion. – The loss of certainty, is however the great pain which results from the change. To feel that the universe may be hurrying blindly towards all that is bad, that humanity may any day cease its progressive development and may continually lose all its fine qualities, that Evolution has no necessarily progressive principle prompting it; these are thoughts which render life almost intolerable. Indeed I doubt whether, if I do not regain my old faith, I shall long be able to hold out against frightful thoughts that crowd in upon my mind. (Russell, 1983, 56)

Here we see the budding philosopher of science reasoning that the ether and first-cause theories are, in a sense, on the same level. This may be Russell's first effort in the subject. He was eighteen.

In the professional sphere, volume 1 of the *Collected Papers* (1983) publishes for the first time Russell's graduate essays in the history of philosophy and epistemology, and reprints his first published writings, all of which are devoted to philosophy of science, particularly to problems about physics and geometry. The latter papers, while essential to understanding Russell's development out of British idealism, have hitherto been virtually ignored. The only modern philosopher of science known to me who has examined any of these writings in print is Lakatos in his essay "Infinite Regress and the Foundations of Mathematics" (the title gives some hint of Lakatos's anti-Euclidean approach to foundations):

> He [Russell] found mathematical proofs shockingly unreliable. "A great deal of the argumentation that I had been told to accept was obviously fallacious" ([Russell, 1959b], p. 209). And he was not quite happy about the certainty of the axioms—geometrical or arithmetical. He was aware of the sceptical criticism of intuition: the *leitmotiv* of his first-ever publication was to fight "the confusion between the psychologically subjective and the logically *a priori*" (Russell [1895], p. 245). How can one know that truth-injections at the top are justified beyond doubt? In pursuing the problem he analysed the axioms of geometry and arithmetic one by one and found that their justification was based on very different sorts of intuition. In his first published paper [1896] Russell analyses the axioms of Euclidean geometry from this point of view.... (pp. 11–12)

While geometry's foundations and their disentanglement from Kantian subjectivity were Russell's chief philosophical interest at the time, he continued to immerse himself in science. Indeed, he records his excitement at the rapid pace of fundamental discoveries in his twenties and thirties (1961, p. 41). His library contains many volumes of current science annotated by him in the margins. (By "his library" I do not mean just the major remnants in the Russell Archives; his science books are scattered far and wide, some as far as the Geophysical Institute at the University of Alaska.) An outstanding classic of science extensively annotated by Russell is William James's *Principles of Psychology*, the two volumes of which he read in 1894 and 1895.[2] Now, in many fields, Russell demonstrated a habit of reading mainly the classics. How he determined in psychology it was worthwhile for him to read James's book (then only four years old) is a mystery, but perhaps it had been recommended by James Ward, his dissertation adviser and himself the author of a classic article on psychology. Russell went on to devote a chapter of his dissertation to James's view of space. Apparently the chapter was judged a disaster in an otherwise outstanding piece of research. The published version of the dissertation omits that chapter, which, with the bulk of the original dissertation, is lost to us. Some quotations from the marginalia of Russell's copy of the *Principles* will illustrate his interest in the philosophy of the new science of psychology.

James was well versed in philosophical issues and the history of philosophy, but he deliberately put them aside in order to produce a textbook in a struggling young science. There is a marked tendency in the book to overlook nice distinctions between categories. He often refers to finding physiological "explanations" of mental phenomena. Russell catches him up on this. On page 499 of volume 1 Russell notes: "Surely psychology is bound to seek a purely psychological solution." On page 594: "Surely this perpetual reference to the brain is a methodological error." And finally, in regard to a summary statement in volume 2, page 449, of the James-Lange theory of the emotions, "that *the bodily changes follow directly the perception of the exciting fact, and that our feeling of the same changes as they occur* IS *the emotion*" (James's italics), Russell comments: "This involves the same materialistic tendency so often shewn before in J[ames]. Surely for psychology such an expl'n is inadequate." And Russell notes that often in experiencing an emotion of his own he is not conscious of bodily changes.

This use of introspective evidence by Russell is, however, entirely in keeping with James's methodology. Throughout the book Russell tests and compares his own reactions with James's reports of *his* reactions. Russell defends the use of introspection as late as *Human Knowledge* (1948), where he even proposes that psychology might be defined as "the science of those occurrences which, by their very nature, can only be observed by one person" (p. 58). The marginalia will be useful to future biographers of Russell. For example, James contrasts visualizers with those who think in auditory images, and Russell reveals that he belongs to the auditory type. James discusses attentiveness to a task and subsequent relief in the "breathing apparatus" upon the task's completion. Russell comments: "I have often found myself panting on getting a solution of a difficulty" (vol. 2, p. 472). Compare this early acknowledgment with his later statement (which I, for one, did not take literally before) that "I concentrated with such intensity that I sometimes forgot to breathe and emerged panting as from a trance" (1954, p. 194). Could James have had an influence here on the way Russell understood himself? Perhaps. There is an affinity in their writing styles, for James's book in many ways is a *History of Western Philosophy* style of textbook, including the constant personal references thrown in to enliven the matter. It is clear, at any rate, that the young Russell was introduced to the use of the experimental method in a science where objectivity is especially difficult to attain as well as to the current state of physiological psychology. However, he admits that he read little psychology during the next twenty years, until he came to write the recently published manuscript, *Theory of Knowledge* (1913), now volume 7 of his *Collected Papers* (1984).

Despite his youthful interest in current science, he was more devoted to philosophy. In a short piece he published under a pseudonym in 1897, he declares: "Nature seldom speaks to me, though it used to very much. Metaphysics, not science, interest my soul" (1983, 1: p. 73). Still, it was philosophy of science above all other branches of philosophy that absorbed Russell in the late 1890s, since he was trying to fit current physics into a neo-Hegelian framework. In *My Philosophical Development* (1959b) he judges that his manuscripts of this period amount to "unmitigated rubbish" (p. 41), which one might think was sufficient reason for not editing them. However, McMaster *is* editing them. The development of a philosophy is not a simple story of stark contrasts, of one whole system being suddenly overthrown for another. We are editing the idealist manuscripts on philosophy of science because in them we expect scholars to be able to trace the arguments that overthrew monism in favor of what Russell usually calls "atomism" or "absolute pluralism" (1918a, p. 111). By using this latter term he emphasizes his new belief that, while there are many things, there is not an organic whole composed of those things (ibid.).

The next decade (following Russell's personal discovery of Peano and Frege) was devoted to *Principia Mathematica*. It was Peano who made the greatest difference to the form Russell's work took. In 1899 he had declined to write on symbolic logic for the *Encyclopaedia Britannica*. He did not know the subject well enough, he wrote, and suggested instead the author of *Universal Algebra* — Whitehead.[3] It is hard to conceive of Russell so declining after his study of Peano.

When Russell completed the logicist program he was, as he says, somewhat at loose ends as to what to do. Then the new developments in physics in the early teens of this century claimed his interest, and he embarked on a study of matter. There are several unpublished papers on matter in the Archives. One of them was revised at great length to please Wittgenstein. Since it was not published, it may be inferred that it never pleased Wittgenstein. Russell was teaching at Cambridge at this time, and would often invite science and mathematics students to his rooms to discuss issues in philosophy of science. He wrote to Lady Ottoline Morrell about the new physics:

> I have been hearing more about the new physics—it is very exciting. The atmosphere of the Scientific world in this age is wonderfully exhilarating as compared to the world of culture—the people are tremendously alive feeling that it is for them to do great things, not at all dominated by past achievements,

tho' they know them thoroughly—all the best people have a tremendous sense of adventure, like the Renaissance mariners. They question everything that has been done, & are willing to pull down because they have enough energy & power to build up again. It is the thing in which our age excels—I am thankful to be able to have a part in it. (no. 873, September 20, 1913; Clark, 1975, p. 213)

The reference to the world of culture is significant. He did not have the science students over to infuse literary culture into them, but rather to build upon what they already had from their study of science.

In the spring of 1913, Russell wrote an essay called originally "Science as an Element in Culture" but retitled "The Place of Science in a Liberal Education" when published in *Mysticism and Logic*. In it he argues that science is not taught to its full cultural potential, there being too great an emphasis upon the merely useful consequences of scientific discoveries. Science's full potential includes the "capacity of producing those habits of mind which constitute the highest mental excellence" (1918a, p. 35). On the intellectual side, those habits of mind make possible "the endeavour to make us see and imagine the world in an objective manner, as far as possible as it is in itself, and not merely through the distorting medium of personal desire" (1918a, p. 39). Later in the essay he expands on just what the scientific outlook is:

> The kernel of the scientific outlook is a thing so simple, so obvious, so seemingly trivial, that the mention of it may almost excite derision. The kernel of the scientific outlook is the refusal to regard our own desires, tastes, and interests as affording a key to the understanding of the world. (1918a, p. 42)

And while Russell's focus on "the kernel of the scientific outlook" may also seem so simple, obvious, and trivial, there is behind it a complex and systematic ethic that pervades and indeed unites much of his technical and nontechnical work, that is based on his early exposure to the neo-Hegelian concept of self, but with its roots further back in the history of philosophy in the *Ethics* of Spinoza. I will not go further into the Spinozistic connection here, except to note Rescher's reference to Russell's "prolonged flirtation with the philosophy of Spinoza, a marked feature of *Mysticism and Logic* and vividly at work in the splendid essay on 'A Free Man's Worship' " (Rescher, 1979, p. 140).[4]

We have now proceeded well into the initial period of Russell's logical constructivism, and his attempt at systematizing epistemology through a concerted application of his principle of acquaintance. Maxwell's well-known phrase, "[Russell's] brief but notorious flirtation with phenomenalism" (Maxwell, 1972, p. 110), recognizes in this period the same sort of intellectual experimentation that Rescher remarks upon in relation to Spinoza. Those interested in clarifying Russell's position on phenomenalism should examine his statement on the physical status of sense-data that he sent to the *Journal of Philosophy, Psychology and Scientific Methods* in 1915, in response to an inaccurate report of his remarks after hearing an Aristotelian Society paper on his alleged phenomenalism. If Russell did come close to solipsism in his exploration of phenomenalism as a method, it was uncharacteristic and temporary, for he always believed in the external world and in later writings insists that he accepts as a datum the view of the universe as presented by the physical sciences. Furthermore, a solipsistic interpretation of his position is ruled out by his postulation of the existence of unsensed sensibilia. (This term inspired at least one salacious limerick [see Clark, 1975, p. 215].) His problem was that of reconciling the fact that some knowledge is public with the fact that only individual knowers are actually acquainted with anything. The problem of perception was to occupy him well past *Human Knowledge*. There is an unpublished note in the Archives on the subject of perception written a decade later. The note is one that Russell sent to Ayer in 1957 with a letter that Maxwell cites (1970, p. 20; 1972, p. 134). Russell attempts again, in this four-page typescript, to explain his ideas on structural isomorphism between perceptual causes and their effects.

The monumental work on epistemology of which the *Theory of Knowledge* manuscript was to form a part was never completed. It was stopped by Wittgenstein's objections and the distraction of the First World War. After the war Russell was influenced by developments in two sciences: the behavioristic movement in psychology, and the acceptance of relativity theory in physics. He was called upon to write popular articles on relativity and even a book. He also wrote a book on the new developments in atomic theory. The less materialistic views of matter among physicists helped him in developing his new philosophy of neutral monism. It is often said that, as a neutral monist, Russell was a mind-body identity theorist, but that interpretation ignores a subtle distinction. Like Spinoza, he held that there is only one kind of substance, namely events, which are neutral as to matter and mind. This view is formulated by Russell in two books of 1927, *An Outline of Philosophy* and *The Analysis of Matter*. (It is at this time, in Maxwell's judgment (1972, p. 169), that the later Russell begins—at least the later philosopher of science.) In a later statement of his views, Russell explains that "if we had more knowledge, the physical and psychological statements would be seen to be merely different ways of saying the same thing" (1956b, pp. 148–49). Presumably, however, the two kinds of statements would still be linguistically independent, and not subject to the sort of mixing the young Russell objected to in William James.

The decade of the thirties was one of general political turmoil, and also personal turmoil for Russell. Aside from a mathematical paper "On Order in Time" (1935) and one on logical form (1938), Russell did not return to philosophy of science proper until he had finished first *An Inquiry into Meaning and Truth* (1940) and then *A History of Western Philosophy* (1945b), that is, until 1943, when he gave a series of lectures at Bryn Mawr College entitled "Postulates of Scientific Method." It is true that, in the meantime, he had written at length *on* science, particularly in *The Scientific Outlook* (1931). There he discloses his valuation of pure science: it "belongs with religion and art and love, with the pursuit of the beatific vision, with the Promethean madness that leads the greatest men to strive to become gods. Perhaps the only ultimate value of human life is to be found in this Promethean madness. But it is a value that is religious, not political, or even moral" (p. 102). It is also true that he developed theories in the social sciences, as in *Power* (1938b); but the main effort left to Russell in philosophy of science took place in *Human Knowledge*. Characteristically he boasted of how little time it took him to work on the latter book—only five hours a day. But the manuscripts give a different impression of his effort. He continually shuffled and rewrote the chapters and, in preparing to write them, amassed a large, coherent quantity of notes that may someday be published. Indeed, he had them typed out a decade later for inclusion in *My Philosophical Development*, but dropped the idea on the advice of Allen and Unwin's editor. I do not know whether *Human Knowledge* is a major creative achievement of Russell's. Certainly he and Maxwell regarded it as such, and just as certainly contemporary philosophers in Britain do not so regard it. At any rate, to judge from the nearly two and a half feet of related manuscripts in the Archives, it was a major creative *effort*.

At the beginning of the chapter on nondemonstrative inference in *My Philosophical Development* (1959b), Russell says that he thinks he was mistaken in not mentioning in *Human Knowledge* "the various perplexities and tentative hypotheses through which I had arrived at my final conclusions...as it made the conclusions appear more slap-dash and less solid than, if fact, they were" (p. 190). In the unpublished portion of the manuscript he went on to say that he was collecting in an appendix various notes he made before reaching the final conclusions of *Human Knowledge*. If he had done so, quite a different book would have resulted. The notes amount to ninety-six pages of typescript and read like a philosophical diary (to adopt a phrase from Ivor Grattan-Guinness commenting on the *Principia* manuscripts). From my perusal I would think they would be extraordinarily interesting to work through. The notes for *Human Knowledge* are due to be edited in the 1990s.

The typescript itself is not a verbatim transcription of the handwritten notes made a decade or more earlier. Unusually for him, Russell revised and corrected the original notes (doing so with a pen he used only in the mid-1950s). Thus the version he thought of printing in *My Philosophical Development* is significantly different from the manuscript. This is particularly true of the section called "Inferences from a Logical Point of View."[5] Most of the time Russell is merely putting into words what he expressed originally in symbols, but partly he is revising. The notes on "Non-Demonstrative Inference" lack his customary literary quality, but still they are laden with interesting points. There is a new and unexpected recollection of D. H. Lawrence[6] in a discussion of recognition through verbal, as opposed to image, memory, and there is a new anecdote about G. E. Moore.[7] There are more extensive discussions of Bayes's theorem than in the book. There is discussion of that all-important topic, the cognitive status of the postulates of scientific inference, and much concerning the analysis of structure under the heading "Causal Laws and Concomitant Variation." The typescript, it must be emphasized, is a selection from the manuscript notes, of which a large portion was not typed. In the manuscript-only portion there is a great deal concerning the mathematical theory of probability and, on the versos of these leaves, extensive computations. It is unlikely that the computations will be included in the *Collected Papers*, but they are interesting as an indication of Russell's mathematical dexterity.

Russell's interest in science continued unabated into his old age. He was awarded the UNESCO Kalinga Prize for the popularization of science in 1957, and he welcomed two new editions of his *ABC of Relativity*, although his knowledge was not current enough to revise it himself. As new weapons systems were developed, his knowledge of physics served him well in the political sphere. Within a few days of the Hiroshima and Nagasaki bombings he published an article on their scientific and political consequences (1945a). He was horrified but not surprised at the vast threat scientific technique now posed, and wrote of it at length in *The Impact of Science on Society* (1951). Yet he never condemned scientists as such, and always ranked them on the same level of human genius as the most creative in other fields of endeavor. In science Russell found that impersonal detachment of inquiry that he so valued and tried to transfer as an ethic to other spheres of human activity.

III

The usual portrait of Russell as a philosopher of science is of one who enjoyed knowing things, both on the particular and the general levels; whose scientific education embraced several of the major sciences, enabling him to keep pace with current developments and to talk on a nearly professional level with practitioners of different sciences; whose methods in philosophy tended to the symbolic and who was given to offering strict proofs; and whose philosophical theories centered on problems of knowledge and were based upon the assumption that current science is more or less true. But there is another way in which Russell is a philosopher of science, a way not usually recognized because it concerns ethics. In what follows I do not mean by "ethics" the study also known as "metaethics," or the formal analysis of ethical concepts. I mean rather normative ethics, or the foundations for a creed of conduct—as Russell says, a doctrine "not of specific duties, but of a way of life, a manner of thinking and feeling, from which it will become plain, without the need of rules, what must be done on each occasion" (1938b, p. 243). There are chapters in several of his books in which Russell discourses on "science and values." The most extraordinary of these is in *The Scientific Outlook* (1931). Although Russell never explicitly formulated his system of values, they nevertheless form a connected one.

While as an ethical philosopher his metaethical subjectivity prevented him from being able to say that there are values that one ought rationally to accept, still his own search for ultimate value was not discarded upon his adoption of emotivism. There are two main values to pure science, in Russell's view. There is first the pursuit of scientific knowledge as an end in itself, and then science as a mental outlook. "The sphere of values lies outside science," Russell says, "except in so far as science consists in the pursuit of knowledge" (1931, p. 275). This is the contemplative ideal of science, as distinguished from the manipulative ideal. The pure scientifist keeps good company:

> The mystic, the lover, and the poet are also seekers after knowledge – not perhaps very successful seekers, but none the less worthy of respect on that account. In all forms of love we wish to have knowledge of what is loved, not for purposes of power, but for the ecstasy of contemplation.... Wherever there is ecstasy or joy or delight derived from an object there is the desire to know that object – to know it not in the manipulative fashion that consists in turning it into something else, but to know it in the fashion of the beatific vision, because in and for itself it sheds happiness upon the lover.... Love which has value contains an impulse towards that kind of knowledge out of which the mystic union springs.
>
> Science in its beginnings was due to men who were in love with the world. (1931, pp. 270–71)

The pursuit of scientific knowledge as an ultimate value is connected with the effect of that pursuit upon one's mental outlook. The phrase Russell uses, the "mystic union," is more than a powerful emotive chant. For him it has content. In *Marriage and Morals* he speaks of supreme personal and sexual love as resulting in the "mingling of personalities." By this phrase he means chiefly the temporary shedding of one's own ego and the escape into something larger. He means much the same thing by "the ecstasy of contemplation" in science, and by the impartiality or impersonality of outlook fostered by scientific inquiry. It is our passions that prevent us from seeing things as they are, and insofar as we can transcend our passions we attain "that submission to fact which is the essence of the scientific temper" (1918a, p. 109), or "the imaginative liberation from self which is necessary to such understanding of the world as man can hope to achieve" (ibid.).

Please note the term "imaginative liberation from self." Russell is not covertly positing a new ontological realm in which liberated scientists and lovers cavort and intermingle without regard for the findings of a level-headed logical empiricism. He is merely looking for ways of communicating an idea that lacks a fixed terminology outside the mystics. He might have used the language of Spinoza, and indeed he often does, for Russell understands the concept of the intellectual love of God in just the way he describes the scientist as lover of knowledge. The root idea here is a kind of impersonal enlargement of the self to include not only the objects of knowledge but also the interests of other persons. In old age Russell wrote an article called "The Expanding Mental Universe" (1959a). He says there:

> Seers and poets have long had visions of the kind of expansion of the ego which I am trying to adumbrate.... If a child develops into a man of science, his world comes to embrace those very distant portions of space and time of which I spoke earlier. If he is to achieve wisdom, his feelings must grow as his knowledge grows. Theologians tell us that God views the universe as one vast whole, without any here-and-now, without that partiality of sense and feeling to which we are, in a greater or less degree, inevitably condemned. (p. 397)

I had never before noticed that Russell might have felt envious of God (supposing that he exists), but of course he would have envied God's impartiality.

The ethic sketched here is, to be sure, not without its difficulties. Russell frequently condemns our human (as opposed to individual) partiality, which is for him the sin of anthropocentrism. It is manifested principally in believing the universe to be attuned to our hopes and fears. He wrote "A Free Man's Worship" partly to counter anthropomorphism's denial of the "trampling march of unconscious power" (1918a, p. 57). We have seen that he wished to imitate in philosophy the modern scientist's refraining from reading into his findings results that would be pleasing to him as a member of the human species. This raised one of the chief difficulties of the ethic. Its feature of impersonality does not allow us to distinguish between the good of those we know and the good of those we do not know—and, by extension, between the good of this and of that group of human beings. This may be what Russell wanted. I think that he had, however, such respect for the motive of individual and collective self-preservation that he did not fear that his ethic could lead to personal or collective self-sacrifice, despite the democratic favoring of all persons that his view inculcates. The ethic seems likely to be useful in promoting generosity (i.e., selflessness in feeling) and rationality (selflessness in thought). These are virtues we sorely need.

Notes

1. The remainder of the letter is as follows. Both portions are quoted with the permission of Mary Lou Maxwell.

> Although I have some reservations about your final list of "Postulates of Scientific Inference," I am convinced that you are correct in holding that much stronger principles than *simple induction* are necessary and, indeed, that the latter is not only not sufficient but is necessary *only* in the sense of being a rather unimportant special case—a rather trivial logical consequence—of the set of principles that *is* both necessary and sufficient. I have no intention of burdening you with details but only to remark that, starting from this point, I believe that I have developed a schema for a theory

of confirmation in which only the frequency interpretation of probability is needed and in which the "single case" probabilities are probabilities that a given hypothesis possesses a specified degree of *closeness* to the truth (verisimilitude, to use K. R. Popper's term) and *not* probabilities that they are true *simpliciter*. In it, your postulates of scientific inference, with the possible exception of *analogy*, would be treated in the same manner as are other laws of nature.

Please allow me to close by thanking you for your admirable efforts in behalf of world peace.
Sincerely yours,
Grover Maxwell
Professor of Philosophy

2. We know what he read from a notebook he kept of his reading from 1891 to 1902. There are 758 entries of monographs and major articles. See his *Collected Papers* (1983), appendix II.

3. Letter to Sir Joseph Larmor, November 20, 1899, Royal Society Archives.

4. See my *The Spinozistic Ethics of Bertrand Russell* (London and Boston: Allen & Unwin, 1985), p. 16.

5. Russell Archives, file 210.006748-F1, folios 9–27. The typescript is in files 210.006901-F6 and 7.

6. Typescript, p. 289.

7. Ibid., p. 250.

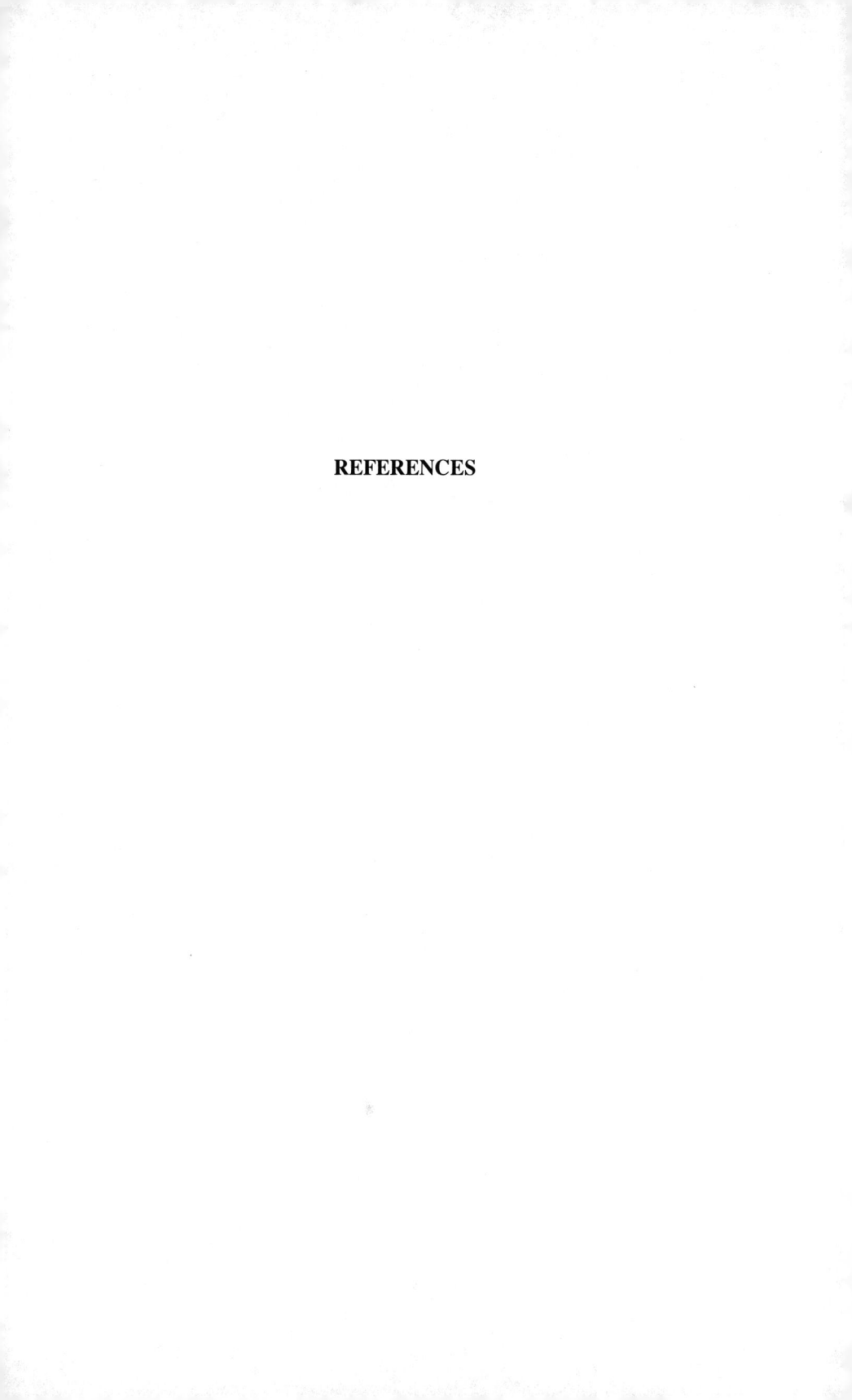

REFERENCES

References

Ayer, A. J. (1972). *Russell*. London: Fontana-Collins; New York: Viking.
Bar-Hillel, Y. (1970). "Indexical Expressions." In *Aspects of Language*. Jerusalem: Magnes Press.
Blackwell, Kenneth (1983). "'Perhaps You Will Think Me Fussy...': Three Myths in Editing Russell's *Collected Papers*," In Heather Jackson (ed.), *Editing Polymaths: Papers Given at the Eighteenth Annual Conference on Editorial Problems, University of Toronto, November 1982*. Toronto: Committee for the Conference on Editorial Problems, pp. 99-142.
Blackwell, Kenneth (1985). *The Spinozistic Ethics of Bertrand Russell*. London: Allen & Unwin.
Broad, C. D. (1924). "Critical and Speculative Philosophy." In J. H. Muirhead (ed.), *Contemporary British Philosophy: Personal Statements*. 1st ser. London: Allen & Unwin, pp. 75-100.
Carnap, R. (1928). *Der logische Aufbau der Welt. The Logical Structure of the World*. Trans. R. A. George. Berkeley: University of California Press, 1967.
Carnap, R. (1931). "On the Logicist Foundations of Mathematics." In P. Benacerraf and H. Putnam (eds.), *Philosophy of Mathematics: Selected Readings*. Englewood Cliffs, NJ: Prentice-Hall, 1964, pp. 31-41. Reprinted in Pears (1972), pp. 175-91.
Carnap, R. (1937). *The Logical Syntax of Language*. London: Routledge & Kegan Paul.
Carnap, R. (1950a). *The Continuum of Inductive Methods*. Chicago: University of Chicago Press.
Carnap, R. (1950b). *Logical Foundations of Probability*. Chicago: University of Chicago Press.
Chisholm, R. (1981). *The First Person*. Minneapolis: University of Minnesota Press.
Church, Alonzo (1956). *Introduction to Mathematical Logic*. Vol. I. Princeton, NJ: Princeton University Press.
Church, Alonzo (1976). "Comparison of Russell's Resolution of the Semantical Antinomies with that of Tarski." *Journal of Symbolic Logic*, vol. 41, pp. 747-60.
Clark, Ronald W. (1975). *The Life of Bertrand Russell*. London: Jonathan Cape and Weidenfeld & Nicolson; New York: Knopf, 1976.
Cocchiarella, Nino B. (1980). "The Development of the Theory of Logical Types and the Notion of a Logical Subject in Russell's Early Philosophy." *Synthèse*, vol. 45, pp. 71-115.
De Finetti, B. (1964). "Foresight: Its Logical Laws, Its Subjective Sources." In H. Kyburg and H. Smokler (eds.), *Studies in Subjective Probability*. New York: Wiley.
Donnellan, K. (1966). "Reference and Definite Descriptions." *Philosophical Review*, vol. 75, pp. 281-304.
Feferman, S. (1964). "Systems of Predicative Analysis." *Journal of Symbolic Logic*, vol. 29, pp. 1-30.
Friedmann, K. and A. Shimony (1971). "Jaynes' Maximum Entropy Prescription and Probability Theory." *Journal of Statistical Physics*, vol. 3, pp. 381-84.
Gödel, K. (1944). "Russell's Mathematical Logic." In Schilpp (ed.), pp. 125-53. Reprinted in Pears (1972).
Goldfarb, Warren (1979). "Logic in the Twenties: The Nature of the Quantifier." *Journal of Symbolic Logic*, vol. 44, pp. 351-68.
Goodman, N. (1979). *Fact, Fiction and Forecast*. 3rd ed., Hackett.

References

Griffin, Nicholas (1981). "The Collected Papers of Bertrand Russell." *History and Philosophy of Logic*, vol. 2, pp. 121-31.
Hacking, I. (1979). "What Is Logic?" *Journal of Philosophy*, vol. 76, pp. 285-319.
Heijenoort, J. van (1967). "Logic as Calculus and Logic as Language." *Synthese*, vol. 32, pp. 324-30.
Heijenoort, J. van (1967). *From Frege to Gödel: A Sourcebook in Mathematical Logic*. Cambridge, MA: Harvard University Press.
Horwich, P. (1982). *Probability and Evidence*. Cambridge: Cambridge University Press.
Huzurbazar, V. S. (1955). "On the Certainty of an Inductive Inference." *Proceedings of the Cambridge Philosophical Society*, vol. 51, pp. 761-62.
Hylton, P. (1980). "Russell's Substitutional Theory." *Synthese*, vol. 45, pp. 1-31.
James, William (1890). *The Principles of Psychology*. 2 vols., New York: Henry Holt & Co.; New York: Dorer, 1950.
Jaynes, E. T. (1968). "Prior Probabilities." *IEEE Transactions on Systems Science and Cybernetics*, SSC-4, no. 3, pp. 227-41.
Jeffrey, R. C. (1983). *The Logic of Decision*. 2nd ed., Chicago: University of Chicago Press.
Jeffreys, H. (1957). *Scientific Inference*. 2nd ed., Cambridge: Cambridge University Press.
Keynes, J. M. (1962). *A Treatise on Probability*. London: Chelsea.
Lakatos, Imre (1978). "Infinite Regress and the Foundations of Mathematics" (1962). In John Worrall and Gregory Currie (eds.), *Philosophical Papers: Mathematics, Science and Epistemology*. Vol. 2. Cambridge: Cambridge University Press, pp. 3-23.
Maxwell, Grover (1970). "Theories, Perception, and Structural Realism." In Robert G. Colodny (ed.), *The Nature and Function of Scientific Theories: Essays in Contemporary Science and Philosophy*. University of Pittsburgh Series in the Philosophy of Science, vol. 4. Pittsburgh: University of Pittsburgh Press.
Maxwell, Grover (1971). "Structural Realism and the Meaning of Theoretical Terms." In M. Radner and S. Winokur (eds.), *Analyses of Theories and Methods of Physics and Psychology: Minnesota Studies in the Philosophy of Science*. Vol. 4. Minneapolis, University of Minnesota Press, pp. 181-92.
Maxwell, Grover (1972). "Russell on Perception: A Study in Philosophical Method." In Pears (ed.) (1972), pp. 110-14.
Maxwell, Grover (1974). "The Later Bertrand Russell: Philosophical Revolutionary." In George Nakhnikian (ed.), *Bertrand Russell's Philosophy*. London: Duckworth, pp. 169-82.
Pears, David (1967). *Bertrand Russell and the British Tradition in Philosophy*. London: Collins.
Pears, D. F. (ed.) (1972). *Bertrand Russell: A Collection of Critical Essays*. New York: Doubleday (Anchor Books).
Quine, W. V. (1969). *Set Theory and Its Logic*. Cambridge, MA: Harvard University Press.
Ramsey, F. P. (1931). *The Foundations of Mathematics*. Edited by R. B. Braithwaite. London: Routledge.
Reichenbach, H. (1971). *Theory of Probability*. Berkeley: University of California Press.
Rescher, Nicholas (1979). "Russell and Modal Logic." In George W. Roberts (ed.), *Bertrand Russell Memorial Volume*. London: Allen & Unwin, pp. 139-49.
Rosenkrantz, R. (1983). "Why Glymour Is a Bayesian." In John Earman (ed.), *Testing Scientific Theories: Minnesota Studies in the Philosophy of Science*. Vol. X. Minneapolis: University of Minnesota Press, pp. 69-97.
Russell, Bertrand (1890-94). "A Locked Diary." In Russell *The Collected Papers*, vol. 1 (1983), pp. 41-67.
Russell, Bertrand (1891-1902). "What Shall I Read?" In Russell *The Collected Papers*, vol. 1 (1983), appendix II.
Russell, Bertrand (1895). Review of G. Heymans, *Die Gesetze und Elemente des wissenschaftlichen Denkens*. *Mind*, n.s. vol. 4, pp. 245-49. Reprinted in Russell *The Collected Papers*, vol. 1 (1983), pp. 249-55.
Russell, Bertrand (1896). "The Logic of Geometry." *Mind*, n. s. vol. 5, pp. 1-23. Reprinted in Russell *The Collected Papers*, vol. 1 (1983) pp. 266-86.
Russell, Bertrand (1897a). "Self-Appreciation." In *The Golden Urn*, no. 1 (March), pp. 30-1. Reprinted in Russell *The Collected Papers*, vol. 1 (1983) pp. 72-73.

REFERENCES   299

Russell, Bertrand (1897b). *An Essay on the Foundations of Geometry*. Cambridge: Cambridge University Press.
Russell, Bertrand (1900). *A Critical Exposition of the Philosophy of Leibniz*. London: Allen & Unwin.
Russell, Bertrand (1903a). "A Free Man's Worship." Reprinted in Russell, *Mysticism and Logic and Other Essays* (1918a), pp. 46-57.
Russell, Bertrand (1903b). *The Principles of Mathematics*. London: Allen & Unwin. 2nd ed., 1937; also published New York: Norton, 1938.
Russell, Bertrand (1905a). "On Denoting." Reprinted in Russell *Essays in Analysis* (1973a), pp. 103-19.
Russell, Bertrand (1905b). "On Some Difficulties in the Theory of Transfinite Numbers and Order Types." In Russell *Essays in Analysis* (1973a), pp. 135-64.
Russell, Bertrand (1906). "On 'Insolubilia' and Their Solution by Symbolic Logic." Reprinted in Russell *Essays in Analysis* (1973a), pp. 190-214.
Russell, Bertrand (1908). "Mathematical Logic as Based on the Theory of Types." *American Journal of Mathematics*, vol. 30, pp. 222-62. Reprinted in *Logic and Knowledge* (1956a), and in Heijenoort (1967), pp. 150-82.
Russell, Bertrand (1910-11). "Knowledge by Acquaintance and Knowledge by Description." *Proceedings of the Aristotelian Society*, vol. 11, pp. 108-28. Reprinted in Russell, *Mysticism and Logic* (1918a).
Russell, Bertrand (1910). "On the Nature of Truth and Falsehood." Reprinted in *Philosophical Essays*. New York: Simon and Schuster, 1968, pp. 147-59.
Russell, Bertrand, and Whitehead, Alfred North (1910-13). *Principia Mathematica*. See Whitehead and Russell (1910-13).
Russell, Bertrand (1911-12). "On the Relations of Universals and Particulars." *Proceedings of the Aristotelian Society*, vol. 12, pp. 1-24. Reprinted in *Logic and Knowledge* (1956a), pp. 105-24.
Russell, Bertrand (1911). "The Philosophical Importance of Mathematical Logic." *Revue de Métaphysique et de Morale*, vol. 19, pp. 281-91. Translation in *Essays in Analysis* (1973a), pp. 284-94.
Russell, Bertrand (1912). *The Problems of Philosophy*. London: Williams and Norgate. New York: Oxford University Press, 1959. Published as Galaxy paperback in 1959.
Russell, Bertrand (1913a). "The Nature of Sense-Data-A Reply to Dr. Dawes Hicks." *Mind*, n. s. vol. 22, pp. 76-81.
Russell, Bertrand (1913b). "Science as an Element in Culture." Reprinted as "The Place of Science in a Liberal Education," in Russell *Mysticism and Logic* (1918a), pp. 33-45.
Russell, Bertrand (1913c). *Theory of Knowledge: The 1913 Manuscript*. In Elizabeth Ramsden Eames and Kenneth Blackwell (eds.), *The Collected Papers of Bertrand Russell*. Vol. 7, London: Allen & Unwin, 1984.
Russell, Bertrand (1914a). "On Scientific Method in Philosophy." Reprinted in Russell *Mysticism and Logic* (1918a), pp. 97-124. Reprinted in Russell *The Collected Papers* (1986), pp. 55-73.
Russell, Bertrand (1914b). *Our Knowledge of the External World*. London: Allen & Unwin. 2nd ed., 1926.
Russell, Bertrand (1914c). "The Relation of Sense-data to Physics." *Scientia*. Reprinted in Russell, *Mysticism and Logic*. Harmondsworth: Penguin, 1953, pp. 138-70; also in *Mysticism and Logic* (1918a), pp. 145-79, and *The Collected Papers* (1986), pp. 3-26.
Russell, Bertrand (1915). Letter on Sense-Data. *Journal of Philosophy*, vol. 12 (8 July), pp. 391-92. Reprinted in Russell *The Collected Papers*, vol. 8 (1986), pp. 87-88.
Russell, Bertrand (1918a). *Mysticism and Logic and Other Essays*. London and New York: Longmans, Green. New York: W. W. Norton, 1929. Reprinted London: Allen & Unwin, 1932 and Harmondsworth: Penguin, 1953.
Russell, Bertrand (1918b). "The Philosophy of Logical Atomism." *Monist*, vol. 28, pp. 495-527, vol. 29, pp. 33-63, 190-222, 345-80. Reprinted in Russell *Logic and Knowledge* (1956a), 1956, pp. 177-281, and in Russell *The Collected Papers*, vol. 8 (1986), pp. 157-244.
Russell, Bertrand (1919a). *Introduction to Mathematical Philosophy*. London: Allen & Unwin.
Russell, Bertrand (1919b). "On Propositions: What They Are and How They Mean." *Proceedings

of the Aristotelian Society, supp. vol. II, pp. 1–43. Reprinted in Russell Logic and Knowledge (1956a), pp. 285–320, and in Russell The Collected Papers, vol. 8 (1986), pp. 276–306.
Russell, Bertrand (1921). The Analysis of Mind. London: Allen & Unwin.
Russell, Bertrand (1923). The ABC of Atoms. London: Kegan Paul, Trench, Trubner.
Russell, Bertrand (1924). "Logical Atomism." In J. H. Muirhead (ed.), Contemporary British Philosophy. Reprinted in Logic and Knowledge (1956a), pp. 323–43.
Russell, Bertrand (1925a). The ABC of Relativity. London: Kegan Paul, Trench, Trubner. 2nd ed. revised by Felix Pirani. London: Allen & Unwin, 1958; 3rd ed., 1969.
Russell, Bertrand (1927a). An Outline of Philosophy. London: Allen & Unwin.
Russell, Bertrand (1927b). The Analysis of Matter. London: Kegan Paul, Trench, Trubner. Reprinted New York: Dover, 1954.
Russell, Bertrand (1929). Marriage and Morals. London: Allen & Unwin.
Russell, Bertrand (1931). The Scientific Outlook. London: Allen & Unwin.
Russell, Bertrand (1936). "On Order in Time." Proceedings of the Cambridge Philosophical Society, vol. 32, pp. 216–28.
Russell, Bertrand (1938a). "On the Importance of Logical Form." In Otto Neurath (ed.), International Encyclopedia of Unified Science. Vol. 1, no. 1. Chicago: University of Chicago Press.
Russell, Bertrand (1938b). Power: A New Social Analysis. London: Allen & Unwin.
Russell, Bertrand (1940). An Inquiry into Meaning and Truth. London: Allen & Unwin. Reprinted Harmondsworth: Penguin Books, 1962.
Russell, Bertrand (1944). "My Mental Development." In Schilpp (ed.), (1944), pp. 3–20.
Russell, Bertrand (1945a). "The Bomb and Civilisation." The Forward (Glasgow), vol. 39 (18 Aug.), pp. 1, 3.
Russell, Bertrand (1945b). A History of Western Philosophy. New York: Simon and Schuster; London: Allen & Unwin, 1946.
Russell, Bertrand (1948). Human Knowledge: Its Scope and Limits. New York: Simon and Schuster; London: Allen & Unwin.
Russell, Bertrand (1951). The Impact of Science on Society. New York: Columbia University Press.
Russell, Bertrand (1954). "How I Write." In Russell Portraits from Memory (1956c), pp. 210–14.
Russell, Bertrand (1956a). Logic and Knowledge. Edited by R. C. Marsh. London: Allen & Unwin.
Russell, Bertrand (1956b). "Mind and Matter." In Russell, Portraits from Memory (1956c), pp. 145–65.
Russell, Bertrand (1956c). Portraits from Memory and Other Essays. New York: Simon and Schuster; London: Allen & Unwin.
Russell, Bertrand (1956d). "Why I Took to Philosophy." In Russell, Portraits from Memory (1956c), pp. 13–18.
Russell, Bertrand (1959a). "The Expanding Mental Universe." Saturday Evening Post, vol. 232, no. 3 (18 July). Reprinted in Robert E. Egner and Lester E. Dennon (eds.), The Basic Writings of Bertrand Russell. London: Allen & Unwin, 1961, pp. 391–98.
Russell, Bertrand (1959b). My Philosophical Development. London: Allen & Unwin; New York: Simon and Schuster.
Russell, Bertrand (1961). "The Pursuit of Truth." Reprinted in Russell, Fact and Fiction. London: Allen & Unwin, pp. 41–46.
Russell, Bertrand (1967). War Crimes in Vietnam. New York: Monthly Review Press; London: Allen & Unwin.
Russell, Bertrand (1967–69). The Autobiography of Bertrand Russell. Vol. 1: 1872–1914; vol. 2: 1914–1944; vol. 3: 1944–1967. London: Allen & Unwin.
Russell, Bertrand (1973a). Essays in Analysis. Edited by D. P. Lackey. New York: Braziller.
Russell, Bertrand (1973b). "Is Mathematics Purely Linguistic?" In Essays in Analysis (1973a), pp. 295–306.
Russell, Bertrand (1973c) "The Regressive Method of Discovering the Premisses of Mathematics," In Essays in Analysis (1973a), pp. 272–83. First written in 1907.
Russell, Bertrand (1983). The Collected Papers of Bertrand Russell: Cambridge Essays, 1888–99.

Vol. 1, edited by Kenneth Blackwell, Andrew Brink, Nicholas Griffin, Richard A. Rempel, and John G. Slater. London: Allen & Unwin.

Russell, Bertrand (1984), *Theory of Knowledge: The 1913 Manuscript*. See Russell (1913c).

Russell, Bertrand (1986). *The Collected Papers of Bertrand Russell: The Philosophy of Logical Atomism and Other Essays, 1914–19*. Vol. 8, edited by John G. Slater. London: Allen & Unwin.

Salmon, Wesley (1974). "Memory and Perception in *Human Knowledge*." In George Nakhnikian (ed.), *Bertrand Russell's Philosophy*. London: Duckworth, pp. 139–67.

Schilpp, P. A. (ed.) (1944). *The Philosophy of Bertrand Russell*. Evanston, IL: The Library of Living Philosophers; LaSalle: Open Court.

Seidenfeld, T. (1979). "Why I Am Not an Objective Bayesian: Some Reflections Prompted by Rosenkrantz." *Theory and Decision*, vol. 11, pp. 413–40.

Shimony, A. (1970). "Scientific Inference." In R. G. Colodny (ed.), *The Nature and Function of Scientific Theories*. Pittsburgh: University of Pittsburgh Press.

Skyrms, B. (1984). *Pragmatics and Empiricism*. New Haven, CT: Yale University Press.

Spinoza, Benedict de (1677). *Ethics*.

von Plato, J. (1982). "The Significance of the Ergodic Decomposition of Stationary Measures for the Interpretation of Probability." *Synthèse*, vol. 53, pp. 419–32.

Weyl, H. (1918). *Das Kontinuum*. Leipzig: Veit.

Whitehead, A. N., and Russell, B. (1910–13). *Principia Mathematica*. vol. I (1910), vol. II (1912), vol. III (1913). Cambridge: Cambridge University Press. 2nd ed., 1925, 1927.

Wittgenstein, Ludwig. (1958). *Philosophical Investigations*. Translated by G. E. M. Anscombe. London: Macmillan.

Wittgenstein, Ludwig (1961a). *Tractatus Logico-Philosophicus*. Translated by D. F. Pears and B. F. McGuinness. London: Routledge and Kegan Paul. First published in 1922.

Wittgenstein, Ludwig (1961b). *Notebooks 1914–16*. Translated by G. E. M. Anscombe. Oxford: Blackwell.

Wittgenstein, Ludwig (1967). *Zettel*. Edited by G. E. M. Anscombe and G. H. von Wright. Translated by G. E. M. Anscombe. Berkeley and Los Angeles: University of California Press.

CONTRIBUTORS

Notes on Contributors

C. ANTHONY ANDERSON is Associate Professor of Philosophy at the University of Minnesota, Minneapolis. He received his doctorate in philosophy from UCLA. He has published articles on intensional logic and philosophy of religion, and is currently completing a book manuscript on the Frege-Church logic of sense and denotation.

KENNETH BLACKWELL has been Archivist of the Bertrand Russell Archives at McMaster University since 1968, when the Russell papers were acquired, and is the editor of *Russell: The Journal of the Bertrand Russell Archives*. He is a founding editor of *The Collected Papers of Bertrand Russell*, and is textual editor of volume 1, *Cambridge Essays, 1888–99* (1983), as well as collaborating editor with Elizabeth R. Eames on volume 7, *Theory of Knowledge: The 1913 Manuscript* (1984). His book, *The Spinozistic Ethics of Bertrand Russell*, was published in 1985. He is currently working on a two-volume bibliography of Russell's writings.

NINO B. COCCHIARELLA is Professor of Philosophy at Indiana University. He has written papers in both formal and philosophical logic and is the author of *Logical Investigation of Predication Theory and the Problem of Universals* and of a volume of essays, *Logical Studies in Early Analytic Philosophy*, on Frege, Russell, Meinong, and Wittgenstein.

WILLIAM DEMOPOULOS is Professor of Philosophy at the University of Western Ontario. He is associate editor of *Philosophy of Science*, the journal of the Philosophy of Science Association. He has published in the philosophy of psychology and the foundations of physics. He is coeditor of *Meaning and Cognitive Structure: Issues in the Computational Theory of Mind* (1986), and of *Language Learning and Concept Acquisition* (1986).

ELIZABETH R. EAMES is a professor in the Department of Philosophy of Southern Illinois University at Carbondale. She is a member of the Society for Women in Philosophy and was the first coordinator of Women's Studies at her university. She has been a Carnegie Fellow and has held research grants from the National Endowment for the Humanities and the American Philosophical Society. Her articles on Russell have appeared in journals in the United States and abroad, and in translation in Italian and Chinese. Her *Bertrand Russell's Theory of Knowledge* appeared in 1969; in 1984 she edited (with Kenneth Blackwell) *Theory of Knowledge: The 1913 Manuscript*, volume 7 of the *Collected Papers of Bertrand Russell*. Her book *Bertrand Russell's Dialogue with His Contemporaries* will appear in 1989.

JOHN EARMAN has taught at UCLA, Rockefeller University, and the University of Minnesota. He is now Professor in History and Philosophy of Science at the University of Pittsburgh. He edited *Foundations of Space-Time Theories* and *Testing Scientific Theories* (Minnesota Studies in the Philosophy of Science, Vols. 8 and 10, respectively). His book, *A Primer on Determinism*, appeared in the Western Ontario Series in the Philosophy of Science in 1986. His *World Enough and Space-Time: Absolute vs. Relational Theories of Space and Time* will appear in spring 1989.

MICHAEL FRIEDMAN received his Ph.D. from Princeton University in 1973. Since then he has worked largely in the philosophy of science and published papers on the the philosophy of geometry, theory of explanation, theory of confirmation, etc. In 1983 he published *Foundations of Space-Time Theories: Relativistic Physics and Philosophy of Science*. He has subsequently concentrated on the history of philosophy of science and has published papers on Kant's philosophy of physics and mathematics and on the development of logical positivism.

RICHARD FUMERTON is Professor of Philosophy at the University of Iowa. He received his Ph.D. from Brown University in 1974. He has published papers in epistemology, metaphysics, philosophy of science and ethics, and is the author of *Metaphysical and Epistemological Problems of Perception* (1985).

WARREN GOLDFARB, Professor of Philosophy at Harvard University, is coauthor, with Burton Dreben, of *The Decision Problem: Solvable Classes of Quantification Formulas* (1979); he is also editor of Jacques Herbrand's *Logical Writings* (1971). He has published articles on mathematical logic, history of logic, and the development of analytic philosophy, in the *Journal of Symbolic Logic*, the *Journal of Philosophy*, *Synthese*, and elsewhere. His article "Poincaré against the Logicists," which treats topics related to his contribution to the present volume, appears in volume XI of Minnesota Studies in the Philosophy of Science.

JAMES HAWTHORNE is a Research Scientist in Artificial Intelligence at the Honeywell Systems and Research Center in Minneapolis, Minnesota, where he is investigating probabilistic and nonmonotonic reasoning for automated systems. Mr. Hawthorne's primary research interests in philosophy involve using formal logics to illuminate issues in the epistemology and ontology of the sciences. His paper in this volume is adapted from his dissertation in philosophy at the University of Minnesota, "A Semantic Theory for Partial Entailment and Inductive Inference."

HERBERT HOCHBERG is Professor of Philosophy at the University of Texas. He has taught at Northwestern, Ohio State, Indiana, Minnesota, and the University of Gothenburg. A former Guggenheim and Fulbright fellow, he is the author of *Thought, Fact, and Reference: The Origins and Ontology of Logical Atomism* (1978) and *Logic, Ontology, and Language: Essays on Truth and Reality* (1984). His translation (with Susanne Hochberg) of three volumes by the Swedish philosopher Ivar Segelberg, along with a monograph commentary, *Qualities, Complexes, Sets, and the Self*, is scheduled to appear as volume 4 in the series Primary Sources in Phenomenology.

PETER HYLTON is Associate Professor of Philosophy at the University of California, Santa Barbara. He was educated at King's College, Cambridge, and at Harvard University. He has published various articles on philosophy of language and the history of analytic philosophy. He is currently working on a book on British idealism, the Moore-Russell reaction against idealism, and the subsequent development of Russell's philosophy.

DAVID PEARS was educated at Westminster School and Balliol College, Oxford, and is Emeritus Professor of Philosophy in the University of Oxford and Emeritus Student of Christ Church, Oxford. He is the author of *Bertrand Russell and the British Tradition in Philosophy* (1967), *Wittgenstein* (1970), *Some Questions in the Philosophy of Mind* (1975), and most recently, *Motivated Irrationality* (1984). With B. F. McGuinness, he is translator of an edition of Wittgenstein's *Tractatus Logico-Philosophicus* (1961). He is a Fellow of the British Academy and a member of the L'Institut Internationale de Philosophie.

R. M. SAINSBURY studied PPE at Oxford and taught there for some years before becoming a Lecturer in Philosophy at the University of Essex (1975-78). He is currently at King's College, University of London. He is the author of *Russell* (1979), and of numerous articles on the philosophy of logic and language.

C. WADE SAVAGE is Professor of Philosophy at the University of Minnesota. He has been a member of the Minnesota Center for Philosophy of Science since 1971, and was its director, 1981-84. He is editor of Volume IX of the Minnesota Studies in the Philosophy of Science, *Perception and Cognition: Issues in the Foundations of Psychology* (1978), and is editor or coeditor of several forthcoming volumes in the series. He is the author of *The Measurement of Sensation: A Study of Perceptual Psychophysics* (1971).

JANET FARRELL SMITH is Associate Professor of Philosophy at the University of Massachusetts at Boston and has also taught at Smith College. In addition to work in philosophy of language on descriptions and demonstratives, she has published articles on the philosophy of language of Bertrand Russell and Alexius Meinong, including "The Russell-Meinong Debate" in *Philosophy and Phenomenological Research* (1985). She is currently at work on a book on Russell's philosophy of language.

INDEX

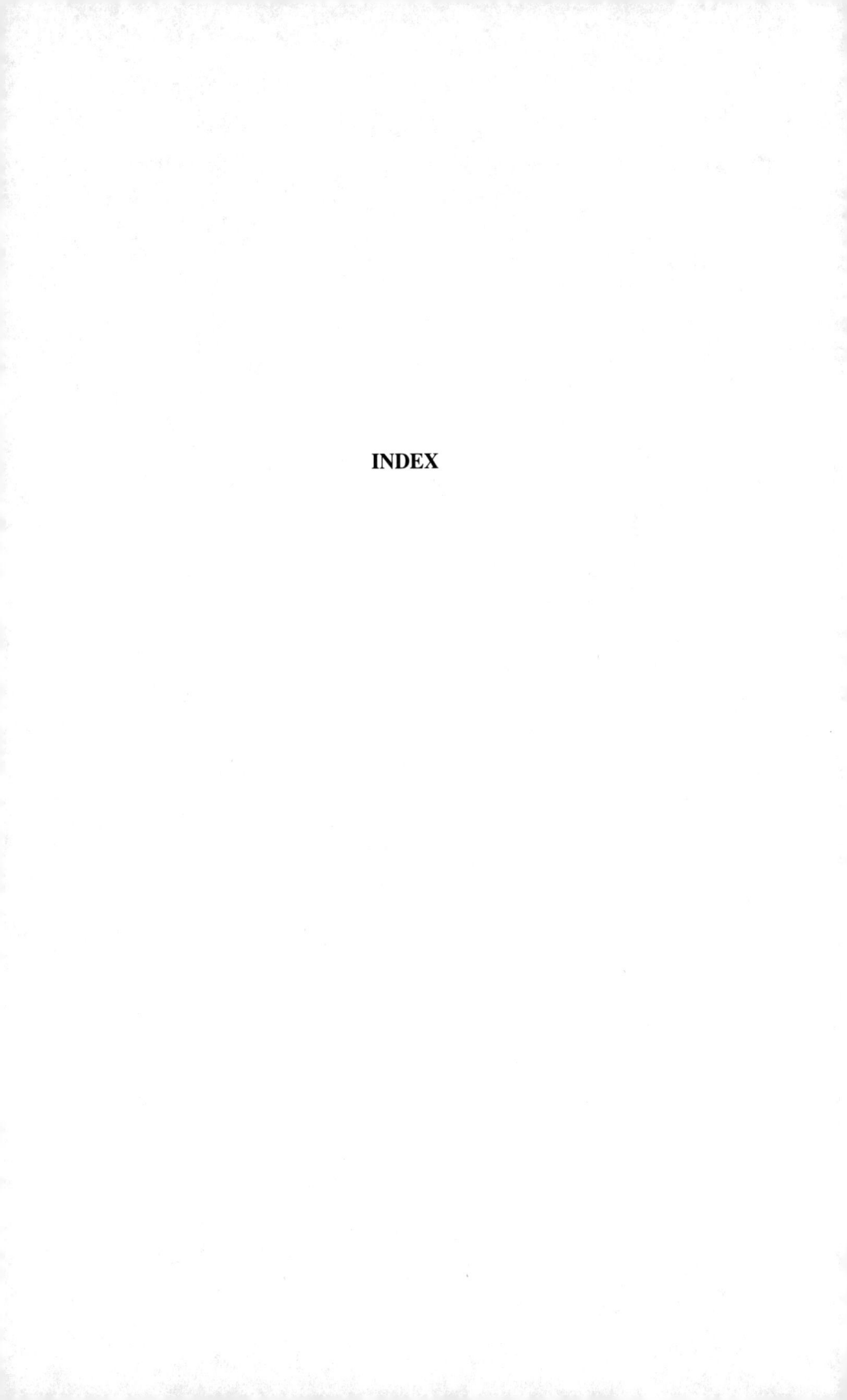

Author Index

Adams, E., 232n
Anscombe, G. E. M., 136n, 301
Aristotle, 282
Ayer, A. J., 7, 149–50, 218n, 288

Bar-Hillel, Y., 13–14, 120, 125–26, 129–30
Benacerraf, P., 21, 261
Bergmann, G., 87n
Berkeley, G., 282
Blackwell, K., 247n
Broad, C. D., 3
Brody, B. A., 117n
Burks, A. W., 135n, 136n

Carnap, R.: 196, 232n, 238–39, 244; concept of logic, 197; constructional system, 186–87; identity conditions, 66; indexicals, 119, 123–24, 128, 134; inductive logic, 222–23, 235, 243; logicism, 39n; names, 14; notion of structure, 195; relativity, 183; scientific theory, 16–17, 24; structural realism, 186–87; theory of types, 59, 79
Carroll, L., 211–13
Castañeda, H., 86n, 136n
Chisholm, R., 129, 135n, 136n, 279n
Church, A., 29, 43–45, 62n, 262
Clark, R. W., 181n, 182n, 287–88
Cocchiarella, N., 86n
Copi, I. M., 87n

Davidson, D., 279n
DeFinetti, B., 223, 225, 231, 232n, 233n, 235
Demopoulos, W., 87n, 137n
Descartes, R., 203, 208, 282
Donnellan, K., 130

Einstein, A., 4

Feferman, S., 38n
Fisher, R. A., 235
Foster, J., 218n
Frege, G.: Bradley's paradox, 75–77; constituents of thought, 106n; indexicals, 136n; influence on Russell, 286; language, 132, 134; notion of level, 62n; laws of propositions, 39n, 58, 90
Friedman, K., 233n
Friedman, M., 137n

Gödel, K., 8–9, 24–26, 32–33, 39, 255
Goldfarb, W., 39n, 199n
Goodman, N., 18–19, 136n, 217n, 229–31, 244, 246
Gratton-Guinness, I., 289
Grice, H. P., 181n
Grossman, R., 86n

Hacking, I., 38n
Hegel, G., 282
Heijenoort, J. van, 39n, 136n
Horwich, P., 233n
Hume, D., 5–6, 144, 205, 213, 243, 268–69, 277, 282
Huzurbazar, V., 228
Hylton, P., 39n

James, W., 138, 144, 262, 284–85
Jaynes, E. T., 231
Jeffrey, R. C., 232n
Jeffreys, H., 221, 228, 235
Johnson, M. L., Jr., 263n

Author Index

Kant, I., 282
Kaplan, D., 106n, 118n
Keynes, J. M., 19, 209, 229, 231, 235, 239, 240, 242
Kim, J., 279n
Kneale, W. and M., 87n
Kolmogorov, A., 222
Kripke, S., 109, 131, 218n
Kyburg, H., 235

Lackey, D., 86n, 95
Lawrence, D. H., 290
Leibniz, G., 4, 273, 281–82
Lewis, G. N., 183
Locke, J., 282
Lyons, E., 135n

McGuinness, B., 181n
Mach, E., ix, 186
Mackie, J., 215, 218n
Maxwell, G.: acquaintance, 264, 278; causal theory of perception, 264; critique of Russell, 236–46, 289; induction, 20, 235–36; letter to Russell, 281–82; prior probability, 246–47; ramification, 271; realism, 264; theory of theories, 183
Meinong, A., 88, 94, 97
Mill, James, 283
Mill, J. S., 269
Misner, C. W., 263n
Moore, G. E., 3–4, 73, 105–6n, 290
Morrell, O., 169, 170, 177, 286

Nagel, E., 135n, 263n
Newman, M. H. A., 16–17, 187–88, 190–91, 196
Neyman, J., 235

Peano, G., 3–4, 26, 286
Pearson, E. S., 235
Peirce, C. S., 135n
Perry, J., 129, 137n
Plato, 282
Popper, K., 232n, 293n
Putnam, H., 17, 111, 127, 131, 193–94

Quine, W. V., 8–9, 24–26, 33, 64–65, 136n, 188, 193–94, 198n, 251

Ramsey, F. P.: inductive logic, 235; infinitary truth functions, 28–29, 39n; nameability, 33; Russell paradox, 79–82; set theory, 255; theoretical terms, 16; theory of orders, 63; theory of types, 8–9, 24, 26, 255
Reichenbach, H., 18–19, 183, 231, 235
Rescher, N., 287
Robb, A. A., 183
Rosenkrantz, R., 230
Ryle, G., 150

Sainsbury, R. M., 106n
Salmon, W., 148, 235
Savage, L., 235
Schlick, M., ix, 186
Schrödinger, E., 183
Searle, J., 117n
Seidenfeld, T., 233n
Sheffer, H., 255
Shimony, A., 232n, 233n
Skyrms, B., 233n
Spinoza, B., 282, 287–88, 292
Strawson, P. F., 219n

Tarski, A., 29, 59
Thorne, K. S., 263n

Urmson, J. O., 7

von Plato, J., 233n

Ward, J., 285
Wettstein, H., 117n
Weyl, H., 38n
Wheeler, J. A., 263n
Whitehead, A. N., 41, 82, 83, 179, 183, 194, 252, 261–62
Wiener, N., 252, 256–57
Winnie, J., 188, 198n
Wittgenstein, L.: axiom of infinity, 197; critique of Russell's work, 3, 6, 11, 15–16, 43, 52, 169, 177, 179, 286, 288; matter, 286; *Notes on Logic*, 170; *Philosophical Investigations*, 7; principle of atomicity, 60, 77; probability, 223; propositions, 106n, 178; reference of language, 132; Russell paradox, 77–84; structure, 195; *Tractatus*, 169, 176, 195, 197, 223

Subject Index

ABC of Atoms, 5
ABC of Relativity, 5, 290
Acquaintance: advance knowledge of form, 174–75; attention as a species of, 156; as combining three constituents of thought, 174; with a complex, 171, 175; with constituents of a proposition, 179–80; extensional, 15, 171–74; with forms, 171, 173, 174–76, 179; and indispensability of indexicals, 125; as intensional, 172, 179; notion of, 103, 139–40, 254, 278; with particulars, 171; with predicates and relations, 171; relations of, 53, 167, 172–73; Russell's doctrine of, 5, 14, 142, 170; with sensibilia, 145–46, 150; simple objects of, 178; specification of the objects of, 172
Aesthetics, 262
"All" vs. "any," 83–84
Ambiguity of scope, 65
Ambiguous statements, 35
Analysis: of analysis, 156; decompositional, 155–56; eliminative vs. noneliminative, 12, 105; infinite regress of, 157; paradox of, 112, 153; translational and decompositional, 155–56
Analysis of Matter: causation, 21, 267–68, 271, 273–75; compresence, 260; instants of time, 20–21, 249, 253–56; location in space-time, 122–23, 269; neutral monism, 145; overlapping events, 254; particulars, 121; physics, 5; realism, 279n; rejection of phenomenalism, 183–84; Russell's later philosophy, ix, 6, 264–65; sense-data, 150, 164, 167; structural realism, 186; theory of theories, 16; Whitehead's "enclosure series," 212
Analysis of Mind: abandonment of sense-data, 138, 143–46, 148, 150, 167–68; causal theory of, 271–72; phenomenalist analysis, 5, 279n; propositions, 56; structuralism, 198n
"Analyzing" postulate, 270
Animal expectation, 204–5, 216–17
Animal inference, 165
Anthropocentrism, 292
"Any" vs. "all," 83–84, 92
Appearance of an object, 272
Arithmetic, derivation of, 10–11
Asymmetric relation of predication, 52–53
Atomicity, principle of, 42, 60–61
Atomistic hierarchy of sentences, 9–10, 42–43, 55, 57, 59–62
Atomistic theory, 58, 286
Aufbau, 195
Awareness. *See* Acquaintance
Axiomatic definitions, 184
Axiom of choice, 21, 254–56, 263n
Axiom of continuity, 222
Axiom of extensionality, 66
Axiom of infinity, 197
Axiom of reducibility, 9, 11, 30, 38, 63, 82–84, 85
Axioms of probability, 224, 231, 237, 239

Bayesian model of inductive inference, 234
Bayes's theorem, 18–20, 221, 226–28, 234–36, 290
Belief, degrees of, 151
Bradley's paradox, 11, 63, 75–79

313

Subject Index

British idealism, 284
British linguistic philosophy, 7

Cauchy-Schwartz inequality, 224
Causal chain, 13, 111, 113, 123, 145, 267, 276
Causal connections (relations), 266
Causal inferences, 265, 275, 276, 278
Causality, 266, 271
Causal judgment, 22
Causal laws, 268, 272-73, 275
"Causal Laws and Concomitant Variation," 290
Causal lines, 265-70, 275-77
Causal order, 122
Causal theory of perception: 134, 183, 264, 267, 271-77; of reference, 12-13, 112
Cause, 21, 214, 264, 267-68, 271, 273, 275, 277
Classes, 30-32, 39n, 60, 101, 107n
Class paradox, 101
Close-minded attitude, 223-25
Coherence theory (of empirical knowledge), 15, 139, 161, 166
Collected Papers, 283-84, 286
Combination (of sentences), 55
Common nouns, 117n
Compactness (of instants of time), 21, 256-57, 260-61
"Complete symbol," 168n
Complexes, 73
Complex object, 141
Complex particulars, 49-50, 53, 66
Complex properties, 66, 84
Complex subject, 145, 147, 151, 181
Comprehension axioms, 32, 64
Comprehension principle (for properties and relations), 47-48
Compresence, complex of, 60, 122, 127-28, 260, 268-69, 277
Confirmation theory, 235-36, 244
Conjunction, 81-82
Constructed theory of instants, 260
Constructionalism, 261-62
Constructions, 264-69, 276-77
Constructivism, Russell's, 25-26, 30-31
Constructivist (antirealist) interpretation of sets, 9
Contingency thesis, 205-8, 211, 216-17, 218n
Contingent facts, 176, 203
Contingent propositions, 15, 17, 170, 175
Continuum of hyperinstants, 257
Coordinate description, 124, 126-28, 135

Coordinate system, 127, 132-33
Co-punctuality between percepts and nonpercepts, 192
Correspondence theory of empirical knowledge, 15, 159
Credibility: based exclusively on data, 203, 214-15; connection to mathematical probability, 160; degrees of, 160, 201-2, 241-42; independent of inference, 161-62, 165; iteration principle applied to, 212; prior assignment of, 243-44; requirement of truth, 208, 216; as supported by principles of evidence, 209-10
Credibility functions, 238-41
Credibility relation, 203-4, 206, 213
C-relation. *See* Credibility relation
Data: credibility of, 213-14; criteria for admissible, 202; and inference, 165-66; as ultimate justification of hypotheses, 200, 203, 214-15; nature of, 200-201; as nonlinguistically possible, 159; as private to the subject, 164; pure and impure, 165-68; Russell's definition of, 159-60, 202; uncertain, 201
Definite descriptions: attributive and referential use, 130-31; application of denoting to, 93; containing indexicals, 120; to define scientific concepts, 187; vs. indefinite, 91; of lambda abstracts, 66; vs. proper names, 116; system of, within object domain, 119; theory of, 100, 108-9
Definitions, 198n
Demonstratives, 117n
Denoting, 90-98, 101
Derivation of arithmetic, 10-11
Descriptions, theory of, 12, 34, 65, 88, 100-102
Designation, rigid and *de re*, 131
Determinism, "billiard ball," 282
Doctrine of logical types, 51, 54
Domain of interpretation. *See* Interpretation
Dualism of universals and particulars, 48-50
Dutch-book arguments, 224, 232n, 237

Emotions, James-Lange theory of, 285
Emotivism, 291
English idealism, 4
Entrenchment theory of projectability, Goodman's, 230
Epimenides' paradox, 28-29, 33
Ethics, normative, 290

Event ontology, Russell's early, ix
Events: and axiom of choice, 254–55; causes from sequences of, 268; construction of, 276; as constructs of the physical world, 265; copunctual, 266; divisibility of, 253; duration of, 258; first and last instants of, 254; located by space-time, 268–69, 276; mental and physical, 268; perceived as real, 266; as percepts, 274; Quine's definition of, 251; recurrence of, 257–59; simultaneity of, 258; theory of, 262
Evidence, 17–18, 203, 205–8, 211–13, 215–17, 285
Exchangeability, 224, 227, 229, 231, 232n
Exemplification, 69, 71–72, 76–79
Exemplification connection, 72, 75–76
"Existential Import of Propositions, The," 95
"Expanding Mental Universe, The," 23, 292
Extensional interpretation of relations, 190
External world, 184–85, 253, 261, 275–76, 288. *See also* Physical world

Facts, 51, 52, 60–61, 72, 76–77, 176
False conclusions, 208–11
First truth/second truth, 37
Form/content division of knowledge, 187, 191
Foundationalist theory of knowledge, 139, 200–3, 214
Foundations of Geometry by Hilbert (1899), 186
Foundedness of relation extensions, 196
"Free Man's Worship, A," 287

Generalization of sentences, 55, 59
Goodman hypothesis, 229
Goodman predicate, 220, 225–26
Goodman's entrenchment theory of projectability, 230
Goodman's "new problem" of induction, 229
Goodman's paradox, 200
Grammar, 103–4
"Greek Exercises," 283
Grelling's paradox, 28–29
Grue classes, 213
Grue predicates, 244, 246

History of Western Philosophy, 213n, 285
Human Knowledge: Its Scope and Limits: causality, 21, 268, 271, 275–76; coordinate replacement, 123–25, 127; as a creative work, 289; credibility, 160–65, 202–3; evidence, 207, 285; fact, 60; foundationalism, 200; Humean empiricism, 6, 234–35; indexicals, 13–14, 119, 123–24, 129; induction, 4, 19–20, 207, 220, 228, 234; language, 127–31; natural epistemology, 260; nondemonstrative inference, 269; notes about, 289; perception, 288; postulates of scientific inference, 236–37; probability, 231, 238, 242; realism, 210; on scientific concepts, 122; sense-data, 149–50, 159; skepticism, 215–16; theory of knowledge, 192, 212
Hyperinstants: continuum of, 257; construction of, 261

Idealism, English, 4
Idealist manuscripts, Russell's unpublished, 286
Identity, 66, 93, 270, 288
Image, 144, 273
Implicit definition, 198n. *See also* Axiomatic definition
Impredicative functions, 79–80
Impredicative predicates, 63
Impredicative properties, 80
Impredicativity, 10–11
Incomplete symbols, 100–102, 107n, 168n
Indexicals: characteristics of, 120, 122; and definite descriptions, 120, 132; designating particulars, 121; egocentric, 124–25; epistemic purity of, 135n; "I," 120, 129–34; indispensability, 127–28, 134; interdefinability, 13, 119, 123, 128–29, 132–33; intersubjective designatum, 133–34; in minimum vocabulary, 119; in *PLA*, 120, 133; proximate and distal, 123; public/private meaning, 14, 132, 134–35; replacement of with space-time coordinates, 119, 123–24, 128–30, 133–34; role of, 128; strict names as a form of, 120–21; subjectivity of, 134; "this," 120, 124–29, 133, 135, 136
Indexical sentence, 120
Indifference principle, 215, 218n
Indispensability of indexicals, 127–28
Individuality of universals and particulars, 49
Indubitability, 162–63
Induction: and Bayes's theorem, 18–20, 226–28; eliminative, 228; enumerative, 211, 220; future-moving, 18–19; general (hypothesis), 18, 220, 226, 229; Goodman's "new prob-

lem" of, 229; in *HK*, 220, 234, 240; instance (particular), 18, 220–22, 225–26, 228–30, 234–36; justification of, 6, 204, 212, 220, 234–36, 269; logical accounts of, 243–44; past-reaching, 18–19, 220, 224–26, 228–30; postulates of, 231; principle of, 207, 232n, 240; and prior probability, 18, 20; simple, 240–42; in *AMa*, 271
Inductive inference, 239–40
Inductive logic, 222–23, 234–35, 240, 243, 244
Inference: adequate data base for, 163–64; "animal," 165, 204; causal, 265; certainty of, 21–22; and credibility, 161; direct, 238–39; as element of knowledge, 166; justification for, 204–5, 211; nondemonstrative, 164; notion of unrestricted similarity, 218n; principles of, 209, 211; Russell's changing view of, 21; and sense-data, 15; statistical, 239; to unobserved causes of perception, 275
Infinite classes, 92
Infinite (disjunctive) functions, 81–82
Infinite regress (in understanding propositions), 176
Infinitary truth-functions, 28–29, 39n
Inquiry into Meaning and Truth: atomism, 10; extensional hierarchy, 6; indexicals, 13–14, 119, 128–29; particulars, 135n; recurrence of instants, 259; sensation and sense-data, 4–5, 146–47, 149–50, 162, 165–66, 278; theory of knowledge, Russell's final, 159–60
Instants (of time): from classes of events, 20–21, 249, 252; compactness of, 21, 250–51, 256–57, 260–61; construction of, 249–52, 257–58, 260; definition of, 253; existence of, 253–56, 262; first and last of an event, 254; as linearly ordered series, 263n; overlapping classes of, 250–54; precedence of, 250; as primitive entities, 249–59, 260; Russell's theory of, 26; Whitehead's enclosure series, 252
Intended references: constraints on, 193–94
Intensionalism, 255
Interdefinability thesis (of indexicals), 120, 132–33
"Interpretation," 189
Interpretation: doctrine of partial, 195; domain of, 193
Intersubjective reference, 131, 133–34
Intervals (time and space), 266–67
Introduction to Mathematical Philosophy, 185

Invariable sequence, 272, 273
"Is Mathematics Purely Linguistic?" 51
"Is Position in Time and Space Absolute or Relative?" 257
Iteration principle, 202–3, 212

James-Lange theory of emotions, 285
Jeffreys's theorem (on future-moving induction), 225, 229
Judgment: about a complex, 180; elementary, 141; as infallible, 153, 158; multiple-relations theory of, 34, 101; of perception, 141–42, 153; and sensation, 151, 153, 166; theory (Russell's) of, 16, 101, 140, 179–81; truth of, 153–54
Judgment empiricism, 19, 243–44
Justification of inductive inference, 6, 214–15

Knowledge: advance, in acquaintance, 174–75; nonstructural, 192; of the physical world, 184–86, 188, 190–91
"Knowledge by Acquaintance and Knowledge by Description," 102

Lambda abstracts, 66–67
Language, 104–5, 126, 127
Laplace's rule of succession, 223
Level, notion of, 62n
Liar's paradox, 115
Linguistic philosophy: British, 7
"A Locked Diary" (1890–99), 283
Logical atomism, 15, 43, 51, 54–55
"Logical Atomism," 54, 60
Logical constructions, 264–69, 276–77
Logical constructivism, 287
Logical fictions, 10, 36, 54, 102
Logical form, 11, 12, 79, 98–100, 103–4, 151
Logical notation (in *PM*), 249, 252
Logical reconstruction of mathematics, 45
Logical subjects, 53, 54
Logical types, 9–10, 51, 54
"Logic and Knowledge," 171
Logicism, 25, 27, 38, 197
Logicist reduction, 27, 30
Love and knowledge, 291

Marriage and Morals, 291
Mathematical axioms, 284
Mathematical logic, 281

"Mathematical Logic as Based on a Theory of Types," 4, 24, 30, 43, 47, 55, 87n
Mathematical properties of the physical world, 185
Mathematics, 197, 290; reduction of logic to, 27. *See also* Logicist reduction
Matrix, 56–57
Meaning, Russell's theory of, 88–89, 98, 102, 113, 115
Mental events, 268
Minimum vocabulary, 119, 124–25, 129, 131–33
Mnemic phenomena, 272–73
Modality: *de re* and *de dicto*, 109
Modus ponens: as premise, 211
Multiple-relations theory, 34, 43, 44–45, 53–54, 56, 101
"My Mental Development," 102, 162
My Philosophical Development: intensionalism, 255; logical positivism, 7, 279n; propositional functions, 41, 60; relations, 61; Russell's development, 3–8, 286; sense-data, 138, 143, 145–47, 159, 165, 278n; solution to paradoxes, 101
Mysticism and Logic, 102

N-adic predicates, 10
Namability, 33, 52, 54
Names: as access to particulars, 118; in "christening ceremony," 121; as definite descriptions, 110–12, 116, 121; determining reference of, 111, 117; as disguised descriptions, 108, 114–15; as disjunctions of conjunctions, 110; as a function of causal origin, 114; parasitic meaning of, 115; proper, 12–13, 120, 127; replaceability of, 14, 125; Russell's descriptivist theory of, 12–13, 116–17; substituting descriptions for, 125
Naming: rigid and nonrigid designators for, 109
Naturalism, 200
"The Nature of Sense Data—A Reply to Dr. Dawes Hicks," 140
Neutral monism, 4, 144–45, 265–66, 271, 288
No-class theory, 30, 46, 101
Nominalism, Russell's, 9–10
Nominalist interpretation of propositional functions, 42, 48, 58
Nominalization, 51

Nonconceptual knowledge ("animal expectaion"), 204
Nondemonstrative inference, 17, 19–20, 269, 271, 289
Noneliminable predicates, 67
Nonindexical language, 136n
Nonperceptible events, 184
Nonrational acceptance of theories, 262
Nonstructural knowledge, 192
Notebooks 1914–16, 177
"Noticing," 146–47, 164–65, 167
Null-class, 94

Objectivity requirement, Carnap's, 187
Observable/unobservable dichotomy, 191
"On Denoting," 4–5, 11–12, 34–35, 88ff, 117n, 125
"On Fundamentals," 106n
"On 'Insolubilia' and Their Solution by Symbolic Logic," 24, 28, 35
"On Meaning and Denotation," 106n
"On Order in Time," 20, 249–63
"On Propositions," 56, 168n
"On Scientific Method in Philosophy," 282
"On the Nature of Acquaintance," 169, 171
"On the Nature of Truth and Falsehood," 142
Ontology, event, ix
Ontology, Russell's, 5
Ordered pairs: 63, 70, 72–75; Wiener-Kuratowski definition of, 11
Ordering property, 74
Ordering relations, 74
Order in time, 20, 260
Ostensive definition, 126
Our Knowledge of the External World: acquaintance, 271; compactness of events, 256; instants of time, 249, 251–52, 254; logical form, 100; order in time, 20; sentence analysis, 12; solipsistic theory of knowledge, 163; structuralism, 198n
Outline of Philosophy, 5
Overlapping instants of time, 250–51, 253–54, 256, 257

Paradox: of analysis, 112; Goodman's, 200; logical, 9; mathematical, 9; semantic, 9, 26, 28, 35; set theoretic, 26. *See also* Bradley's paradox; Grelling's paradox; Liar's paradox; and Russell's paradox
Partial interpretation: doctrine of, 195

Subject Index

Particular induction: principle of, 232n
Particulars: complex, 49–50, 53, 73; egocentric, 129, 135n; hypothesized, 265; as individuals, 49, 53, 55; naming of, 52; in physics and psychology, 272; and properties, 85; Russell's notion of "ultimate," 121; simple, 60–1, 135n; as units of analysis, 265
Perception: belief in external cause, 269; distortion of, 274; judgment of, 141–42; Russell's definition of, 165, 282; and sensation, 141, 147; sensational core of, 147, 149–50, 273, 276, 278
Percepts, 192, 267, 279n
Phenomenalism: Russell's early, 4–5, 184, 191; Russell's rejection of, 183
Philosophers: motivation of, 282
Philosophical framework for science, 264–65
Philosophy: Russell's reason for studying, 282–85
Philosophy of Logical Atomism, 10, 52–56, 104, 119–21, 127, 133, 170, 173
Physical objects, 21, 102
Physical world, 185, 264–65, 267–68. *See also* External world
Physics, 21–22, 183, 265, 272, 286
Picture theory: of meaning, 16; of propositions, 179
"Place of Science in a Liberal Education, The," 287
Polyadic logic, 198n
Portraits from Memory, 162
Postulate of structure, 275
Postulates of induction: Russell's five, 231
Postulates of scientific inference, 200, 203, 218n, 234, 236–37, 245–46, 290
"Postulates of Scientific Method," 289
Power, 289
Predicate abstracts, 66–67
Predicates as properties, 65–67
Predication, 52–53, 63, 67, 75, 87n
Predicative functions, 40n
Predicatives, 10
Predicativity, 24–25, 36, 38, 63ff
Predictability, 245
Presentability of entities, 33
Primary and secondary qualities, Locke's, 186
Primitive proposition, 84
Principia Mathematica: analysis, 153–55, 157; axiom of infinity, 197; comprehension axioms, 32; influence on reception of later works, 6; notion of order, 62n; Peano and Frege, influence of, 286; predication, 63, 67; primitive proposition, 84; propositional functions, 10, 42–43, 47–53, 56–57; science of mathematical logic, 281; symbolic logic, 3–5, 22; theory of knowledge, 182n; theory of types, 24, 41
Principles of Mathematics: constituents of a fact, 52; on denoting, 87n, 90–4, 96, 98–99, 103; on properties and relations, 41, 47, 49–50; on propositions, 10, 46; theory of description, 12
Prior probability, 231, 235–37, 239–40, 242–44, 246–47
Probabilistic inference, 242, 247n
Probability: axioms of, 224, 231, 237, 239; constraints of logic on, 238; degree of credibility, 224, 237–38; frequency theory of, 207, 210, 247, 293n; logic of, 236, 242; mathematical, 237–38; and predictability, 245; posterior, 241–42; "single case," 293n; subjectivist, 19, 237–38; theory of, 239, 241, 290
Problems of Philosophy: acquaintance, 171–72; certainty of sense-data, 15, 139–41, 151–57; induction, 4, 232n; inference, 163; proper names, 117n; Russell's metaphysics and epistemology, 5; self-evidence, 161; theory of knowledge, 182n; theory of truth, 49
Projectability, 18–19, 222–24, 225–27; 230–31
Proper names, 117n, 120
Properties: 11, 47, 70, 75, 79; and relations, 41, 46–47, 77–78
Properties of the physical world: mathematical, 185
Properties vs. particulars, 85
Propositional functions: comprehension axioms for, 32; constructivism, 9; as logical subjects, 10, 48; nominalist interpretation of, 42, 48, 58; predicative, 50; as properties, 41, 46–47, 86n; properties of, 31, 100; of ramified types, 44–48, 59; in Russell's logic, 28; as single entities, 36, 47, 62; as universals, 47; variable, 46, 56
Propositional theory, 33
Propositions: assertibility of, 29; atomic, 56; constituents of, 89–92, 94, 96–99, 105, 171, 175, 178; contingent, 15, 102, 170, 175, 180; entirely general, 177–78, 180; first truth/second truth, 37; general laws of, 27; infinite regress in understanding of, 176;

SUBJECT INDEX

intensional nature of, 34; as logical fictions, 10, 36; logical form of, 72, 97-99, 103-4; matrix of, 56; primitive, 84; pure-data, 167-68; quantified, 37-38; and sentences, 103-5; as single entities, 43-47, 51; specification of, 31-32, 34; and variables, 34, 37; Wittgenstein's critique, 170
Psychology, 285, 286, 288
Pythagoreanism, 188

Qualities: Locke's primary and secondary, 186
Quantification, 80-81
Quasi-permanence: laws of, 270

Ramification, 9, 24
Ramified abstracts as properties, 85
Ramified second-order logic, 42, 48, 57, 59-60, 62n
Ramified theory of types. *See* Theory of types
Ramified types, 52-55, 57-58, 62n
Ramsey sentence, 183-84, 195, 271
Rationality, 210
Realism, 195, 210
Recurrence of instants of time, 261. *See also* Events
Redundancy theory of truth, 29
Reference, 12-13, 113, 193-95
"Regressive Method of Discovering the Premises of Mathematics, The," 47
Relational abstracts: as blocks to the Russell paradox, 85
Relational extensions: foundedness of, 196
Relational order, 11, 63, 86n, 87n
Relational predication, 75
Relational properties, 72-73
Relation of exemplification, 76-79
Relation of self- and non-self-exemplification, 70, 71
"Relation of Sense-Data to Physics, The," 143, 163, 198n, 211, 278n
Relation of temporal precedence. *See* Temporal precedence
Relations, 11, 72, 74-75, 173, 190
Relations of acquaintance. *See* Acquaintance
Relations on a given domain, 189
Relation words, 61
Relativity: theory of, 21, 259-61, 288
Religion, Russell's view of, 22-23, 283-84, 292
Representation of properties, 70
Representation theorem, 223, 233n

Rigid designator, 13, 109, 131
R-types. *See* Ramified types
Rule of replacement, 68. *See also* Indexicals
Rule of succession: Laplace's, 223
Russell's paradox, 10, 37, 46, 58, 63ff, 115
Russell property, 67-70
Russell relations, 70-71

Science: cultural potential of, 282-83, 287, 290; as religion, 22-23, 289; Russell's popularization of, 290
Scientific inferences, Russell's postulates of. *See* Postulates of scientific inference
Scientific knowledge: value of, 291-92
Scientific ontology, ix
Scientific Outlook, The, 289, 291
Scientific properties, 16
Scientific realism, 267, 271
Scientific theory, 16-17
Scope, ambiguity of, 65
Self, Russell's concept of, 287
Self-evidence, 154, 157-58, 160-62, 177-78
Self-identity, 71
Self-predication, 86n
Self-reference, 114
Semantic paradox, 9, 26, 28, 35
Sensation, 141-48, 153-54, 166, 273
Sensational core of perception, 147, 149-50, 273, 276, 278
"Sensational datum," 149-50
Sense-data: certainty of, 14-15, 139, 151-52, 158-59, 160-63, 165; as grounds for empirical judgment, 142-43, 163; infallibility of, 151-52; physical status of, 287-88; purity of, 22; reliability of analysis of, 154-57; Russell's abandonment of, 14, 138-50, 160; Russell's definition of, 140; separability from inference, 15; simple vs. complex, 140, 142
"Sensible presentations," 140
Sentences and propositions, 104-5
Sequence, 173, 272, 274
Sets: constructivist interpretation of, 9
Set theory, 255, 256
Simple particulars, 60, 135n
Simples, 54, 55
Simple theory of types. *See* Theory of types
Simultaneity of events, 258
"Single-entity" propositions, 168n
Skepticism, 185, 215, 216-17, 224

Solipsistic theory of knowledge, 163, 165, 288
Space-time, 122, 132, 268. *See also* Coordinate description; Coordinate system
Statistical inference, 239
Statistical syllogism. *See* Inference, direct
Strict names, 120–21. *See also* Indexicals
Stroke-function (of atomic propositions), 57, 59
Structuralism, 191
Structural isomorphism, 288
Structural knowledge, 184, 186
Structural postulate, 270, 275
Structural properties, 16, 186, 188ff
Structural/quality division, 190–91
Structural realism, Russell's, 16–17, 185, 186
Structure, 185, 188–97, 265
Substitution: principle of, 55, 59
Substitutional theory, 28, 35–36
Symbolic logic, 4–5
Symbolism, theory of, 104

Technical logic, 5
Temporal precedence: relation of, 253, 257–59
Theoretical Knowledge: theory of, 187
Theoretical vocabulary, 193–95
Theory confirmation, 235–36, 244
Theory of Knowledge: acquaintance, 171, 174; decompositional analysis, 156; doubt and certainty, 151–52, 161; forms and universals, 173; propositions, 168n, 173–74; psychology, 286; relational predication, 72; theory of knowledge, 170, 288; Wittgenstein's criticism of, 5, 11, 15–16, 52, 169–70, 288

Theory of theories, 16, 183, 188
Theory of types: extensionalized, 255; ramified, 8–9, 11, 43, 54, 79–83, 85; Russell's, 64; Russell's new in *PM*, 42–43, 62, 100; simple, 8–10, 24, 26, 39n, 59, 85, 255
Thought, 115, 171, 174
Time, 20, 259, 260
Time-like and space-like intervals, 266–67
Time, local, 259, 261
Truth, 29, 210, 213

Understanding, 31, 177, 178
UNESCO Kalinga Prize, 290
Universals and particulars, 48–50

Variable propositional functions, 46, 57–58
Variables, 35–37, 44, 49, 57, 59, 84, 92, 195
Vicious-circle principle, 9, 32, 49, 63, 79–80
Vietnam, Russell's book on, 7

War Crimes in Vietnam, 7
Well-ordering principle, 254, 263n
Wiener-Kuratowski on ordered pairs, 11, 63, 70, 72–75
Words, 89, 96, 98, 103–4
World War I, 5–6, 288
World War II, 290

Zermelo-Fraenkel set theory, 256
Zorn's lemma, 255–56